Foundations of Public Contracts

STUDIES IN COMPARATIVE LAW AND LEGAL CULTURE

In today's shrinking world it's important to extend our horizons and increase our knowledge of other people's laws. This series publishes in-depth volumes covering various aspects of private and public law in diverse legal traditions. Additionally, it seeks to encourage improved techniques and methods of comparative legal research, including the use of interdisciplinary studies. Individual volumes may deal with the law and culture not merely of well-known and frequently studied countries, but also with lesser-known, mixed, religious, and plural systems of the world. The focus ranges from important aspects of legal history, culture, and institutions to local experience and evolving legal trends.

Titles in the series include:

Foundations of Public Contracts

A Comparative View

José Guilherme Giacomuzzi

Professor of Law, Department of Public Law and Jurisprudence, The Federal University of Rio Grande do Sul, Faculty of Law, Brazil

STUDIES IN COMPARATIVE LAW AND LEGAL CULTURE

 Edward Elgar
PUBLISHING

Cheltenham, UK • Northampton, MA, USA

Published by
Edward Elgar Publishing Limited
The Lypiatts
15 Lansdown Road
Cheltenham
Glos GL50 2JA
UK

Edward Elgar Publishing, Inc.
William Pratt House
9 Dewey Court
Northampton
Massachusetts 01060
USA

A catalogue record for this book
is available from the British Library

Library of Congress Control Number: 2022932831

This book is available electronically in the **Elgar**online
Law subject collection
http://dx.doi.org/10.4337/9781800880924

Printed on elemental chlorine free (ECF)
recycled paper containing 30% Post-Consumer Waste

ISBN 978 1 80088 091 7 (cased)
ISBN 978 1 80088 092 4 (eBook)

Printed and bound in the USA

To my daughter, Anita, for having re-founded my life by colouring our journeys with grace, joy and love

Wise men should bring together and compare the legal framework of all states, or of the more famous states, and from them compile the best kind.

Jean Bodin

in *Method for the Easy Comprehension of History* (1566)

Contents

Acknowledgements

'Language, it seems, was invented only for average, middling, communicable things', wrote Nietzsche in *Twilight of the Idols* (IX, §26). I owe so much to so many people for helping me for so long that I'm sure my words won't be enough to thank them all the way I should.

Some people open doors and minds. GW Law School doors were opened to me by Joshua Ira Schwartz, my mentor, from whom I received more attention than I could ever pay back, and Bob Cottrol, with whom I've been learning about American and Brazilian history since we first met some 20 years ago. Dalia Tsuk has taught me American Legal History from the Realists' perspective, opening my mind to legal comparison. At Georgetown University, Joshua Mitchell showed me, then a snoopy auditor, the importance and depth of Tocqueville, Hobbes and Rousseau. In France, I thank Laurance Folliot-Lalliot for the delightful conversations we've had in Washington, DC and Paris about *le droit administratif*. I also thank her for helping me access la Salle du Droit Public at the University of Panthéon-Assas. I'd also like to thank Professor François Rangeon for sending me a copy of his out-of-print book, which was central to my argument.

This work was completed during the Covid-19 pandemic, one of the most challenging times of the past hundred years. From Brazil, eager to address my lack of knowledge in many areas of law, I've sent emails to people I've learned much from over far too many years, but whom I've unfortunately never met. Their generosity has confirmed my belief that knowledge can unite instead of separate. I thank James Gordley, James Whitman, Stefan Vogenauer, William Ewald and Uwe Kischell for exchanges about comparative law theory, and Brian Leiter, Dan Priel, Joseph Raz, Martin Loughlin, Pierluigi Chiassoni and Ralf Poscher for legal theory and jurisprudence.

In Brazil, where I live, two friends and colleagues read the whole manuscript and rescued me from some pitfalls: José Reinaldo de Lima Lopes, one of my pilots in legal history and jurisprudence, and Egon Bockmann Moreira, whose generosity I wish I could pay back someday, were the best readers I could have had. My gratitude also goes to two of my soul brothers: Claudio Ari Mello, with whom I've been sharing most of my thoughts for the past two decades; and Jorge Cesa Ferreira da Silva, my guru for private law issues since the previous century, when we were young, curious law-school students at the Federal University of Rio Grande do Sul, in Porto Alegre, RS, Brazil (UFRGS), our *alma mater*. At UFRGS, where I teach nowadays, I learn from two colleagues and friends, Wladimir Barreto Lisboa and Paulo Baptista Caruso MacDonald, both legal philosophers. No one mentioned above is responsible for the remaining irresponsible ideas in this book.

I must mention two librarians who were my guardian angels: Suzanna Louzada (Porto Alegre, RS, Brazil) and Mary Kate Hunter (Washington, DC, USA). Without both, this book wouldn't have seen the light.

Finally, I would say I'm a lucky man: two of my generation's most cultivated Brazilian administrative law scholars, Itiberê de Oliveira Rodrigues and Luiz Gustavo Kaercher Loureiro, are my friends. I've been learning with and from them for more than a decade. In addition, all of us are fortunate enough to have been students of the late, ever missed Professor Almiro do Couto e Silva (1933–2018), a Brazilian jurist of incomparable culture, integrity and kindness, and former Dean of the Faculty of Law of the UFRGS, to whose illuminating memory this book is also dedicated.

Porto Alegre, RS, Brazil, September of 2021
JGG

Abbreviations

BACEN	*Banco Central do Brasil* (Brazilian Central Bank)
CCP/2018	*Code de la Commande Public of 2018* (French Code of Public Contracts)
CCPCom/2021	*Code de la Commande Public commenté*, edited in 2021
CE	*Conseil d'État* (French State Council)
CFB/88	*Constituição Federal do Brasil de 1988* (Brazilian Federal Constitution of 1988)
Em	Emile (Rousseau's book)
FAR	Federal Acquisition Regulation
GAJA/2021	*Les grands arrêts de la jurisprudence administrative*, 21st ed, edited in 2021 by Dalloz
GAPJA/2019	*Les grands arrêts politiques de la jurisprudence administrative*, 1st ed, edited in 2019 by Dalloz
LGC/1995	Lei nº 8,987/1995, *Lei Geral de Concessões* (Brazilian General Law of Concessions of 1995)
LLCA/2021	Lei nº 14.133/2021, *Lei de Licitação e Contratos Administrativos* (Brazilian Law of Bids and Administrative Contracts of 2021)
LLCA/1993	Lei nº 8.666/2021, *Lei de Licitação e Contratos Administrativos* (Brazilian Law of Bids and Administrative Contracts of 1993)
PPP/2004	Lei nº 11,079/2004, *Lei de Parcerias Público-Privadas* (Brazilian Law of Public-Private Partnerships of 2004)
SAD	Sovereign Acts Doctrine
SC	Social Contract (Rousseau's book)
STF	*Supremo Tribunal Federal Brasileiro* (Brazilian Supreme Court)
STJ	*Superior Tribunal de Justiça* (Brazilian Superior Court of Justice)

Traité 1	Laubadère, André de et al (1983), *Traité des Contrats Administratrifs*, vol 1 (LGDJ, 2nd ed)
Traité 2	Laubadère, André de et al (1984), *Traité des Contrats Administratrifs*, vol 2 (LGDJ, 2nd ed)
TRF	*Tribunal Regional Federal* (Federal Regional Court)
U.S.C.	United States Code
WN	The Wealth of Nations (Adam Smith's book)

Introduction to *Foundations of Public Contracts*

It was spring 2004. I had just chosen the topic of my doctoral dissertation and was in Professor Joshua Schwartz's office at the George Washington University Law School to have our first meeting after he had agreed, to my great honour, to serve as my supervisor.

The office was located on the fourth floor of a remodelled building in downtown Washington, DC. The 20×18-foot room (or something like that; I've never got feet-inches-pounds right) has an 8- or 9-foot-high ceiling and accommodates quite a few shelves. In the US, each law school professor usually maintains an office filled with books and decorated with personal belongings. Highly modern, double-paned glass windows isolate that space from noise and wind, and the heating and cooling systems maintain a constant temperature throughout the year. Furthermore, the electronic facilities shorten all distances from computers to telephones, making each office a delightful, private working space, no matter how strange the ambience appeared to my sensibilities.

At the time, I'd just finished the LLM degree at GW Law – it took me a year to find my feet in trying to understand a new way of thinking about law, based upon an unfamiliar form of reasoning. My previous encounters with my supervisor had revealed that we belonged to different legal systems and worked with different assumptions not only about government contracts law but also about the law as a whole. However, the topic I had chosen, a comparative study of exceptionalism in government contracts, sounded familiar to us both. Or so I thought.

Schwartz once wrote that in the US '[t]here is a tradition of "exceptionalism," which emphasizes that, because of its sovereign status, unique functions, and special responsibilities, the government, as a contracting party, is not subject to all of the legal obligations and liabilities of private contracting parties'.[1] That would be opposed to the 'tradition of congruence', which would embody 'the tendency to construe the obligations and liabilities of the Government under

---

[1] Schwartz 1996: 637. The expression 'exceptionalism' in American law was coined, and has since been developed, by Schwartz: see Schwartz 1997: 489–92; 2000: 1192–3 and note 61; 2002: 117–18; 2003: 864; 2004: 16–30.

its contracts to conform to those of private parties under purely private agreements'.[2] Having been trained in Brazil's civil-law system, heir to the French
legal tradition, I intuited that exceptionalism would have a similar meaning to
what French and Brazilian jurists call exorbitance/*exorbitância*, a notion that
for centuries has implied superiority of the public over the particular interest.
I'd found, or so I thought, the red thread for my research, a liaison between
our minds, or at least a starting point to explore – a 'functional equivalent', in
comparatists' lingo.

I hence began the conversation by sharply saying: 'To me, your idea of
exceptionalism in American government procurement law corresponds to
what we civil-law jurists call "supremacy of the public interest"!' To my
dismay, Professor Schwartz wrinkled his brow and replied: 'I've never suggested any superiority of the public interest, and this is not what I mean by
exceptionalism!'

Three months later, I was in Paris to meet with Doctor Étienne Picard,
Professor of Public Law at the Panthéon-Sorbonne. Monsieur Picard was
generously waiting for me at the entrance of a singular hall on the second floor
of the *Université*, a building now more than 800 years old, located behind the
Panthéon, in the charming Quartier Latin.

At the Sorbonne, professors have no private offices; most rooms are thus
public and impersonal, as are most French universities. Professor Picard kindly
guided me to an office empty of books, with no shelves, computers or telephones. The contrast with my supervisor's office in the US was striking. The
room was a square, 7×8 metres, and the ceiling was around than 9 metres high
(I quickly measured it with my eyes; it looked like many rooms of the Federal
University of Rio Grande do Sul, Brazil, from which I graduated in 1993 and
where I teach nowadays). Nothing but three heavy chairs and one wooden table
decorated the sober room, and I sensed that many generations of scholars and
students had enjoyed the same impersonal, traditional atmosphere. Although
I had never entered that particular room before, I experienced a sort of numi-
nous intimacy once inside.

In my rudimentary French, I tried to explain to Professor Picard (whom
I had never previously met) the subject of my research. Unsurprisingly, this
proved to be an easy task: we shared a similar legal epistemology. Brazil
imported the French idea of *droit administratif* and its corollaries as the notion
of *contrat administratif*. We spoke the same language.

At a certain point in the conversation, I decided to play devil's advocate.
I said that a Portuguese scholar had published a book in the 1990s (with
a suggestive title: 'requiem for the administrative contract') which had become

---

well known in Brazil, implying that the French understanding of *contrats administratifs* as different from private contracts was a historical accident and that all efforts undertaken over more than a century by French scholars and courts to find a correct and determinative criterion to separate private contracts from public contracts were but an illusion, or, more crudely, a waste of time.[3] Professor Picard, who thus far had been speaking perfect English to compensate for my flawed French, said very clearly in his native tongue: '*Il faut que vous compreniez que la France est un État Administratif!*' ('You must understand that France is an Administrative State!').

I intend these two personal stories to aid in setting the tone for all that follows. My words to each professor touched on a set of sacrosanct assumptions upon which the US and French legal systems rely. I will attempt to show that the two scholars' intuitive reactions reveal significant prejudgements about the law of public contracts.[4] In a way, this book attempts to explain why the two professors reacted in the ways they did; in short, I will explore the law in their minds.[5]

States are treated differently when they contract with a private party in the US or France or Brazil.[6] In these three legal systems, the state enjoys the power to unilaterally change contracts or even terminate contracts for its convenience, and the power to supervise the contract and apply sanctions and penalties to the contractor. Besides, when acting in its sovereign capacity, the state possesses the power to escape from some contractual responsibilities, while contractual duties almost always bind private parties. These privileges deviate from private law parameters. In this sense they are exceptional, *exorbitantes*.[7]

But this is all too trivial. Colin Turpin (1928–2019) enumerated and explored these and other peculiar characteristics of public contracts in the International Encyclopedia of Comparative Law four decades ago.[8] My concern is different: Where do these prerogatives come from? How were they constructed? How do they operate within the legal systems? In short, what are the foundations of these exorbitant powers?

By foundations, I mean the underlying philosophical, historical, political and social reasons why the government is treated differently when it contracts

---

[3]   See Estorninho 1990.
[4]   See Gadamer 2004: 268–78.
[5]   See Ewald 1998: 704 (full argument in Ewald 1995).
[6]   For Drago (1990: 117), the different treatment seems to exist in all legal systems. But see Fromont 2010; Hourson & Yolka 2020: 33–4.
[7]   For overviews on the three public contract law systems, which may not be up to date, see Schwartz (US), Naguellou (France) and Sanches & Angel (Brazil), in Naguellou ed 2010.
[8]   See Turpin 1982.

with a private party. As I will explain in Chapter 1, the word 'foundations' encompasses the civilian idea of 'material', 'substantial' sources of law,[9] sometimes treated interchangeably as 'the creative forces of law' – *les forces créatrices du droit*,[10] an expression consecrated in 1955 by Georges Ripert (1880–1958).[11]

Material sources are at work whenever the law is created, either by legislators or judges or administrators or agencies; they inform the content of the 'formal' or 'dogmatic' sources of law, be they mandatory, like statutes (*lois*) and legal precedents (*jurisprudence*), or optional, like scholarly work (*la doctrine*) and customary law. However unfamiliar to the Anglo-American jurists nowadays, this use of the term 'sources' conveys, I believe, ideas that bear a resemblance to what Roscoe Pound (1870–1964) tried to explain by speaking of forms and sources of law.[12] Accordingly, I will emphasize sources (civilians' material or substantial sources) over forms of law (civilians' formal or dogmatic sources) in this book.

At the core of Schwartz and Picard's above-flagged sacrosanct assumptions about public contracts lie two opposing ideas about the state and the individual and two different forms of reasoning. More crucially, at the foundations of public contracts in the American, French and Brazilian legal systems lie two different conceptions of the general interest, a central concept in political philosophy that generated two disputing conceptions, as revealed by a French official 1999 document, the *Rapport public du Conseil d'État* on the *intérêt général*: a transcendental, French conception, called voluntarist, versus a utilitarian, Anglo-American conception.[13] Any work on the foundations of public contracts must deal with this crucial dispute.

These divergent assumptions implicate differences in crucial legal concepts and structures.

In French (and to a lesser scale Brazilian) law, classifying a contract as a *contrat administratif* instead of a *contrat privé* has profound practical implications,[14] and establishing the criteria that distinguish one from another is an endless theoretical battle.[15] As we will see in due course, this battle was

---

[9]   See Dufour-Kowalska 1982: 200; Amselek 1982: 253; Bergel 2012: chapter 2; Jestaz 2015: 1, 3.

[10]   See Bergel 2012: 57. But see Jestaz 1993: 74–5.

[11]   See Ripert 1955.

[12]   See Pound 1946; 1933; 1931.

[13]   See *Rapport public du Conseil d'État* 1999: 245–61.

[14]   For the differences in private law underlying conceptions of contracts and *contrats*, see Sacco 1991a: chapter 3; 1991b: 12–13.

[15]   In France, the first book on the subject, although not a general theory, is Perriquet 1884. Jèze dedicated part of volumes III (1926), IV (1934), V and VI (1936) of his *Principes Généraux du droit Administratif* to *les contrats administratifs*. But the first

strengthened by the advance of the European Union's liberal ethos, which, by shaking the tectonic plates of the French idea of State, invites us to discuss the entire notion of *droit administratif*, including one of its pillars, *le contrat administratif*.[16] As Jacques Caillosse recently warned, *le droit administratif* cannot be indifferent to the *théorie de l'État*.[17]

In contrast, there has been little effort to build a theory of public contracts law based upon abstract principles in the US.[18] Instead, American public procurement law has dealt more with practical questions than with abstract ideas.[19] The late Chief Justice William Rehnquist (1924–2005) suggestively referred to the 'somewhat mundane law of government contracts'.[20]

Yet to understand the foundations of public contract law, we must do more than analytically describe and criticize the case law to predict future decisions or simply compare statutory and regulatory norms whence differences or similarities eventually arise. 'You say that what the courts pronounce is law. So it is; but it is no less important to know the sources whence it derives', Harold Laski wrote to Oliver Wendell Holmes Jr on 8 December 1917.[21] Following Laski, we must try to comprehend the material sources from which the law derives.

Accordingly, I will focus less on the case law or practical questions than a regular common law lawyer would expect, and I will prefer a theoretical over

---

general theory was the *thèse de doctorat* of Péquignot 2020 [1945]. On the importance of Jèze's and Péquignot's works, see Plessix 2003a: 740–2. In 1955, a three-volume *Traité* combining the earlier efforts was written by André de Laubadère (1956). The *Traité* was updated by Franck Moderne and Pierre Devolvé and became a two-volume second edition in 1983/4, which is still a major reference (in this book, I will refer to this work as *Traité 1* and *2*). For a more complete bibliography, see Plessix 2020: 1219–22. For a doctrinal history of *contrats administratifs*, see Friedrich 2016. See also a historical study by Bezançon (2001) on the *concessions*. In specialized handbooks, see Richer & Lichère 2019: 87–130. Brazilian government procurement law has been theoretically influenced by French doctrine, but Brazil has produced considerably less. For theoretical approaches, see Giacomuzzi 2011; Almeida 2012; Moura 2014; Loureiro 2020.

[16] See Amilhat 2014. For studies about the impact of the *droit communautaire* on the basic notions of French public law and on French legal structure, see Dubouis 1996; Picard 1996; Terneyre 1996.

[17] See Caillosse 2017: 29–32.

[18] The first book is Shealey (1919), who did not offer a theory of public contracts. The third and final edition of the book (1938), although more elaborated and updated, differs little in its structure from the first. Donnelly (1922) wrote a 'treatise' on the subject following the same non-theoretical path. The scenario has not changed significantly. For a more theoretical survey in the US public contracts law, see eg Schwartz 1996; 2004; Schooner 2001; 2002.

[19] See Mairal 2003: 1716; Langrod 1955: 330, 333.

[20] *U.S. v Winstar Corp.*, 518 US 839, 932 (1996) (Rehnquist CJ dissenting).

[21] *Holmes–Laski Letters* 1953: vol. 1, 116.

a practical approach.[22] 'Legal practice is law without theory',[23] and this book will not serve as a guide for lawyers' briefs; nor is it an exhaustive enumeration of all specific forms of public contracts in the three systems under scrutiny.

The choice of these three legal systems is not casual.[24]

'Human thought develops by antagonism', wrote the Canadian philosopher John Watson (1847–1939) in 1892.[25] Theories in any domain of law, being products of human thought, develop by antagonism, too. This dialectic departs from the idea that understanding comes from contradicting one another, being 'daughter of debate not of sympathy', as Gaston Bachelard (1884–1962) has stated about the truth.[26] It is a truism that the more the comparatist knows about the foundations of a particular topic in a culture that upholds opposing values, the more she will understand her own legal system.[27] Thus, comparative law is always dialectical.[28]

Among the influential Western liberal cultures, the two that differ most sharply are the American and the French. As early as 1927, André Tardieu (1876–1945), an influential French *homme d'État*, stated that in many distinctive characteristics such as physical composition, moral trend, the rhythm of growth and volume of production, the world offers no analogy to the United States – 'But if antithesis be sought, France provides it'.[29] Comparing American and French foundations of public contracts law fits into this broad scenario.

Leaving aside personal reasons, as the third legal system under scrutiny I've selected the Brazilian, this being perhaps the Western country that most reflects both of the opposing Anglo-American and French legal systems. Throughout its history, Brazilian law, particularly its public (contracts) system, has revealed a desultory pendular move from one leading model to

---

[22] Dworkin (2006 [1997]: 49–51) wrote that the practical approach, which 'seems so down-to-earth, so sensible, *so American*', shall be rejected, because it 'suffers one commanding defect: it's wholly impractical'. The theoretical approach, he adds, 'is not only attractive but inevitable' (emphasis added).

[23] Hoecke 2017: 273.

[24] Siems (2018: 18) points to three countries as a frequent suggestion for comparison.

[25] Watson 1892: 9.

[26] Apud Bourdieu 1991: 3.

[27] See eg Samuel 2011: 186.

[28] See Clark 2012: 1.

[29] Tardieu 1927: 13.

another,[30] a move that only enriches the delicate topic of 'legal transplants', which has fascinated comparatists.[31]

It may be shocking that comparative lawyers still have to justify their purposes. And yet, comparative law studies may have multiple aims.[32]

As is the case for many in comparative law, the primary purpose of this study is to act as a building block for a better understanding of public contracts, primarily in the American, French and Brazilian legal systems.[33] Although I consider it an exaggeration to claim that comparative law is indispensable for legal knowledge, I join those who believe that legal knowledge may benefit from the comparison.[34] It is interesting, however, that until very recently, public contracts law was subjected to comparative studies only sporadically,[35] notwithstanding collections of articles regarding the so-called globalization of

---

[30]   For the intellectual influence of Anglo-American and mostly French ideas in Brazil until the 1950s, see Costa 1956; Perrone-Moisés ed 2004.

[31]   See Alan Watson (1983) and Kahn-Freund (1974) for opposing views on legal transplants. Legrand (1997), using cryptic language, advocates the impossibility of legal transplants. I follow Kischel (2019: 62) on Legrand's unacceptable conclusions. For a French bibliography on *emprunts juridiques*, see Plessix 2003a: 12, note 4.

[32]   See Kischel 2019: chapter 2; Husa 2014: 53.

[33]   The building block metaphor is from Kischel 2019: 34. I wrote 'primarily', as the study may be useful in systems influenced by American or French law.

[34]   See Kischel 2019: 46, 53; Husa 2015: 20, 22; Jacquemet-Gauché 2013: 11.

[35]   See JDB Mitchell 1954 (PhD dissertation studying British, American and French government contract laws); 1950; 1951. Turpin (1982, chapter 4) wrote the chapter on Public Contracts in the *Comparative Law Encyclopedia* and focused mainly on British, American and French systems; see also Hadfield 1999 (examining American and Canadian government procurement law); Langrod 1955 (analysing the important distinctions between Anglo-American and civil law systems, especially the French, of government contracts); Mairal 2003 (a comparison between US and Argentine's government procurement laws, exposing the French influence on Argentine's law); Mewett 1958 (considering the theory of government procurement, or the lack of it, in France, Britain and the US); Pfander 2003 (comparing the institutions and law of government accountability in England, France and Romania, but reserving less than one page for government's responsibility in contracts). In Portuguese, see Estorninho 1990 and Sérvulo Correia 1987 (historical comparative perspectives on the theory of government contracts, but not studying the common law tradition). For periodical references, see compilations by Noguellou 2010 and Auby 2006 (a précis of some specific points and problems about public contracts, dealing with the main European legal systems and occasionally mentioning American law). Collections of articles on public procurement addressing foreign legal systems have been published recently, in English or in French: see eg Noguellou 2010; Arrowsmith & Trybus eds 2003; 1999.

public procurement.[36] That is perhaps a characteristic of all comparative public law,[37] except for constitutional law.

While explaining the similarities and differences among the three legal systems, much of the job, as said, will be to explain why lawyers and jurists think the way they do about public contracts law and try to understand why it would be difficult for them to think diversely. Understanding the styles of legal thinking and knowing the prejudices and prejudgements behind them may help us better understand why similarities and differences exist in the three juridical cultures.[38]

Thus, this study won't seek practical answers to specific problems,[39] however useful they may be.[40] Although the law, as I take it, is constructed to guide conduct, and legal theory is constructed to decide concrete cases, I am not interested primarily in providing practitioners with formulae to help lawyers.[41] Comparative law's first goal may not necessarily be developing new solutions to hard cases.[42] Still, it may indirectly be helpful to improve arguments eventually used to tackle issues covered by the subject under study.[43]

Moreover, this is a non-neutral work in two critical ways. First, I will make choices while interpreting and explaining legal concepts, norms and institutions. Second, while I have a doctoral law degree gained in the US, and although American law has influenced Brazilian law for decades, I cannot drop my civilian baggage at will.[44] I'm conscious that 'the important thing is to be aware of one's own bias so that the text can present itself in all its otherness and thus assert its own truth against one's own fore-meanings'.[45]

Since legal sources of public contracts law have changed, particularly in France and Brazil, this book's structure and content differ from the original work, presented as a doctoral dissertation in July 2007 at GW Law.

---

[36]   See eg the collection of articles in Arrowsmith & Trybus eds 2003, particularly Schwartz's.

[37]   Exceptions are eg Villain-Courrier 2004; Jacquemet-Gauchet 2013; Gabayet 2015; Jordão 2016.

[38]   On *Vorverständnis*, ie pre-understanding (fore-meanings, in some translations), see Gadamer 2004: 268–310, especially 270–2, 295. On hermeneutics and law, see Poscher 2019. On hermeneutics in modern comparative law, see Whitman 2003b; Kischel 2019: 156–62.

[39]   See Husa 2015: 22.

[40]   Favouring studies for practical purposes, see Hourson & Yolka 2020: 33.

[41]   See Ewald 1995: 2045; Nehl 2006: 20.

[42]   Compare Pfersmann 2001: 276–7; Grossfeld 1990: 12–13.

[43]   See Husa 2015: 22.

[44]   See Husa 2015: 23; Frankenberg 1985: 415–16.

[45]   Gadamer 2005: 271–2.

As to the most essential continental law formal sources, in France, a new *Code de la commande public* of 2018 (CCP/2018),[46] effective since 1 April 2019, covers the two main categories of *contrats administratifs*: *les marchés publics* and *les concessions*, both being this book's focus. *Les marchés*, largely equivalent to the American government procurement,[47] encompass *les marchés de travaux*, *de fournitures* or *de services*, *de partenariat* and *de défense et de sécurité* and are the most important public contracts in practice.[48] *Les concessions* are, however, theoretically the most expressive, as we will see.

Brazil has a peculiar combination of laws regulating public contracts. Two laws deal with the so-called collaboration contracts (*contratos de colaboração*), containing the basic general norms for bidding and procurements dealing with public works, services, purchases and disposals: Federal Law 14,133, effective since 1 April 2021, called the Law of Bids and Administrative Contracts (*Lei de Licitações e Contratos Administrativos* – LLCA/2021); and Federal Law 8,666, of 21 June 1993 (LLCA/1993), valid until 1 April 2023.[49] In addition, Federal Law 11,079/2004 regulates Brazilian Public–Private Partnerships (PPP/2004). These three laws are equivalent to the French *marchés publics*. Finally, Law 8,987/1995, called the General Law of Concessions (*Lei Geral de Concessões* LGC/1995), is equivalent to French concessions.

More important, however, are the changes in material sources. The neoliberal wave that overtook many Western legal systems over the past four decades didn't spare France or Brazil. The growing influence of European Union liberal norms has shaken the dominant assumption about the 'essence' of *contrats administratifs*.[50] Underneath the surface rests, again, the dispute about the conceptions of the general interest. No wonder that recent French scholarly studies (*la doctrine*) have revived and investigated its most fundamental administrative law concept, *l'intérêt général*,[51] and tried to theorize about the phenomenon of *l'exorbitance*.[52]

Is the *contrat administratif* as *exorbitante* as the French have been gasconading for so long? Does the 'essence' of public contracts remain intact, or should the private contracts philosophy speak for all? As Benoît Plessix recently stated: 'fashion is the unity of law, and the contract appears as the

---

[46] I will use the second edition of the CCP commented upon under the direction of Eckert 2021 (CCPcom/2021).

[47] See Brown & Bell 1998: 204.

[48] See Plessix 2020: 1237.

[49] From 1 April 2021 to 1 April 2023, the public administration can choose which law applies.

[50] See Amilhat 2014.

[51] See Clamour (2006); Coq 2016.

[52] See Saillant 2011.

common concept's archetype.'[53] Unity of law means, briefly, equating public and private contracts with mastering private law parameters. As a reaction, Plessix stated, revealingly, that the *Conseil d'État,* the French institution par excellence, is 'culturally, the best rampart to the Anglo-Saxon utilitarianism'.[54] Being as French as it gets, that idiom is, for a comparatist, tremendously rich.

In Brazil, the 'superiority of the public interest' – which, as we will see, has been considered the founding public law principle since Brazilian independence from Portugal in 1822 – has been questioned from the late 1990s onwards. Moreover, various changes in law's formal sources have occurred in public contract norms in the past two decades.

Put crudely: to what extent is the Anglo-Saxon Liberalism influencing the French idea of Law and State, and, consequently, the very concept of *contrat administratif*? How does the ever-oscillating Brazilian law fit in this scenario?

None of these questions was tackled in the original work some 15 years ago, three years after the first meeting mentioned earlier, in which I thought I had found, and then immediately lost, the red thread that would lead me to the foundations of public contracts law. In searching for them, I have followed the same line. It is up to the reader to decide whether I've kept the thread or lost it again.

Before I proceed, three qualifications on terminology are in order. First, I shall use – as part of the French doctrine still does – *contrat publics* and *contrats administratifs* as synonyms to mean contracts governed by public law norms. Nowadays, however, some scholars prefer the expression *contrat public* (originally a doctrinal idea) to denote *le contrat administratif* and *le contrat privé de l'Administration,*[55] that is, ordinary contracts between the State and contractors. Second, I shall use government contracts, public contracts and administrative contracts as equivalent expressions. Third, I shall use state and government as synonyms, although clearly they are not.

---

[53] Plessix 2020: 1221; also 2011: 54–6.
[54] Ibid: 618.
[55] See ibid: 1227, 1266–7; Lichère 2020: 7; Hourson & Yolka 2020: 47; Ubaud-Bergeron 2019: 28.

1. A comparative public law approach: setting the tone

'Comparative Law is an enigmatic, paradoxical and elusive subject in that, just as one thinks one has mastered it, another puzzle appears on the horizon',[1] wrote Esin Örücü in the opening sentence of a book whose title, *The Enigma of Comparative Law*, speaks for itself. There is no agreement as to the structure, scope, role, function, object of inquiry, aims, epistemology and methodology of comparative law research.[2]

This is not a book on comparative law theory or methodology, and any method justifies itself only a posteriori.[3] However, the fuzziness of the scenario calls for qualifications on some theoretical and methodological assumptions.

1. THE VARIOUS APPROACHES AND METHODS OF COMPARATIVE LAW

There have been multiple approaches to comparative law. They usually carry labels, sometimes reflecting opposing ideas and ideals: 'textual' versus 'contextual', 'traditional', 'functional' versus 'cultural', 'integrative' versus 'differential', 'post-modern', 'socio-legal', 'numerical', 'statistical', and others.[4] Some of these approaches may overlap.

Yet, there are no magical formulae for comparative law, notwithstanding disputes about conducting sound comparisons.[5] Moreover, it seems overly pretentious to downgrade a comparative law study for (not) being 'cultural' or

---

[1] Örücü 2004: 1.

[2] See eg Pfersmann 2001: 275; Hoecke 2004; Glenn 2006; Ponthoreau 2005: 8; Samuel 2014a; 2014b. For an overview of the present debate, see Mousourakis 2019: 12; Hoecke 2011; 2015.

[3] See Beaud 1994: 14.

[4] For recent textbooks, see eg Siems 2018; Kischel 2019.

[5] Legrand (2017) uses unfortunate, needless rhetoric to disqualify other approaches. See elevated rebuttals in Gordley 2017; Whitman 2017. We should keep in mind Crick's comment in 1962: 'I'm constantly depressed by the capacity of academics to overcomplicate things' (1992: 7).

'functionalist' or whatever label it holds. 'The key point', as Kischel put it, 'is that different questions correspond to different methods'.[6]

Comparative law studies, whether conducted by functionalists, traditionalists, culturalists, textualists (you label!), have been helping with legal change (perhaps for the better), enhancing knowledge (hopefully), throwing light on practical problems (maybe indirectly), unifying law (when peoples so wish).

One aspect of comparative law methodology, however, deserves closer attention.

2.   SIMILARITIES OR DIFFERENCES?

'What is striking and mysterious in comparing two legal systems', wrote Karl Llewellyn (1893–1962) in 1933, 'is the ways they are similar and the ways they are different'.[7] Simple as it is, the core idea remains true: comparative law has always been about explaining and exploring to what extent similarities and differences between rules and institutions of two or more legal systems exist.[8]

In the past four decades or so, there has been a dispute over the importance of similarities and differences in comparative law, thus summarized: the defenders of an 'integrative comparison' pay more attention to similarities between legal systems than to differences, which would, in contrast, defend a 'differential comparison'.[9] In searching for commonalities, an integrative comparison would construct an epistemological apparatus to find them; by presuming similitude (*praesumptio similitudinis*) it would search and find a 'functional equivalent' (*équivalent fonctionnel*) for all comparison, concluding that 'practical results are similar',[10] that is, similar problems would deserve similar solutions in all legal systems.[11] The role of comparatists would be to unify law.[12] This type of comparison was frequently equated to 'functionalism',[13] which is the target of criticism for being superficial, naïve, culturally neglective, uninteresting, meaningless, without epistemological value.[14] Pierre

---

[6]   Kischel 2019: 156.
[7]   Llewellyn 1989 [1933]: 1.
[8]   See Sacco 1991b: 5.
[9]   See Ponthoreau 2005: 10.
[10]   Zweigert & Kötz 1998: 40.
[11]   See Zweigert & Kötz 1998: 39–40; Sefton-Green 2002: 91–2. For the first sharp criticism, see Frankenberg 1985: 436–40.
[12]   See Zweigert & Kötz 1998: 24.
[13]   See ibid: 34. For a more elaborated idea about 'functionalism' in comparative law, see Michaels 2019.
[14]   See Legrand 2002: 225, 228; Samuel 2003: 35–6.

Legrand asked: 'What is the point of comparative law if all that comparatists see are similarities?'[15]

That is an exaggeration.[16] As James Whitman put it, 'scholars who perceive only "difference" in the world tend to get a little dizzy, a little unsteady on their scholarly feet'.[17] Of course, searching for differences doesn't amount to being profound or exciting, much as searching for similarities doesn't mean being shallow or fastidious. The point, again, is always about the *purpose* of the comparison. The interesting questions are *why similarities and differences exist, what function* they play within the legal systems and *what their epistemological role is* in shaping the law.[18]

Thus, if I dedicate little effort to comparing the black letter laws and not much to legal decisions (for common law standards), it is because I'm convinced that the safer path for a more profound comprehension of the way jurists think and operate, that is, the safer route for *this research*, is to explore the different foundations of public contract law in each legal system. Accordingly, I repeat, I will emphasize material over dogmatic sources of law. Moreover, contrary to what seems still to be the mainstream in comparative law theory, I believe that positivism (adequately understood and explained below) is the most precise methodology.

3. A POSITIVISTIC APPROACH TO COMPARATIVE LAW AND THE CONFUSION OF LABELS: IN PRAISE OF CLARITY

Parallel to the debate over similarities and differences, much ink has been spilled over against what has been pejoratively classified as a 'descriptive',[19] 'textualist',[20] 'traditional',[21] merely 'practical' – in short, a 'rule-model' – comparative law viewpoint. This approach, so the critics say, would consist in an enumeration of side-by-side 'rules' between two or more legal systems; being a 'rule-model' legal knowledge,[22] this approach would produce many

---

[15] In Sefton-Green 2002: 86.
[16] Kischel (2019: 166–73) shows that the critics attack functionalism as a bogeyman.
[17] Whitman 2003b: 314.
[18] See Michaels 2019: 368–85.
[19] See Zweigert & Kötz 1998: 11.
[20] Sefton-Green (2002: 86) has described the text–context dichotomy as 'classic' and says that *les contextualistes* 'explain comparative law in terms of environmental factors: society, economy, politics, etc'. The deeper idea of 'law as culture' would fit into 'contextualism'.
[21] See Van Hoecke & Warrington 1998: 496.
[22] See eg Samuel 1998: 820–5; 1995.

comparative law doctoral dissertations deemed as poorly descriptive,[23] and comparative law studies deemed as reductionist, less attractive, less strenuous, 'a very comfortable kind of activity'.[24] Following this line of thought, the rule-model approach has been labelled 'positivistic'. The conclusion comes quickly: '[T]he juridical comparison must necessarily be anti-positivist.'[25]

In contrast to the 'rule-model', 'positivistic' approach, there would be a more desirable, 'theoretical', 'cultural', 'hermeneutical', 'principled' or 'jurisprudential', deeper approach of comparative law – the only one worth pursuing.[26] In one way or another, many comparatists who have been challenging the 'rule-model', 'traditional' approach favour a deeper, 'hermeneutic' approach, indebted to Hans-Georg Gadamer (1900–2002).[27] Positivism is linked to a textual, rule-model, superficial, traditional, neglectable approach; in contrast, 'hermeneutic' equates to a contextual, cultural, principled, deep, worth-pursuing approach.

Following Leslie Green's warning, I don't want to make too much of the label 'positivism'.[28] However, since the term has been pivotal to mainstream comparative law, I'd like to dwell upon it here.

Linking 'positivism', without qualification, to a rule-model, superficial, textualist approach of comparative law, if not deceitful, adds little to gaining knowledge of (comparative) law or legal theory, which is, for many comparatists, the primary purpose of most comparative law work.[29] But, more important, I do believe that a positivist methodology (as exposed below) would help to clarify the 'enigmatic' subject of comparative law.

Much of the anti-positivist mood among comparative law theorists is due, I think, to the debate over rules and principles that took place between H.L.A. Hart (1907–92) and Ronald Dworkin (1931–2013) from the late 1960s on. In 1995, at the peak of the discussion – which continued after Hart's death – William Ewald, in a pathbreaking, book-length article entitled *Comparative Jurisprudence*, claimed that a mere study of 'rules', from an external point of view, with no attention to 'principles', was insufficient for a proper understanding of legal systems.[30] By expressly invoking Dworkin,[31] the hinted line of thought was: Hart → rules → positivism versus Dworkin → principles →

---

[23]　Hoecke 2017: 276.
[24]　Merryman, in Legrand 1999a: 4.
[25]　Cassese 2000: 20.
[26]　See Grossfeld 1990: 8; Ewald 1995; Valcke 2004; Legrand 1996c: 234.
[27]　See Curran 1998; Legrand 1999b.
[28]　See Green 2021: 39.
[29]　See Zweigert & Kötz 1998: 15; Kischel 2019: 46.
[30]　See Ewald 1995 (summarized in 1998).
[31]　See Ewald 1995: 1895, 1996 (footnote 7).

anti-positivism. That liaison, I think, has aided the disdain for 'positivism' among (at least Anglo-American) comparatists, not because it was original, but because it came along with the impressive, exuberant prose Ewald deployed in that iconoclastic article, which ultimately dealt with the philosophical origins of the German Civil Code.

The liaison, however, besides being parochial,[32] is nowadays unfair to jurisprudence, even *within* the Anglo-American world, *pace* its eventual defenders. It accepts the flawed, very early dismantled distinction between rules and principles and ignores that positivism, in the very perspective of Hart's 'internal point of view', is intrinsically 'hermeneutical', as many jurisprudents and comparatists have been noting for decades.[33]

Yet, after all, defenders would pose, aren't rules 'brittle', 'largely ephemeral and inevitably contingent'? Isn't it correct to say that concepts represent realities attached to specific contexts, being necessarily relative and subjective, urging comparatists to research beyond the 'rules'?[34] And isn't positivism exclusively concerned with *posited* norms, thus neglecting the *underlying reasons* (principles? culture?) from which legal norms derive?

Not so fast. 'Legal positivism' is a misleading term. From Alf Ross (1899–1979) to Joseph Raz (1939–), many legal philosophers have examined the various uses of 'legal positivism' in the juridical lexicon.[35] There are, in fact, too many traditions of legal positivism, so much so that self-proclaimed positivists of different juridical cultures sometimes appear not to be talking about the same thing.[36] As Michel Troper claimed in 2021, it wouldn't be accurate to translate *positivisme juridique* into 'legal positivism'.[37] The positivism of Norberto Bobbio (1909–2004), author of the 'standard view about legal positivism in contemporary Latin legal cultures',[38] is in many aspects similar to the positivism of Hans Kelsen (1881–1973), which is in

---

[32] At a more general level, Anglo-American comparative law has been considered parochial. See Glendon et al 1994: 1; Hoeflich 1997: 131; Reimann 1998: 737, 644. For a classic essay expounding the historical insularity of English law, a precursor of American parochialism, see Kelley 1974.

[33] See Hart 1983: 13–15; Hacker 1977: 12–18; Postema 1998: 330–5, 353–6; Bix 1999: 176; MacCormick 2008: 46–58, 184, 203–6; Bell 2011: 169; Chiassoni 2016: 400–3; Priel 2020: 11–12. Even William Ewald recognized that Hartian positivists would have agreed with what he said in his seminal article, as he kindly wrote to me in electronic exchanges.

[34] See Legrand 1996b: 55–6; Hoecke & Warrington 1998: 49–502.

[35] See eg Chiassoni 2021; 2016: 64–78.

[36] See eg Spaak & Mindus 2021: 5.

[37] See Troper 2021.

[38] Chiassoni 2021: 331.

turn, nevertheless, different from John Austin's (1790–1859).[39] It would be challenging to find a resemblance between the works, for instance, of Carré de Marberg (1861–1935), who tried to combine a *théorie positive du droit* that was also prescriptive,[40] and Andrei Marmor (1959–), who fiercely advocates that positivism is a descriptive theory of law.[41] And in fact, there is perhaps one single proposition shared by all positivists, the one 'isolated' by John Gardner (1965–2019): 'In any legal system, whether a legal norm is legally valid, hence whether it forms part of the law of that system, depends on its sources, not its merits.'[42] Apart from that, 'legal positivism' encompasses too many views. Thus, which version of 'legal positivism' is confined to a 'rule-model', superficial (comparative law) approach?

Perhaps we can equate 'positivism' to a rule-model approach if we restrict 'law' as being confined to black letter rules written in statutes, such as the *positivisme* proclaimed by the nineteenth-century French *École de l'Exégèse*, which advocated a strict interpretation of the text provisions of the 1804 Napoleonic Civil Code,[43] or the nineteenth-century German *Staastsgesestzespositivismus*, that is, a naked 'legalistic' positivism.[44] True, as Paul Amselek mentioned in 1982, a *positivisme juridique de type classique* glorified itself for not looking beyond law's 'formal sources'.[45] And also true, the Exegetical School and the German Historical School have forgotten, for political purposes, the theory of 'sources of law' while separating, although unclearly, material and formal sources. In this vein, strict legalistic positivism, a *positivisme juridique de type Classique*, could be fairly criticized. Unfortunately, however, nobody who has thought carefully about positivism and its nuanced history defends this version of positivism any longer; comparative law scholars, therefore, attack a strawman.

I also concede that a black letter rule-model approach may be reductionist if it merely provides the reader with a descriptive list of the similarities and differences between the legal systems under scrutiny or restricts itself to the analysis of the legislative text. Although such lists may be pretty helpful for lawyers interested in practical answers (which is not neglectable per se), or even for satisfying lawyers' curiosity, they ultimately help little if we want to know the foundations of law.[46] But this has nothing to do with legal positivism

---

[39] See Bix 1999: 169.
[40] See Mineur 2010.
[41] See Marmor 2006.
[42] Gardner 2001: 199.
[43] See Troper 2021: 140.
[44] See Chiassoni 2016: 66; 2021: 333; Lesaffer 2009: 461–3.
[45] See Amselek 1982: 253.
[46] See Legrand 1995b: 265; 2002: 226–8, 244.

as a theory of law that contends that the legal validity depends (exclusively or not) on norms' sources, not on their merits.

It is not my intention to talk anyone round to the soundness of positivism; nor, I repeat, is legal theory or jurisprudence the subject of this book. Lollygagging, therefore, isn't my business. However, I do think that a legal positivistic methodology has, adapting Pierluigi Chiassoni's metaphor, the 'discrete pleasure' of clearness.[47]

I will now elaborate a bit on the meaning of 'sources'.

4.   SOURCES OF LAW AS FOUNDATIONAL

'Sources of law matter. They serve to separate the province of law from the realm of non-law.' These are the introductory words of Stefan Vogenauer's article on 'Sources of Law and Legal Method' for the *Oxford Handbook of Comparative Law*.[48] But 'sources of law' is an expression of many meanings, as Vogenauer himself shows.[49] It is also an 'enlightening' if 'dangerous notion'.[50]

It is dangerous for, as a hydrological metaphor, it evokes a *natural* sense to law, as a fountain from which the water would necessarily spring.[51] No wonder that Kelsen, the greatest continental legal positivist of the last century, famously wrote that 'sources of law' is a 'figure of speech' with 'more than one meaning', a 'highly ambiguous expression' that 'seems to render the term rather useless'.[52] Kelsen thought law would stem from nature (or God or Reason) only for the natural law doctrine. The word 'sources', evoking nature as it does, runs against Kelsen's positive law theory.[53]

On the other hand, however, the notion of sources is illuminating. It throws light on the normative character of law, on its non-palpable texture, which facilitates the understanding of the liaison of law and its origins.[54] And here lies a good deal of the battle in jurisprudence, mainly in Anglo-American literature. Does the law have a divine source? Or is it derived from Reason? Or from human nature? Does it come from a supposedly existent Objective Morality?

---

[47]   See Chiassoni 2016.
[48]   Vogenauer 2019: 878.
[49]   See ibid: 884–6. See also Jestaz 1993: 73–5; Amselek 1982: 251–2.
[50]   Amselek 1982.
[51]   See ibid: 254–5.
[52]   Kelsen 1967 [1960]: 232–3; 2006 [1949]: 131–2. See also Amselek 1982: 252.
[53]   See Kelsen 2006 [1949]: 390–400. On Kelsen and sources, see Bobbio 1982.
[54]   See Amselek 1982: 257–8.

Remember the word 'sources' in the positivists' 'sources thesis' mentioned in the previous section. The iconic positivistic phrase 'legal validity depends on sources, not merits', meaning that law is a matter of social sources, not of moral merits, encapsulates the previous section's battle. It is a specific, perhaps slightly different use of the word 'sources', but an illuminating one anyway. It reflects the idea that law is a human construction, an artefact.

In this book, as mentioned in the Introduction, I will use the notion of sources, mainly of the dichotomy between *material* and *formal* sources, in the same way continental jurists have been doing since the 'theory of sources' was originated as a new paradigm of law, a positivistic construction forged by the Exegetical School in France and the Historical School in Germany in the nineteenth century.[55] This methodology, I hope, deflates the claims of those who accuse positivism of not being concerned with 'principles' or 'contexts' or 'culture'.

I cannot recollect the history of these two schools of law.[56] Yet it is essential to see them together as a political movement against the then reigning natural order, of which natural law was part. Both schools flourished simultaneously with the Codification movement, not coincidentally when the Roman law was revived. In France, *la loi*, now located at the epicentre of the Modern State, dethroning the King's will, was considered the only source of law, its *source formelle par excellence*. This position, advocated by the Exegetical School in the nineteenth century, did not prevail, in its crudity, among positivists in the twentieth century.

In Germany it was the very idea of Codification, *das Gezets* as the source of law, that two eminent Romanists – Friedrich Carl von Savigny (1779–1861), the leading figure of the School, and Georg Friedrich Puchta (1798–1846), Savigny's pupil – fought against; for them, the source of law was the *Volksgeist*. The Historical School has helped to forge the division, unclear but existent, between *sources formelles* and *matérielles*, the latter coined to separate form and substance. The material sources 'provide substance to the norms' ('*fournissent aux normes leur matières*').[57] For a classical natural law theorist, the question of sources is not quite posed: 'the law *is* [revealed] by gods, the God, the Reason, Nature, the human nature, etc'.[58]

When positivists like Georges Ripert, 'the most respected French civil law scholar of the first half of the [twentieth] century',[59] and Gaston Jèze

---

[55]   See Frydman 2011: 363–5.
[56]   In this and the next three paragraphs, I freely derive from Dufour 1982; Beauthier & De Broux 2012; Ruelle 2012.
[57]   Bergel 2012: 57.
[58]   Papaux & Cerutti 2020: 113; Dijon 2012:
[59]   Batiffol, in Sourioux 1982: 35.

(1869–1953), the French publicist who elevated the idea of *service public* to its apogee at the time, presented their legal theories, it was already evident in France that the formal sources were insufficient to understand the law.

'Law is voluntarily created by men', wrote Ripert in his classic work, and 'each people gives itself the law, hence the law it deserves'.[60] *Les positivistes* take law as being only the posited rules, that is, rules given by the political Power, while sociologists and philosophers discuss and investigate the foundations of law; however, continues Ripert, considering only posited legal rules doesn't prohibit jurists from researching why the Power has given the rules. Quite the contrary: we must analyse the 'secrets of the creation' of posited norms precisely because we no longer believe in their transcendent character.[61]

In 1925, in the Preface to the third edition of his *principes généraux du droit administratif*, Jèze wrote that what matters in the study of law is researching the 'conditions in which legal problems are posed', which is even more important than 'the solution that prevails momentarily'. To solve the problem, Jèze continued, one must '*research the social, economic, political, historical environment in which the legal question is presented*'.[62]

True, for positivists of Kelsenian lineage, I insist, all that is extra-normative is unimportant to law as it is 'meta-juridical', social facts being 'strangers to law'.[63] But for Kelsen's normative jurisprudence,[64] 'source of law' can mean the reason for the validity of law: in his pyramid of norms the basic norm is the ultimate reason of a legal order, and the constitution, the 'higher positive legal norm', is the 'source of the general legal norms created by legislation or custom'; in short, 'to a positivistic theory of law', only law can be a source of law.

Adjusting Kelsen's terminology, *material sources* (an expression he never used) were 'sources' only in a 'nonjuridic sense', meaning 'moral and political principles, legal theories, expert views' that may influence either law-creating or law-applying functions; these sources wouldn't be mandatory, 'unless a positive norm delegates them as legal sources', that is, *formal, dogmatic sources*, in my language. In short, *material sources* would be a matter for sociologists, historians, political theorists, philosophers. Jurists would deal

---

[60] Ripert 1955: 71. Ripert's positivism fits into Gardner's 'isolation thesis': 'A bad law is as binding as the most perfect law' (ibid: 74).

[61] See ibid: 74–5, 78.

[62] Jèze 2005 [1925]: II.

[63] See ibid: 79.

[64] Much of what follows in this subsection I have learnt from email exchanges with Pierluigi Chiassoni, to whom I owe more than these lines. Sometimes, I only paraphrase his insights. For citations of Kelsen's work, see 1967 [1960]: 232–3; 2006 [1949]: 131–2.

only with *formal, dogmatic sources*, which are 'the sources in the sense of the positivistic law theory', the only legally binding ones.

Kelsen's legal theory is still hugely influential in the continental law world, and his ideas on sources remain valid for many positivists.[65] However, one may easily see that Kelsen can't ignore moral and political principles, legal theories, expert views (for him, sources in a 'nonjuridic sense') either in law creation or interpretation. These 'nonjuridic' sources are always optional but may become mandatory if a positive norm obliges.

No legal positivist ignores *material sources* or *les forces créatrices du droit*. For positivists, material sources are to be taken into account as factors that affect formal sources. 'From the viewpoint of legal methodology, the material sources permit to determine the *content* to ascribe to the rules emanated from the formal sources.'[66] To use Ripert's metaphor, the political Power doesn't give the laws out of its pleasure; it is the source of law, but the source only pours from the subterranean pressure of the groundwater – and this is what is interesting to unfold.[67]

But how do material sources influence law?

Positivists usually recognize *interpretation* as the activity through which material sources go into the meaning of legal provisions. 'Method', as Vogenauer put, 'is usually employed to refer to the "path" or the "way" from an existing source of law to the decision on a particular legal issue in a given situation'. And here comes the crucial part: 'Understood in this sense, it concerns the application and the interpretation of the law and is a synonym for the "legal reasoning" that is more frequently used in common law systems.'[68] Put differently, legal methodology (*méthologie juridique*), sources of law and legal reasoning are intimately related concepts.

Thus, from a positivistic theory of law, there is no doubt that material sources are at work whenever new law is created, either by legislators or judges or administrators or agencies. In that sense, material sources are part of the law, whenever and no matter how law-makers consider them. Thus, knowing of material sources is essential to understand the law of a given community. Simply put, that is why, for positivists of any lineage, it is important to know about material sources, *pace* Kelsen's considerations about the character of these 'sources', whether mandatory or optional.

It is a fact that, following modern Anglo-American debate between exclusive and inclusive positivists, the comparatist can still debate the moral value

---

[65] In Brazil, see Dimoulis 2016: 170–96 (on sources); 2006 (on positivism).
[66] Papaux & Cerutti 2020: 116.
[67] See Ripert 1955: 80.
[68] See Vogenauer 2019: 890.

of legal sources.[69] Would they count as valid laws even if they are morally wrong? Or shall they necessarily be morally valuable in order to count as valid law? Exclusive legal positivists would answer positively for the first and negatively for the second question. In contrast, inclusive legal positivists would have a more nuanced answer for both questions: the moral content of the legal source should be considered if a legal norm in the system so requires. But *that answer* doesn't restrain the interpreter from searching for the material sources of law. On the contrary, it requires knowing them.

Exclusive and inclusive positivists cannot simply dismiss material sources. For example, in evaluating the validity of a legal norm, inclusive legal positivists would consider the moral merit of material sources, while exclusive legal positivists wouldn't. Yet, again, *that* specific nuance doesn't interfere with the fact that material sources, for positivists, are to be searched for and comprehended.

Understood in that way, positivism can't ignore the *context* (moral, social, political, historical) in which the *text* is inserted.[70]

Following positivism of the Hartian lineage, this book does not ignore that law and adjudication are intrinsically political and that jurisprudence is part of a more general political theory.[71] So are comparative public law and legal theory. While not falling into the trap of a murky concept of 'culture', the positivist methodology of conceptually *separating*, but not *isolating*, formal and material sources is a tool that helps us to understand our legal institutions better, not merely to know them.[72] Hart himself thought that natural law has a great merit of showing 'the need to study law in the context of other disciplines and foster[ing] awareness of how unspoken assumptions, common sense, and moral aims influence the law and enter into adjudication'; but all that, Hart thought, 'can be taught in other ways'.[73]

Yet it does not follow from this that law hands over its authority to morals, social sciences, history or political theory. On the contrary, the law may draw upon concepts from other disciplines, which does not mean that law incorporates them *tout court*. What happens, as Ralf Poscher claimed, following Max Weber's methodological teaching, is that the law, in a *preliminary analysis*, shares common concepts with the other disciplines; still, later, the law may,

---

[69]   I thank Joseph Raz for email exchanges about the subject of this and the following paragraph.
[70]   In French *droit administratif* nowadays, this idea is expressed by Pleassix 2020: XII–XIII.
[71]   See Green 2012: xv (on Hart's message).
[72]   See Hart 1983 [1954]: 21 ('In law as elsewhere, we can know and yet not understand').
[73]   Hart 1983: 11.

and pervasively does, transform them, through legal methods and from the doctrinal and institutional necessities of the law itself, into legal conceptions, which ultimately ends up deflating the Hart–Dworkin debate about law and morality.[74]

In any event, the primary purpose of the conceptual separation of law from other realms is, therefore, *clarity*: it is by separating – but not isolating – law from morals and different assumptions behind the law that we can morally criticize the law and eventually improve it. Clarity is also the primary purpose of separating 'law' and 'non-law', 'formal' and 'material' sources of law.

From the viewpoint of any lawyer, what is the point of knowing how the *Conseil d'État* has decided or would decide a case about state liability in torts or contracts if one has little idea that the state liability in France was developed in the wake of the construction of a new theory of State, and in response to particular necessities with regard to the role of the state in French society? Take the *Blanco* case, decided by the *Tribunal des Conflits* in 1873 – perhaps the best known in the French public law history – which has 'emancipat[ed] French public law from the restrictions imposed by private-law concepts'.[75] Nevertheless, *Blanco*'s ruling, crucial to French law, is only a formal source of law.

But formal sources – from norms posited in statutes, by-laws and regulations to legal decisions and scholarly opinions – are better understood, in public contract law, if we conduct, as Jèze would have taken it, research on the different philosophies (Empiricism versus Rationalism) and forms of reasoning (systematic versus non-systematic), as well as research on the opposing notions of state and individual and on the contrasting conceptions of public interest. And these social aspects are historically and politically situated. These subjects will be tackled in due course.

In Chapter 2, I will present a sketch of the black letter exorbitant rules and some formal sources. First I would like to make one last observation about the comparative law approach, however obvious it may appear.

5.   THE GENERAL CHARACTER OF COMPARATIVE LAW

The epigraph of this book features a phrase from Jean Bodin (1530–96), the father of the modern idea of public law, taken from his *Method for the Easy Comprehension of History* (1566) – a deceiving title.[76] By deploying a *proces-*

---

74   See Poscher 2009.
75   Bernard Schwartz 1956: 251.
76   See Loughin 2018: 988.

sus comparatiste, Bodin tried to understand the public law, *le droit politique*, through the comprehension of historical facts – not the profusions of facts' details, but their 'spirit' – thus anticipating Montesquieu's idea of highlighting what the times and peoples would take as typical and constant. To be able to judge other men, historians should be open to generalization.[77]

Politics is not an exact science, as we have known since Aristotle. 'Therefore in discussing subjects and arguing for evidence', Aristotle wrote about politics, 'we must be satisfied with a broad outline of the truth to indicate the truth with a rough and general sketch'. And later on, he concluded that 'demanding logical demonstrations from a teacher of rhetoric is clearly about as reasonable as accepting mere plausibility from a mathematician'.[78]

All that applies to statements and discussions about the law, mainly to a comparative public law study: thus, throughout this book, broad claims will be made, but none is absolute. For instance, I'll claim that Americans believe in and live by a *positive* conception of individualism, whereas French and Brazilians hold a *negative* conception; that America is a 'stateless society' whereas France and Brazil are 'State societies'; that the French conception of *intérêt général* is Rousseauian, while the American is utilitarian (and Brazil is searching for one). These claims, of course, may not fit *all* American, French or Brazilian individuals. It is possible, for instance, that in Louisiana or the countryside of Texas, there's a community that holds communitarian values more strongly than a group of businessmen in Bordeaux or São Paulo city. Nevertheless, generalizations, so long as they are accurate, are a necessary component of comparative law. Again, I will compare, not pontificate.[79]

---

[77] See Goyard-Fabre 1989: 66–7.
[78] *Nicomachean Ethics*, B I, Ch 3, 1094b.
[79] See Whitman 2003a: 16.

2. Black letter rules and formal sources: an overview of exceptionalism

States' different treatment in the three legal systems runs from the formation stage through performance of contracts. Below are only some of the critical norms similarly encountered at the black letter law level.

1. CONTRACTS' FORMATION

At this stage, states usually have additional obligations and duties to perform. Perhaps the most important is the duty to promote full and open competition in awarding most public contracts,[1] which considerably diminishes governments' freedom to contract.

Yet some remarks are noteworthy: only in the US and Brazil is full and open competition expressly consecrated in laws and regulations,[2] Brazil even having elevated the norm to constitutional status.[3] In France, *l'Administration* was freer to contract, generally enjoying its *liberté contractuelle*.[4] The standard doctrine usually mentioned that the *Conseil d'État*, in *Chambre synd. des agents d'assurance des Hautes-Pyrénées* (1984) and confirmed in *Ville de Paris* (2010), established that there was no general principle mandating the *personnes publiques* to undertake any bidding process (*concurrence*) to contract, and that the obligation of *mise en concurrence* should be established either by law or by regulation.[5]

---

[1]   In the US, see Schwartz 2010: 630–7.

[2]   'Full and open competition' is required in the US by 10 USC § 2304(a)(1)(A) (regarding military and NASA contracts); 41 USC § 253(a) (regarding contracting by most civilian agencies). In Brazil, art. 11, II, of the LLCA/2021 reads: 'The bidding process has as goes: […] II. To assure […] open competition'.

[3]   Article 37, XXI ('with the exception of the cases specified in law, public works, services, purchases and disposals *shall be contracted by public bidding proceedings* that ensure equal conditions to all bidders, with clauses that establish payment obligations, maintaining the effective conditions of the bid, as the law provides, which shall only allow the requirements of technical and economic qualifications indispensable to guarantee the fulfilling of the obligations') (emphasis added).

[4]   See Richer & Lichère 2019: 131; Hourson & Yolka 2020: 40–1; Ubaud-Bergeron 2019: 60–8.

[5]   See Lichère 2020: 73. See also Richer & Lichère 2019: 132, 405.

However, this freedom was never absolute in France,[6] and recent changes in posited norms have almost standardized an obligation of public competition under the growing influence of the liberal ethos embedded in the Directions of the European Union.[7] Thus, even though there is still no explicit legal norm imposing an obligation on the government to *mise en concurrence* in contracting,[8] whether or not to submit all *contracts publics à objet ou à effet économique* to competition is a matter of great controversy in French *droit des contrats publics*.[9]

Moreover, a vast quantity of norms fix special requirements of government procurement formation in the three countries. Scholars label them 'reverse' or 'positive' exceptionalism in the US[10] and *sujétions exorbitantes* in French;[11] they are given no specific name in Brazil. These requirements and limitations are extensively regulated in all three legal systems and deal with various types of competitive procedures, as well as the manifold consequences that spread from them: when, how and under what circumstances to conduct (or to dismiss, or make flexible, when and if possible) a sealed bidding or a competitive negotiation; the requirements for the bidding process per se, when applicable; its types, formats, exigencies, general rules for solicitations; its rules of publicity (conditions of posting, timing, locality, format); the bidder's pre-qualifications or special technical requirements, and so on. Scrutiny of all these contingencies may reveal various similarities and differences in the three legal systems according to the numerous distinct goals and objects of each legal order and type of contract. As already stated, since they impose extra obligations and duties on the government, I won't conduct an enumeration of these requirements or a side-by-side comparison of rules in this book.[12] Ultimately, all these requirements shall respond to similar legal principles of efficiency, transparency and equality of opportunity for bidding, consecrated in similar language in laws and regulations in the three countries.[13]

---

[6]   See Ubaud-Bergeron 2019: 64–5; Dufau 2000: 12133; Traité 1: § 553.

[7]   For an overview of the battle between *liberté contractuelle* and *mise en concurrence*, see Ubaud-Bergeron 2019: 223–39. See also Amilhat 2014: 251. For a concise overview of the formation of *contrats administratifs*, see Hourson & Yolka 2020: 86–98.

[8]   See Ubaud-Bergeron 2019: 225.

[9]   See Plessix 2020: 1307; Amilhat 2014: 182–7.

[10]   See Schwartz 2004: 5, 30–43.

[11]   See Dufau 2000.

[12]   For the US, see Cibinic et al 2011: chapters 3–7. For France, see Hourson & Yolka 2020: chapter 3. For Brazil, see Justen Filho 2019: chapters 2–4; 2021: 256–1188.

[13]   In the US, FAR 1.102 provides 'guiding principles for the Federal Acquisition System' that do not differ much, in textual form, from the principles established in the

2.   CONTRACTS' PERFORMANCE

Exceptionalism/*exorbitance/exorbitância* as a prerogative *enjoyed* by the state is located in contracts' performance. I will briefly explain 'internal' or 'direct' and 'external' or 'indirect' forms of exceptionalism for organizing purposes.

2.1   Internal or Direct Exceptionalism

In the *International Encyclopedia of Comparative Law* (1982), Turpin begins the analysis of 'prerogatives of the public authority' in public contracts by affirming that 'the element of public interest' is 'significantly more prominent in the sphere of public contracting' than in private contracts; these prerogatives are vested in the administration due to the apparent interest in ensuring that the public funds committed to the procurement of goods and services are carried out with efficiency and economy.[14]

Turpin then delineates the main prerogatives: '(1) control or direction of the contract (including the variation of contractual conditions); (2) unilateral termination of the contract; and (3) sanctions against the contractor (including re-adjustment of the contract price or recovery of excess profits).'[15] In broad terms, the list is accurate.[16] We may call Turpin's examples 'internal' or 'direct' exceptionalism since they relate to the power that governments exercise *within* the contract. It is noteworthy that internal exceptionalism is similar in all three systems studied here (and many others), as far as the posited rules are concerned.

In the US, the Federal Acquisition Regulation (FAR),[17] effective as of 1 April 1984, is the source of most of the rules applicable to government procurements of all federal agencies that do not have a specific exemption (such as the Federal Aviation Administration and the Postal Service). For example, the FAR provides, in its fundamental changes clause, that '[t]he Contracting

---

French CCP/2018 or the Brazilian LLCA/2021. None of these specific norms will be covered here.

[14]   Turpin 1982: 36.

[15]   Ibid: 37.

[16]   Particularities of a given legal system and personal preferences in cataloguing the exceptional rules can make the list shorter or longer, but not substantially different. For instance, Schwartz (2004: 18) expressly includes the power to 'suspend or defer the performance of a government contract' in his examples of exceptionalism.

[17]   Throughout this book, *all* information about the FAR, either in the text or in footnotes, is taken from the *Government Contracts Reference Book* by Nash et al 2021 and will be cited/quoted without quotation marks. The FAR is published in Title 48 of the Code of Federal Regulations, and I'll henceforth omit the '48 CFR' and replace it only with 'FAR'.

Officer may at any time, by written order, and without notice to the sureties, if any, make changes within the general scope of this contract',[18] specifying the circumstances in which changes can be made.[19] But suppose the change 'causes an increase or decrease' either in cost or in time required for the performance of the contract. In that case the Contracting Officer 'shall make an equitable adjustment in the contract price, the delivery schedule, or both, and shall modify the contract'.[20]

There was no statute or regulation expressly dealing with the problem of changes in France until very recently. But the CCP/2018 has consecrated, upon compensation, the *pouvoir de modification unilatérale* in its Article L.6-3°, L.2194-2, and L.3135.2. As in the US, the modifications cannot affect the contract's 'essential conditions' (*conditions essentielles*).[21] However, very early in French law – in the case *Compagnie nouvelle du Gaz de Deville-Lès-Rouen*, decided by the *Conseil* in 1902, and especially after *Compagnie française des tramways*, decided in 1910[22] – the power to make unilateral changes was granted to the Administration, provided that the changes do not affect the 'financial clauses', and subject to the requirement for compensation for prejudice modifications.[23] There were indeed years of doctrinal discussion and somewhat ambiguous decisions.[24] Still, ultimately the power to make changes was unambiguously recognized by the *Conseil d'État* on 2 February 1983, in *Union de transport public urbains et régionaux*.[25]

Similarly, the Brazilian LLCA/2021, Article 104, I, and LLCA/1993, Article 58, I, confer on the government the power to change a contract to adjust the contract in the public interest, provided that the changes respect the contractor's rights. In addition, LLCA/2021, Article 124, I, and LLCA/1993, Article 65, I, qualify the previous general rule and permit unilateral changes by

---

[18]   FAR 52.243-1(a) (fixed-price) and FAR 52.243-2 (a) (cost-reimbursement). On changes in the American law, see Cibinic et al 2016: chapter 4; Schwartz 2022: 755–71; 2010: 638–9.

[19]   See FAR 52.243-1 and 2 (a)(1–3). There then follow five alternates with minor modifications providing for in-service contracts. There is a similar, separate clause for fixed-price construction contracts in FAR 52.243-4.

[20]   FAR 52.243-1(b).

[21]   See Richer & Lichère 2019: 252 (citing cases). For a classic discussion, see *Traité 2*: §§ 1167–78.

[22]   See *Traité 2*: § 1173.

[23]   See Richer & Lichère 2019: 250–3; Ubaud-Bergeron 2019 : 379–96; *Traité 2*: § 1173.

[24]   For an inventory of the doctrine and its tendencies, as well as a brief survey of the decisions before 1983 about the power to make changes in the *contrats administratifs*, see Llorens 1984; *Traité 2*: § 1174; Richer & Lichère 2019: 250–3.

[25]   See eg *Traité 2*: § 1173; Richer & Lichère 2019: 251; Lichère 2020: 112.

the government in two situations: (a) to better adjust, technically, the project to its goals; and (b) when it is necessary to quantitatively modify the price of the contract, within the statutory limits and the scope of the contract.[26] Finally, Article 130 establishes that when the change causes the increase of contractors' duties, the Administration must re-establish the contract's 'financial equilibrium'.[27] This last rule is designed to balance the power to change with the obligation to compensate. In short, Brazilian 'financial equilibrium' is the functional equivalent to the 'equitable adjustment' clause in the US procurement system.

Another internal exceptional feature common to all three public contracts systems is governments' power to inspect contracts' performance. The FAR grants the government a broad authority to perform its inspections in various contracts in the US.[28] In France, this power was deemed to be encompassed by the *pouvoir de contrôle et de direction*,[29] accepted and acknowledged by most of the doctrine as a general rule applicable to the *contrat administratif*, even if the contract was silent.[30] Courts, however, were reluctant to admit such a power when the contract is silent,[31] or if there was no legislative or regulatory source.[32] The CCP/2018 expressly states the authority in Article L. 6, 1°. In Brazil the power to inspect is inherent to a broader State prerogative to 'control' the contract's performance, expressly stated in Article 104, III of the LLCA/2021.[33]

---

[26]   Articles 65, § 1° (LLCA/1993) and 125 (Law 14,133/2021) establish that the contractor must accept unilateral changes made by the government in public works, services and purchases provided that the changes are up to 25 per cent of the initial value of the contract, and up to 50 per cent in the specific case of remodeling a building or equipment. Art. 65, § 2° (LLCA/1993) prohibits any changes superior to the aforesaid limits. On changes in Brazilian law, see Guimarães 2003: chapters 2–5; Justen Filho 2019: 1275–1361; 2021: 1405–18.

[27]   Equivalent to Art. 65, § 6°, LLCA/1993.

[28]   FAR 52.246-2 through -8 and -10 require the contractor to (1) provide and maintain an inspection system that is acceptable to the government, (2) give the government the right to perform reviews and evaluations as reasonably necessary, and (3) keep complete records of its inspection work and make them available to the government. On inspection in American law: see Cibinic et al 2016: chapter 9.

[29]   See Hourson & Yolka 2020: 115–16; Richer & Lichère 2019: 255–7.

[30]   See Traité 2: §§ 383–7; Péquignot 2020 [1945]: 284–96.

[31]   CE, 3 Apr 1925, *Ville de Mascara*, cited by Richer & Lichère 2019: 257.

[32]   CE, 18 Jul 1930, *Compagnie des Chemins de fer PLM et autres*, cited by Richer & Lichère 2019: 257.

[33]   Equivalent to Art. 58, III, LLCA/1993.

Also, in the US, the FAR provides the general clause for 'default termination' by the government,[34] which exercises the government's right to wholly or partially terminate a contract because of the contractor's actual or anticipated failure to perform its contractual obligations. A vital element of exceptionalism is the so-called strict compliance doctrine, which holds that the government is not forced to accept performance that is not strictly up to contract specifications, termination for default being possible even if the performance is substantial even in the case that any defect is non-material.[35] In France, the government power of *résiliation pour faute* ('default termination') is usually present in French *contrats administratifs*, and courts imply its existence even if the contract is silent.[36] Moreover, when the *contrat administratif* enumerates the motifs for *résiliation pour faute*, the judge will consider the enumeration non-exhaustive.[37] In Brazil, a similar rule in Articles 104, IV and 137, I of the LLCA/2021 gives the government the power to apply sanctions caused by a contractor's default, even if it is only partial.[38]

Yet the best example of internal exceptionalism, the 'most radical of special prerogatives enjoyed by the administration', is the power governments have to terminate the contract for its convenience, 'a widespread feature of national systems of procurement', in Turpin's language.[39]

In the US, almost all government contracts contain the standard Termination for the Convenience of the Government clause, which, using inclusive language, grants the government the right to terminate the contract when it is 'in the Government's interest'.[40] That is '[p]erhaps the single most striking example of the exceptionalist phenomenon, and one that most clearly reflects its characteristics'.[41] If the contract is silent about termination for convenience, the courts read the contract as if it were included, as established by the '*Christian* doctrine', set in *G.L. Christian and Associates v the US* (1963).[42]

---

[34]   FAR 52.249-8 through -10. On default termination, see Cibinic et al 2016: chapter 10; Schwartz 2022: 803–16; 2010: 641–2.

[35]   See Schwartz 2004: 18–20, specifically note 15.

[36]   CE 30 Sep. 1983, *SARL. Comexp.*, cited by Richer & Lichère 2019: 246.

[37]   See Richer & Lichère 2019: 246. On default termination in France, see Traité 1: §§ 763–5; Hourson & Yolka 2020: 133–4.

[38]   Equivalent to Arts 58, IV, and 77, LLCA/1993. See Justen Filho 2019: 1230–1, 1398–1421; 2021: 1285–6, 1464–7.

[39]   Turpin 1982: 40.

[40]   FAR 52.249-1 through -5.

[41]   Schwartz 2004: 26.

[42]   The '*G. L. Christian* doctrine' is applicable not only to the termination-for-convenience clause but also to all mandatory clauses, which are to be read into the contract even if they have been omitted by mistake. See Cibinic et al (2011, Ch. 1, Section II); Schwartz 2022: 122; 2010: 639–41; 2004: 24, 679. Before *G.*

In France, *le pouvoir de résiliation unilatérale sans faute* in the name of the *intérêt général* has long been recognized as a general rule applicable to the *contrats administratifs*, being recently labelled as 'perhaps the *prérogative exorbitante par excellence*'.[43] Georges Péquignot (1914–2003), author of the first *Théorie Général du Contrat Administratif*, wrote in 1945 that this is 'one of the less contested Government's rights [*droits the l'Administration*] in our field',[44] accepted as it had been since the mid-nineteenth century at least.[45] Like in the US, this prerogative is considered granted to the Administration even if the contract is silent.[46] Nowadays, this power is 'carved on the marble of the CCP/2018',[47] in Articles L. 6, 5°, L. 2195-3 2°, L. 2195-6 and L. 3136-3 2°.

In Brazil, the LLCA/2021, Articles 104, II and 137, VIII, consecrate the unilateral rescission of the contract by the government for 'reasons of public interest, justified by the maxim authority of the administrative agency'. They correspond to Articles 52, II and 78, XII, of the LLCA/1993 (for 'reasons of high relevancy, well known public interest, [provided that these reasons are both] justified and determined by the head of the agency to which the contractor is subordinated and taken in the respective administrative proceeding').

The doctrines above diverge significantly from those applied to private contract law in analogous circumstances. In this book's final chapter I will explore, albeit briefly, the prerogative of termination of contracts for the government's convenience.

There are, however, other examples of exceptionalism that are more far-reaching in scope than the ones mentioned previously (except for termination for convenience). They trigger more fundamental questions in terms of the legal epistemology and jurisprudence of public contracts. I will now introduce these other examples of 'external exceptionalism', which will be the object of deeper scrutiny throughout this book.

2.2   External or Indirect Exceptionalism

Under the label 'indirect impairment of performance', Turpin's comparative analysis also explains that an alteration of the regular contractual performance

---

L. Christian, however, if the government terminated a contract for its convenience in the absence of a statute or regulation, or when the contract was silent, government could be held in breach, and the contractor could recover anticipated profits. See Beauregard 1965: 259.

[43]   Plessix 2020: 1353.
[44]   Péquignot 2020 [1945]: 360.
[45]   See Richer & Lichère 2019: 238 (citing cases); Hourson & Yolka 2020: 130–2.
[46]   See Richer & Lichère 2019: 238.
[47]   CCPcom/2021: 462.

may result from governmental acts that are in their nature extraneous to the contractual relationship. This risk, to which contractors are exposed, is inherent to public contracting. When the government enters into a contract, it never leaves aside its sovereign status or its general responsibilities in pursuing public welfare.[48]

Imagine, for instance, that the state passes a new statute regulating the production, transportation and storage of specific products considered dangerous to public health. Further, imagine that the government has contracted, under the old rules, with one or several firms to perform one or all of these activities now regulated by a new statute. Finally, consider that none of these activities was regulated (or that they were regulated differently) at the time of the original contract and that the new law or regulation impairs each contractor's position compared to the original contract. Or suppose that a state, pursuing the legitimate interest of defending its internal economy, adopts an economic policy to prohibit, for a certain period, the importation of, say, agricultural products from a foreign country, thus affecting or even barring the performance of all government contracts aimed at delivering food for the needy, or for troops stationed abroad. Is the government responsible for damages resulting from this obstruction of performance? If so, to what extent is the government accountable? Does the government responsibility have anything to do with the cause of the policy adopted?

Now think of a policy being adopted in response to a natural disaster, or during wartime, or a pandemic such as SARS-CoV-2. Does that make any difference? How about changes in government policies for 'merely ideological' reasons? Think of all economic plans, handed down sometimes abruptly in either developing or developed nations, which, even if ostensibly aimed at the public good, end up harming contractors. Economic plans can be (and often are) based on different conceptions about the state's role in societies, contrasting theories that are always based on political economies and philosophies. In all these cases, which could effortlessly be multiplied in kind and complexity,[49] does the state have the duty to compensate the injured contractors? Is there any difference if the 'sovereign act' derives from the executive or the legislative power? Which, if any, are the criteria or standards that courts should use when facing these problems?

These examples raise the complex problem of state responsibility for sovereign acts. In juridical terms, a state sovereign act is not a specific, direct change

---

[48]   See Turpin 1982: 39.
[49]   For examples in American law, see Cibinic et al 2016: chapter 3, section VI (citing cases in which the Sovereign Act Doctrine ('SAD') was successfully used to bar contractors' claims for damages).

caused by the 'internal' government's power to modify public procurements but an indirect alteration to the contract caused by an 'external' regular governmental activity. A state sovereign act interferes with the normal course of the contract, which leads to the old, highly complex theme of state liability, or, more specifically, to the problem of state liability *without fault*. This – the issue of 'external exceptionalism' – must be analysed within the context of state liability.

In the US, such questions fall under the theory of 'Sovereign Acts Doctrine' or 'Sovereign Acts Defense' (SAD) and its variation, the 'Unmistakability Doctrine'. The SAD, in brief, is said to shield the government from contractual liability 'for acts performed by it in its sovereign capacity'.[50] This doctrine, recognized by the Supreme Court as early as 1924 in *Horowitz v US*, holds that the government is not liable for breach of contract damages resulting from its 'public and general acts as a sovereign'.[51] Applying similar principles of sovereignty, the Unmistakability Doctrine, articulated in 1982 by the Supreme Court in *Merrion v Jicarilla Apache Tribe* and in 1986 in *Bowen v Public Agencies Opposed to Social Security Entrapment* (*POSSE*),[52] holds that government 'contracts should be construed, if possible, to avoid foreclosing [the] exercise of sovereign authority', and that 'sovereign power, even when unexercised, is an enduring presence that governs all contracts subject to sovereign jurisdiction, and will remain intact unless surrendered in unmistakable terms'.[53]

The French/Brazilian 'functional equivalent' of SAD and the Unmistakability Doctrine seems to be the theory of the *fait du Prince/fato do Príncipe* (literally, 'Fact of the Prince', or, in Turpin's translations, 'Act of Sovereignty').[54] But caution is in order here, for the very use of a functional equivalence must be adequately understood in public law. Moreover, although conceived as playing a role similar to these American doctrines,[55] the assertion of equality between SAD and *fait du Prince* may be somewhat misleading, as I will explain shortly. In any case, for the moment, it is essential to mention two general points briefly.

---

[50] Latham 1975: 30.

[51] *Horowitz v US*, 267 US 458, 461 (1924). See Turpin 1982: 40.

[52] 455 US 130 (1982); 477 US 41 (1986).

[53] 477 US at 52–3 (quoting *Merrion v Jicarilla Apache Tribe*, 455 US 130, 148 (1982)).

[54] Turpin 1982: 40, 44–5.

[55] See Turpin 1982: 40. Turpin doesn't use the term 'functional equivalent'. But he dealt with the SAD and *fait du Prince* under the same item, called 'indirect impairment of performance'. However, Turpin treated with greater care the theory of *fait du Prince* in another item, called, suggestively, 'relief of the contractor', perhaps conscious that the equivalence between the SAD and *fait du Prince* would be somehow misleading.

The first is the practical problem of whether the contractor injured by a sovereign act is entitled to compensation. In France (and Brazil), this problem is treated by the theories of *fait du Prince* and *imprévision*. In the US, the issue is treated by SAD and the Unmistakability Doctrine. In this sense, the American and French (or Brazilian) theories are equivalent. The second point is that in none of the three legal systems would a contractor be entitled to compensation if the 'sovereign act' is considered 'public and general': in this broad sense, all theories are similarly structured.[56]

Moreover, under the umbrella of 'external exceptionalism', besides *fait du Prince/fato do Príncipe*, another critical theory constitutes French/Brazilian exorbitant public contract law systems: the theory of *imprévision/imprevisão* (unforeseen contingencies).

However, to deal with the 'sovereign acts' – the core exceptionalism[57] – we need to dig into the foundations of public contracts, and to do so will take the rest of the book. So I'll try, first, to justify the comparative law approach I will undertake, thus preparing the argument for the next chapter.

3. DIGGING DEEPER

Two theories deal with the problem of sovereign acts. They are the core of public contracts in the US: the 'Sovereign Acts Doctrine' or 'Sovereign Acts Defense' (SAD) and the 'Unmistakability Doctrine', which are, according to Schwartz, 'the true apotheosis of exceptionalism'.[58] Their French and Brazilian 'functional equivalents', I repeat, would be the theories of *fait du Prince/fato do Príncipe* and *imprévision/imprevisão*.[59] The issue in all these

---

[56]   See Turpin 1982: 44–5 (examining only French law).

[57]   No wonder that SAD appears in the title, and permeates the whole work, of Schwartz's (1996) seminal article about the issue, suggestively labelled *Liability for Sovereign Acts: Congruence and Exceptionalism in Government Contracts Law* and the finest scholarly effort in the US towards a theoretical understanding of the nature of public procurement.

[58]   Schwartz 2004: 26.

[59]   As we will see in Chapter 8, Brazilian law has imported the French notions of *fait du Prince* and *imprévision*, with some qualifications. In this section I will use only the French words. I will show later in this chapter that, according to part of the French doctrine, *fait du Prince* may also encompass what was *supra* called 'internal' power to change contract, that is, *fait du Prince* would be the genus of which the power to make changes (*pouvoir de modification unilatérale*) would be the species. See eg the classic book by Badaoui 1955, who nevertheless used the same idea of 'internal' and 'external' modification to refer to the same phenomena I am dealing with. In this book, I will refer to *fait du Prince* only with respect to external changes. *Traité 2*: §§ 1291–3 also remarks that the expression *fait du Prince* can be understood *lato sensu* and *stricto sensu*.

theories is whether the state is liable for damages when otherwise lawful government activities, carried out in the state's sovereign capacity, cause the contract's impairment.[60]

While searching for similarities and taking advantage of the idea of functional equivalence, the comparatist, in examining the three systems, may conclude that the problem of state responsibility for sovereign acts receives similar treatment in the US, France and Brazil.

The three legal systems appear to work, in broad terms, within the following two-part structure. First, we should ask whether the external government activity that impairs the contract is 'public and general',[61] and whether the loss suffered by the contractor is not 'special'. If these two inter-related conditions obtain, then the contractor is not entitled to recover any damages. Thus, under this scenario, the remaining question in the three legal systems would be to find out what 'public and general' and 'special loss' mean.

Second, the comparatist who undertakes a quick survey of the doctrine and court decisions (law's formal sources) in either legal system perceives that no clear-cut formula exists to determine what a sovereign act would be. The 'public and general' standard and the 'special loss' formula are open-ended criteria to guide courts. As we will see, in the US, the 'public and general' standard is said to have been invoked 'mechanically'.[62] Moreover, the Supreme Court has not yet provided clear guidance to clarify what a 'public and general' act means; in France and Brazil, the scenario is similar. French doctrine and courts continue to inquire about the nature of the government action to determine what government action would be exempt from compensation, but no clear guidance is provided.

From this perspective, the comparatist may also conclude that similar practical consequences attach to comparable situations in all systems. For instance, in American law, the enactment of legislation or the promulgation of regulation to alter or remove price controls, establish or modify minimum wage or implement monetary or fiscal policy are usually considered 'sovereign acts' by boards and courts.[63] Therefore, if the government takes any of these actions during contract performance, no compensation is due even if the contractor is

---

[60] Sovereignty and state are connected concepts. See Loughlin 2010: 184 ('the notion of the "sovereign state" is tautological'); 2003: 73 (citing Charles Loyseau). See also Beaud 1984: 13; Heuschling 2002: 419.

[61] The 'generic quality of the interfering act' is deemed to be 'the most important factor' to be analysed to establish or negate government liability for breach of contract. Schwartz 1996: 698.

[62] Schwartz 1996: 666.

[63] I paraphrased examples from Latham (1975: 34) (citing many boards' and courts' decisions). See also Cibinic et al 2016: chapter 3, section VI.

adversely affected. The consequences of these sovereign acts are roughly the same in France, but not quite so in Brazil. What differs radically is the epistemology behind the practical results.

Yet the equivalence between SAD or the Unmistakability Doctrine and *fait du Prince* or *imprévision* is, I insist, beguiling. The very use of 'functional equivalents' in comparative public law is, if anything, riskier than in private law, the branch for which the notion of functional equivalent was devised. Private law directs its attention mainly to the relations between arguably coequal parties; it deals with the so-called relationships of coordination,[64] being designed to cope primarily with problems of corrective justice.[65]

In contrast, public law is 'particularly ideological',[66] more 'closely connected to the national political and administrative process';[67] it has stronger historical, political particularities and deals mainly with distributive justice.[68] Public law 'is even more national-specific than private law to the extent that it's more closely imbricated in the distinctive policy prevailing at local level';[69] it deals with political issues more closely; it reflects, again, political philosophy and political disputes more clearly than private law. *Le droit politique*, an expression still used by many, is perhaps the best example.[70] Accordingly, the function of legal theories in public law becomes more openly 'politicized' than in private law. Public law, Martin Loughlin wrote bluntly, 'is simply a sophisticated form of political discourse', and 'controversies within the subject [of public law] are simply extended political disputes'.[71]

That is a crucial point, and jurists are not willing to admit it. In France, the political character of the decisions of the *Conseil d'État* and the *Tribunal des Conflits* was brought to light and scrutinized by a group of scholars in a recent

---

[64] See Radbruch 1950 [1932]: 153. In Brazilian doctrine, see Loureiro Filho 2001: 203.

[65] This is an oversimplification of a complex issue. I stick to the classic Aristotelian idea of corrective and distributive justice in Book V of *The Nicomachean Ethics*. Private law as the proper realm of corrective justice is Aristotle's idea. See Weinrib 1995: chapter 3. But in all private law issues, which are supposedly related mainly to corrective justice, there is always a minimal apportionment of distributive justice. To isolate private relations from any distributive element of justice is hardly possible. My intention is only to emphasize that *political* issues relate more closely to public than to private law.

[66] Kischel 2019: 36.

[67] Bell 2002: 244.

[68] See Plessix 2003a: 494–8; 2020: 714.

[69] Legrand 2002: 246. Of course, private law has its historical and cultural particularities as well. Again, I am only emphasizing the 'more political' features of public law uniqueness.

[70] See Loughlin 2003: 71; 2010: 231–7; 2018: chapter 5.

[71] Loughlin 1992: 4; 2003: 132. See also Triepel 1986 [1926].

book entitled *Les Grands arrêts politiques de la jurisprudence du droit administratif* (GAPJA). At the beginning of GAPJA, Jacques Caillosse criticizes the traditional way jurists comment on administrative courts decisions, a method that neutralizes the role of the political in law – *'une sorte de grammaire du neutre'* practised in the French *doxa doctrinale*. The GAPJA, writes Caillosse, exposes the vulnerability of this model of thinking and advocates an approach that evidences the inseparability of the legal and the political character of *la jurisprudence administrative*.[72] I will try to take GAPJA's message seriously.

In the next section, I will briefly expose the extent and the scope of this research, and explain how the arguments will be organized in the upcoming pages.

4.   COMPARING THE *FOUNDATIONS* OF PUBLIC CONTRACTS: WHAT ARE WE TALKING ABOUT?

From the list of the primary examples of exceptionalism in public procurement in the three countries under scrutiny, one might conclude that the similarities between the systems are many. Were this a dogmatic, formal-sources comparative law work, it would suffice to describe the leading cases, perhaps quoting scholarly comments, and add a short conclusion conceding, correctly, that those listed prerogatives are granted to the government 'in order that the public interest may be protected'.[73] It is now a truism that public contract law norms empower governments with prerogatives that depart from the norms of private contracts – norms that we call exorbitant.[74]

Yet my goal is not to update Turpin's descriptive work from 1982, adding Brazil to the legal systems scrutinized. Instead, a deeper theoretical comparative study of the foundations of public contracts may aid a better understanding of the subject.[75] As Schwartz has argued, 'the exceptionalism/congruence spectrum has the potential to be a particularly useful device for comparative law studies of public procurement law, transcending some of the conventional difficulties associated with comparison in isolation of seemingly parallel portions of disparate legal systems'.[76]

---

[72]   See Caillosse 2019: 21–3.
[73]   Turpin 1982: 36.
[74]   Schwartz (2004: 13) warned us of the danger of comparing the degree of exceptionalism or congruence of two or more legal systems without previously making a study of this particular feature within the same legal system.
[75]   See Hoecke 2004: 191.
[76]   Schwartz 2004: 7, 11–15.

We will see that the three systems of public contract law are different at the epistemological level. They differ in the ways jurists and lawyers *perceive* and *understand* both the world and the law (of government contracts). American lawyers and French or Brazilian jurists have, so to speak, divergent *mentalités.*[77]

Instead of lawyers, I'll stick to *jurists* to refer to French and Brazilian legal actors. The difference is as acceptable as it is revealing: while jurists were very influential in many continental law nations, such as Prussia, Portugal and France, lawyers were crucial to the formation of common law countries such as England and the US.[78] Jurists trained in Roman law aimed to justify the Roman tradition and forge legal arguments supporting the royal and, later, state power and bureaucracy. Jurists at Sorbonne and Coimbra played this role. In contrast, lawyers, with their practical conception of the world, and trained in the English Inns of Court as they were, were the by-product of the Anglo-American pragmatic culture. This difference helps to understand the prominent *normative* role of the scholarly work (*la doctrine*) in forming public law in France and Brazil. Nothing similar has happened in the US.

When an average American lawyer faces a problem about exceptionalism, say, whether the contract termination for convenience of government grants contractors the right to total compensation, she will analyse the issue from *individualistic values* dominating in private/common law philosophy.[79] If trained in government procurement law, the lawyer will sense that the government must be treated differently from a private party. Still, the public–private law dichotomy *structure* won't control her mind. 'Attitudes and assumptions are corollaries', Örücü correctly stated.[80] A lawyer trained in government procurement law would probably come up with a practical reason to justify treating government differently. Still, she would not, as a French or Brazilian lawyer would, start by *classifying* the case as a 'public law case' and, *based on that*, assume there is a transcendent public interest to be protected.

Political theorists say that this American attorney functions within a 'stateless society' rather than a 'state society'.[81] It is not by chance that a comparative lawyer and social theorist have recently examined political economies of the US, UK, Germany and France and concluded that the US was the most market-centred and France the most state-centred.[82] For an American lawyer, any 'social' or 'communitarian' philosophy is unwelcome.

---

[77] See Legrand 1996b: 60.
[78] See Carvalho 2006: 36.
[79] Lucy (1997) suggestively took 'common law' and 'private law' as synonyms.
[80] Örücü 1987: 314–15.
[81] See eg Dyson 1980: 51–8; Jones 1993: Chapter 1; Nettl 1968: 561.
[82] Reitz 2012. See also Siems 2018: 172.

In broad terms, Americans' *mentalité* is a theoretical structure previously conceived to tackle 'private law' and 'public law' cases in the same manner. For centuries, lawyers have praised the *equality of the parties*. And they are very proud of it. Since Edward Coke (1552–1634), they have conceived sovereignty and Rule of Law (whatever they might mean by that) as incompatible concepts.[83] Albert Venn Dicey (1835–1922) thought that government and individuals must be subjected to the same law; if the lawyer is minimally trained in comparative law, she also knows that, following Dicey, different treatment for public and private entities is a horrendous thing that can only apply to the 'unfortunate countries of the Continent, especially France'.[84]

American judges are predisposed to see a hypothetical termination for convenience as a practical problem between two equal parties calling for a pragmatic solution, not for abstract theories, which are almost useless. Their cognitive apparatus is trained to 'use discrete inductive ideas capable of functioning only within limited factual spheres'.[85] Whether the decision fits within a systematic thought is unimportant; the American mind evolves by analogies, and all a judge needs is to find an *authoritative precedent* to support his outcome.[86] Since Americans disregard the Romanist-based public–private law dichotomy (for them, this is at best an academic debate between 'Legal Realists' and the so-called Classical Legal Thinkers), they are bound to apply the same law to all. Our judge may have recently heard Loren Smith, Senior and Former Chief Judge of the US Court of Federal Claims, reaffirming a common law credo: '[t]he very meaning of the rule of law is that rules bind all, government and citizens, in their conduct.'[87]

Hence, an average American lawyer, even if trained in government procurement law and therefore conscious of the cases that have established 'exceptional' treatment by courts, will, more likely than not, approach the hypothetical according to the 'private law' paradigms. Of course, she knows the introductory lesson: 'government contracts generally are not subject to the private law of contracts in the US.'[88] However, the worldview she grew up with *favours congruence, not exceptionalism.*

The paradigms navigated by the French (or Brazilian) jurist are different because her epistemological assumptions about the world have been different for centuries. In 1934 Lord Macmillan delivered a lecture at the University of

---

83   See Friedrich 1939: 20.
84   Shklar 1987: 6 (qualifying Dicey's conception of the Rule of Law as an 'unfortunate outburst of Anglo-American parochialism').
85   Legrand 1996b: 65.
86   See generally Legrand 1996b: 65–7.
87   Smith 2003: 774.
88   Schwartz 2010: 625. See also Fromont 2010: 268.

Cambridge, entitled *Two Ways of Thinking*, opposing civilian deductive and common law inductive thought, a contrast applicable to law and religion and economics and philosophy. Code-law and the case law system, 'the two great systems of law which thus divide the civilized world', said Lord Macmillan, 'exemplify the *two main types of mind*, the type that searches for the principle and the type that proceeds on precedent. The two methods are the results of widely *divergent temperaments*.'[89] Tardieu's words are definitive: '*We don't think alike*. The axes around which we revolve are not pointed in the same direction.'[90]

The French (or Brazilian, though nowadays to a lesser extent) jurist praises the State over the individual. Political theorists say they live in 'State societies'.[91] As we will see, liberalism means egoism for the average French and (to a lesser degree) Brazilian jurist. It is up to the State to lead the Nations' fate. For that reason, I will retain the capital 'S' when referring to French or Brazilian States and use a small 's' in reference to an American state or the 'state' in general. It is not a coincidence that the ideological concept of *service public*, central to the ideas of *contrats administratifs*, was constructed in the Golden Age of *droit administratif* (1880–1930), being embedded within a new political theory about the State. Concepts such as *solidarité social, responsabilité devans les charges public* and *responsabilité sans faute*, as we will see, are corollaries of the same ideology.

In their first year of law school, French and Brazilian students learn that administrative law and public contracts belong to *le droit public*, or *droit politique*, an expression still preferred by some in France.[92] This is the terminology chosen by Montesquieu and Rousseau.[93] In that sense, *le droit administratif est exorbitante*.[94] As Saillant has recently put it, *l'exorbitance* conciliates the law and the political, thus legitimating State power.[95]

Law professors tell French and Brazilian students that the separation of law in public and private has Roman origins. Public law is governed by norms that differ from private law, called ordinary law.[96] The very first paragraph of

---

[89] Macmillan 1937: 76, 81.

[90] Tardieu 1927: 64 (emphasis added).

[91] As stated below, from now on I will use capital 'S' when referring to French or Brazilian States, and small 's' for American states. I'll maintain use of the small 's' for 'the state' in general. Nettl (1968: 567) has remarked on the uniquely French capital letter in *L'État*.

[92] See Dabin 1969: 140–2; Goyard-Fabre 1997: 1; Loughlin 2010: 231–7. For the place of *droit politique* within a 'political jurisprudence', see Loughlin 2017: 74–108.

[93] See Dabin 1969: 140.

[94] See Saillant 2011, from which I derive massively.

[95] See ibid: 607–8.

[96] For a historical view, see Bigot 2002: 18–26; Mestre 1985.

the Digest (Book 1.1.1.1), the most critical part of the *Corpus Iuris*,[97] reads as follows: 'A law student at the outset of his studies ought first to know the derivation of the word *jus*. Its derivation is from *justitia*.' And right after that (Book 1.1.1.2): 'There are two branches of legal study: public and private law. Public law is that which respects the establishment of the Roman common-wealth, private that which respects individuals' interests, some matters being of public and others of private interest.'[98]

It follows that *le droit public*, not the *ius commune*, is to be applied to the State, which always acts in the name of the public interest. Thus, public law norms bear a distinguished purpose: they assure the 'triumph of the *intérêt général* over the private egoism'.[99] This seed turns into the idea of 'supremacy of public interest', which shall govern students' *mentalité* whenever they face a public law case. Brazilian Supreme Court has still been affirming the 'principle of the supremacy of public interest' for decades, despite the intense academic debate in the past 30 years.[100]

In Brazil, remarkably, two posited rules fuel the public interest ethos and the public–private law dichotomy: (i) the Federal Law of Administrative Procedure no 9,784/1999 has consecrated the 'principle of public interest' (Article 2°), which, for many, means '*supremacy* of the public interest', a principle that could be found in the General Theory of State.[101] Hence, for the students, it is the whole administrative law that is *exorbitante*, and it *has to be so* because a *Administração* acts, I repeat, constantly in the name of the superior public interest, and students are very proud of it; (ii) the LLCA/1993 (Article 54) and the LLCA/2021 (Article 89) expressly rule that public contracts obey 'public law precepts', while the 'dispositions of private law' are applicable only supplementarily, thus separating the public and private realms.

Moreover, in contrast to her American colleague, the French or Brazilian judge who faces our termination-for-convenience-of-the-government hypothesis will face it as an academic enterprise. The judge praises and invokes theory and systematic thinking, so much that she can't even think of a case without fitting it into a broader 'intellectual scheme that goes beyond the raw classification of case law decisions around salient facts'.[102] Facts give way to abstract principles. The judge will try to apprehend the legal question at

---

[97] See Schiavone 2017: 8.
[98] Alan Watson's translation. Identical words in the *Institutiones*, 1.1.4.
[99] Plessix 2020: 713.
[100] Debate and sources in Giacomuzzi 2017b.
[101] See Nohara & Marrara 2018 (commenting on article 2°); Meirelles et al 2020: 98–9. *Contra*, see Justen Filho 2021: 134–6.
[102] Legrand 1996b: 65. About the importance of systematic thinking for exceptionalism, see Chapter 2.1.2.

stake,[103] understand what principles stand behind it, and finally organize the thought so that the answer can be deduced from a coherent, logical theory. Her first concern will not be to scrutinize the facts, although she won't (can she?) neglect them. Immediately, the judge's *mentalité* will first classify our hypothetical as a public law case, and this classification will serve as the fundamental assumption. But, of course, she is aware of the fact that the State, whose interest is 'superior', has limited power, and the judge must accommodate this paradox.[104]

After citing Dicey, the common law coryphaeus, Bertrand de Jouvenel (1903–87) drew the line that divides common law and French political philosophies: while the former places Law over power, the latter places Power over law.[105] Of course, this idea is an oversimplification, but it's helpful to frame the scenario in which public contract law fits.

If I had unlimited space, I could expand on all of the examples of exceptionalism mentioned above. Yet this enterprise would be contradictory to the purposes of this book. So, I will explore only one of the 'internal exceptionalism' comparisons, namely the doctrine governing termination for convenience of the government, and I will do so only briefly, in the final chapter. Instead I will deal more deeply with the external exceptional doctrines, SAD and Unmistakability, together with their continental 'functional equivalents', *fait du Prince* and *imprévision*. Let me minimally justify these choices.

Termination for convenience and SAD are, in the US, 'the most dramatically exceptionalist doctrines'.[106] Their functional equivalents in France and Brazil, *fait du Prince* and *imprévision*, together, touch the heart of exceptionalism most deeply. In short, they are the distinctive doctrines that make public contracts exceptional.

But the foundations of public contracts are hidden beneath doctrines, which are still formal, dogmatic sources. We must dig deeper and comparatively contextualize them historically, thus grasping the contrasting political philosophies and ideologies they serve. The uniqueness of each legal system under scrutiny is to be found in the material sources of law.

---

[103] See Legrand 1996b: 66.
[104] See Bigot 2002: 47.
[105] See Jouvenel 1993 [1945]: 345; Loughlin 2000: 12–14.
[106] Schwartz 2004: 29. Also Schwartz 1997: 558 (SAD is 'at its core, profoundly exceptionalist').

3. Public contracts' *mentalités* and ideologies

On 2 November 1930, Harold Laski wrote to Justice Holmes:

> I also read a very interesting treatise on French constitutional law by [Maurice] Hauriou. Curious in [sic] the complete mental difference from Dicey. You wouldn't think they were discussing the same *fonds* [content] at all. And his own comments show that he himself, having read Dicey, was completely bewildered by *'L'empiricisme anglais'*. He can't understand a constitution which lays down no general principles and is not, so to say, out there to be philosophized about. He wants metaphysics and can't find them in Dicey and is clearly genuinely upset.[1]

Laski touched on a crucial point in comparative legal theory: a *mental difference* between the continental and Anglo-American jurists. Even when they are dealing with the same subject, it may seem that they are not discussing the same content. This mental difference, or *mentalité*,[2] is patent when one compares American, French and Brazilian government contract law. Some of these differences were glossed over in Chapter 2 and will be treated more carefully here.

There is a relation between the notion of *mentalités* and the broader hermeneutical concept of pre-understanding (or fore-meaning, fore-structure).[3] The idea of *mentalités* originated in intellectual history in the twentieth century from (mostly) French historians. It may be roughly understood as a 'code name for what used to be called culture',[4] a rather 'losing word' to be avoided. There is also a close link between *mentalité* and the ideas of *'longue durée'* and 'community',[5] as well as 'history'.[6]

Several interconnected factors contribute to differences in *mentalités*. First, there is a difference in origin. In the US the *specific* phenomenon of wartime

---

[1]   *Holmes–Laski Letters* 1953: vol. 2, 1223.
[2]   I will stick with the term *mentalité*, following Furet 1984: 16 (the French word *mentalités* 'has no equivalent in other languages').
[3]   Gadamer 2004: 268–78.
[4]   Hutton 1981: 237.
[5]   See Legrand 1995a: 313.
[6]   See Furet 1984: 1–23; Guldi & Armitage 2014.

difficulties triggered exceptionalism,[7] whereas in France or Brazil this circumstance played a minor or indirect role. Instead, in these countries, exceptionalism is a phenomenon that permeates the *entire legal structure.*

As James Nagle and Joshua Schwartz have noted, exceptionalism in the American government contracts regime is tightly connected to the historical centrality of military contracts in the US procurement system.[8] Schwartz shows that it was in response to the particular necessities of the army during wartime (or upon the cessation of hostilities) that exceptionalist norms arose and developed; all of the seminal cases that initially granted exceptional prerogatives to the American government either arose from military procurement cases or were somehow influenced by wartime circumstances. True, exceptionalism later spread 'as a Trojan horse' to civilian government procurement, and American government contract law is today, in general, a unitary body of law.[9] But it was initially because of the wartime circumstances that exceptionalism flourished in the US. That is why I call American exceptionalism 'circumstantial'.

How much weight this historical factor has played in shaping American government procurement law is, I concede, an important, debatable question. For instance, in *Torncello v US* (1982), a seminal case in termination for convenience (to be explored in Chapter 9), the historical wartime origin of 'exceptionalism' carried heavy weight in the 'congruential' outcome. *Torncello* was a post-war case. According to the causal and historical argument suggested by Schwartz, linking exceptionalism to wartime circumstances, were *Torncello* a wartime case, the decision probably would have been different. Moreover, another point can be raised in favour of Schwartz's historical argument about the centrality of the military procurement in the development of the 'exceptionalist' tradition of US government procurement law and in favour of my thesis about the circumstantial character of American government procurement law: state law of government procurement, which *doesn't deal* with military procurement, is considerably 'less exceptionalist' than federal government procurement law. In short, *but for* the military circumstances, the US government procurement law would be entirely dominated by 'congruence' philosophy.[10]

---

[7]   This is the thesis of Schwartz 2004. The centrality of military procurement in the US was noted first in a historical study by Nagle (1999), on which Schwartz (2004: 50–4) relied. Nagle's work is mainly descriptive; the causal, systematic connection between wartime circumstances and 'exceptionalism' in the US government procurement law is Schwartz's.

[8]   See Nagle 1999; Schwartz 2004: 49–83.

[9]   See Schwartz 2004: 49–86.

[10]   I thank Schwartz for this federal/state comparative point.

The origins of exceptionalism in France and Brazil are different and broader in scope.[11] Exorbitant norms have been directly related, as mentioned earlier, to the central role played by the State in the whole structure of law and society. The Administration has always 'needed' special norms to reasonably exercise its power (*puissance public*), one that was, in short, *demanded* and *accepted* by society.

These special norms have been developed since before the French Revolution.[12] The special norms form a systematic body of law, *le droit administratif*, which is part of the *droit public*. As such, the whole *droit administratif* is exceptional, *exorbitante*, in the sense that it is constructed upon principles that are essentially different from the principles that govern *le droit privé*[13] – in the Brazilian case since the Empire (1822–89), when the Brazilian elite wished to *be* French and the Brazilian State tried to mirror the French State.

In France, the central idea is that the *intérêt général* prevails over the private interest, imposing a particular treatment regime that only special judges (*le juge administratif*) can implement.[14] Briefly, the sovereign (*l'État*) is subjected to special norms (*droit public*, *droit administratif*, *contrat administratif*), to be applied by special judges (*le juge administratif*), who sit on special courts, at the summit of which is the *Conseil d'État*. As early as 1849, the structural *exorbitance* was explained by Alexandre-François Vivien (1799–1854) before a commission charged with the function of examining a project about the *Conseil d'État*:

> The laws and the *contrats administratifs* belong to an order of principles, ideas, and interests *completely strange to ordinary jurisdictions*; to apply this set of norms it's necessary [to have] the practical knowledge, the legal studies that we don't find in ordinary jurisdictions. It would be dangerous to the Administration to be submitted to judges who are not aware of its necessities, its uses, its needs, [judges] who, by a matter of obligation, are concerned almost exclusively with private law, and whose invasion in the administrative domain would soon destroy the controlling principle of separation of powers.[15]

---

[11]   It may seem an oversimplification to treat French and Brazilian systems interchangeably. However, as far as the structural reasons for exceptionalism are concerned, the treatment is fair: Brazil has followed the French idea of public–private law dichotomy and 'imported' the French idea of both *droit administratif* and *contrat administratif*, as I have tirelessly emphasized.

[12]   See generally Bigot 2002: 13, 18–26; Mestre 1985; Plessix 2003a: 355–74.

[13]   In the Brazilian doctrine, see Cretella Jr 1990: 243. Exploring the different functions of public and private law, see Bell 2002: 236.

[14]   See Sandevoir 1964: 303–5.

[15]   Apud Burdeau 1989: 290 (emphasis added).

In an important sense, Vivien has echoed Montesquieu in Book 26, Chapter 16 of the *Spirit of Laws*: 'It's ridiculous to claim to decide the rights of kingdoms, nations, and the universe by the same maxims used to decide among individuals a right concerning a drain pipe.' This spirit remains alive in France.[16]

Revealingly, in 1999, the *Rapport Public du Conseil d'État* on *l'intérêt général* stamped the following words about liaison between the necessity *le juge administratif* and the voluntarist conception of *intérêt général*:

> In the French political tradition, the *intérêt général* inserts itself in the voluntarist, republican filiation, which conceives the unitary State as its protector […] *L'intérêt général* inspires the government's politics and justifies the administrative action, attentively controlled by the *juge administratif*. The very existence of *juge administratif*, distinct of the common judge, which is the *juge judiciaire*, ensures the specific function of *l'intérêt général*, which won't be reduced to a simple social composition between divergent interests.
>
> The existence of a *droit public* and a State endowed of its own judges renders, in fact, the conviction that *l'intérêt général* will be entirely served by the *droit privé*, even if the proceedings of *droit privé* can reveal themselves as conforming to *l'intérêt général*. It's in this interest only that the Administration enjoys exorbitant powers […] and imposes constraints to the administered […] [*L'*]intérêt *général* is never simply an addition of a series of particular interests. It introduces an element of rationality that is sufficient to create something different from the sum of its elements.

A few pages later, the *Rapport* deals with the notion of the *contrat administratif*:

> [An] unequal relation between parties in the contrat […] constitutes one of the specificities of *le contrat administratif* compared to *le contrat privé*. It's in the name of *l'intérêt général* that the contracting administration has at its disposal certain means of unilateral actions, hence the power to make unilateral changes and increase contractors' charges, financial ones included, or even the power to unilaterally terminate the contract in the interest of the public service.[17]

As we will see in due course, and as has already been noted, the French conception of *intérêt général*, Rousseauian in its essence,[18] is key to French thought and conceptions of State and law. This conception contradicts the utilitarian conception of 'public interest' reigning in the US; in short, they represent *contrasting ideologies*.[19] As Plessix sensibly suggests, at the foundations of the autonomy of *le droit administratif* (and of *contracts administratifs*)

---

[16] See Plessix 2020: 713–25.
[17] *Rapport public du Conseil d'État* 1999: 265–6, 279.
[18] See Plessix 2020: 617.
[19] See Rangeon 1986: 13–38, 107–207.

lies 'a faith in a Society that doesn't limit itself to the Market, in a State that is irreducible to all other forms of collective life'.[20]

The whole issue of exceptionalism in the French legal system is to be understood around the public law normative principles. The idea of *contrat administratif* as something different from the *contrat de droit privé* is at the core of *le droit administratif*.[21] *L'Exorbitance* is part of a broader structure, *le droit politique*. Thus, French exceptionalism is 'structural', not 'circumstantial'.

This structural sense gives to the word *exorbitance* a new meaning: in *droit politique*, to say that a legal rule (*règle du droit*) is *exorbitante* means not simply that the rule derogates the common rule; the word *exorbitante,* explains Élodie Saillant, has 'an autonomous and proper sense in *droit public*; it has lost its synonymy with derogation […] It has turned into a true notion representing the autonomy of *droit administratif's postulate.*'[22]

Any debate about the very notion of the *contrat administratif,* or the 'existence' of *contrats administratifs* as a separate theoretical entity, is necessarily a debate about the exact structure of both legal and political systems.[23] Thus, it is not circumstantial that Saillant's book links *l'éxorbitance* with 'political power's specificity and superiority'.[24]

Hence, to argue against the existence of the different theoretical structure of the *contrat administratif* is tantamount to questioning the French law itself. You remember my question to Professor Picard, reported in the Introduction to this book. To say to a French public law professor that the *contrat administratif* is a 'historical accident' is to shoot him in the heart, questioning the very French identity; it is to attack the whole *système exorbitante*, upon which France has built its Nation.

Brazil followed, in general, the French ethos. True, Brazil has no administrative justice in the sense France has. Brazil's State Council, which was never so magnificent as the French model, closed its doors with the proclamation of the Republic in 1889, when Brazil for the first time officially moved the pendulum towards the American political philosophy, and a Supreme Court, inspired by the US model, was designed. The ethos, however, of Brazilian administrative law has remained largely the same for many decades.

Another factor to be mentioned is the public–private law dichotomy. There is an indisputable fundamental opposition between the *political functions* that American and French (or Brazilian) legal systems have granted to the (lack of)

---

[20]   Pressix 2020: 715.
[21]   See Traité 1: § 179. On the criteria to distinguishing the two types of *contrat*, see ibid: §§ 84-182.
[22]   Saillant 2011: 56.
[23]   Restricted to legal, see generally Drago 1990: 119.
[24]   Saillant 2011: 608. See also Plessix 2020: 713, 716.

public–private law dichotomy, as we will see. It's not a coincidence that John David Bawden Mitchell (1917–80), the English professor of constitutional law and author of the first Anglo-American comparative work on public contracts, published in 1954, was an admirer of the French legal system and a critic of the ideas of Albert Venn Dicey (1835–1922), a common law jurist and a fierce opponent of the French public–private dichotomy.[25]

Put broadly, while the dichotomy has played a minor role in legal epistemology in the common law world, quite the contrary has occurred in continental law systems, France being the paradigmatic example. Brazil has followed France. This crucial difference is taken for granted in comparative law literature. Still, lawyers and jurists have often belittled its implications – with a few exceptions, to be mentioned in due course. This issue is a critical factor for a better comprehension of how lawyers and jurists think about government contract law in the US, France and Brazil.

The third factor fuels and is fuelled by the first two. The conceptions of state and the individual are different in the three countries. In short, while in the US the state is generally viewed 'negatively' and the individual 'positively', in France the opposite holds. Brazil lies somewhere in the middle ground between these two poles. If what makes public contracts different from private contracts is the presence of the state in the contractual relation, it would be surprising if legal systems that hold different conceptions of state and grant other functions to it could base their public contract law regimes on similar foundations.

Finally, the state liability systems in America, France and Brazil have been constructed upon different pillars. This difference results from the third factor, that is, the different conceptions of the state.

These are very delicate topics, and caution must be exercised from the very beginning.[26] Although I will explore the problem of state liability in Chapter 5, I would like to advance a few comments now.

In America, sovereign immunity is still a real presence, being influential both in courts and in legal doctrine and structuring the legal reasoning accordingly. In contrast, in France and Brazil, sovereign immunity has no force whatsoever. The norms establishing State responsibility for its wrongdoings, either in torts or in contracts, are set to such an extent that no-fault liability on behalf of the State has been broadly accepted (in Brazil, the no-fault liability of the State in extra-contractual cases is found in a constitutional norm, Article 37,

---

[25]   See Mitchell 1965. On Mitchell's legal thought, see Loughlin 1992: 191–7. On Dicey's thought and its lasting influence in the common law world, see Loughlin 1992: 140–65; 2000: 102–3; 2003: 131–4; 2010: 440–5.

[26]   No other significant theory on public liability has been developed since Borchard's last article in 1928.

§6, CFB/88). This different foundation of State liability facilitated the creation and development, in France and Brazil, of the 'exorbitant' public law norms that many Anglo-American scholars have recognized to offer, remarkably, better protection to the individual than the common law system, including in the domain of government contract law. Edwin Borchard (1884–1951) and Harold Laski are the most remarkable examples.

In a lengthy study conducted in the 1920s, Borchard provided an invaluable service for comparative law in eight articles about government liability in torts.[27] In the seventh part of his work, Borchard mentioned that the role of the public–private law dichotomy was crucial to the French construction of a system of public responsibility that differed mainly from the Anglo-American private law parameter.[28]

Laski was a connoisseur and admirer of French law. In 1919, he co-translated a book written in 1913 by Léon Duguit entitled *Les Transformations du Droit Public*. The translation received the name *Law in the Modern State*. Additionally, Laski was the only non-French jurist to write an article about Duguit's work in the prestigious *Archives de Philosophie du droit et de Sociologie juridique*, which in 1932 dedicated a special double volume to studies on Duguit (died in 1928), whom Laski suggested had influenced a generation in the same way that Montesquieu had two centuries earlier. In this work, Laski expressly recognized having been 'profoundly influenced by [Duguit's] conceptions'.[29]

On 13 July 1917, Laski wrote a letter to Justice Holmes concerning administrative law. Laski said he '[had] been buried in administrative law', and that 'the French stuff [was] very impressive'. Laski was also 'absolutely amazed by Dicey's muddleheadedness about it'. About Maurice Hauriou's book entitled *Droit administratif*, Laski wrote that '[it] is one of the most suggestive books I ever read'.[30] A few months later, on 28 November, Laski wrote to Holmes again: 'I'm convinced that French system of administrative law is today *infinitely superior* in its results so far as the liberty of the subject goes that Dicey's rule of law, which is today so theoretical and so beset on all hands by exceptions as to be hardly applicable at all.'[31]

---

[27] See Borchard 1924; 1926; 1927a; 1927b; 1928a; 1928b.
[28] See Borchard 1928a: 604.
[29] See Laski 1932: 1, 22. About Duguit's influence on Laski, see also Allison 1996: 82.
[30] *Holmes–Laski Letters* 1953: vol 1, 93.
[31] *Holmes–Laski Letters* 1953: vol 1, 113 (emphasis added).

My goal here is not to prove which system is 'better', for whatever purpose.[32] However, scrutiny of the reasons why one system would be preferable for whatever purpose could help, dialectically, to better understand the foundations of public contract law.

The comparatist cannot understand the central doctrines of external exceptionalism, namely SAD and the Unmistakability Doctrine, 'the true apotheosis of exceptionalism', if she detaches these doctrines from the American 'negative' vision of the state or from the medieval canon of sovereign immunity, whose spirit, I repeat, springs from the ashes whenever the state raises its sovereign defences in courts. In government contract cases, sovereign immunity appears under a different name, be it SAD or the Unmistakability Doctrine, but the role of these 'modern' doctrines remains ultimately the same.[33]

I argue that, viewed from a comparative perspective, sovereign immunity functions as a counterweight to the extremely powerful individualism that reigns in the Anglo-American world. In a sense, it serves as a vehicle to introduce, below the radar, the civilians' idea/principle of public interest's superiority into the common law regime. Thus, my comment to Professor Schwartz, reported in the Introduction, that 'exceptionalism' would be equivalent to the 'supremacy of the public interest' was governed by my civil law *mentalité*. Had I a common law mind I would have never asked such a 'nonsensical' question, to which I received the most probable common law answer.

Similarly, the French and Brazilian *responsabilité sans faute* (no-fault liability) cannot be understood if severed from the vision of a positive State and a more communitarian perspective of State liability. We must never forget that the widely respected French theoretical system – a system that many common lawyers recognize as 'superior' to the Anglo-American as far as the protection of individual rights is concerned – is based on a political philosophy that never ceased to confer significant power to the State. In broad terms, as posed by Jacques Chevallier, the ideological foundations of *droit administratif* and *contrat administratif* have oscillated from *puissance public* to *service public* – hence, within *public* boundaries[34] – two notions that are rather complementary,

---

[32] In fact, whether French or Brazilian systems protect contractors better than the American system in practice is a question to be empirically explored, a survey that I won't undertake here. Empirical research is necessary to confirm the hypothesis of some Anglo-American scholars that the French system protects the individual better than the American system, and I believe that comparatists must take the suggestion seriously. If the suggestion is correct, then the ironic fact is that the French model shouldn't be abandoned or criticized by American Liberals, but rather should be carefully studied. Accordingly, the comparatist should ask the following key question: which legal system is really 'exceptionalist' and favours the state over the individual?

[33] See Sisk 2016: 325–31.

[34] See Chevallier 1979.

as Jean-Arnaud Mazères has brilliantly shown in a recent study on the *political* importance of a seminal *droit administratif* case decided by the *Conseil d'État* in 1910 called *Compagnie générale française des tramways*,[35] already mentioned in Chapter 2 and to be explored in Chapter 7.

In fact, *le droit administratif* is a by-product of an ideological counteraction between the ideas of *puissance* (power) and *service*, a duet of forces that would work in a dialectic movement, as we will see. But, for the moment, I must say that Chevallier's explanation of public power and public service is very revealing, for it sets the tone of the debate from the very beginning: the 'movement of dialectic opposition' occurs *within public boundaries*. By avoiding framing the question in terms of 'public versus private' domain, 'State versus individuals' or 'power versus rights', Chevallier unfolded the French ideology and shed light on comparative studies: French ideas of puissance and service are both accompanied by the adjective *public*.[36] As myths that lead France, *le mythe du service publique* doesn't eradicate *le mythe de la puissance publique*; on the contrary, they reinforce each other.[37]

Unlike SAD and the Unmistakability Doctrine, construed in the US to protect state acts, the theories of *fait du Prince* and *imprévision* were constructed in France *to protect contractors* and represent a backlash against a legal philosophy which confers on the State a power that must be compensated. Of course, conclusions on this complex topic require qualification, which I offer in Chapter 7. I believe, however, that one can already understand Laski's insight: it seems that Americans, French and Brazilians are not talking about the same *content* when they talk about exceptionalism in government contract law.

John Bell has stated: '[t]he legal mechanisms and the way of legal thinking to achieve them are the most important feature of difference between legal systems.'[38] I have shown that this observation is remarkably accurate and meaningful when one compares American and French or Brazilian (public) laws, specifically government contract law. 'Ways of legal thinking' can be replaced by *mentalités*, 'a state of mind, a way of seeing the world'.[39]

Three dichotomies reflect this mental difference fairly.

---

[35]   See Mazères 2019: 92.
[36]   See Chevallier 1979; Amilhat 2014: 280.
[37]   See Chevallier 2019: 550–1.
[38]   Bell 2002: 237.
[39]   Samuel 2003: 64.

1.   THE THREE DICHOTOMIES

1.1   Empiricism versus Rationalism

American lawyers are the best modern example of the common law mind,[40] for they see the law as a *technique* to solve practical problems, courts existing, as mentioned, to decide the dispute presented by the parties; in general, common lawyers welcome theories only to the extent that they are helpful to resolve the issue before the court, a problem that appears to them *as* and *from* a set of facts. The common law propositional question is '*Quid facti?*' (What are the facts?); as a consequence, common law is mainly reactive. American Legal Realism unsurprisingly held that 'in deciding cases, judges respond primarily to the stimulus of the facts'.[41]

On the contrary, a continental mind tries to construct an abstract theory before deciding any particular case, and jurists ask for the principles first, the propositional question being '*Quid iuris?*' (What is the law?); consequently, the continental mind is more proactive or projective.[42]

Tocqueville described this difference as early as 1835, in *Democracy in America*: 'The English or American lawyer seeks out what has been done before, whereas the French lawyer inquires what we ought to do; the former looks for judgments, the latter, reasons.' And a few pages later: 'The American mind keeps its distance from general ideas and doesn't direct its attention to theoretical discoveries.'[43] Accordingly, these differences represent a different way of thinking and different philosophical views of the world.[44]

It is a truism nowadays that common law and continental law may be viewed as conveying, respectively, the 'empiricist' and the 'rationalist' way of living, the former 'meaning your lover of facts in all their crude variety', the latter 'meaning your devotee to abstract and eternal principles'.[45] In Martin Rogoff's contrasting picture '[t]he French Cartesian tradition places a premium on abstract thinking with a corresponding lack of attention to empirical detail',

---

[40]   See Mattei 1992: 4.
[41]   Leiter 1997: 269.
[42]   See Legrand 1996b: 66.
[43]   Tocqueville 2003 [1835]: 311, 352.
[44]   As Legrand (1999b: 6) puts it, 'it's not by chance that the English law as we know it, free from systematic and rule thinking, but concrete and pragmatic [...] has been constructed in the country of John Stuart Mill and Herbert Spencer, which is neither the country of Descartes nor the one of Kant'.
[45]   James 1975 [1907]: 12.

while 'American pragmatism has an instinctive distrust of abstractions and values actual experience'.[46]

Yet, the empiricist–rationalist dichotomy should not be oversimplified. 'No one', said William James (1842–1910), 'can live an hour without both facts and principles, so it's a difference rather of *emphasis*; yet it breeds *antipathies* of the most pungent character between those who lay the emphasis different-ly.'[47] The italicized words are essential, in the sense that in American, French and Brazilian laws, *they act as a magnet*: a common law mind focuses *mainly* on facts and tends to pay less attention to principles and abstract theories. In contrast, a civil law mind focuses *primarily* on principles and is more willing to neglect facts.[48] As a result, Anglo-American lawyers have *antipathies* for abstract, systematic thought, while continental jurists have *antipathies* for facts. It cannot be surprising that this difference is also reflected in government procurement law. The 'somewhat mundane law of government contracts', to recall Justice Rehnquist's suggestive words quoted in the Introduction, is only a reflection of the empiricism and the mainly reactive character of the common law mind.

1.2 Systematic versus Non-Systematic Thinking and the Role of the Doctrine

An interrelated point to be noted is the unsystematic or less systematic feature of common lawyers instead of civil law jurists' more systematic ideal of law.[49] Llewellyn emphasized the American substantive law's 'notoriously unsystem-atic character' and noted that 'what has been written – in opinions themselves, by and large – has not been systematic. Rather, it consists of scattered, unsys-tematic fragments worked up and ad hoc to provide grounds for, indeed to justify, the decisions at hand.'[50]

Although commonly mentioned,[51] the importance of the difference in systematic thinking has been underestimated. David Gerber correctly wrote:

---

[46] Logoff 1997: 27.

[47] James 1975 [1907]: 12 (emphasis added).

[48] See James 1975 [1907]: 13.

[49] For a position noting the more 'obvious roles' played by 'idea-systems' in civil law countries, but recognizing the increasing importance of the systematic thought in specific American law disciplines such as American legal history, see Gerber 1992: 167. In this article Gerber (at 165–76) correctly remarks upon the political significance of systematic thought (or the Idea-system, as he prefers) as a theoretical enterprise.

[50] Llewellyn 1989 [1933]: 1–2.

[51] Örücü (1987: 313–18) contrasts and explains assumptions of civil law and common law (and socialist) traditions: 'philosophy of systematizing' versus 'empiri-cal' philosophy; 'framework laid down' versus 'free individual'; 'paternalistic legisla-

'[t]he extent to which ideas within a legal culture are systematically related to each other may have a far greater influence on the characteristics of that culture than is generally supposed.'[52] I believe this is particularly true concerning the field of government contract law.

I use the idea of 'system' in the strong sense in which civil law jurists have understood it at least since the nineteenth-century codification process. That is, I use 'system' not only as an internally coherent, consistent, hierarchically ordered, interrelated set of principles, rules and concepts from which lawyers will 'deduce' the law,[53] but also as the 'only possible way through which the human cognition can know the truth'.[54] For civilians, systematic thought is an essential condition to *understand* the law. Common law lawyers, in contrast, have never considered the idea of system as a *conditio sine qua non*.[55]

These features have deep historical roots. The common law's less systematic *mentalités* can be traced back to Bracton's era,[56] while systematic continental thought, culminating with the codification movement of the nineteenth century, has its seeds in Roman law.[57] The European nineteenth-century codes may be seen as the positivization of modern jurists' idea of law as a *system*,[58] but 'continental scholars', Gordley states, 'were systematic before they had codes'.[59] We know there is more than one form of systematization, but the codification is undoubtedly 'the most efficient and the most laden with consequences'.[60] The lack of a successful codification movement in the

---

tor' versus 'liberal society'; 'law lays down rules of conduct' versus 'law used more for dispute resolution'; 'codes' versus 'remedies'.

[52]   Gerber 1992: 153.

[53]   For a very similar notion, see Örücü 1987: 310.

[54]   Larenz 1997 [1991]: 21. Dworkin's 'praise of theory' (2006 [1997]: chapter 2), if not Dworkin's entire 'system', has a lot in common with continental legal thinking, in spite of his revealing insularity in the common law tradition.

[55]   See Legrand 1996b: 65; Bernard Schwartz 1952: 433.

[56]   In a historical perspective, Holdsworth (1983 [1925]: 29–30) indicates that at the end of the thirteenth century, English courts, unlike French law, ceased to draw from Bracton, who used Roman sources and doctrines to construct a system of law. From that point on in history, English judges have been in contact with leading practitioners in day-to-day courts, losing touch with continental legal learning and becoming insulated in their own system. For that reason, '[a] native development of common law was ensured; but the result was that, in the fourteenth and fifteenth centuries, law tended to become more and more technical, and less and less rational'.

[57]   Some trace the origins of the French Civil Code of 1804 and the German Civil Code of 1900 to the imperial codes of Theodosius and Justinian. See Ost & Kerchove 1994: 72.

[58]   See Sève 1986: 81.

[59]   Gordley 1998: 735.

[60]   Ost & Kerchove 1984: 72. See also Legrand 1995a: 318, 322.

Anglo-American world in the nineteenth century is only the most recent man-ifestation of this cultural contrast.[61]

The German Civil Code (1900) – a by-product of the German Pandectists, by scholars who had perused the already cited Digest of Justinian (published in 533 AD) – had German Idealism as its leading philosophy.[62] René Sève finds in Hegel's philosophy the inspiration for codification. Hegel explicitly made a claim for codification, which would provide individuals with a 'coherent system'. In Hegel's words, 'the infinite urge of our times is precisely to sys-tematize, i.e., to raise to the universal'.[63]

The Pandectists undertook a highly abstract, systematic study of Roman law and 'undoubtedly represented one of the most extreme forms of formalism [and systematic thought] applied to law'.[64] If German private law has been thence-forth the most fertile source of 'systematic thinking',[65] the German predomi-nance by no means diminishes the importance of the idea of 'system' in French thought. However, it is important to note that the intellectual origins of French and German 'systems' were different. While the framers of the Napoleonic Code were inspired by the natural law 'system' of the seventeenth-century jurists, the Germans drew from the nineteenth-century natural lawyers.[66]

The notion of 'system' implicates the interrelated notions of coherence and consistency. Of course, *all* legal systems seek coherence and consistency to some degree.[67] By saying that common law is less systematic than continental law, I'm suggesting neither that the former is purposely incoherent nor that common lawyers do not intend to have a more comprehensive, coherent 'system of law', or that they don't reason consistently. Nor am I taking sides in the famous Anglo-American jurisprudential battle between those who under-

---

[61] What is labelled in the US as a 'Code' is nothing more than a compilation of laws ordered chronologically. See Legrand 1995a: 323. On Anglo-American codifica-tion, see generally Pound 1956; Reimann 1989; Talon 1998. For a comparison between French and English laws on codification and systematic thought, see Allison 1996: chapter 6. American Restatements of Contracts may be viewed as an attempt to sys-tematize contract law. For a comparative view of the French and German Codes and American Restatements, see Gordley 1981.

[62] See Ewald 1995.

[63] Sève 1986: 81. I relied on HB Nisbet;s translation for Hegel 1991 [1821] § 211: 243.

[64] Ost & Kerchove 1994: ix. See also Schmidt 1965.

[65] It's no coincidence that a classic German book on systematic legal thinking was translated into Portuguese by a Portuguese private law scholar. See Canaris 2002 [1983].

[66] See Gordley 1981: 142–5. Linking codification with the intellectual tradition of the state, see Dyson 1980: 112.

[67] Coherence is used here in its more 'familiar value', that is, in the sense of 'intel-ligibility'. See Raz 1992: 276–7.

stand the law, or rather adjudication, as a necessary coherent enterprise,[68] and those who think coherence is unachievable in law, either because of the society and law's inherently political feature and necessary conflicting interests,[69] or because of the so-called authoritative character of law.[70] Coherence, I take it, is better understood as an effort we put into legal reasoning and ultimately into law than as an intrinsic characteristic of the law. It's a purposive enterprise upon which we depend to make sense of legal texts, judicial decisions and legal doctrine, or whatever the source of law may be in a given society. My focus is on the purposes a legal system wants to achieve; consequently, a 'less systematic thought' emerges. The American 'circumstantial exceptionalism' and the French or Brazilian 'structural exorbitance' are ideas intimately related to the less and more systematic ways of thinking of Anglo-American and continental legal thought and must be understood under this light.

Achieving a perfectly coherent system of law has not been common law's *primary goal*. Building an *a priori* coherent body of rules and principles that could be the starting point to solve cases would run against the common law *mentalité*. Essentially, their primary focus is not the system's logic but the practical solution of the case. Therefore, a less coherent,[71] less systematic body of rules and principles results from a traditional mental activity that rejects abstractions. 'A pragmatist', said James in 1907, 'turns his back resolutely and once for all upon a lot of inveterate habits dear to professional philosophers. He turns away from abstractions and insufficiency, from verbal solutions, from bad *a priori* reasons, from fixed principles, closed systems, and pretended absolutes and origins.'[72]

A necessary consequence of the lack of a more coherent law system is that the courts' decisions appear to be based more on the court's authority than on

---

[68]   In American jurisprudence, Dworkin's theory of law as 'Integrity' (1986: chapters 6–7) is an excellent example.

[69]   American critical legal cholars champion this view. See eg Unger 1983: 571.

[70]   See Raz 1992: 297.

[71]   Raz (1992: 283) seems to acknowledge that 'while it's possible that some legal systems display considerable coherence, there surely can't be a general reason to suppose that they all do'.

[72]   James 1975 [1907]: 31. For an argument opposing James and Kant's epistemologies, see Kloppenberg 1986: 57–9. Of course, the contrasting pragmatic versus abstract or Pragmatism versus Idealism way of putting things is a crude simplification of a much more complex issue. German Idealism was not a univocal movement; it has encompassed a 'subjective' or 'formal' version in Kant and Fichte's thought, and a contrary, 'objective' or 'absolute' version among the so-called Romantics (Hölderlin, Novalis, Schlegel, Schelling, and the young Hegel). See Beiser 2002: 11.

reason.[73] 'Exaggerating somewhat', Kischel wrote, 'one might say that the common lawyer looks not for the best argument, but rather the highest-ranking authority'.[74] Accordingly, 'tradition' becomes the only explanation at hand to deal with problems such as exceptionalism.

Nobody can deny the importance of tradition in legal thinking. The idea of *mentalité* also carries the notion of 'pastness', in the sense employed by Martin Krygier to explain the law. 'In every established legal system', says Krygier, 'the legal past is central to the legal present'. In law, this past, represented by 'beliefs, opinions, values, decisions, myths, rituals', is 'deposited over generations' and 'institutionalized', almost 'sacralized'. The presence of the past, which Krygier calls 'authoritative presence', is 'frequently unnoticed by participants'. It's viewed as 'obvious' and 'natural'.[75] This tradition is then transmitted through generations. As Gadamer put it: 'We stand in traditions, whether we know these traditions or not.'[76]

Yet traditions may be unreasoned. Some say that this is the case with the sovereign immunity doctrine in US law. 'The strongest support for sovereign immunity', wrote Kenneth Culp Davis (1908–2003), 'is provided by that four-horse team so often encountered – historical accident, habit, a natural tendency to favor the familiar, and inertia'. Susan Randall agrees: 'Time and tradition have, of course, embedded the mistake of sovereign immunity in our culture'.[77]

What can a book on comparative public contracts derive from that? Isn't it true that *le droit administratif* was constructed by a court, *le Conseil d'État*? Isn't it a remarkable characteristic of *le droit administratif*, in opposition to private law, that it was developed *without* a Code?

The answers pass through the crucial role of the doctrine in shaping the French and (to a lesser extent) Brazilian legal systems. It's a glaring historical mistake to think that systematic thought didn't pervade continental public law or that *droit administratif* is less systematic because it doesn't have a Code.

Although continental public law has never been systematized in a Code, the idea of systematization pervades all of civil law thought. The very notion of

---

[73] I'm not denying courts' authority *qua tale*, but opposing 'arguments of authority' to 'arguments of raison', in the sense of 'authority versus reason'. See Fletcher 1997: 1599–1600; Haarscher 1998. In French public law, see Troper 1994.

[74] Kischel 2019: 247.

[75] For Krygier (1986: 240–51, quotations at 241, 246), there are three elements of every tradition: pastness, authoritative presence and transmission. For a perspective linking the inherent historical character of the law with the history of philosophy, see Villey 1962: 17-2.

[76] Gadamer 2001a: 45.

[77] Davis 1970: 384; Randall 2002: 6.

Rechtsstaat in Germany or *État de Droit* in France is a by-product of rationalistic thought, a product of systematic theories.[78] Kant was also influential on the so-called golden age of *droit administratif* (from the 1880s to the 1930s), having broadly influenced the French concept of State in that period.[79] The notion of 'system' has become so strong among civilian countries that it is part of civil law jurists' idea of law as a whole.[80] *Le droit administratif* is an excellent example of that.[81]

In France, the systematization of public law has been performed not only by the most prestigious French institution, the *Conseil d'État*, which has been shaping the *droit administratif* since around the mid-nineteenth century, but also by *la doctrine*, which since the 1820s, but mainly since the 1880s, has been playing a decisive role in systematizing the *droit administratif*.[82] It is a 'choir of two voices', as Jean Rivero (1910–2001) famously wrote in 1955.[83]

Comparatists must therefore be cautious not to stereotype *le droit administratif* as administrative judge-made law, as many scholars have suggested,[84] thus inducing a belief that the *droit administratif* is as unsystematic as or less systematic than common law. *Le droit administratif*, and consequently *le contrat administratif*, has been influenced by empiricism and conceptualism since the beginning of the eighteenth century.[85] Yet conceptualism became predominant. The considerable effort made by the *Conseil d'État* and the French *publicistes* to systematize and ultimately construct the *droit administratif* would never have been possible if the French (jurists) *mentalités* hadn't favoured abstraction and systematization over practical reasoning.[86]

As the Italian administrative law historian Bernardo Sordi illustrated, the *doctrine-jurisprudence* duet has shaped French administrative law in such a way that '*l'interpretatio probabillis* of the doctrine becomes *interpretatio necessaria* thanks to the administrative jurisdiction'.[87] Accordingly, since the end of the nineteenth century, a specific continental model, a system of *droit administratif*, has imposed itself in Europe (France, Germany, Italy, Austria).

---

[78] On the German constitutional law, see Ewald 1995: 2046–65 (expounding that the German *Rechtsstaat* is a by-product of Kantian rationalistic, a priori moral system).

[79] See Dyson 1980: 160.

[80] See Whitman 1990: 121.

[81] See eg Cassese 2000: 27; Saillant 2011: 213–17.

[82] See generally Plessix 2003a: 309–486; Fortsakis 1987.

[83] In Sordi 2014: 178–80.

[84] See eg Brown & Bell 1998: 2–3; Bernard Schwartz 1952: 436; JDB Mitchell 1954: 167.

[85] See Bienvenu 1985: 159; Chevallier 2001: 603; Jestaz & Jamin 2004: 109–20; Fortsakis 1987: 36; Duxbury 2001: Chapter 4.

[86] See generally Fortsakis 1987: 285–6.

[87] Sordi 2014: 179.

This model mirrors the German Pandectism and tried to create a 'general part' (*allgemeiner Teil*) of administrative law. This is the epoch of the *grandes catédrales du droit administratif*, its *belle époque*. Not coincidentally, it is also the time of the construction of a 'disciplinary status' of administrative law by Maurice Hauriou (1856–1929) and Léon Duguit (1859–1928) in France, by Otto Mayer (1846–1924) and Fritz Fleiner (1867–1937) in Germany, by Vittorio Emanuele Orlando (1860–1952) and Santi Romano (1875–1947) in Italy, and by Hans Kelsen (1881–1973) and Adolf Merkl (1890–1970) in Austria.[88]

Even if only France matters to our analysis, we cannot disregard the cross-fertilization of ideas in Europe already in place at the time, and, more important, the ever dominant 'systematic thinking' in all these countries. Yet what matters most now is to single out the role of *la doctrine* in systematizing *le droit administratif*. As Sordi highlighted, from the beginning of the twentieth century on, it was no longer possible to distinguish which part of the duo was the master: *La doctrine* gained such high-level status that it influenced the very conception of the *État de droit*, the rule of law, which conserves its 'doctrinal matrix' via its plural form, of *doctrine jurisprudentielle*, of *doctrine écrite* and of *doctrine enseignante*.[89]

Brazilian administrative law and public contract law, having been influenced by European *mentalité* and mainly French administrative law since its very beginnings, has also operated under similar influences, praising systematic thought. Of course, Brazilian law school students may have read none of the authors mentioned above (except Kelsen). Still, they will have heard of them (and even read some in post-grad courses) before they will have heard of (let alone read) the Brazilian jurists, who themselves only copied their European masters, as we shall shortly see. In contrast, the role of the doctrine in shaping *le droit administratif* and *le contrat administratif* is not comparable to the lack of influence of the US doctrine in moulding government procurement law.

We cannot forget, however, as Élodie Saillant demonstrated,[90] that the notions of *droit administratif* and *contrat administratif*, whose *exorbitance* is the *raison d'être*, are not given facts but *political* choices, which are, in France, shaped systematically. As a human creation, an instrument, *l'exorbitance* can be used for ideological reasons. The argument that 'nature' would require

---

[88] See Sordi 2014: 181–2.
[89] See ibid: 185–6.
[90] See Saillant 2011: 316–36.

exorbitance and special courts is simply flawed, judicial review in England and the US being the best proof of this. In a country like France,

> the exorbitance acts circularly: the necessity to command puts the Administration above the administered to satisfy the public needs, which constitutes the superiority and specificity of the political power. But this superiority and specificity, once constituted, contribute, in their turn, to legitimate and give authority to the command power of the State because we [French] obey better those in whose superiority we invariably believe.[91]

L'exorbitance, in France, represents the superiority of the *pouvoir politique*; this political power, incarnated by the State, must intervene and use its exorbitant legal means to promote *l'intérêt général*, thus conciliating power and law.[92] Thus, in public contracts, all exorbitant powers, from the internal to the external exceptional norms described in Chapter 2, must be understood within this theoretical framework. 'Civil law and common law represent, therefore', wrote Alexander Pekelis (1902–46) in 1943, 'not only the two main legal systems of Western civilization, but also two fundamental trends of human nature'.[93]

Let me now turn to the deepest stage of public contract law foundations.

1.3   Two Conceptions of the General Interest

The concept of public or general interest is 'essentially contested', as Walter Gallie (1912–98) famously put it.[94] Any use of a concept carries an assumption of agreement as to the meaning, that is the content or conception, of the concept. As to the concept of public interest, French and American law assign different content to it – as Laski would say, they aren't talking about the same *fonds*.

Briefly, as suggested in the Introduction to this book and as reported in the *Rapport public du Conseil d'État* on the *intérêt général* in 1999, the French law conception holds an abstract, transcendental idea of the concept, while Anglo-American law assigns to it utilitarian content. To explain this difference I will follow Brian Leiter's theoretical framework of law's two main moral theories in contrasting the two ideologies,[95] as sketched below.

Leiter opposes Moralism and Realism. For him, the recent American jurisprudential debate between Ronald Dworkin (1931–2013) and Richard Posner

---

[91] Ibid: 333.
[92] Ibid: 525–6, 554, 556, 607–8. See also Coq 2015: 41, 170.
[93] Pekelis 1943: 692.
[94] See Gallie 1956. See also Rangeon 1986: 7.
[95] Leiter 2012.

(1939–) was not new; it was only a modern version of a much older political and philosophical dispute: Plato versus Thucydides, Kant versus Nietzsche, Hegel versus Marx and Rawls versus Geuss. The real dispute about the concept of law would be, for Leiter, between those who depart from a theory about how things *should be* and those who depart from a theory about how things *are in reality*.[96] Leiter's illuminating work is a valuable tool for framing the problem of the opposing conception of general interest.

Nothing I will say here is new to political philosophers but it can, I think, help us to better understand administrative and public contract laws in the three systems. No wonder that the leading study about the concept of general interest, foundational to the French public law, came not from a law professor but from a political philosopher. In 1986 François Rangeon published *L'idéologie de l'intérêt général*, in which various conceptions of the general interest were deployed. Rangeon's work has not only guided all public law works dealing with the subject ever since but has also served as the major reference for the Rapport mentioned above.

What follows is not an armchair enterprise.

The 3° International Colloquium of the *Centre de Droit Public Comparé* was held in Paris in May 2016, with the following subject: *L'intérêt général dans les pays de* common law *et de droit écrit*. The *Conseiller d'État* Jacques-Henri Stahl said that the notion of *intérêt général* leads us to the heart of *le droit administratif*; that it is its *raison d'être*, almost its essence, undoubtedly the most fundamental of the entire *droit administratif*, for it locates itself in the roots of all others: it founds the action of the administration, giving it its legitimacy and its finality, being also at the foundation of *les contrats administratifs*, as well as the *responsabilité sans faute*.[97] Therefore, this book cannot avoid dealing with the subject at the philosophical level.

One last remark is in order. Recall Weber's methodological teaching and the *preliminary analysis* flagged in Chapter 1. Various branches of thought, according to Weber, could share preliminary concepts. So, 'due to the advanced state of the development of legal thought', Weber wrote that 'important branches of the empirical sociocultural sciences, especially political and economic disciplines, employ legal concepts for terminological purposes […] of what may be called a *preliminary* analysis of their own subject matter'. However, when 'a political or economic inquiry undertakes to conceive its subject matter in terms of the "problematic" of politics or economics', then

---

[96]　See Leiter 2012: 867–8.
[97]　Stahl 2017.

'the inquiry is no longer at the level on which a preliminary analysis is undertaken by employing legal concepts'.[98]

In other words, politics and economics colours legal concepts with different meanings. The reverse is obviously true and applies to the relationship between morality and law.[99] The law may, preliminarily, share concepts with other disciplines, but later it transforms them into legal conceptions.

Thus, in what follows, I do not want to imply that French or American law has handed over its authority to any specific moral theory. But that does not indicate that (the meaning of) a moral theory that lies at the foundation of a legal concept is unimportant. On the contrary: how could we understand the *legal* meaning of a juridical concept without fully grasping the origins, philosophical as they may be, of that concept?

My intention is not to analyse Rousseau's or Smith's or any other philosopher's corpus, but only to stress the contrasts apropos their ideas of general interest to reach the foundations of the law (of public contracts) in which their thoughts have reverberated.[100] What must be clear upfront is, as Rangeon demonstrated, the political and ideological character of the concept of general interest.

2.   FRANCE: ROUSSEAU AND THE TRANSCENDENT CONCEPTION OF *INTÉRÊT GÉNÉRAL*

Simone Goyard-Fabre emphasized, about Rousseau's *œuvre*, that the problem of *sources* is central to his thinking, from the *origins* and *foundations* of inequality in the Second Discourse to the *principles* of political law in the Social Contract.[101]

In Rousseau's lineage, the general interest is an abstract ideal.[102] Based on his 'doctrine of ideas', Plato's metaphysics supported the view that two worlds exist, material and immaterial. This 'metaphysical dualism' came with an ontology: immaterial ideas were constant, invariable, transcendent. Natural law, natural rights, moral realism, all of them being canons of the legal and political thought in the Western world, derived from the Platonic idea of situating norms and moral ideas *above* the contingent, artificial world. This

---

[98]   Weber 1977: 136.

[99]   That insight is Poscher's (2009), from whom I draw the analogy.

[100]   In the next two sections, I derive freely from my previous work (Giacomuzzi 2017b).

[101]   Goyard-Fabre 1982: 78.

[102]   See Williams 2007: xix–xxx, from which I derive this and the next paragraph.

dimension was crucial to Rousseau's moral and political philosophy, of which the general interest was the most critical concept.[103]

Unsurprisingly, Thucydides opposed his realism to Plato's idealism, which would have been captured, in Leiter's theory, by Nietzsche's *Twilight of The Idols*:

> Plato is boring. — Ultimately my distrust for Plato runs deep: I find he has strayed so far from all the fundamental instincts of the Hellens, he is so spoilt by morality, so proto-Christian — the already has the concept 'good' as his highest concept — that to describe the whole phenomenon of Plato I would use the harsh term 'superior swindle', or, if it sounds better, idealism, in preference to any other. [...] My recuperation, my preference, my *cure* for all Platonism has always been *Thucydides*. *Courage* in the face of reality is what ultimately distinguishes between such types as Thucydides and Plato: Plato is a coward in the face of reality — *therefore* he takes flight into the ideal; Thucydides has *himself* under control, therefore he keeps things, too, under his control.[104]

In a book about the legacy Thucydides left for Western culture, the Spanish scholar Juan Carlos Iglesias-Zoido – a specialist in Greek philology – claimed that Thucydides initiated a *pragmatic* history of humanity; he was, says Iglesias-Zoido, conscious that the historical methodology at his disposal was of no *utility* to explain the past, and thus abandoned all fictional accounts.[105] Leiter recalls that, for Thucydides, political leaders are driven by selfish motives such as power, fear, and wealth – they are 'creatures for whom moral considerations and rhetorical window dressing rather than reasons for actions'.[106]

Many centuries later, Thucydides the realist historian changes to a model of political thinker.[107] In 1629 Hobbes translated the *History* from Greek into English, which was 'a political action in part'.[108] In this translation, which antedates *Leviathan* by two decades, Hobbes offers the germ of his thought by underlining, in the Introduction, the pragmatic finality of Thucydides, warning the reader that in the *History* the author does not lose himself in digressions, but instead sticks to the *facts, to reality.*[109]

It's the same Hobbes, the materialist, that opposes himself to Platonic dualism. At the end of *Leviathan*, in chapter 46 (a suggestive title: *Of the Darkness from Vain Philosophy and Fabulous Traditions*), after saying that

---

[103] On the ontological essence of *l'intérêt général*, see Coq 2015: 153–70.
[104] Nietzsche 1998 [1888] 77–8 (emphasis in original).
[105] Iglesias-Zoido 2011: 43.
[106] Leiter 2012: 871.
[107] Iglesias-Zoido 2011: 196.
[108] Martinich 2005: 5.
[109] See Iglesias-Zoido 2011: 200–5.

the 'Greek school' was useless, Hobbes blames Plato's and Aristotle's metaphysics: 'We are told there be in the world certain essences separated from bodies which they call *abstract essences* and *substantial forms*.' This was a mistake: 'The world (I mean not the earth only, that denominates the lovers of its worldly men, but the universe, that is, the whole mass of all things that are) is corporeal (that is to say, body) and hath the dimensions of magnitude (namely, length, breadth, and depth).'[110]

To those who wish to know why those subtleties would be present in the *Leviathan*, Hobbes is clear:

> It is to this purpose: that men may no longer suffer themselves to be abused by them that by this doctrine of *separated essences*, built on the vain philosophy of Aristotle [and Plato], would fright them from obeying the laws of their country with empty names, as men fright birds from the corn with an empty doublet, a hat, and a crooked stick.[111]

Rousseau fought against materialism. Hobbes' doctrine was gaining terrain in cultivated society. In France, when materialists like Diderot and Voltaire spoke of 'rationalizing the laws', thus attacking the Church and its dogmas, their goal was primarily political: dethroning the laws of God and putting the laws of men in its place. Diderot and his friends wanted to build a new society on a materialist basis, thus negating traditional moral dogmas such as God, free will, the soul and transcendental ideas. They tried to 'enlighten' the world.[112]

In his *Encyclopédie*, Denis Diderot (1713–84), the most significant French materialist, followed Hobbes in affirming that human beings are purely material. Julian de La Mettrie (1709–51), impassioned by Descartes' *Description du corps humain* (1664), extirpated the immaterial element of Descartes' duality in publishing *L'Homme Machine* (1747), in which La Mettrie maintained that the 'the big mistake' of philosophy was metaphysical dualism; we are only substance, said Le Mettrie, unsurprisingly mentioning his archfoes Leibniz, Malebranche and Fénélon – all of them Rousseau's heroes.

Claude Helvétius (1715–71) published his masterpiece *De l'esprit* (1758) anonymously, trying to find a philosophical basis for La Mettrie's metaphysics, bringing together empiricism and materialism – for Helvétius a natural marriage. In the book, Helvétius maintained that there were only two sources of ideas: sensation and memory. Moreover, he used the concept of *utilité publique* as a weapon in his polemic against religion and the concept of human

---

[110] Hobbes 1998 [1651]: 458–9. On Hobbes's materialism and anti-Platonic moralism, see Williams 2007: chapter 2.

[111] Ibid: 460.

[112] In the next four paragraphs, I follow Williams 2007: 61–2.

social nature, suggesting that the ancient idea of public interest was but a *myth*; the only existent interest was the *particular*, and public utility was nothing but 'the sum of all particular interests'.[113]

Also anonymously, Paul-Henry D'Holbach (1723–89) published *Système de la Nature* (1770), in which he agreed with La Mettrie on the unity of substance: men were only a combination of material substance, and religious doctrines that proclaimed immaterial ideas were dangerous, for they replaced authority by reason, thus contributing to tyranny. There's no free will, said the atheist D'Holbach, who, like Helvétius, united empiricism and materialism. Instead, the most important among material causes was the will to preserve our own lives and self-interest. D'Holbach's utilitarianism was straightforward: once free will doesn't exist, the only thing we can do is to maintain what we can see: happiness.

Rousseau reacted to all of this. His Platonic metaphysics (existence of God, free will, immaterial soul, transcendent ideas) and epistemology (suspicion of senses and confidence on 'internal sentiments') are revealed in the *Emile* when the Savoyard Vicar wants to *educate* the youth about the traditional morality of Plato, Descartes, Malebranche, Fénélon and Lamy, to destroy the materialist foundations that were then emerging.[114]

In *Emile*, Rousseau's enemies are *les philosophes*. 'I am not a great philosopher. And I care little to be one' (Em 266).[115] Materialists, for Rousseau, 'are indeed deaf to the inner voice crying out to them in a tone difficult not to recognize. A machine does not think; there is neither motion nor figure which produces reflection' (Em 280).

In this part of *Profession of Faith*, Rousseau explains why a man cannot be simply a material substance, with no spirit and movement. There must be something superior to material substance, to everything, something that would give sense and order to the universe. 'This Being which wills and is powerful, this Being active in itself, this Being, whatever it may be, which moves the Universe and order all things, I call *God*' (Em 277).

Rousseau says: 'I perceive God everywhere in His works. I sense Him in me; I see Him all around me' (Em 277). It's this superior Being that makes free will possible, not the material body. And 'after having discovered those attributes of the divinity by which I know its existence', Rousseau adds,

> I find myself by my species incontestably in the first rank; for by my will and by the instruments in my power for executing it, I have more force for acting on all the

---

[113]   In Rangeon 1986: 108.
[114]   See Williams 2007: 62.
[115]   I use Alan Bloom's translation of *Émile*.

bodies surrounding me, for yielding to or eluding their actions as I please, than any of them has for acting on me against my will by physical impulsion alone. (Em 277)

This metaphysical conviction encompasses the body/soul dualism. For Rousseau, the soul is made by God and can have 'sublime ideas'. The existence of God, the soul/body duality and the conviction that nothing comes from material substance enable Rousseau's belief that there is a sense of justice 'innate in [the] human's heart' (Em 279). I can't find better words to exemplify this Platonic passage: 'There is in the depths of souls, then, an innate principle of justice and virtue according to which, in spite of our own maxims, we judge our actions and those of others as good or bad. It is to this principle that I give the name conscience' (Em 289).

We are away from the *real* world. Nothing in Rousseau's work is *tangible, material*. Accordingly, the general interest is an immaterial idea, which is *postulated, transcendent*. But Rousseau did not define *l'intérêt général* throughout his work.

We all know the two passages in the Social Contract: 'general will is always in the right, and always tends to the public welfare', and soon after, 'There is often a difference between the will of everyone and the general will; the latter is concerned only with the common interest, while the former is concerned with private interests, and is the sum total of individual want' (SC 66).[116] They help little. Why didn't he give us a clearer vision of his 'most successful metaphor, [which] conveys everything he most wanted to say'?[117]

Because he didn't need to. As Patrick Riley (1941–2015) has brilliantly shown,[118] Rousseau used a *theological* notion of the general will, which was well known and defended by French Platonic moral theologists for longer than 70 years (1644–1715), among them Antoine Arnauld (1612–94), Nicolas Malebranche (1612–94) – Rousseau's great inspiration – and others. Their basic idea was that the *volonté général* expressed a will possessed by God to decide about man's destiny, a kind of God's justice. What Rousseau did was transform this theological notion into a *civic* one. Here is how Rousseau made this change.[119]

Early modern theologians were concerned with reconciling God's will to save everyone, as put in Paul's first letter to Timothy, with the belief that only some would be saved. Would God not have a *volonté général* that would save us all? Why would He wish to save some and condemn others? Notions of

---

[116] I use Christopher Betts' translation of the Social Contract.
[117] Shklar 1969: 184.
[118] See Riley 1986; 2001; 2015.
[119] What follows is based on Riley 2015; Williams 2014; 2015; and Shklar 1969.

volonté générale and *volonté particulière* were part of the larger question of God's justice, which was as old as Christian philosophy.

Malebranche gave ample theological attention to the notions of *volonté générale* and *volonté particulière*. God would act 'by *volontés générales* when he acts as a consequence of general laws which he has established', and 'does not act at all' by *volontés particulières*, 'by lawless and ad hoc volitions, as do "limited intelligences" whose thought was not "infinite"'. For Malebranche, to act by *volontés particulières* shows limited intelligence, while to act by *volonté générale* shows wisdom. God acts only by *volonté générale*, even if there are 'monstrous' children and unripe fruit, which are not *themselves* wished by God. There is a 'constant and regulated order' in the laws of God, who does not act in the name of *volontés particulières*; those who think this way, said Malebranche, 'imagine that God at every moment is performing miracles in their favor'; this 'flatters the self-love which relates everything to itself' and 'accommodates itself quite well to ignorance'.[120]

Malebranche, 'the undisputed greatest Platonist of Modern France', separated body and soul and thought that God was 'the primary causal agent of the universe'.[121] In Malebranche, there is an eternal, immutable conception of Justice, to which even God's will must confirm. Contrary to the 'bizarre' idea of Hobbes, there was nothing arbitrary in God's will, Malebranche thought, and each act of will for their particular pleasures is 'unjust, it is ungrateful, it is blind'.[122] Rousseau took these ideas seriously.

The *volonté* represents Rousseau's conviction that 'civil association is the most completely voluntary of acts' (SC 137), that 'to remove the will's freedom is to remove all morality from our actions' (SC 50). Only free men act voluntarily, and free will is not an end in itself. It is *necessary* to the implementation of the social pact, which becomes a political body. This *volonté*, for Rousseau, must be *général*. And here lies the crucial point for Rousseau's moral and political theory: contrary to God's will, which was *natural* to Malebranche and other theologians, in Rousseau it would be *produced* by familiar and *civic* education.[123] As Riley said, 'it's not an accident that education (domestic and civic) is everything in Rousseau'.[124]

Thus, the notion of *volonté général*, a theological expression common to the seventeenth-century French theologists, was transformed by Rousseau's genius into a fundamental civic notion, around which men should unite themselves to construct a society. The *volonté général* is an amalgam that pulls

---

[120] Riley 2015: 14–16 (Malebranche quotations are Riley's).
[121] Williams 2007: 35, 36.
[122] Williams 2015: 247 (Malebranche quotations are Williams').
[123] See Riley 2001: 125.
[124] Riley 2001: 126.

men out of themselves as individual *qua tale*. The individual is, in Rousseau, associated with egoism and to *amour propre*.

What is crucial to administrative law scholars is this: the *Emile* is Rousseau's treatise on *education*, through which the author intends to turn a man into a *citizen*, who will act not out of egoism, of self-love, of individual interest, but in the name of the community, the *volonté générale*, the public interest. As Williams said: 'The point of the general will is to make "good man" by this measure – to make citizens order themselves for the whole, rather than precisely the opposite'.[125] The general will is not natural but *constructed* through education, which can never, for Rousseau, be based on materialist philosophy.

But if there is no Heaven, no God, what is all this jargon for?

We are all familiar with the answer, which has most brilliantly come from the legal historian Pierre Legendre,[126] thus summarized by Plessix: by taking God's place, the State is the paternal figure which structures the political power and orders society. But, moreover, in communities that anchor their systems in the *summa divisio* public–private law, public law is the terrain in which we encounter the virtues, the impartial aims, the sublime values such as *l'intérêt général* and *le service public*,[127] not individual rights.

In modern times, for the French, the general interest must rest 'in an abstract, untouchable place, of no other reality but conceptual: the nation and/or the State'.[128] We are always in the terrain of abstractions, and there is a dialectical relation between the three ideas: Nation, State and general interest. All three concepts are thus amalgamated. It is the State, in the end, that incites and guides people in the name of and towards the general interest, which *transcends* particular interests.[129] The State is the vehicle of the public interest, which is the principle of the social order whose application springs out of the State authority.[130] As Gilles Guglielmi put it recently, this conception of the general interest is developed '*par le droit public français en soi la quitessence*'.[131]

Civilians, heirs of *droit administratif, understand* this rhetoric. But unfortunately, ironies like that shown in Cohen-Tanughi's comment about France, 'this singular country in which each – and the State first – knows, or thinks to

---

[125] Williams 2014: 24–5.
[126] See eg Legendre 1992; 2005.
[127] See Plessix 2020: 8.
[128] Rangeon 1986: 15; Chevallier 2015: 84.
[129] See ibid: 18-29, 121.
[130] See ibid: 133–40.
[131] Guglielmi 2017: 18.

know, with a remarkable ease, where the general interest is',[132] pass over this rich tradition of Rousseau's thought.

One last word on terminology before examining the US conception of public interest. French law has always maintained the adjective *général* instead of *publique*. That is not casual, as Didier Truchet remarked in the same colloquium mentioned earlier: 'Undoubtedly, it's necessary to see in the adjective "général" an implicit reminiscence of the "volonté générale" that founds the French conception of democracy.'[133]

It is Rousseau whispering.

3.   THE US AND THE UTILITARIAN CONCEPTION OF THE GENERAL INTEREST

The word 'liberalism' acquired a political sense in the nineteenth century. In the previous one it had an economic sense in the work of the Physiocrats and Adam Smith (1723–90), the father of modern economics, having flourished first in the United Kingdom, Smith's soil, and later in France and the US.

In France, liberalism attacked the idea of a planned economy, *économie dirigé*. In the UK, in 1776 Smith published *The Wealth of Nations* (WN), in which he famously claimed that the private interest is the motor of the economy. Therefore, the State should recognize that personal interests are to be left to the marketplace.[134] Below are the famous words:

> It is thus that the private interests and passions of individuals naturally dispose them to turn their stock towards the employments which in ordinary cases are most advantageous to the society. But if from this natural preference they should turn too much of it towards those employments, the fall of profit in them and the rise of it in all others immediately dispose them to alter this faulty distribution. *Without any intervention of law*, therefore, *the private interests and passions of men naturally lead them to divide and distribute the stock of every society*, among all the different employments carried on in it, as nearly as possible in the proportion which is most agreeable *to the interest of the whole society*. (WN, Bk4, Ch7, Part3, §88) [emphasis added, footnote omitted]

This passage, says Rangeon, clearly announces the economic and political principle: if we leave each to pursue the individual interest, the economy of the whole society will grow, and so the general interest. The fundamental turn of this vision is 'to give an economic justification to a political principle'.[135] The

---

[132]   Cohen-Tanugi 1985: 117.
[133]   Truchet 2017: 214.
[134]   See Rangeon 1986: 155–6; Clamour 2006: §§ 187, 191, 192.
[135]   Rangeon 1986: 155–6.

individual interest, for Smith, consisted in 'bettering our condition, a desire which […] come with us from the womb, and never leaves us till we go to the grave' (WN, Bk2, Ch3). Smith's idea is that the individual interest is fundamentally in conformity to the good of society.

In the *Emile*, Rousseau used a similar image: 'The sole passion natural to man is *amour de soi*' (Em 92), 'the source of our passions, the origin and the principle of all the others, the only one born with man and which never leaves him so long as he lives is *amour de soi* – a primitive, innate passion, which is anterior to every other, and of which all others are in a sense only modifications' (Em 212–13). Here lies a crucial difference that helps explain the opposing mottos of the two authors: while Rousseau's expression (*amour de soi*) denotes a concern with human nature, Smith's (bettering our condition) conveys a concern with human economic activity.

Accordingly, Smith's idea of bettering the human condition, which 'the greater part of men propose and wish', is through 'an augmentation of fortune' (WN, Bk2, Ch3), thus attributing to the particular interest an economic sense. And so it is as to the public interest. Prosperity, for Smith, is the key to the general interest, as seen in the chapter entitled, revealingly, *Of the Wages of Labour*:

> It deserves to be remarked, perhaps, that it is in the progressive state, while the society is advancing to the further acquisition, rather than when it has acquired its full complement of riches, that the condition of the labouring poor, of the great body of the people, seems to be the happiest and the most comfortable […] The liberal reward of labour, as it encourages the propagation, so it increases the industry of the common people. (WN, Bk1, Ch8)

Smith's society is one of exchange, and it is the particular interest that moves society to the common good, that is, to prosperity. 'The natural effort of every individual to better his own condition', he said, 'when suffered to exert itself with freedom and security, is so powerful a principle, that it is alone, and without any assistance, not only capable of carrying on the society to wealth and prosperity, but of surmounting a hundred impertinent obstructions' (WN, Bk4, Ch5).

In the UK, utilitarianism, from Bentham onwards, would profit from Smith's philosophy. This, coupled with an 'individualist fiber' which is 'impermeable to the public interest' and 'was well anchored at the time [of Dicey] and […] is still today',[136] meant the UK became impermeable to Rousseau's conception of *intérêt général*. Contrary to France, where national sovereignty is connected to the *intérêt général*, in the UK the public interest is a legal *and* political prin-

---

[136] Duffy-Meunier 2017: 49, 54.

ciple that designates the majority of the electors in the Parliament – hence, the public interest changes over time.

The American version of the public interest follows the common law path, in contrast with France. There's no transcendence in it, no abstractions. The American ideological understanding of the general interest is *materialist*; it is a product of human *agreement*, not a pure ideal; it is *pluralist* and *immanent*. There must be a harmonic compromise among the many, *changeable* public interests. All private interests are *politically* legitimate to concur to the formations of the common good, which isn't given by any force external to society, let alone the state; hence, it is *procedural*, and the divergence of private interests compounds the collective good. The private interest is not demonized as an enemy; on the contrary, it governs the public policy. Business competition in the marketplace constructs the public interest better than the State.[137]

Nothing could be further from the transcendent ideal of Rousseau, to whom the *volonté générale* is not produced by deliberation, let alone market forces, but is found in the heart of men.[138]

Perhaps Elizabeth Zoller has touched the heart of the matter in saying, in the avant-propos of the colloquium mentioned earlier, that the general interest was the motor of the *État legal*. Still, it could no longer be the motor of the *État de droit*. In the Rule of Law, the engine is the individual rights, the particular interests.[139]

Many Brazilian jurists would nowadays agree.

4.   THE BRAZILIAN SWING

Brazilian law has rarely discussed public interest foundations, contenting itself with simple ideas uncritically imported from abroad. And courts repeat, like a monologue, that the general interest is superior to the private interest. It's the uncritical tradition at its peak – and perhaps the main reason why Brazilian administrative law has been historically so desultory.

Celso Antônio Bandeira de Mello (1936–), professor of administrative law and famous for his (recent) leftist engagement in politics, is the most notorious defender of the supremacy of the public interest.[140] Not by chance, he is one

---

[137] See Rangeon 1986: 200–1; Chevallier 2015: 85–6; Coq 2015: 162; Custos 2017: 67–74.

[138] See Perrin 2014: 167.

[139] See Zoller 2017: 13.

[140] But he is by no means the only one. He parts company with – among many others – for instance Maria Sylvia Di Pietro (1943–), probably the best-selling Brazilian handbook author in the field, mentioned in Chapter 8. About Brazilian 'publicists', see Sundfeld 2014: chapter 3.

of the greatest admirers of French State philosophy and all its corollaries; throughout his work, he berates Anglo-American Liberalism and the associated legal system. And, curiously enough, in opposing the US system of precedents as sources of law to the continental system, he explains that scholarly works guide courts' decisions, not vice versa.[141] Remarkably, he is one of the living authors most frequently quoted by the STF, the Brazilian Supreme Court.

In his very influential *Handbook of Administrative Law*, Mello simply claims that the genuine public interest is 'the interest of all', 'the public dimension of private interests',[142] and not reducible to the mere sum of them. Mello doesn't mention Rousseau in his discussion of the public interest. Still, in another part of the book, he states (without *any* further comment) that the 'ideological basis of Administrative law is […] the concourse of two lines of thought: of Rousseau and Montesquieu'.[143]

In the 1990s, however, the Liberal wave returned and overtook Brazilian public law entirely, having a massive impact on public law scholarly work, particularly in the areas of administrative law and public contracts. Finally, a seminal work published in 1998, if only in dogmatic terms and *completely* ignoring material sources, touched the heart of the problem and questioned the sacrosanct principle of 'superiority of the public interest', suggesting the opposite would hold: in the abstract, the Brazilian system would support the prevalence of private interests/rights over the public interest.[144] This launched a debate that continues to this day.

It would take another chapter, at least, to comment on this battle.[145] It is remarkable, however, that for the first time in Brazilian legal history, the tectonic plates of administrative law seem to have been shaken. Beneath the surface lies the real battle between the two conceptions of the general interest deployed in the two previous items.

Although never touching the ground of the philosophical level, what matters to us is that this battle has, unsurprisingly, been influencing the formal sources on public law, particularly public contracts, as we will see in Chapters 8 and 9.

5.   A PERSONAL ANECDOTE

I'd like to end this chapter with one more personal story.

It is about something that happened at NYU Law School in the Fall of 2005, during a seminar conducted by Professor Ronald Dworkin on Legal, Political,

---

[141] See Mello 2021: 38.
[142] See ibid: 50–2.
[143] Ibid: 42.
[144] See Ávila 1998.
[145] I examined the battle in Giacomuzzi 2017b (full of sources).

and Social Philosophy, which I attended as an auditor while I was a visiting researcher at Columbia. The seminary was part of a broader colloquium, joined by many scholars in New York City.

On a specific day, we were to discuss a paper presented by Benedict Kingsbury, Professor of International Law at NYU, entitled *The Problem of the Public in Public International Law*.[146] One point to be addressed was the concept of 'public interest', central to the paper, and I sensed that for most students, especially Americans, there was a difficulty in grasping why and in what sense a concept like public interest could be central to the paper, given its lack of concreteness. But a French student stood apart from the chorus: 'I don't understand', he said, 'why you're so sceptical. In France, the concept of public interest structures the whole legal system and is foundational to administrative law specifically.' Professor Dworkin intervened and asked for more arguments.

Convinced that I could help, I tried to do so as concisely as possible (an auditor, I thought, was not supposed to talk): I mentioned the Roman origins of the public–private law dichotomy, in which the public interest is central; its influence in the civil tradition; and its importance in civilians' *mentalité*. After the class, Professor Dworkin kindly approached and privately told me: 'I've got your thesis, but you need arguments to support it.'

I nowadays see that my explanation to Professor Dworkin could bear a germ of correctness but was essentially superficial. More than 15 years later, I still can't offer a public interest theory, let alone a concept. Yet I'm convinced that if my explanation had begun with Rousseau, then Dworkin, a moralist, would have taken it as familiar.

As we know, in his constitutional theory, mainly exposed in *Freedom's Law*, Dworkin opposed his 'moral reading' of the American constitution to the 'majoritarian premise' of democracy.[147] To make sense of his theory, Dworkin needed a new conception of democracy to refute the majoritarian idea, according to which democracy corresponded to the majority vote. For Dworkin, if 'collective action' were to be understood statistically, that is, as the mere sum of individuals one by one, the majority could oppress the rights of minorities. This was, essentially, why Dworkin created a new conception of democracy, called 'constitutional', based on a 'communal' idea of collective action, famously exemplified with the metaphor of an orchestra, which is not merely the statistical sum of many sounds, but a collective action that produces a symphony that a single musician cannot play.

---

[146] Available here: www.law.nyu.edu/centers/lawphilosophy/colloquium/fall2005. The paper was never published, as far as I know.

[147] See Dworkin 1996: 1–38.

It is not a coincidence that the example invoked by Dworkin to illustrate his communal conception of democracy was Rousseau's general will[148] – Rousseau the moralist, the anti-positivist, who elevated the *volonté général* above the *volontés particulières*, a general will that is not the mere sum of particular instruments of an orchestra.

What matters is that underneath Rousseau's general will, or the public interest in the French and Brazilian administrative and public contract law, there will always be something unpalpable, immaterial, unexplained by reason alone, something apprehensible only (if indeed it is) by senses. These ideas are better understood and accepted in countries that have lived by abstract notions inherited from Plato and Rousseau. More often than not, these people presuppose all that these two giants did.

It is not difficult to recognize the emotional plea of these ideas – they take a byway to the heart. 'Whatever may be our opinion of his merits as a thinker', Bertrand Russell (1872–1970) wrote of Rousseau, 'we must recognize his immense importance as a social force. This importance came mainly from his appeal to the heart and to what, in his day, was called "sensibility".'[149] I believe that this plea to the heart still lives in French and Brazilian *mentalités*, at least in those *publicistes* that advocate the public interest's supremacy. We need something to unite us in this chaotic, violent world, even if it is only an ideal.

But nor is it difficult to see that this ideal is wholly severed from the *real world*. In this pluralist universe we inhabit – whose history is made of massacres, wars, cruelty and inequality – to think there is a natural order of things and beings, a good that we could call common, a public interest that would amalgamate us as a Nation, all sounds like a piece of childlike music, a dream which inhabits the realm of pure ideas. Thucydides told us this story more than 2,500 years ago – Thucydides, the grandfather of Hobbes the materialist, the precursor of Smith and Bentham and the father of utilitarianism, all archfoes of Rousseau.

Again, Moralism versus Realism, Leiter's illuminating framework, is in play.

---

[148] See ibid: 20.

[149] Russell 1972 [1945]: 684. Revealingly, Russell affirmed that 'Hitler is an outcome of Rousseau; Roosevelt and Churchill, of Locke' (at 685).

4. The public law–private law dichotomy in the context of public contracts

'It would be a serious error to imagine that the distinction between public law and private law is merely a classificatory device that can be used or discarded as seems most convenient', warned Nigel Simmonds in 1984. 'The distinction', he correctly put it, 'is an element of a *much wider political theory* and its acceptance or rejection as a valued doctrinal category depends upon how the legal order is to be *philosophically construed*'.[1]

Simmonds' warning is simple and profound. It captures an often neglected aspect of the dichotomy, which I will emphasize shortly: the *political character* lurking behind the *choice* made, consciously or not, by those who have or have not adopted, constructed and perpetuated a law system based or not based on the dichotomy. Georges Burdeau (1905–88) touched the core of the matter: 'Indeed, political universe is not given by nature; it's inseparable of a human thinking that creates it while conceiving it.'[2] Whether to uphold the dichotomy is a *political choice* that has normative consequences. But let me first start with a trivial, descriptive remark.

Of all the exciting things that attract continental jurists' attention when studying the common law system, particularly the American system,[3] few may be viewed as more fundamental than the almost complete lack of a methodological dichotomy between public and private law. Indeed, what strikes civil law jurists is that the public–private law dichotomy is at the core of civil law jurists' method of thinking whenever they face any legal problem. Yet, at the same time, common law lawyers almost neglect the dichotomy.[4]

---

[1]   Simmonds 1984: 121 (emphasis added).
[2]   Burdeau 1980: 25.
[3]   The English doctrine has been more attentive than the American to the issue of the public–private law dichotomy, particularly with respect to administrative law. See generally Allison 1996: chapter 5. Since the late 1970s, a scholarly debate has taken place over whether or not to adopt the public–private law dichotomy. For criticisms, see eg Harlow 1980. Favouring dichotomy, see eg Samuel 1983; Amhlaigh 2015. For an overview, see Freedland 2004. The point should not be whether or not to have the dichotomy, but *for what reasons* we should or should not have it.
[4]   The common law feature has obviously historical roots. On English law, see Loughlin 2013: 14; JDB Mitchell 1965. Allison (1996: 4–12, 77–81) has highlighted

Moreover, when Americans do not neglect it, they usually attach different content to it and imply different consequences. It is crucial to understand why this difference exists and to discern the implications that follow from that. What matters is the normative function of the division in lawyers' and jurists' way of thinking.

For centuries, civilians have been thinking from and through the public–private law 'great dichotomy',[5] the *summa divisio*. 'The distinction structures completely the teaching of French law and the French research about law.'[6] Although the dichotomy has, unsurprisingly, been under severe attack since at least the 1950s, Merryman's words are still vivid: 'The [civil] law student, who encounters this sweeping division at the outset of his career, tends uncritically to absorb it. It quickly becomes basic to his *Rechtsanschauung* [legal perception].' And despite the challenges to it, the civil law student '*knows* that public law and private law are *essentially* different'.[7]

In sharp contrast, Merryman continues, 'American lawyers, American law and American legal scholarship seem to get along without any conscious use of the great division between public and private law'.[8] From the beginning of their course, students in the US law schools are not introduced to the *summa divisio*. While civilians have implied a prevalence of public law over private law, Americans invert the poles of the dichotomy, if they do not just gloss over it. What is the importance of that difference? What values are behind it?

Ultimately, the difference in treatment reveals that civil law jurists and common law lawyers *have assumed different moral and political values*, the values upon which different legal systems were constructed. Jacques Chevallier noted that the public–private distinction 'appears as a category of thought in the western societies' imagination' and that the dichotomy 'is

---

that Bracton, Sir Matthew Hale, Blackstone, Austin, Markby, Holland, Pollock and Dicey generally ignored, rejected or gave little importance to the public–private law dichotomy. But see Kischel 2019: 319.

[5]   See Bobbio 1985, chapter 1.

[6]   Auby 2004: 20; also Cailosse 1996: 955–6.

[7]   Merryman 1968: 3 (emphasis added). See also Merryman & Pérez-Perdomo 2007: 92. Merryman's article demonstrates that the dichotomy was becoming fuzzy in the mid-1960s. It is nevertheless still valid. See also Allison 1996: 70.

[8]   Merryman 1968: 4. This characteristic of Anglo-American law has been largely recognized. See eg Fromont 2010: 267; Samuel 2003: 243; Allison 1996: 1; Pierce Jr et al 1999: 3; Borchard 1928a: 604; Pollock 1923: 256; Pound 1937: 20 (referring to public law as 'something quite unknown to the received common law'); Bernard Schwartz 1956: 250; M Shapiro 1972: 411; Slesser 1936: 19. *Contra*, but for very different teleological reasons, see M Cohen 1927: 8. For a thoughtful historical explanation apropos the lack of public–private dichotomy in English law (which can be used to also explain the American scenario), see Samuel 1988: 278–85.

expressed by the submission of each sphere to different *systems of values* and different *normative system*';[9] this contrast of distinct values 'is, no doubt, more or less marked according to the country: strongly marked in continental Europe, *and notably in France*, it's less apparent in Anglo-Saxon countries, *and notably in the US*'.[10] It is therefore not a coincidence that France is the civil law country in which the public–private law dichotomy has received more attention,[11] while the US is the common law country in which the dichotomy has had less importance.[12]

Yet, the public–private law dichotomy is a multifaceted topic. It can be viewed from many different vantage points, triggering various criticisms. So, I must identify my target to avoid misunderstandings. What matters about the public–private law dichotomy is not whether a given legal system recognizes it or not, but *for what purpose* a legal system supports or dispenses with the dichotomy.

In France and Brazil, the *summa divisio* has been working as a necessary, although not sufficient, condition to support the normative structure of *droit politique* and all its corollaries, from legal and moral principles such as the superiority of the public interest to legal concepts such as *contrat administratif*. In the US, the (very parochial and restricted) debate over the dichotomy is influenced by the opposite view: the Liberal philosophy that enhances private interest at the expense of the public interest. In Anglo-American Liberalism (which I capitalize to indicate that I mean to include both American Liberalism and conservatism), it is the private law philosophy that prevails. The purpose of the dichotomy encompasses, ultimately, *a political and moral debate*.

---

[9]   Chevallier 1995: 6, 7 (emphasis in original). See also Bobbio 1985: 5.

[10]   Chevallier 1995: 7 (emphasis added). See also Cailosse 1996: 956–7.

[11]   See eg Beaud 2004: 30–1 (the dichotomy is in France a 'scientific division of law', which is reinforced by the way the French teach law and the way the professors are recruited: to teach either public or contract law); Caillosse 1996: 955–7 (highlighting the central function played by the *summa divisio* in French law in contrast to other continental law and common law systems); Testu 1998: 347 (referring to the ideological aspect of the division); Plessix 2003a: 15–16.

[12]   In American law, besides the historical criticism made by the so-called Critics about the public–private dichotomy, the distinction has been an issue within feminist jurisprudence. See eg Gavison 1992 (examining the feminist critique of the dichotomy). It also appears in the constitutional law arena with respect to the correct identification of what would be a 'state action', to which two key constitutional provisions, namely the Bill of Rights and the Fourteenth Amendment, would apply, as opposed to 'private action', to which the same constitutional provisions would not. See eg Alexander 1993 (holding that a conceptual critique of the public–private dichotomy does not lead to a normative collapse of the distinction). Neither the feminist nor the constitutional law critique will be the object of my concern in this book.

First, I will explain two perspectives of the dichotomy: (i) *a priori* to the very concept of law (the 'ontological' view) and (ii) an instrument to reach specific political goals (the 'teleological' perspective). I will argue that only the teleological view is relevant. Second, I will explore the purposes of the dichotomy for the theory of public contract law.

1. THE 'ONTOLOGICAL' AND THE 'TELEOLOGICAL' QUESTIONS

As already asserted in Chapter 3, the *summa divisio* comes from the *Corpus Iuris* of Emperor Justinian. Public law was concerned with the organization of the Roman state, while private law was about the well-being of individuals.

However controversial the meaning and role of the dichotomy through-out the centuries,[13] and no matter how complex the political and historical debate about the boundaries of *ius privatum* and *ius publicum* has been,[14] it is crucial to note that, among civilians, common sense about the methodological public–private schema has suggested – at least from the Middle Ages onwards – a mutual implication of both spheres: the public realm ends where the private domain begins; if the former augments, the latter will necessarily diminish.[15]

Moreover, there is an intimate relationship between the idea of state and the *summa divisio*. Wherever the conception of state is lacking, as in feudal Europe, the dichotomy is lacking. If the notion of state is weak, like in the Middle Ages, the public–private dichotomy is also weak.[16] Norbert Elias (1897–1990) demonstrated that in the Middle Ages, primarily at the beginning of the era, the decentralizing forces of society overcame the centralizing tendencies.[17] Henri Legohérel (1937–2019) remarked that in ninth to twelfth-century France, unlike in Germany and England, 'the blossoming of feudality was accompanied by a decline of the royal power and the central authority', and that '[t]he notion of State and the idea of sovereignty undergo

---

[13] See Chevrier 1952: 6–11; Roubier 1951: 295–300; Rigaudière 1997; Jones 1970: 140; Allison 1996: 42–9.

[14] See generally eg Birocchi 1996; Merryman & Pérez-Perdomo 2007: 95.

[15] See Bobbio 1985: 4.

[16] See Rigaudière 1997: 83 (arguing that the 'opposition between *jus privatum* and *jus publicum* lost progressively its entire value in the medieval society', because custom gradually took the place of the rules emanating from the then dispersed and contested authorities who enacted them); Troper 2004: 193; Ullmann 1975: 137 ('The concept of the State was as far removed from the mind of the high Middle Ages as the steam-engine and electricity'). See also Allison 1996: 112–14; Gaudemet 1995: 16; Jolowicz 1978 [1957]: 52; Jones 1970: 141, 143; Plessix 2003a: 399; Radbruch 1950 [1932]: § 16, 155); Samuel 1988: 278; Simmonds 1984: 123; Pires 2005: 358–9.

[17] See Elias 2000 [1939]: 197–208.

a long eclipse; what remains is found within the most simple notion of patri-
mony'.[18] No wonder that in the Middle Ages the dichotomy has played a much
smaller role in law, which explains the well-known modern linkage between
the medieval or feudal character of the common law,[19] as well as its neglected
attention to the public–private law dichotomy. Accordingly, it is not surprising
that a 'stateless society' like the American one has dedicated little effort to
building a state theory and has constructed its legal system without paying
much attention to the Roman *summa divisio*. Once 'programmed' in American
lawyers' *mentalités*, all that must be taken into consideration when the comparatist faces any legal problem.

In contrast, civilians, particularly in French law (followed by Brazilian law),
have historically presented a very different viewpoint. The modern idea of
the State, considered from the late seventeenth century onwards (but whose
seeds were planted in Roman times and had fermented since the fourteenth
century),[20] has served as a vehicle for strengthening the public–private law
dichotomy.[21] As Otto von Gierke (1841–1921) stated, the separation of *ius
publicum* from *ius privatum*, which 'had at one time seemed to [men] hardly
more than a matter of words', became, with the idea of the superiority of the
State, 'even more decisively a main outline in the ground-plan of all constructive Jurisprudence'.[22] Since the Enlightened Revolutions, the debate over
the idea of the State, its functions and its relations to law has controlled the
public–private law dichotomy.

The 'statenessness' was fuelled by the *summa divisio*, and *le droit administratif* was, according to Olivier Beaud,[23] the matrix of the autonomy of *le droit
public* at the beginning of the Golden Age of administrative law, that is, around
the 1870s. At the time, the role of *la doctrine* became even more relevant in
French public law, and it is little wonder that *les publicistes* worked their way
out through publishing.

In 1894, when the *Revue de droit public et de la science politique* (which
became one of the best legal publications in France) appeared, its founder,
Ferdinand Launarde, then professor of *Droit Public Général* at the *Faculté de
Droit* in Paris, wrote that the State was a decisive element in the definition of
public law and that the object of study of the new Review was the structure of

---

[18]   Legohérel 1991: 30.
[19]   See Pound 1999 [1921]: chapter 1; 1937: 16–23; Dyson 1980: 115; Heuschling
2002: 177, 419; Radbruch 1962: 5; Roubier 1951: 300.
[20]   See Creveld 1999: Chapter 2.
[21]   See Jones 1970: 145.
[22]   Gierke 1900 [1881]: 83–4.
[23]   See Beaud 2004: 34–8, from which I derive freely in this paragraph and the next.

the State and its relations with particulars (in response, *les privatistes* created the *Revue trimestrielle de droit civil* in 1902).

In 1932, Hermann Kantorowics (1877–1940) wrote: '[T]he State is one of the elementary concepts of jurisprudence, and is closely related to the highest concept of legal science, namely the concept of law itself.'[24] In identifying the reasons for the (lack of) a public–private law dichotomy in French and English law, Allison suggests that the concept of state, well developed in post-revolutionary France, was and still is lacking in England.[25] Olivier Dubos is correct: '*Le droit administratif* is a son of the Theory of State.'[26] So it is *le contrat administratif*.

The dichotomy has been so crucial to continental law that some have considered it, until very recently, *a priori*.[27] In this sense, the dichotomy would be part of the essence of the law. 'In fact', wrote Gustav Radbruch (1878–1949), the coryphaeus of this vision, 'the distinction between private and public law is anchored in the very concept of the law'.[28]

But positivists are suspicious about 'ontologies'. And of course, for a positivist comparative analysis, it does not matter whether the public–private law dichotomy is congenital to the concept of law; to be fair, most continental law jurists nowadays are doubtful about the idea of the dichotomy as being *a priori*.[29] What matters is the uncontroversial fact that French and Brazilian jurists still think about law *as if* the law necessarily encompasses the dichotomy, regardless of how malleable the dichotomy has become or how substantial the challenges against it have been. No wonder the civilians who advocate the collapse of the whole theoretical notion of public contracts, trying to melt them into the theory of private contract, also support the destruction of the public–private dichotomy. Julian Barnes' recent words are on point, whatever one thinks of the dichotomy: 'At present, the public/private divide is one of the greatest challenges for administrative law scholarship.'[30]

---

[24] Kantorowics 1932: 1.
[25] See generally Allison 1996: chapters 4–5.
[26] Dubos 2019: 135.
[27] See Radbruch 1950 [1932]: 152. See also Máynez 2000 [1940]: 131) (citing Radbruch's philosophy); Pires 2005: 359–61 (analyzing Radbruch's philosophy).
[28] Radbruch ibid.
[29] Radbruch himself (ibid) mentions that some continental legal systems have not even recognized the dichotomy. About the history of the dichotomy and its decline, see Estorninho 1999: 139–58; Raiser 1990; Barnes 2019. On its origins in French law, see generally Chevrier 1952. On its axiological dimension, see Chevallier 1979: 12–13. For recent debates, see Auby & Freedland (eds) 2004; Auby 2021.
[30] Barnes 2019: 90.

However, the most important point is that the dichotomy serves as a tool to achieve specific *political goals*.[31] It is, therefore, the *teleology* of the dichotomy that will concern us.

I will use an American law example not only to explain the instrumentality of the dichotomy but also to elucidate the previous claim that the dichotomy has appeared in the US more commonly as an argument used by a specific group of scholars with one particular *political* target in mind than as an epistemological feature that structures the average American-law lawyers' *mentalité*. Of course, I'm talking about the Critical Legal Scholars' story,[32] according to which the public–private law dichotomy was an ideological weapon used by the late nineteenth-century conservative 'formalism', the so-called Classical Legal Thought, to avoid social changes in American society.[33]

Briefly, the Critics, a Leftist movement in American legal academia, contend that conservatives used the dichotomy to protect the private, non-political, 'rights' of the 'haves'. For Classical Legal Thought, these rights would be 'natural'; they would be confined and pertain to private law and could not be infringed by the political power, that is, by the public law. The public–private dichotomy, so the Critics' argument goes, was deployed by the American elite to maintain the status quo.[34] By defining the private sphere, in which the individual rather than the state had 'natural', absolute rights, and by avoiding an inter-disciplinary approach to a supposedly 'pure' law,[35] the elite tried not only to keep the state out of business and the populace (societal workers at that time) away from corporations' profits but also to avoid any sort of redistribution of wealth. 'The distinction between public and private law', Morton Horwitz wrote, 'was in part a culmination of more long-standing efforts of conservative legal thinkers to separate the public and the private realms in American political and legal thought'.[36]

---

[31] See generally Máynez 2000 [1940]: 135.

[32] For an overview of Critical Legal Studies as a 'movement', a 'school', or a 'theory of law', see Kennedy 1997: 8–13.

[33] The term Classical Legal Thought has been commonly attached by the 'Critics' to Christopher Columbus Landgell (1826–1906), Dean of Harvard Law School from 1870 to 1895. About the structure of Classical Legal Thought, and for a criticism of it, see Horwitz 1992: 9–31. See also Tsuk Mitchell 2007; 37–9; Lobban 2018: 419–26.

[34] See Horwitz 1992: 10–11; 1982; Gordon 1983; Kennedy 1982. For critiques of Critics, see Leiter 1997: 273.

[35] See Gordon 1983: 74.

[36] Horwitz 1992: 11. See also Tsuk Mitchell 2007: 39. The subject can get much more nuanced than this broad simplification. For instance, in the field of corporations, the public–private dichotomy was key to understand American legal history. However, the idea that conservatives employed the dichotomy *to protect private property*

There is an assumption to be disclosed in this story. The public–private dichotomy is usually linked, mainly in common law systems, to the political philosophy of 'Liberalism',[37] which most Critics argue against.[38] Yet, there are many forms of Liberalism.[39] By 'Liberalism', I mean the commonsensical economic and political philosophy committed to free market values, limited state, representative government and pluralism, a philosophy that bases society mainly on property and liberty.

Once again, Radbruch's doctrine is illuminating.[40] He expounded as early as 1932 the relationship between the public–private law dichotomy and Liberalism. For Liberalism, 'private law is the heart of all law, with public law as a narrow protective frame laid around private law and especially private property'.[41] The Liberal idea of a social contract, he continues, attempting 'to trace super- and subordination in the state to an agreement between the originally coequal individuals', aims 'to dissolve public law fictitiously in private law'.[42] That is, roughly put, the Anglo-American vision of law, and it is this Liberal view that the Critics criticize.[43] Their criticism isn't directed to the public–private dichotomy *qua tale*. Critics knew that the dichotomy was only a device to achieve specific ends. The dichotomy per se is irrelevant, but it became relevant since it was used to protect specific political interests. Therefore, the Critics argue against the public–private dichotomy *because* they see it as an instrument used to carry out a political purpose or philosophy they dislike; they target the dichotomy as an *instrument* politically manipulated by the 'American elite' to maintain the status quo.

This line of criticism is hardly new. In 1927, when Morris Cohen (1880–1947) wrote about property and sovereignty and linked these concepts to *dominium* and *imperium*, his goal was to criticize the laissez-faire liberalism that saw property as an absolute value, which defended the view that public

---

remained the same. See Frug 1980: 1101–5, 1129–49. I owe this nuance to Professor Tsuk.

[37]   See eg Cane 1987: 57; Kramer 1999: 112.

[38]   Marx's dialectic critique of the public–private dichotomy is at the basis of some Critics' arguments against the dichotomy. See Turkel 1988.

[39]   See eg Rosemblatt 2019.

[40]   Radbruch's doctrine has been neglected by the common law scholars who have dealt with the subject of public–private law dichotomy. The exception is Pound 1939.

[41]   Radbruch 1950 [1932]: 153.

[42]   Ibid. One may object that this liaison between Liberalism and the dominance of private law (the 'heart of all law') is fair *only if* one speaks of nineteenth-century Liberalism, which was represented in American law by 'formalism'. Yet if we consider Pound (1939) as an anti-formalist and as a precursor of Legal Realism, one will easily perceive that my point is not about words.

[43]   Pound (1939: 472) noted that 'skeptical realists' would agree with Radbruch.

authority should abstain from intervening in the private sphere. For Cohen, not even private contracts were independent of public policies or political theory. The dichotomy, which separated *dominium*/property/private law from *imperium*/sovereignty/public law, was thus only indirectly criticized. That is, the dichotomy was criticized *because* it was a political instrument.[44]

This criticism's teleology is crucial to better understand the epistemological importance of the dichotomy in legal reasoning. For the comparatist, there is a significant contribution to take from the Critics' story. In American lawyers' *mentalités*, whenever the dichotomy appears in the legal debate, it becomes infused by the following fore-meaning: Liberalism implicates a conception of the public–private dichotomy in which the private sphere is preeminent.

Nevertheless, suppose the comparatist concedes that the dichotomy can play different roles in society and uphold different purposes, as it has done throughout civil law's history. In that case, she must conclude that the distinction between public and private law can protect private property and carry out redistributive policies. 'It shouldn't be thought', Peter Cane aptly argued, 'that the public-private distinction finds a place only in the views of those who would popularly be called "liberals"'.[45] It all depends upon the assumptions one holds about the dichotomy and what political goals one wishes to achieve.

As Radbruch noted, 'Conservative and Social' views supported the distinction too, holding opposing conclusions nevertheless. 'From this standpoint, private law appears but as the scope left, provisionally and revocably [sic] within all-embracing public law, to private initiative, which is granted in the expectation that it will be used dutifully and may be withdrawn as soon as that expectation is not fulfilled.'[46] Public law would then overcome private law. Hence, contrary to the assumptions held by Liberalism, the 'social' view of the law emphasizes public law over private law.

> [Social law] replaces the liberal idea of equality with the social idea of equalization; it brings to the fore *distributive instead of commutative justice*; and since equalization by distributive justice necessarily supposes a *superior authority above the individuals*, it supersedes self-help by the help of organized society, *especially the help of the state*. This, however, involves the emergence of that *great figure* of organized society, *the state*, behind even the most private individual legal relations and their private participants, as the third and chief participant, always observant, ready to intervene, and frequently intervening. It involves a conception of even the most private legal relation as more than merely a concern of private persons participating therein, as a social-legal relation related to *public law*.[47]

---

[44]   See Cohen 1927. But see Kramer 1999; Leiter 1997: 273.
[45]   Cane 1987: 57.
[46]   Radbruch 1950 [1932]: 154.
[47]   Ibid (emphasis added).

Yet, again, things can be more nuanced than that. Radbruch's explanation of 'social law' goes on. It emphasizes the same point that Critics made about the distinction, suggesting that a 'social–legal order' wouldn't juxtapose, but rather would overlap, public and private laws. He also exemplifies this overlap with labour law and business regulation. [48] Morris Cohen and the Critics would undoubtedly applaud that.

However, what matters here is to remark that Radbruch's viewpoint is helpful to emphasize that the critical issue is, again, the *purpose* of the dichotomy, not the dichotomy *qua tale*. Whether a legal system accepts the dichotomy is less important than knowing the *purpose* for which the dichotomy is defended or attacked: if the dichotomy holds, which sphere is considered preeminent, and for what reasons. Unfortunately, Roscoe Pound seems to be the only American scholar who paid attention to Radbruch's insights.[49]

Unlike in American Liberalism, in French and Brazilian 'State societies' jurists have historically understood and accepted the dichotomy *as an instrument to exalt the State power*, which is deemed to lead to the public good, the 'general interest'. This view is based on a more 'social' conception of society, to borrow Radbruch's previous notion. Therefore, unlike American Critics, most French and Brazilian jurists who attack the dichotomy *support* Liberal philosophy. Bobbio reprised the idea of using the dichotomy to promote the public sphere; unsurprisingly, he exemplified it by quoting a Roman text:

> [T]he original differentiation between public and private law is accompanied by the statement of the *supremacy* of the first over the second, as attested by one of the fundamental principles which govern the system where the great division is in force – the principle according to which *ius publicum privatorum pactis mutari non potest* [*Digesto*, 38.2.14] or *privatorum convention iuri publico non derogat* [*ib.*, 45, 50, 17].[50]

This notion is of critical importance to my argument. As Bobbio stated, wherever 'the great division is in force' – that is to say, in most of the civil law world, *and specifically in France and Brazil* – the following implication will

---

[48] See ibid.
[49] See Pound 1939.
[50] Bobbio 1985: 5 (emphasis added). Mestre (1985: 128) mentions the same portions of the *Digest* (D., 2. 14. 38) to exemplify 'the public utility over private conventions'. Batiffol (1979: 377–8) also remarks that Romans knew well that the notion of *publica utilitas* should trump the idea of *privatorum commode*. But see Troper 2004: 189 (stating that the dichotomy had no legal effect in Roman law, and that the distinction was only pedagogic). Troper is a jurist influenced by Kelsen, who negates the dichotomy. One sees in the (Roman) texts whatever one wishes to see. Contra, see Testu 1998: 353–4 (advocating – under liberal assumptions – private's law superiority over public law).

be in force too: *in public law, there is alleged supremacy of the public interest over the private interest.*

As the political philosopher Nannerl Keohane wrote:

> The maxim *utilitas publica prefertur utilitate privatae* – that public utility should be preferred to private – had been voiced by innumerable writers from Tacitus to Saint Thomas. Sometimes the phrase was a vague admonition to look out for the general welfare; in other instances it came close to a full-blown formulation of what was later known as *raison d'état*. In any case, it was generally accepted long before the seventeenth century that public utility – whether as the utility of the largest number of individuals, or as the good of some entity larger than the sum of individuals – took preference over private utility where the two were in direct conflict.[51]

Herein lies the key to the public–private law distinction in the French and Brazilian legal systems. The public–private law dichotomy has facilitated the adoption of the cardinal principle of public law, the *supremacy* of the public over the private interest. Inchoate in civilians' *mentalité* is an *idealist* conception of State, which incarnates virtues that would be absent from the earthly, egoistic private sphere; the *summa divisio* is viewed as axiomatic for that reasoning.[52] If we add the Rousseauian conception of public interest to that structure of thinking, we are prepared to understand the whole idea of *droit administratif*. All of that is absent in Anglo-American legal systems.

Roscoe Pound has captured this nuance. He argued that Radbruch's idea that public law was a 'law of subordination',[53] which would subsume 'individual to public interests', was against the common law. Speaking of Radbruch's thoughts, Pound pictured the German philosophy as if it '[had] reverse[d] the common-law conception in which the King rules under God',[54] thus making everyone equal. 'Granting that it was the mission of Reformation', Pound wrote in 1921, 'to "give life to individual freedom", individual freedom through the state and society were quite as possible means of achieving this mission *as the Anglo-American exaltation of abstract individual freedom above the state and above society*'.[55]

In the same vein, the French philosopher Paul Roubier (1886–1963) – in Chapter III of his classic book on General Jurisprudence, whose subtitle is

---

[51] Keohane 1980: 156.
[52] See Plessis 2020: 8.
[53] Pound 1931: 471. The idea of subordination is pervasive in continental law. To explain the public–private law dichotomy, German doctrine has developed the 'theory of subordination or of subjection', also known as 'theory of infra-ordering and of supra-ordering' (*Subjektionstheorie*). See Estorninho 1999: 144. According to this theory, public law is principally law of subordination.
[54] Pound 1939: 472.
[55] Pound 1999 [1921]: 38 (emphasis added).

Histoire de Doctrines Juridiques et Philosophie des Valeurs Sociales – links individualism to 'the legal regime of coordination', to contracts and commutative justice, while statism is related to 'the legal regime of subordination', to the role of institutions and distributive justice.[56]

The relation between Liberalism and individualism is not casual. And it is not a coincidence that Pound – always him – while speaking about 'Puritanism and the Law' in 1921, linked the uniqueness of the common law with an ultra-individualism. 'For individualism, in and of itself, has not been peculiarly English or peculiarly American. What is peculiar to Anglo-American legal thinking', he concluded, 'and above all to American legal thinking, is *ultra-individualism*, an uncompromising insistence upon individual interests and individual property as the focal point of jurisprudence'.[57]

So, unsurprisingly, almost a century later, leading political psychologists have, based on empirical evidence, similarly linked an 'American Moral Exceptionalism' to a uniquely Puritan heritage; the fact the US values moral individualism more than any other country in the world is not due to a supposedly existent reasoned process that would reflect a conscious effort, but because of an intuitive, spontaneous, effortless operation.[58]

For Pound and his fellow thinkers, the common law tradition does not accept the idea of subordinating law, public law. Accordingly, common law would be historically refractory to any notion of *a priori* supremacy of public interest or superiority of the state. No wonder Pound concluded his article on public and private law by insinuating that Radbruch's idea of the dichotomy encompassed a 'revival of absolutism'.[59] This spirit still lurks behind the American *mentalité* whenever they face a case in which the state plays a part.

2.   THE POLITICAL PURPOSES OF THE DICHOTOMY AND ITS APPLICABILITY TO PUBLIC CONTRACTS

The idea of equality of the parties reverberates in American government contract law cases, that is, in formal sources of law.

An illuminating example is a well-known 1934 Supreme Court case, *Lynch v US*: 'When the US enters into contract relations, its rights and duties therein are governed generally by the law applicable to contracts between private individuals.'[60] The American courts have invoked the rhetorical force of this

---

[56]   See Roubier 1951: 231–52. See also Samuel 2018b: 16.
[57]   Pound 1999 [1921]: 37 (emphasis added).
[58]   See Uhlmann et al 2009: 33–4.
[59]   Pound 1939: 482.
[60]   292 US 571, 579 (1934).

congruential jurisprudence since the early eighteenth century.[61] Accordingly, scholars have reflected it at least since the beginning of the twentieth century.

Robert Shealey (1874–1949) stated in 1919 that '[i]n a broad sense and subject to statutory limitations, the US, when it contracts with its citizens, is controlled by the same laws that govern citizens under similar conditions, and all obligations which would be implied against citizens under the same circumstances will be implied against it'.[62]

In 1922, James Donnelly (1887–1970) wrote:

> When the sovereign engages in business and the conduct of business enterprise and contracts with individuals, when such contract comes up before the court for construction, the rights and obligations of the parties must be adjusted upon the same principles as if both contracting parties were private persons. Both stand upon equality before the law and the sovereign is merged in the dealer, contractor and suitor.[63]

Donnelly's statement was made in the section that dealt with 'rescission of contract', nowadays named 'termination for convenience'. First, Donnelly writes, citing an appropriate case, '[p]ublic bodies have no sovereign right to rescind agreements at their mere pleasure. Such contracts can only be rescinded under the same conditions and subject to the same liability as natural persons'.[64] The fundamental assumption comes earlier in the book: 'Our concept of government is founded on the principle of *individualism*.'[65]

These are telling statements, showing that the controlling philosophy of private law lurks behind the scenes. Moreover, no distinction between public and private contracts has existed in the US, at least not one systematically exposed in scholarly works. 'Public contracts', wrote Donnelly, 'are no different from private contracts. The obligations of each endures are under the law, and the former are governed by the same canons of interpretation as applied to contracts between natural persons.'[66]

It is true that, nowadays, termination for convenience of the government is present either in the military or in civilian procurements in the US. However,

---

[61] See *US v Tingey* (1831). Shealey (1938: 4) cites 11 other cases, from 1836 to 1925. Schwartz (2004: 60–1) remarked that *US v Tingey* reflected a 'significant and distinctive application of a congruence-oriented approach, rather than an exceptionalist approach'.

[62] Shealey 1919: 4. But he also warned that 'there [were] several limitations to the rule', and that '[i]n certain respects the government, when it appears as a contractor, is regarded quite differently from the private parties'.

[63] Donnelly 1922: 353 (citing *People v Stephens*). See also Herman James 1946: 3; Turpin 1982: 31–2 (citing, among other American cases, *Lynch v US*).

[64] Donnelly 1922: 353 (citing *People ex rel. Graves v Sohmer*).

[65] Ibid: 50 (emphasis added).

[66] Donnelly 1992: 273 (citations omitted).

in the 1920s, when Donnelly wrote his treatise, the Supreme Court had already decided *US v Corliss Steam-Engine Co.*,[67] an 1875 case in which the Court recognized the government's prerogative to terminate the contract in the public interest. The Court stated:

> [T]he discharge of the duty devolving upon the secretary necessarily requires him to enter into numerous contracts for the public service; and the power to suspend work contracted for, whether in the construction, armament, or equipment of vessels of war, *when from any cause the public interest requires such suspension*, must necessarily rest with him.[68]

Why didn't *Corliss* become the leading case for termination for convenience in the US?

One plausible explanation is that *Corliss* was a case in which the military context was preeminent, and as such, it couldn't be extended to civilian procurement.[69] However, as Judge Bennet of the former Court of Claims explained in *Torncello v US* in 1982,[70] the case-law history shows that termination for convenience remained restricted to military procurement for almost a century.[71] Only with the FAR in 1984 did American law incorporate the termination for convenience into civilian procurement.

All that is in sharp contrast with the French principle, held by *les Tribunals Administratifs* from the mid-nineteenth century on (nowadays consecrated in articles L. 2195-3, 2°, 2195-6 and L. 3136-6, as well as article L. 6, 5° of the CCP/2018), that *le pouvoir de résiliation unilatérale sans faute* in the name of the 'general interest' should be admitted as a general rule applicable to the *contrats administratifs*, even in the silence of the contract.

---

[67] 91 US 321 (1875). On the importance of *Corliss* in the US, see Schwartz 2004: 56–67; on *Corliss*' history, see Page 2008: 4.

[68] 91 US at 322 (emphasis added). Schwartz (2004: 60) quotes the same part of *Corliss*.

[69] See Schwartz 2004: 59–63. Forty-four years later the Supreme Court decided *US v Purcell Envelope Co.*, 249 US 313 (1919), in which the Court 'establishes', said Schwartz (2004: 63), 'one of the leading congruence-influenced doctrines concerning federal government contract formation: that a contractor's offer, coupled with an acceptance effectuated by a government official possessing the requisite authority results in a contract binding on the US'. 'The *Purcell* Court', Schwartz concludes (ibid: 44), 'in a routine civilian procurement, can find no reason to depart from the private law regime in which an acceptance of an offer yields a binding contract'.

[70] 681 F.2d 756 (1982).

[71] Schwartz (2004: 65, note 101) states that Judge Bennet's opinion in *Torncello* 'remains a uniquely careful record of the history of the development of the termination for convenience doctrine, and an important sign post as to its proper scope'.

In fact, *le droit politique* has upheld the principle of the public interest's supremacy since the early times. In the Middle Ages, when the seeds of *droit administratif* were planted, the discourse in favour of the distinctiveness of the State was the French hallmark. The 'privatization' of the rules of *droit administratif* has never prevailed, and the French legal system has always felt that unique principles were necessary to govern *le droit public*.[72] Historically, the notions of *police* and *politique* were invoked in a somewhat interchangeable fashion in the fourteenth century by Boutillier and in the sixteenth century by Bodin and Domat, to differentiate the *droit public* from the *droit privé*.[73] After the Revolution, the baron Joseph-Marie Gérando (1772–1842), who in 1819 became the first tenured administrative law professor at Paris University,[74] remarked that, within the *droit administratif*, the relations of public and private interests, the obligations and reciprocal rights were governed by 'special rules, and not according to ordinary law rules'.[75] This maxim has been repeated ever since. More recently, Pièrre Sandevoir wrote that 'the preeminence of the general interest over the private interests requires a special treatment of the administrative procedure that the judges of the regular courts can't provide'.[76] An American scholar overstated: 'French "public law" itself instructs judges to favor the interests of the state over those of individuals when conflicts between the two arise.'[77]

Indeed, *le droit public* has long embraced the inequality of parties, considering the State as 'superior' to the individual.[78] *Le droit administratif* – and consequently, *les contrats administratifs* – has been historically considered as a 'law of privilege' (*droit de privilège*), since it is founded on an unequal relationship between the administration and the administered.[79] However, as we will see shortly, from the beginning of the twentieth century on, a new theory of State was constructed by scholars and courts to meet economic, social and political necessities related to matters such as industrialization and concentration of means of production, poverty and demands for social justice.

---

[72] See Mestre 1985: 159–60.

[73] See generally Mestre 1985: 162–3. The first *publicistes* in France, those who tried to systematize *le droit public* for the first time, were in service of the State power. See Plessix 2003a: 314.

[74] See Burdeau 1995: 107; Jestaz & Jamin 2004: 110–11.

[75] Gérando 1829: vol. 1, 63.

[76] Sandevoir 1964: 303.

[77] Shapiro 1981: 33.

[78] See Gérando 1829: vol. 1, 62–3; Plessix 2003a: 282; Bigot 2000: 532; Guglielmi 1991: 213.

[79] See Chevallier 1988; Caillosse 1996: 957; Gaudemet 2020: 25; Langrod 1955: 330.

As a construction of human intellect, like all academic disciplines,[80] *le droit administratif* was a byproduct of a new political ideology designed to meet all mentioned needs; the highly political and ideological concept of *service public*, based on the idea of social solidarity and having Léon Duguit at the forefront, has redefined not only the discipline but also the theory of State.[81] The remarkable success of the highly ideological and political concept of *service public* in the first decades of the twentieth century influenced the formation of a theory of *contrats administratifs*. There is always a political ideology behind public law concepts.

In the 1920s and 1930s, when Shealey and Donnelly deployed the congruential philosophy mentioned above, Gaston Jèze, '*le fondateur du droit des contrats administratifs*',[82] wrote bluntly at the beginning of his *Les principles generaux du droit administratif*, Tome 2 (1930) that the idea of *service public* was 'intimately linked' to the proceeding of public law (*procédé du droit public*), which had special legal rules and legal theories (*règles juridiques spéciales, théories juridiques speciales*), which are attached to 'the following essential idea: the particular interest must bow to the general interest' (*l'intérêt particulier doit s'incliner devant l'intérêt général*).[83]

In Brazilian law, the supremacy of the public interest as a legal principle has been loudly proclaimed since the start of Brazilian independence in 1822. During the Empire (1822–89), whose model was the French State, virtually all administrative law scholars have followed the French doctrine.[84] Pimenta Bueno (1803–78),[85] an extraordinary commentator of the first Brazilian Constitution (1824), wrote in 1857:

> Public Law, *jus publicum, quod ad statum reipublicae spectat*, deals with all relations between citizens and State, relations of *general interest*, and thus not belonging to the private realm. Public Law organizes the conditions of the common good; its aim is the *salus publica suprema lex*; [it] takes into consideration and protects specially the collective interest, *bene esse civitatis* and for its love [Public Law] *despises the individual interest* in those cases in which individual interest is *subordinated* to the collective interest.[86]

---

[80] See Plessix 2011: 47.
[81] See Chevallier 2018: chapter 1.
[82] Plessix 2003a: 741.
[83] Jèze 2004 [1930]: 2–3.
[84] See Moreira Neto 2014: 61.
[85] For a historical view about Pimenta Bueno, see Guandalini Jr 2016: 202–4.
[86] Pimenta Bueno 1978 [1857]: 6. See also Lopes 2004: 236 (quoting the same excerpt).

Bueno starts from Justinian *summa divisio* and even maintains the Latin words. In the next paragraph, Bueno defines private law again using Latin: '*Jus Privatum, quod ad singulorum utilitatem spectat*, deals with relations [...] between individuals [...] and takes care of the general well-being but secondarily.'[87] Based on this clear division, Bueno immediately explained that 'from this important classification and division of interests' spring naturally different jurisdiction powers, namely the administrative and the judicial, with other attributions, 'which shall never be confused'.[88] In short, *direito administrativo*, as part of the public law, takes care of the *superior interests*, which would easily be linked with, or represented by, the State. These were all French ideas.

The same thought springs from the first great administrative law professor of the Brazilian Empire,[89] Paulino Soares de Souza (1807–66), born in Paris. After travelling to Europe and visiting mainly France and England, Souza revealed his Frenchness in the preamble of his book, one of the first written in Brazil about *direito administrativo*: 'I've re-joined and study, if not all, almost all scholars who wrote about French *droit administratif*, which is *the most complete and developed*.'[90]

The public–private dichotomy and its corollary, the supremacy of the public interest, are apparent throughout Souza's work, which begins with a chapter entitled 'Definitions – Divisions – Distinctions', defining, *à la française*, the public and private spheres of law, emphasizing that the former deals with the *reipublicae*.[91] Following Chauveu Adolphe's (1802–68) doctrine, Souza claims that '[t]o wish applying to the State the maxims of ordinary law and

---

87   Pimenta Bueno ibid. See also Lopes ibid.
88   Pimenta Bueno 1978 [1857]: 7.
89   Souza was 'the most significant author of the [Brazilian] Empire'. Moreira Neto 2014: 61. For Carvalho, Souza was 'the most important thinker of [Brazilian] monarchical conservatism' (2005: 83). See also Guandalini Jr 2016: 216–32.
90   Souza 1960 [1862]: 8 (emphasis added).
91   See Souza 1960 [1862]: 16–17. The author used the same Roman formula, *ad statum reipublicae spectat*, quoting Laferrière. Souza expressly said that he adopted Laferrière's definition of *droit administratif* because it was 'the most comprehensive and satisfactory' (ibid: 19). Louis Firmin Lafferrière (1778–1861), Professor at Rennes University, wrote the *Cours théorique de droit public et administratif*, published in 1849. Of the many emerging French professors of *droit administratif*, Lafferière was the one who began to write on the subject. Others were Émile-Victor Foucart, professor at Poitiers; Adolphe Chaveau, at Toulouse; François Alfred Trolley, at Caen; and Alexis Desiré Dalloz, Louis Pierre Cabantous, Alfred-Pierre Blanche, Jean Chantagrel, R Gandillot and JM Boileux, besides Joseph-Marie de Gérando and Louis-Antoine Macarel, respectively the first and second professors of the discipline at Paris University. Impressively enough, Souza cited all these authors and is said to have read all their books in the process of writing his. About the blooming of the literature on *droit administratif* in France, see Burdeau 1995: 108–10.

the handicaps of the ordinary jurisdiction would be to neglect the most vulgar rules of society'.[92] To submit the State to ordinary laws would be to succumb to 'sterile egoism, sacrificing the national greatness'.[93] The public administration should be subordinated to public law principles and take care of the public interest, overcoming private interests.[94] Souza then writes that there are some standard necessities in all societies that 'must be satisfied by the public power'. The end of public administration is to 'provide these collective necessities and guide social interests, either general or local'. Based on the thought of French authors, Souza stated that the *direito administrativo* is 'the proper public law, which comprehends individual rights'[95] and deals with 'social interests'. In contrast, private law takes care of private interests.[96] Remarkably, no case is cited throughout Souza's entire work. Instead, scholars systematize the law, an activity that was not only descriptive but also normative: being a jurist and a politician, Souza wanted to forge a State that mirrored *l'État français*.

Although not without upheavals, the philosophy of supremacy of the public interest has survived throughout the twentieth century in France and Brazil as the basic principle of administrative law.

A fair example is a classic work on government contracts written by José Cretella Júnior (1920–2015), who was an administrative law professor at the University of São Paulo. In its eighteenth and last published edition (2006), the author bluntly maintains, based on the French doctrine, that the '*public* prevails over the *private*. The *public interest* is prevalent over the *particular interest*'. This principle, he continues, is *fundamental* to the comprehension of the *direito administrativo*; it is '[i]mpossible' to understand the legal regime of public law if one detaches it from its 'principled foundations'. Thus, 'Public Law institutions have special configurations, which don't look alike with the Private Law configurations'.[97] This idea forms the *mentalité* of most Brazilian public lawyers and is still abundantly mentioned by the Supremo Tribunal Federal (STF), the Brazilian Supreme Court.[98] Accordingly, it also governs public contract law, being at the basis of all exceptional norms.

The public–private law dichotomy fuels the classic division between the two types of *contrats de l'Administration* (*contratos da Administração*) the State

---

[92]　Souza 1960 [1862]: 61.
[93]　Ibid.
[94]　See ibid: 56.
[95]　Ibid: 22, 18.
[96]　See ibid: 36.
[97]　Cretella Júnior 2006: 128–9. This position is still held by many Brazilian scholars.
[98]　See eg STF, ARE 826.377 AgR, 10 Sep. 2018; ARE 1.036.631 AgR, 8 Aug 2017; ADI 1.626, 15 Dec. 2016.

can perform: (i) *contrats administratifs/contratos administrativos*, governed by public law principles and subject to the *droit administratif/direito adminis- trativo*; (ii) *contrats privés* or *de droit commun de l'Administration /contratos privados da Administração*, governed (mainly) by private law principles and subject to the ordinary rules of the Civil Code.[99] But, of course, the focus of this book is only on the *contrat administratif*, which is a specific, 'public' type of *contrats de l'Administration*.

Interestingly enough, the general criteria to distinguish the two types of *contrats de l'Administration*, either in France or Brazil, is the following: *con- trats administratifs* are those contracts that contain 'exorbitant clauses'. Courts define these clauses as the clauses that give parties rights or impose duties that are 'in its nature strange to those susceptible to being freely agreed by the parties in civil and commercial law frame'.[100] Simply stated, the *clauses exor- bitantes du droit commun* are the *raison d'être* of the French (and Brazilian) *contrats administratifs*.[101] *Clauses exorbitantes* in French and Brazilian laws have been said to instantiate supremacy of the State interest over the private contractor, which creates a position of 'inequality' between parties.[102]

René Chapus (1924–2017) famously wrote that *clauses exorbitantes* are of two categories: (i) forbidden in private relations; (ii) founder of inequalities. The latter is the most common, and they 'submit the co-party to the control, or even to the authority, of the public power'; their lawfulness is established case by case, but courts have decided that the 'control of the public power' over the private can occur in 'general terms' or more 'precise terms'. For instance, in a case of exploitation of a velodrome, the State may have control over the profits; in the case of restaurant management, the State may have the control over employees and prices; in a case concerning the exploitation of the Palais de Glace in Paris, the State has the right to request the dismissal of the employee. Furthermore, the control may manifest itself in certain specific obligations of the contractor, such as the duty to ask for government permission in certain transactions or the responsibility to stop, upon the government's request, the exploitation of the lease of an establishment. Alternatively, *clauses exorbi-*

---

[99] In French law, see eg Gaudemet 2020: 351–62; Frier & Petit 2020: 488–505. In Brazilian law, see eg Cretella Júnior 2006: 60–2; Meirelles 2010: 249–52.

[100] Chapus 2001: vol. 1, § 724. In Brazilian doctrine, see eg Cretella Júnior 2006; 61; Meirelles 2010: 248–9; Câmara 2019: 325–36; Justen Filho 2019: 1167.

[101] See eg Chapus 2001: vol. 1, §§ 722–7; Saillant 2011; 96–102, 266–7. But see Canedo 2004. In Brazil, see eg Cretella Júnior (ibid); Câmara (ibid); Justen Filho (ibid). In English, explaining French law (also applicable to Brazilian law), see Brown & Bell 1998: 141–3 (citing the classic cases in which the criteria of the *clauses exorbitantes* were established).

[102] See Péquignot 2020 [1945]: 249; Chapus 2001: vol. 1, § 724; Cretella Júnior 2006: 61; Meirelles 2010: 248, 251, 256–63.

tantes can request a permanent performance by the contractor, for example, relative to the type of show and its frequency in the municipal theatre. Finally, *exorbitantes* are also clauses that establish a 'termination under the law' (*réso-lution de plein droit*), which can occur even without the contractor's fault, regardless of whether the contractor is entitled to damages.[103]

But what is the difference between this continental idea about the supremacy of the public interest and Turpin's statement that what triggers government prerogatives in government contracts is the protection of public interest? Don't they reflect similar ideas about government contracts?

There are two crucial differences between the two ideas. The first lies in the word *supremacy*. No legal system maintains that the public interest is to be neglected. But to hold that the public interest is *superior* to the private interest establishes an unspoken hierarchy, having a robust normative func-tion. The second, more crucial and already examined, deals with the different *conceptions* of public interest in the French (and Brazilian) versus the US legal systems.

Yet, one should not conclude that there is a dogmatic postulate among French or Brazilian jurists; nor is the supremacy of the public interest the only consequence of the public–private dichotomy. Instead, it is the poli-tics and teleology of the dichotomy that matter most. I contend that, unlike Anglo-Americans' Liberal *mentalité*, civil law jurists *understand and use* the dichotomy as a tool that facilitates the idea of public supremacy over private interests. The dichotomy fuels an ideological presumption in favour of the collective, the State; it acts as a 'default rule'. Whoever challenges the idea has the burden of proof.

Nevertheless, there are backlashes against the American and French or Brazilian conceptions of the public–private dichotomy. As stated in the Introduction, theories develop by antagonism. I will show that this tension applies where state liability for sovereign acts is concerned. The opposition between Anglo-American and continental cultures is again very telling. We need to understand what forces push the pendulum to the other side.

---

[103] For all the examples of this paragraph and others see Chapus 2001: vol. 1, §§ 725–6. The examples apply to Brazilian law.

5. Liability for sovereign acts: an overview

It was mentioned previously that a government contract can be unilaterally changed by the government during its performance as long as the changes remain 'within the general scope of the contract', as written in clauses commonly used to allow unilateral changes. This problem must remain unexplored.

My subject under the umbrella of 'sovereign acts' is broader in scope and considerably more complex. I will deal with the problem that arises when, in the course of regular state authority, government actions (whether executive or legislative) indirectly alter a public contract's performance, impairing the contractors' situation; hence, I will call it 'indirect impairment' of contract or 'external exceptionalism'. Again, the two theories dealing with the problem in the US are the 'Sovereign Acts Doctrine' or 'Sovereign Acts Defense' (SAD) and the 'Unmistakability Doctrine', and the French and Brazilian 'functional equivalents' are the theories of *fait du Prince/fato do Príncipe* and *imprévision/imprevisão*.

Like *fait du Prince* and *imprévision*, SAD and the Unmistakability Doctrine respond to each legal culture's *political and ideological* necessities. They are parts of legal systems that, as already suggested, encompass different ideas of the state and state responsibility. As explained in Chapter 4, while in France and Brazil the dichotomy has fuelled the Roman maxim *utilitas publica prefertur utilitate privatae* (public interest has preference over the private interest), in the US this maxim is seen as outlandish. Thus, for a French or Brazilian jurist, public law issues must follow different legal principles, principles that *recognize* an allegedly State *superior* position, and (only in France) different, specialized judges, who sit in different courts, must judge public law cases, fuelled by a conception of *intérêt général* that owes its content primarily to Rousseauian philosophy.

This logic is foreign to American lawyers. For them, legal principles in public and private law are similar, although not necessarily identical; the state is not superior; no special judges or courts exist, and a utilitarian philosophy of public interest dominates. The creation of the Court of Claims in 1855 (split in 1982 into the Court of Appeals for the Federal Circuit and the Court of Federal Claims) to judge cases against the government has nothing to do with the idea behind the creation, in France, of the *tribunaux administratifs*, which belong not to the judiciary but to the executive power.[1] SAD and the Unmistakability Doctrine are, accordingly, theories operating in a legal system that generally favours congruence and equality. At the same time, *fait du Prince* and *imprévision* are theories in a legal system that severed public and private law and created a special branch, *le droit administratif*, which is *exorbitante* and favours inequality. Based on that premise, the French and Brazilian systems of State responsibility would, theoretically, favour the State at the expense of the individual. In contrast, American law would operate in the opposite direction. Notwithstanding, the law has evolved otherwise.

In fact, because of the growth of capitalism, the increase in state economic activity and rapid social change at the beginning of the twentieth century, all legal systems were concerned with state liability. As a result, the *Conseil d'État*, alongside French publicists, developed, particularly in the 'Golden Age' of *droit administratif* (*l'Âge d'Or*, roughly from the late 1870s to the 1930s), a strong and relatively coherent system of public law liability, either for torts or for contractual relations,[2] that has been applauded worldwide and has served as a model for various nations,[3] including Brazil.

By contrast, American law has remained faithful to the medieval English maxim 'the king can do no wrong', whose spirit still echoes in some cases in which the government takes part. In other words, French public law has built a complex system of legal norms that, generally speaking, is deemed to offer better protection to individuals than is provided by Anglo-American systems. Concerning public contracts, Georges Langrod wrote in the 1950s that, 'contrary to the opinion of those who support the common law, it's in France, through the *régime administratif*, rather than in Anglo-American countries, that actual means of protecting individuals who contract with the state, consistent with reasonable safeguard of the public interest, have been found'.[4] Undoubtedly, the alleged superior protection offered by the French system is the reason why so many Anglo-American scholars, dating back more than two generations, have shown profound admiration for the *Conseil d'État* and the French system of public law as a whole.[5]

---

[1]   On the creation of the Courts of Claims, see Richardson 1882. For a classic comparative study between Anglo-American and French systems of administrative adjudication, see Diamant 1951.

[2]   As for contractual relations, see Terneyre 1989. In the Preface of Terneyre's book, Frank Moderne states that '[o]ne of the merits of Mr. Terneyre's dissertation – and it's not a neglectable one – is to have shown that the State Council has succeeded in elaborating, discreetly, a real "system" of contractual liability of public entities' (at iii).

[3]   See generally Pinto Correia 1988: 56–62; Shapiro 1981: 153.

[4]   Langrod 1955: 334.

[5]   In addition to Borchard's and Laski's works cited in the previous chapter, see Brown & Bell 1998: 1, 25; Loughlin 1992: 161; JDB Mitchell 1954: 164–5; Shapiro 1981: 154; Rohr 1995: 252–4.

John Rohr (1934–2011) nicely captured the implications of sovereign immunity and the French system of state responsibility. While commenting on the famous *arrêt Blanco*, decided by the *Tribunal des Conflits* in 1873,[6] he stated: 'This [State liability] is a principle that even to this day has not been established in the US *because of* sovereign immunity.'[7]

True, an American lawyer might contend that my claim about sovereign immunity is misleading or, worse, simply a gross mistake, a false starting point for comparison. She may quote statutes and cases to support the contention that sovereign immunity in government contract cases was waived, at least for some types of litigation, very early. After the Court of Claims was created in 1855,[8] and with the enactment of the Tucker Act in 1887,[9] the American law has waived its immunity for contract claims. According to this argument, the waiver belies my starting point.

Nonetheless, this rebuttal is as linear as it is erroneous. As Gregory Sisk explains, sovereign immunity 'lies in the background' of all cases in which government is involved. 'Even when the government has waived sovereign immunity through legislation, the doctrine influences the manner in which the courts interpret and apply such statutes (although increasingly less so).'[10] The spirit of sovereign immunity is undoubtedly still alive in the US,[11] notwithstanding the Supreme Court's vacillating interpretation of the doctrine,[12] whose 'meaning is contested and contestable'.[13] By contrast, sovereign immunity is no longer alive in France and Brazil, and contrary ideas are in force.

Here lies an apparent paradox: SAD and the Unmistakability Doctrine are theories that operate within a legal system that privileges individuals, a system governed by a private law philosophy. This same system has, however, been historically reluctant to admit state responsibility for its wrongdoings. My thesis is that American law *needs* sovereign immunity as a form of compensation to its Liberal ethos.

In contrast, the theories of *fait du Prince* and *imprévision* operate within a culture that has historically favoured State power over the individual and has built a unique system of State responsibility and protection of individuals'

---

[6]   For a classical reading of *Blanco*, see Chapus 1999; for a recent, political reading, see Bigot 2019.

[7]   Rohr 1995: 243.

[8]   See Krent 1992: 1564–5; Sisk 2016: 232–3.

[9]   28 USC § 1491(a)(1). See Krent 1992: 1565. For a general historical view of the claims against the US, see Shimomura 1985.

[10]   Sisk 2016: 69. See also Jackson 2003: 569–70.

[11]   See generally eg Sisk 2016; Rohr 1995: 242–5. Brown & Bell (1998: 184) say that the principle 'the king can do no wrong' still prevails in English legal theory.

[12]   See generally eg Pierce Jr 2002: 1.337–86.

[13]   Jackson 2003: 523.

rights. These apparent contradictions can nevertheless be explained. To do so, I will now turn to the crux of the matter: the differing foundations of public liability in the American and French or Brazilian legal systems.

1.   STATE RESPONSIBILITY FOR 'SOVEREIGN ACTS': SOVEREIGN IMMUNITY VERSUS *RESPONSABILITÉ DE LA PUISSANCE PUBLIC*

State responsibility is a vast topic, even if confined to its dogmatic sources. It is possible to divide the subject into subcategories: torts and contractual breaches; illicit and licit actions; responsibility for executive, legislative or judicial activities – each being governed, arguably, by specific norms and standards of reasoning, triggering various defences. However, tackling all these subjects would make this survey too broad. Accordingly, this book is limited to contractual relations.[14]

As mentioned previously, instead of providing the reader with a detailed analysis of the various sorts of state liability or with a careful study of the case law, that is, dogmatic sources, the foundations of public contracts are better understood through the study of material sources of each legal system.

The first essential proposition is as trivial and broad as it is fundamental. Since the conception of the state differs within the legal systems under comparison, it would be surprising if the US and France (or Brazil)[15] had adopted the same epistemological starting points. While the US legal system still gives significant force to the idea of sovereign immunity and some degree privileges state *irresponsibility*, French and Brazilian legal systems build upon a contrasting philosophy of state *responsibility*. We need to understand the foundations of the disparate assumptions beneath the formal sources.

The most intriguing difference between American and French legal treatment of state liability is the pervasive role that the 'mysterious' doctrine of sovereign immunity,[16] whose constitutional provenance is deemed 'obscure'[17] or contradictory to the notions of 'equality and accountability',[18] has been

---

[14]   On tort liability in a comparative perspective, see articles in Fairgrieve et al (eds) 2002.

[15]   Unless otherwise indicated, the treatment given to State liability in France is applicable to Brazil.

[16]   See Borchard 1924: 4; Rohr 1995: 242. Courts have been registering this 'mysterious' character of the maxim. See Judge Traynor's opinion in *Muskopf v Corning Hospital District*, 359 P.2d 457 (1961); see also Justice Brennan opinion in *Owen v City of Independence*, 445 U.S. 622, 654 (1980) (quoting Borchard, ibid). My attention was drawn to the courts' decisions by Randall 2002: 4, note 2.

[17]   Jackson 2003: 522.

[18]   Seife 1996.

playing in the US law,[19] being yet 'solidly anchored in the Supreme Court precedent'.[20] Allegedly originated from the medieval English maxim 'the king can do no wrong', sovereign immunity will serve as the starting point for my analysis of government contract law in US law.[21]

Jurists all over the globe, including most American jurists, have recognized and criticized this American uniqueness,[22] which at first sight runs against the American *mentalité* of individualism. However, I believe this idea is simplistic and that the contrary holds: American individualistic philosophy, I repeat, *fuels* state irresponsibility and *asks for* sovereign immunity.

My contention, to put it clearly, is that in an ultra-individualistic society such as the American one, which doesn't accept or doesn't 'understand' the collective idea of a transcendent *l'intérêt général*,[23] the doctrine of sovereign immunity (and its offshoots, such as SAD and the Unmistakability Doctrine) are to be viewed as necessary precisely to *protect* the 'public interest', sometimes conflated – unsurprisingly, in a country that favours a utilitarian concept of public interest – with 'public money'. No wonder then that, in the past decade, when sovereign immunity has been the subject of ferocious attack, some scholars who favour sovereign immunity attached a more palatable American catchword to it: sovereign immunity exists to protect 'democracy'.[24]

In contrast, the French legal system has abandoned the analogous maxim of *le Roi ne peut mal faire* and turned it into an empty adage without any force. Moreover, French law gave way to an opposite doctrine, *la responsabilité sans faute de la puissance public*, State liability without fault. In France, State liability has been one of the most illuminating constructions of the *Conseil d'État* since at least 1873.[25] On the other hand, Brazil established in its Constitution of 1934 joint and several liability between the State and its functionaries in case

---

[19]   See Jackson 2003: 527, 540, 542. See also generally Krent 1992.

[20]   Sisk 2010: 899. See also Jackson 2003: 523.

[21]   See generally Hadfield 1999: 471.

[22]   The classic criticism is Davis 1970. Among the few defenders, see eg Krent 1992; Sisk 2003; 2010; 2016; Brettschneider & McNamee 2015.

[23]   My intention is neither to defend nor attack sovereign immunity, the SAD or the unmistakability doctrine. I only intend to contextualize these doctrines and explain why a 'stateless', individualistic society like the American one 'needs' such doctrines, while 'state societies' don't.

[24]   See Brettschneider & McNamee 2015; Sisk 2016: 71–2, 76.

[25]   In torts, *Blanco, Tribunal de Conflit* 1873, is the leading case. In the area of *contrats administratifs*, the 'waiver' of sovereign immunity occurred earlier. See Terneyre 1989: 7.

of the latter's fault.[26] Moreover, Article 37, § 6 of CFB/88 consecrated State strict liability as a default rule in torts.[27]

Therefore, while in America the state is still, in principle, generally immune from suit without its consent, thus not responsible, in France or Brazil the opposite holds. Therefore, the theories of the SAD and the Unmistakability Doctrine in the US, and *fait du Prince* and *imprévision* in France or Brazil, must be understood within this dialectic opposition.

Understanding this fundamental point will take some work. Let me start with the first pair of opposing conceptions.

2.   OPPOSING CONCEPTIONS OF STATE AND INDIVIDUAL

'We shall begin', wrote Karl Mannheim (1893–1947), 'with the fact that the same word, or the same concept in most cases, means very different things when used by differently situated persons'.[28] It is the same idea of different conceptions of a concept that was conveyed by Gallie and explored in Chapter 3.

The words 'culture' and 'civilization' are perhaps the best example of this phenomenon. Norbert Elias (1897–1990) has shown that these terms meant different things in England, Germany and France.[29] Additionally, some words are so powerful that they seem to bear an entire culture. As Arieli has stated, these words 'are constituent parts of the image the individual and society have of themselves and the world around them. As such they are instruments of orientation and action, norms of behaviour, and guides toward personal and social attitudes.'[30] As will be discussed, *state* and *individualism* are two of these concepts.

State and individualism are meaningful words that encompass a robust set of ideas, which have been used since at least the eighteenth (state) and nineteenth (individualism) centuries by historians, philosophers, jurists and sociologists to represent a way of thinking, to stereotype peoples, to criticize or applaud attitudes and to uphold social and philosophical theories – *thus shaping the*

---

[26]   See Dias 1995: 570. In the nineteenth century, Brazil had two Constitutions (1824 and 1891); neither consecrated State liability. However, many statutes established State liability for damages in various cases. See Loureiro Filho 2001: 225–6.

[27]   'Public legal entities and private legal entities rendering public services shall be liable for damages that any of their agents, acting as such, cause to third parties, ensuring the right of recourse against the liable agent in cases of malice or fault.'

[28]   Mannheim 1954: 245; also Legrand 2002: 232.

[29]   See Elias 2000 [1939]: chapter 1.

[30]   Arieli 1964: 2.

law. Moreover, they are concepts that have carried an inherent meaning and could become influential forces of social cohesion and action.[31] As Mannheim suggested, '[w]e belong to a group [...] because we see [the] world and certain things in the world the way it does (i.e. in terms of the meanings of the group in question)'.[32]

2.1   'State Societies' and 'Stateless Societies'

In 1970, the former French President George Pompidou (1911–74) uttered to his ex-colleagues of the *Conseil d'État*:

> For more than a thousand years [...] there has been a France only because there was the State, a State to bring it together, to organize it, to make it grow, to defend it not only against external threats, but also against group egotisms and rivalries. Today, more than ever, the State's force is indispensable to assure the nation's future and its security and to assure the individual his liberty.[33]

In 1986, US President Ronald Reagan (1911–2004), in a speech to a Joint Session of Congress stamped in the *New York Times* of 5 February, said that '[p]rivate values must be at the heart of public policies'.[34]

Pompidou's words would offend Anglo-American sensibilities and even perhaps seem fatuous. To the French people, however, they sounded and still sound quite sensible.[35] Similarly, President Reagan's phrase sounds strange to a Frenchman, while it was and is quite familiar to an American. Taking for granted that '[i]n large measure, collective identity is created and perpetuated through public discourse',[36] these two former presidents' excerpts are revealing.

The sense of 'stateness' in France is perhaps more vital than in any other modern Western country,[37] while in America the opposite holds. France has been developing a theory of State or political science *par excellence* since the sixteenth century.[38] As Tardieu wrote in 1927, '[i]n France the whole history of

---

[31]   See ibid: 2–3.
[32]   Mannheim 1954: 19. My attention to it was called by Arieli 1964: 3.
[33]   Quoted by Dyson 1980: 83–4.
[34]   Quoted by Wolin 1989: 25.
[35]   According to Frankenberg (1998: 185), 'Statism still prevails in France, defending the "general interest" as represented by the state against claims to a wide participation in government by the citizenry'.
[36]   Wolin 1989: 9. 'Public discourse consists of the vocabulary, ideologies, symbols, images, memories, and myths that have come to form the way we think and talk about our political life.' Ibid.
[37]   See Voegelin 1989 [1936]: 49.
[38]   See ibid: 53.

the country has been built up around the State and by it. The State was counted on and counted with, in every act of public and private life.' Soon afterward, he contrasted this model with the American distaste for the state: 'Far from considering the central Government as a watchful providence to look after him, the American tinges with distrust what little thought he gives it.' This contrast reflects what must be recognized as 'two essentially different political worlds'.[39]

As the decades went on, these observations achieved the status of a truism among comparatists, whether jurists, political or social scientists, French or Anglo-Americans. In 1985, Laurent Cohen-Tanugi contrasted the two models of state regulation. He emphasized that in France, 'society is structured entirely by and around the State, which plays a role of impulsion and exercises, on the contrary, its stranglehold on society'. In contrast, he added, the US offered 'the other model', in which society regulates itself. 'In such a model, society has an autonomous life to the State and has at its disposal its own instruments of regulation.'[40] In 1995, John Rohr wrote that '[i]n French, the word *state*, *l'État*, has a strongly normative force one seldom finds in its English equivalent'.[41] In 2003, James Whitman, writing about criminal punishment in the US and Europe, noted that America, 'of all Western countries, is the one that is most consistently suspicious of state authority',[42] emphasizing soon after that France has a 'much stronger state than ours [Americans]'.[43] In 2019, Jacques Chevallier put it in definitive words: 'The vision of an all-powerful State, overhanging civil society and dominating it from the above, doesn't have course in the US and UK; and, correlatively, the administration cannot refuge itself behind *l'intérêt général, la puissance public* or *le service public* for protecting its authority from all contestation.'[44]

This opposition reflects two different world visions and has deep, ancient roots. It will also have profound consequences in public contract law. The roots can be traced back to medieval times and linked to two different conceptions of sovereignty.[45] This difference persists today and is at the core of French (or Brazilian) and American concepts of public law, retaining a grip on government procurement law as well.

---

[39] Tardieu 1927: 39.
[40] Cohen-Tanugi 1985: 5.
[41] Rohr 1995: 24. The author capitalizes *État*, but writes *state* with a small *s*. On the difference between France and US with respect to the idea of State, see generally ibid: 24–9.
[42] Whitman 2003a: 4.
[43] Ibid: 13.
[44] Chevallier 2019: 552.
[45] See Beauté 1992: 114–15; García-Villegas 2006: 369.

I am not suggesting that the French (or Brazilian) public contracts system has not changed since the Golden Age. What I am suggesting is that, in France (and Brazil to a lesser degree), the leading force of statenessness abides and pervades the whole political spectrum, *le droit administratif* included. Legal history may help.

Although the modern concept of state didn't exist in the Middle Ages, a brief review of historical contrasts helps capture the roots of the opposition between state and stateless cultures.[46] Two interconnected factors must be mentioned. First, the difference in the 'kingship model' would influence the notion of sovereignty in Anglo-American and French cultures. Second, the lack of influence of Roman law concepts in Anglo-American legal systems should be noted.

2.1.1   Two opposing kingship models

A sociogenesis of the English culture in the Middle Ages reveals that British society has never abandoned the values of pluralism, respect for individuality and diversity. The UK has been ever reluctant to accept any kind of centralization of power; the British have shown an aversion to any privilege for the state and exhibited strong continuity of medieval ideas and institutions, such as diffusion of power, confidence in customary practices and reliance on social and cultural heritage instead of on ordered abstract principles.[47] Unlike the French 'theocratic' ruler, the English 'feudal kingship', to use Walter Ullmann's terminology, had to work *with the consent* of the council of barons and magnates, despite the resulting inefficiencies.[48] The English medieval 'state' has never succumbed to the alleged 'absolutism' which reigned in France.[49] The ultimate source of law was consent, either implicit or explicit, and not the king's will,[50] which was always limited in the UK.[51] This practice, Ullmann implies, suggests relative equality between the king, lords and vassals and indicates that the king's authority came not from his superior position or interest but from membership in the community.[52]

The seventeenth century presented a fair picture of what I above called 'two visions of the world'. For the common law theorists, including Edward

---

[46]   For a classic study about the sociogenesis of the medieval state and state formation in Europe, see Elias 2000 [1939]: 187–362.

[47]   See Dyson 1980: 52; Allison 1996: chapter 5; Beauté 1992: 114; Heuschling 2002: 177; García-Villegas 2006: 370.

[48]   See Ullmann 1975: 154–5; García-Villegas 2006: 370.

[49]   See Beauté 1992: 114; Bobbio 1995: 33.

[50]   See Dyson 1980: 114.

[51]   See Beauté 1992: 123.

[52]   See generally Ryan 2003: 56–7.

Coke,[53] the social order would be a *Cosmos*; it would be an order that springs spontaneously from the bottom up, from the society itself, maturing as time goes on.[54] For the other group – people such as King James I (1566–1625), his counsellor Francis Bacon (1561–1626), Thomas Hobbes (1588–1679) and to some extent John Locke (1632–1704) – society would be a *Taxis*; it would be conceived by men themselves, perhaps only one man, and would have rules axiomatically deductible from abstract principles handed down by Reason.[55] Cartesianism, which had strongly forged Jean Domat's legal and political philosophy,[56] inspired the second group.[57] In the Glorious Revolution, the common law vision buried the Stuarts' attempt to import the French model of kingship and consecrated individual rights, rather than political power, as the real source of power.[58]

Accordingly, the contractual element was the leading force of relationships between the king, lords, and subjects; *this contractual element lasted as the foundation of Anglo-American public law*,[59] being still at the core of American *mentalité* about public contract law. The seeds of 'congruence' in Anglo-American societies, their passion for equal footing, the equivalence of forces in procedural questions (the so-called adversary litigation), the aversion to any a priori idea-force of a transcendentally conceived 'supremacy of the public interest' (the king was not *above* the lords or vassals, but *side by side with* them) and other alike principles are all combined here. In this contractual model, what prevails is corrective justice, the leading philosophy of private law.

As for this first factor, the French model of theocratic kingship presented a remarkable contrast.[60] It is true that from around the ninth to the twelfth century, with the decline of royal power and the central authority alongside a long eclipse of the idea of State, theocratic kingship was absent even in France.[61] After that, however, a tendency toward centralization and an increasing willingness to rely on State power became the hallmark of the French

---

[53] Coke was 'the most typical English lawyer'. Cohen 1936: 697.
[54] See Heuschling 2002: 175; Legrand 1999b: 42–3.
[55] See Heuschling ibid.
[56] See Church 1967: 16–22.
[57] See Heuschling 2002: 175.
[58] See García-Villegas 2006: 370. Charles I (1625–49), the second Stuart after James I (1603–25), was decapitated on 9 February 1649. See eg Beauté 1992: 118. When examining Radbruch's idea of 'subordinating law', Pound (1939: 472) remarked that '[c]ertainly Bacon, James I, and Charles I would have agreed with [Radbruch]'.
[59] See generally Pound 1944: 1195. For a comparison between the French and the English models of state, see Cassese 2000: 14–20.
[60] See Ullmann 1975: 155; Pound 1944: 1218–19.
[61] See Elias 2000 [1939]: 257–61; Loughlin 2003: 73.

State.[62] Roughly put, since the high Middle Ages France has been the model of a 'State society', in which a centralized government runs the country at all levels.

French feudalism was dominated by the so-called theocratic ruler rather than the English 'feudal overlord'.[63] 'It's surely not surprising', wrote Walter Ullmann, 'to find that the modern concept of sovereignty had its birthplace in France'.[64] No consent between kings and subjects appears in French historical surveys. On the contrary, French kings, suggestively called 'the holy kings of France',[65] incarnated a superior authority, of which the king was the sole source.[66] Moreover, the king in feudal France 'enjoyed certain mystical advantages denied to less-developed monarchists, such as the ability to perform miracles, especially those of thaumaturgical variety';[67] the king was also 'credited with having "all the laws in his breast"'.[68] These 'absolutist' ideas were generally not only accepted by the uneducated,[69] but also ultimately backed (perhaps not entirely and not in its allegedly divine force, but certainly concerning the purposes) by jurists, who have formed the traditional elite and have played a leading role in Western Europe, particularly in France, since the twelfth century.[70]

From the fifteenth to the seventeenth centuries, French jurists such as Barthélemy de Chasseneuz (1480–1541) upheld the view that the Prince's right should prevail over persons and property; the Prince had, therefore, the

---

[62]   One cannot understand French culture or French (public) law without paying attention to the phenomenon of centralization of government. For a historical view of the phenomenon up to the first two decades of the twentieth century (during the 'Golden Age' of *droit administratif*), see Garner 1919.

[63]   See Dyson 1980: 53.

[64]   Ullmann 1949: 14; also Chevallier 2019: 144.

[65]   Ullmann 1975: 155.

[66]   See Parker 1989: 38. 'It's from me alone', said Louis XV (reigning 1715–74) to the *parlement* of Paris, 'that my courts derive their existence and authority […] and it's to me alone that supreme and undivided legislative power belongs' (ibid).

[67]   Keohane 1980: 55. Ullmann (1975b: 155) also mentions the 'so-called thaumaturgical, i.e., miracle-working and healing powers by which the royal *mystique* was considerably fostered'. It was said that the French king Clovis bathed with a holy oil 'brought down straight from heaven'. See ibid. 'The right of supreme power had been acquired by the French kings: "*Jus summae superioritate in regno suo totaliter acquisitum*".' Ullmann 1949: 14.

[68]   Ullmann 1975: 156. Pound (1999 [1921]: 39) attributes a similar phrase to Boniface VIII in the fourteenth century.

[69]   Goubert estimates that '[p]erhaps four-fifth of the French population in 1685 were completely illiterate'. In Greenberger 1979: 146.

[70]   See generally ibid: 144–56. Greenberg explains that most lawyers didn't share the vision that kings acted in God's name, but they all believed in the capacity of kings to do good and act fairly and in the public interest.

right to decide at will whether and when taxes were necessary for the State and to act accordingly.[71] Charles Loyseau (1564–1627), the first, remarkable French publicist, exalted sovereignty and said it was the only *seigneurie* of State, thus becoming the *seigneurie publique supreme*.[72] Cardin Le Bret (1558–1655), in his book *De la souveraineté du Roy* (1632) – a real peroration favouring the glory of kings' rights – compared the king to a shepherd that *guides and watches over* the people.[73] Thus arose the model of the king – and later the State – who should act not arbitrarily but candidly, with prudence and moderation: a vision that the *Conseil d'État* helped to keep alive throughout the centuries.[74]

Jean Domat (1625–96), 'the greatest French jurist during the reign of Louis XIV'[75] and author of the most influential work about the principles of jurisprudence at the time, *Loix civiles dans leur ordre naturel*, discussed royal authority by generally mentioning the king's power 'for the maintenance of justice and public tranquillity'.[76] Domat then enumerated various royal prerogatives, among them the power to make laws, not without remembering, however, that the sovereign was to be prudent and act for the 'good order in the State';[77] a king's rank 'obliges him to subordinate his personal interest to the general good of the state which it is his glory to regard as his own'.[78] All these works were synthesized by Claude Fleury (1640–1723), who instantiated better than anyone the role of a publicist in defence of the Power.[79] His principal works, the *Institution au droit Français* and *Droit Public de France,* were directed to 'the education of the Princes'.[80]

Domat and his contemporaries felt no necessity to speak of legislative sovereignty,[81] as the British did; it was God, so Domat argued, that delegated His powers to the French kings, and 'it is by Him that they reign'.[82] The Ulpian's phrase *Quod prince placuit legis habet vigorem* (*Digesto*, 1.4.1), 'what pleases

---

[71] See Keohane 1980: 55.
[72] See Plessix 2003a: 321–2.
[73] See ibid: 323. See generally Borchard 1927b: 1048.
[74] See Keohane 1980: 55.
[75] Church 1967: 13.
[76] In Parker 1989: 47.
[77] In Plessix 2003a: 324.
[78] In Church 1967: 21.
[79] See Plessix 2003a: 324–5.
[80] Ibid: 325.
[81] See Parker 1989: 47.
[82] Parker 1989: 47. See also Plessix 2003a: 324–5.

the prince has force of law', gained force in France. The effect of this maxim, together with the *princeps legibus solutus est*, wrote Keohane,

> was to put the king above the law, which then became an instrument of his will in governing. To appreciate the revolutionary implications of this development, it is important to recall the quite different sense of law in medieval times. Law was synonymous with right and with custom, the moral sense and traditional social pattern of a community. Law developed and changed imperceptibly; it was not 'made' by human will to deal with novel situations.[83]

The same Roman maxim remained odious in England.[84] This maxim provided the source for the French *si veut le roi, si veut la loi; car tel est notre plaisir* ('what the king wills, the law wills; for such is our pleasure'),[85] suggesting not coordination of movements between the king (later, the State) and his subjects, but rather a *superiority* of the former's will (later, interests) over the latter's. Viewed by many as the representative of God as He was, superior in power and with a clearer mind, willing to take care of the common good (which was his own), the French king's interest,[86] and not the British consent, was the source of law. Wouldn't *la puissance public* 'naturally' become a material source of law in the modern French State? Isn't it comprehensible that modern French publicists advocate that the State defend individual rights? As we will see, *Fait du Prince* and *imprévision* are corollaries of this ethos.

Additionally, it is important to note that at the beginning of its conception, the notion of 'interest' had little or nothing to do with the interest of ordinary men. It was only connected to the discourse about *states*.[87] In a chapter entitled 'Public Utility Preferred to Private: Mercantilism and *Raison d'État*', Keohane wrote, '[t]he most common formulations were "the interests of the prince" and the "interests of the state", taken as synonymous, and used to denote national power and glory'.[88] Keohane expanded: from the sixteenth century on, the expression *les intérêts publiques*, together with older terms like *le salut public* and other phrases used to designate the ancient *bonum publicum*, was employed as a synonym of princely and state interests.[89] Keohane adds: 'In

---

[83]   Keohane 1980: 57.
[84]   See Borchard 1927b: 1066.
[85]   See Loughlin 2003: 75.
[86]   See Keohane 1980: 174–5. About *les intérêts publiques*, Richelieu wrote, in his *Testament politique*, that only 'the monarch and his advisors can perceive the public interest; and it's the business of the king to be sure that this prevails over others at all times' (ibid: 175). 'The public interest has an objective reality of its own, visible to those charged by God with responsibility for the state' (ibid: 176).
[87]   See Greenberger 1979: 154.
[88]   Keohane 1980: 154.
[89]   See ibid.

some contexts, "public interests" were interchangeable with "public welfare"; but for many publicists, the new term was more concrete and meaningful in its referents than the older ones.'[90]

For Plessix, Nicolas Delamare (1639–1723) was the founder of an ancient *droit administratif*, the first publicist to systematize the field, being the model for the science of *droit administratif* in the nineteenth century.[91] In the eighteenth century, in his *Traité de la Police*, a four-volume work published between 1705 and 1738, Delamare set the tone for what France would become: *un État administratif*, that is, a centralized, unified and hierarchical State whose public law *served* to achieve the common good.[92] In the Preface, Delamare wrote that the public law's goal was 'the general, common good of Society'; the *droit de la police*, that is, the police power, was a part of public law whose 'the only object consists in conducting man to the perfect happiness he can enjoy in life'.[93]

Interestingly enough, at the beginning of the first chapter of the *Traité*'s first volume, Delamare clearly states on the *summa divisio*: 'Among these laws, there are those whose object is the general and common good of society, and those that concern only to the interest of the individuals. Through time, such a natural distinction has formed what we call the Public law and the Private Law.' Moreover, he added: 'All Nations well established have followed this fair division of laws.' Nevertheless, the Greeks, he continued, 'whose Language among all others has always been abundant in energetic names, would give the one of Police to the Public Law yet'.[94] This is because Police and Public Law were energetic names to convey society's general and common good.

Therefore, from the first systematic Treatise on Public Law, French publicists have seen the authority of the State, and not its authoritarian character, underneath the royal power and as the foundation of *le droit public*. The king was both legislator and administrator because he was, primarily, just.[95] Even under Louis XIV (1638–1715), the so-called Sun King and utterer of the famous phrase '*l'État c'est moi*', the notion of 'public power' held by the King never ceased to mean that 'it was the duty of the king to serve the general welfare, the common good, and not his "own" interest'.[96] This character of French kingship has passed through the centuries and, after being transformed

---

[90]   Ibid. See also Chevrier 1952: 16.
[91]   See Plessix 2003b.
[92]   See Plessix 2003a: 336–42; 2003b: 123.
[93]   Delamare 1705: II. My attention to this passage is due to Plessix 2003a: 340.
[94]   Delamare 1705: 1–2.
[95]   See Plessix 2003a: 347.
[96]   Rowen 1961: 88.

by historical metamorphoses, remained in the French *mentalité*. In 1789, the absolute king was dethroned as a result of the Revolution, and 'the Nation' was substituted in his place. Nevertheless, the philosophy of the *Ancien Régime* remained, partially at least.

For our comparative purposes, it is crucial to consider what the ancient French monarchy aimed to be: a war machine against the feudal regime, which encompassed many privileges and defended no sovereign State.[97] The centralized State, with its force and sovereignty, coupled with the divine power of kings blessed with prudence and willingness to do good in the name of all (the British would quickly label it 'absolutism'), was a vision totally different from the ever individualistic philosophy hold by most common law lawyers. These ideas passed throughout the centuries and reached modern times. Interestingly enough, they have, as often happens in history, remained substantially unaltered.

The seeds of French *droit administratif* – and consequently of *contrat administratif* – come, therefore, from the conceptions of State and public law of the Middle Ages.[98] It is thus a mistake to think either of *droit administratif* or of the French State as if they were a miracle invented in 1789. Moreover, as demonstrated, at the inception of *droit administratif* in the Middle Ages, an umbilical cord linked public law (*droit administratif*) and the idea of sovereignty.[99]

That is not to say that the French Revolution did not alter French law. As Sheldon Wolin explained, '[a] revolution wants to begin history, not to continue it'[100] – and this was particularly true of the French Revolution.[101] Virtually all recognized the revolutionary liberal mood,[102] and no one can doubt that the Revolution changed France, inaugurating a 'novel era' in public law and *droit administratif*.[103] Nevertheless, an entire and abrupt break with the past is hardly possible. One cannot empty the human spirit by decree, and coups of the guillotine are not enough to sever the *mentalités* of many generations. History, therefore, should not be accommodated in separate, disassociated blocks for men who need to organize their thoughts, perhaps aiming to find a new

---

[97]   See Plessix 2003a: 325.

[98]   See generally Plessix 2003a: 319–49; Mestre 1985: 17.

[99]   See Plessix 2003a: 332. Plessix is emphatic in concluding that the modern authors of *droit administratif* didn't do else than 'to perpetuate the great tradition of the *science de la police*, inaugurated by the great Delamare' (at 373).

[100]   Wolin 1989: 2.

[101]   'In 1789 the French made the greatest effort ever undertaken by any people to disassociate themselves from their past, and to put an abyss between what they have been and what they wished to become'. Tocqueville 1998 [1856]: vol. 1, 83.

[102]   See eg Burdeau 1995: 106; Plessix 2003a: 354.

[103]   See Burdeau 1995: 42; Plessix 2003a: 351–3; 2003b: 125.

beginning. Hence, the French Revolution is said to have somehow revived the past without completely altering the conception of State,[104] if only concerning habits, feelings and even ideas, as Tocqueville has brilliantly suggested.[105]

2.1.2 The Roman law influence

The second interrelated factor to be mentioned is common ground in legal analysis. While Anglo-American societies have lived relatively free of the influence of the Romanist tradition,[106] it was imbued in French and Brazilian societies. If sweeping, the following contrasting observation is crucial: by inheriting Roman law, France incorporated a set of maxims and principles that, in encompassing public notions – *res publica*, State, public interest, *imperium* – became so important to the French 'State society' that these maxims have never left French *mentalité*, having permeated legal reasoning ever since. On the contrary, American law remained stuck to private law principles and philosophy.

The Roman tradition implanted much of the rhetorical force of 'stateness' in French legal thought. The distinction between public and private affairs (*res publica* and *res privata*), *imperium* and *dominium*,[107] from which the public–private dichotomy was derived, has moulded the French legal mind. Unlike in American law, French jurists have operated for centuries with a *mentalité* that tends to make abstract connections between State and individual, construct its political–legal theory outside the private law domain and use the notion of *imperium* to shape its public law.[108] The emphasis on *imperium* (as in France), rather than on *dominium* (as in the common law world), elevates the group's

---

[104] See Jaume 2005: 29. Burdeau (1995: 44) wrote that the first revolutionaries culti-vated a doctrine 'even more statist' than the ancient monarchy used to defend. See also Plessix 2003a: 364–9.

[105] The well-known main thesis of *The Old Regime and the Revolution*, depicted in its Preface, is that the French have 'retained from the old regime most of the feel-ings, habits, and even ideas which helped them make the Revolution that destroyed it. Unintentionally, they used the debris of the old regime to construct the framework of their new society.' Tocqueville 1998 [1856]: vol. 1, 83. See also Plessix 2003a: 351; 2003b: 115.

[106] I'm not suggesting that Anglo-American law received no influence from Roman or civil law whatsoever. See Helmholz 1992; Hoeflich 1997; Kelley 1974: 30–40; Allison 1996: 122–8. I'm suggesting that the strong Roman rhetoric in favour of the state or public interest or *res publica* or any concept triggering 'Stateness' was absent in Anglo-American world. Of course, the lack of influence doesn't come out of the blue; rather, it is the outcome of many factors, one of which is the positive spin Anglo-American culture gives to the concept of individualism, as I will explore shortly.

[107] For a study on the notions of *dominium* and *imperium* in ancient Roman law, see Gaudemet 1995.

[108] See generally Samuel 1988: 281–3.

importance, the collective, the State, rather than the individual.[109] The Middle Ages French jurists, led by Domat, used Roman law precepts to build the ideas of State and sovereignty.[110] Once this structure was accepted, it was not difficult to link State power and public welfare.[111] 'Governing was concerned with the care and custody of *res publica*, the common and the public interest.'[112]

Norbert Foulquier has shown all the intricacies and upheavals embedded in French legal history that contributed to the problematic emergence of the concept of right (*droit subjectif*) in *le droit administratif*. 'In France, the administration has always had its Law, legitimated by the principles and superior authority, be it either the King or the Nation.'[113] Thus, an individualistic legal concept like that of 'right', central to the law as it is nowadays, has had to fight long battles against the collectivist ethos that continues to reign in the *droit administratif*, be it represented by Duguit's rejection of what he called a 'metaphysical idea' that opposed solidarity, which was behind the notion of *le service public*, Duguit's alfa and omega of *droit administratif*, or be it represented by *la puissance public*, Hauriou's idea-force, to briefly mention the two most famous scholars of French public law.

All this lingo (except, of course, for the rights talk) is almost absent in the common law world. Anglo-American law has developed without emphasizing abstract concepts like state or *imperium*.[114] Proud of the insularity, uniqueness and pragmatic character of the Common Law, English lawyers and jurists, Coke at the forefront, have historically rejected Roman and civil law influences that would menace the purity of the common law, supposedly the only system genuinely able to protect the native liberty of the English (and later American) people.[115]

---

[109] See Samuel 1998: 835; also generally Cohen-Tanugi 1985: 5–28.

[110] See generally Church 1967: 16.

[111] Bluntschli, a common law writer, registered this liaison in the nineteenth century: 'The Romans saw the real function of the State in the *public welfare*. Their two expressions, *res publica* and *salus publica*, are logically as well as verbally connected; they are, in fact, as substance and quality, as potentiality and realization' (1885: 299).

[112] Dyson 1980: 115.

[113] Foulquier 2003: 219. See also Jacquemet-Gauché 2013: 316–20.

[114] Loughlin (2003: 76–7) noted that the classical distinction between *res publica* and *dominium* was 'suppressed in English political thought, not least because of Whig assumptions, underpinned by the work of Locke, that property is a pre-political category and that the chief end of government is to ensure its preservation'. And he emphasized: 'The maintenance of this distinction between political power and the power exercised through property is essential to an understanding of property.' See also Duffy-Meunier 2017: 47.

[115] See generally Kelley 1974: 25–39. Pound (1937: 8) remembered that Sir Henry Maine spoke of peoples ruled by the civil law as having 'built the debris of the Roman rules into their walls!'

For Coke, sovereignty and rule of law were incompatible.[116] 'Magna Carta [was] such a fellow that it will have no sovereign', Coke warned Charles I in 1628.[117] Hobbes put in Cokes' mouth the following words: 'We love to have our king amongst us, and not be Govern'd by Deputies, either of our own, or another Nation.'[118]

More than four centuries later, Albert Venn Dicey (1835–1922) offered the 'most influential restatement of the Rule of Law since the 18th century'.[119] Unsurprisingly, Dicey's narrow-minded rejection of *droit administratif*, together with all that it encompasses – the public–private dichotomy, the special administrative courts, the superiority of the public interest's ideology, the notion of sovereignty, and the like – lasted almost unmodified throughout his life,[120] and continues to be highly influential in Anglo-American law.[121] Historically evaluated, Dicey's defence of the common law, together with his bitter criticism of 'collectivism' or 'despotism' allegedly existent in French law, was an unavoidable consequence of the nature of the English medieval

---

[116]   See Friedrich 1939: 20.

[117]   Beauté 1992: 118. As for the American respect for Magna Carta, it is useful to quote the following excerpt: 'Although England had proceeded on the path to parliamentary supremacy, the American colonists were more inclined to resuscitate the Magna Carta and its libertarian underpinnings against a recalcitrant English Parliament'. Hutchinson & Monahan 1987: 104.

[118]   Hobbes 2005 [1666]: 16 (footnotes omitted).

[119]   Shklar 1987: 5. See also Mestre 2021: 33.

[120]   The disagreement in the common law doctrine over whether Dicey modified his opinion about *droit administratif* has remained vivid. Allison (1996: 18–23) claims there were minor, unsubstantial modifications of Dicey's positions from the first edition of his *Law of the Constitution* (1885) to the eighth edition (1915), the last published while Dicey was alive. But see Loughlin 1992: 155–6 (suggesting a change in Dicey's position). Contra Lobingier 1942: 37 (affirming, by quoting excerpts from Robson and Jennings' work, both that Dicey was convinced by the work of his 'French friends' – Gaston Jèze mainly – that his views about *droit administratif* were obsolete and that Dicey eventually abandoned the positions he had held over his life). In any event, what is important is that, as Loughlin recognizes, 'Dicey's [first] approach, nevertheless, lived on in the minds of lawyers' (ibid: 161).

[121]   See eg Allison 1996: 11, 23; Freedland 2004: 115 ('I think that the spirit of Albert Venn Dicey lives on, to the effect that public law still has to fight for its place in English law'); Heuschling 2002: 240–1; Loughlin 1992: 140, 156, 161; 2003: 43, 133; Dimock 1933: 42 ('A. V. Dicey's misconception and prejudices were transplanted to American soil'); Frankfurter 1938: 517–18 (lamenting that '[g]enerations of lawyers and judges were brought up in the mental climate of Dicey', whose 'misconceptions and myopia' have 'crossed the Atlantic' and 'placed scholarship and authority behind uncritical American legal abstractions'); B. Schwartz 1952 (analyzing the then underdevelopment of American administrative law as opposed to French *droit administratif* and generally criticizing Dicey's view due to its legacy for the common law system).

legal thought.[122] Hence, the almost absence of any systematic theoretical effort to separate public from private contracts in the Anglo-American world, in sharp contrast to the French law, can be viewed, historically, as a corollary of Dicey's political philosophy and violent attack upon the *droit administratif*.[123]

In short, the seeds of egalitarianism between the state and citizens, the lack of any public–private law distinction and the absence of an alleged superiority of the public – first represented by the king and later by the state – in the common law world are found in this brief historical inspection. America has inherited all of these values.[124] Anglo-American political and social theories had 'no room for any valid notion of state' from very early on.[125] The historically 'stateless' American society would nevertheless use the notion of sovereignty immunity and SAD or the Unmistakability Doctrine as antidotes to its statelessness. I will show why in due course. For the moment, suffice it to state that the 'public' should find its way. First, the opposing conception of 'individualism' will be presented.

2.2   Positive and Negative Conceptions of Individualism

Although the terms 'individualism', 'socialism' and 'communism' are nineteenth-century expressions,[126] *individualism* itself is much older as a philosophical enterprise. Some scholars trace its genesis to early Christianity.[127] Yet my point here is to trace neither the history nor the roots of individualism. Whomever its 'father' was, whether Ockham in the fourteenth century, as

---

[122] See generally Loughlin 1992: 146–53 (indicating the line of English legal thought from Coke to Dicey); Heuschling 2002: 242–6 (expounding Dicey's methodology and linking it to Coke's ideas). Unsurprisingly, the pioneer of English administrative law, William Robson (together with other thinkers like Harold Laski, Sir Ivor Jennings, JA Griffith and Patrick McAuslan), was considered by Loughlin (1992: 159–206) as a thinker who held a more socialist view of the world. See also Heuschling 2002: 262–3.

[123] See Mewett 1958: 233.

[124] Pound (1999 [1921]: 1–31) highlighted the 'feudal element' of American law in 1921. See also Borchard 1927b: 1059 ('The essence of the feudal system of government was contractual'); Dyson 1980: 53.

[125] Nettl 1968: 20. For the author, this feature 'only highlights a problem that is much older' (id). The Anglo-American reticence about the word 'state', which can be traced back to Hobbes and Locke, reveals the liberal, anti-state philosophy. See Beaud 1990: 122.

[126] See Lukes 2006: 19. See also Swart 1962: 78. My attention to the importance of the topic was first drawn by Lukes (1971), later published in a book of 1973, with a new edition (2006), from which I derive massively.

[127] See Villey 2001: 96–109.

Michel Villey insistently had it,[128] or Hobbes and Locke or any other chosen figure or epoch,[129] we are nowadays all children of individualism. The point is to know what we take it to mean.

Americans not only like individualism, but have built a country upon this concept. 'Above all', wrote Yehoshua Arieli, '[in America] individualism expressed the universalism and idealism most characteristic of the national consciousness. This concept evolved in contradistinction with socialism, the universal and messianic character of which it shared.'[130]

On the contrary, French people not only dislike individualism but, more importantly, see it as a threat.[131] 'The evil which plagues France is not unknown; everyone agrees in giving it the same name: *individualism* [...] All for each, each for all, that is society; each for himself, and each against all, that is individualism',[132] wrote Louis Veuillot (1813–83), a French Catholic antiliberal writer.

My central argument is this: in law, the American 'positive' notion of individualism has been used to fuel any theory that happens to be related to American values, such as capitalism, free market and liberal democracy – values embedded in American culture. As Steven Lukes wrote:

> It was in the US that 'individualism' primarily came to celebrate capitalism and liberal democracy. It became a symbolic catchword of immense ideological significance, expressing all that has at various times been implied in the philosophy of natural rights, the belief in free enterprise, and the American Dream. It expressed, in fact, the operative ideals of nineteenth- and early twentieth-century America (*and indeed continues to play a major ideological role*), advancing a set of universal claims seen as incompatible with the parallel claims of the socialism and communism of the Old World.[133]

Whichever brush one chooses to paint American history with, individualism generally receives bright colours. As Arieli has shown, individualism 'supplied the nation with a rationalization of its characteristic attitudes, behaviour patterns, and aspirations' throughout American history.[134] Of course, one will

---

[128] See Villey 1964: 98; 1957: 89.

[129] See Swart 1962: 77.

[130] Arieli 1964: 345–6. See also Bird 1999: 1.

[131] Brazilians' idea of individualism is very complex. In broad terms, it's nevertheless fair to say that Brazilians are closer to the French conception of individualism than to the American philosophy of positive individualism. My intention in this section is to analyse only the two extremes, and that is why the Brazilian idea of individualism won't be mentioned.

[132] Quoted by Lukes 2006: 24.

[133] Lukes 2006: 37 (emphasis added).

[134] Arieli 1964: 345. See also Whitfield 1988: 480–1.

find various connotations of the term individualism in the US. Lukes' perusal of Emerson's, John Draper's, Walt Whitman's and William Summer's works have shown these various connotations.[135] However, Lukes' last word on the issue is borrowed from James Bryce (1838–1922), to whom 'individualism, the love of enterprise, and pride in personal freedom' have represented to Americans 'not only their choicest, but their peculiar and exclusive possession'.[136]

Ironically, it was a Frenchman who gave American individualism the most distinguished complexion. Alexis de Tocqueville (1805–59) painted American individualism so positively that his ideas about it have influenced every work on American culture and its uniqueness. His masterpiece *Democracy in America*, which 'remains the best book ever written about Americans',[137] is (among many things) a comparative sociological work in which he describes the French version of individualism in a very negative way.

Tocqueville's insights about American individualism have contributed enormously to what I have been labelling a positive view of it. He linked individualism with democracy,[138] equality and the free market, and this liaison has taken a firm grip on American culture. Individualism was fuelled by other hand-in-hand ideas, the 'premier facts' or 'generative facts', which Tocqueville put at the centre of his theoretical enterprise.[139] These facts 'served to connect, explain, and signify each part of the theory', thus exercising 'a certain kind of power' over other facts.[140]

'Individualism is a recent expression given birth by a new idea. Our fathers knew only egoism.'[141] With these words, Tocqueville made a critical claim. He set out a crucial comparison, which will be explored further – namely, individualism-democracy *versus* egoism-aristocracy – a claim that has been presented in this book as very meaningful and representative of the US and French spirits. American individualism, in Tocqueville's mind, 'is a consid-

---

135 See Lukes 2006: 39.

136 Quoted by Lukes 2006: 40.

137 Whitfield 1988: 480.

138 See Tocqueville 2010 [1840]: 881–94.

139 See Wolin 2001: 98.

140 Ibid. Wolin mentions that 'among the most important of these were: liberty, centralization, participation, majority tyranny, individualism, Cartesianism, and political culture'. Ibid.

141 Tocqueville 2010 [1840]: 881. In *The Old Regime*, Tocqueville (1998 [1856]: 162–3) presents an analogous view: 'Our ancestors lacked the word "individualism", which we have created for our own use.' *Individualisme* was such a novel term in 1840 that the first English translator had no alternative but to maintain the French term, 'however it may seem to an English ear'. Whitfield 1988: 480. Tocqueville didn't coin the term, but defined and developed it. See Schleifer 2010: 881.

ered and peaceful sentiment',[142] while '[e]goism is a passionate and exaggerated love of oneself, which leads man to view everything only in terms of himself alone and to prefer himself to everything'.[143] Alternatively, in even more definitive words, '[e]goism is a vice as old as the world. It hardly belongs more to one form of society than to another.' In its turn, '[i]ndividualism is of democratic origin, and it threatens to develop as conditions become equal'.[144]

The effort of coupling individualism with both democratic liberalism and law prevailed in America. Tocqueville's American democrat is an individualist in a positive sense, not an egoist. He is a self-reliant man, and Tocqueville is credulous about this modern human being, described as a '*convinced* individual who believes as dogmatically in his own uniqueness as he does in the sanctity of his individual soul and its preciousness in the eyes of God'.[145] Although closely related to individualism, egoism could only lead to selfishness if narrowly, negatively understood. On the contrary, democratic individualism, adequately understood, leads to equality and freedom.

It is not difficult to see the solid ideological character of Tocqueville's theory. He inverted the old sense of 'narrow' individualism and put a positive spin on it. Individualism turned out to be 'the philosophical method of Americans'.[146] This decisive shift – from negative to positive – in the meaning of individualism and the coupling of it with democracy and equality may well serve as a landmark point between French and American ideas about the issue. While American democracy fuelled equality, French aristocracy severed the nation; and 'men who live in aristocratic countries', he added, 'are often disposed to forget themselves'.[147] For Tocqueville, '[a]ristocracy had made all citizens into a long chain that went from the peasant up to the king; democracy breaks the chain and sets each link apart'.[148]

Alexis de Tocqueville, the most sensitive comparatist of France and America of all times, has shown better than any other theorist that the *memory of the past* plays a definite role in the development of the nations. It suffices to quote him once more: 'The great advantage of the Americans is to have arrived at democracy without having to suffer democratic revolutions, and to have been born equal instead of becoming so.'[149] Thus, the memory of the past, an aristocratic past, impeded France from making the same move.

---

142 Tocqueville 2010 [1840]: 882.
143 Ibid.
144 Ibid: 882–3. See also Wolin 2001: 216.
145 Wolin 2001: 351.
146 Ibid.
147 Tocqueville 2010 [1840]: 883.
148 Ibid: 884.
149 Tocqueville 2010 [1840]: 886.

French individualism conveys the opposite idea. In France, the term individualism 'usually carried, and indeed still carries, a pejorative connotation, a strong suggestion that to concentrate on the individual is to harm the superior interest of society'.[150] Historically, French people have condemned individualism across the entire political spectrum, from the very right to the very left.

Conservative thinkers shared scorn for the individual's 'private stock of reason';[151] among the theocratic Catholic reactionaries, as Joseph de Maistre (1753–1821) ('[t]he most brilliant writer of French counter-revolutionaries)[152] pointed out in 1884, the individual reason was 'of its nature the mortal enemy of all associations'.[153] In 1796, Louis de Bonald (1754–1840) had already stated that 'man only exists for society and society only educates him for itself';[154] and Hugue de Lamennais (1782–1854), arguing against the *philosophes*, who had according to him inspired the Revolution, said that man 'lives only in society' and that 'institutions, laws, governments draw all their strength from a certain concourse of thoughts and wills'. However, individualism, he emphasized, 'destroys the very idea of obedience and duty, thereby destroying both power and law'.[155]

As Steven Lukes shows, the ideas of Claude Henri Saint-Simon (1770–1825) had a pervasive effect on French thought. Saint-Simonism shared counter-revolutionary reactionary thoughts, such as 'their critique of the Enlightenment's glorification of the individual'.[156] Locke, Reid, Condillac, Kant, d'Holbach, Voltaire and Rousseau were 'defenders of individualism' in Saint-Simonians' eyes, and individualism was used to 'refer to pernicious and negative ideas underlying the evils of the modern critical epoch'.[157] Mazzini, an Italian nationalist who borrowed Saint-Simonian's ideas, said that the individualism of the French Revolution had only 'a negative value' and had led to 'egotism and nameless immorality'.[158] In short, for Saint-Simonism, Locke *et caterva* 'preached egoism'.[159]

Along the same lines, French socialists have contrasted individualism 'with an ideal, cooperative social order, variously described as "association", "harmony", "socialism", and "communism"'.[160] Lukes quotes several authors

---

150 Lukes 2006: 23.
151 Ibid: 21.
152 Swart 1962: 78.
153 Quoted by Lukes 2006: 21–2.
154 Quoted by ibid: 22.
155 Quoted by ibid.
156 Lukes 2006: 22.
157 Ibid.
158 Quoted by Swart 1962: 80.
159 Lukes 2006: 23. See also Swart 1962: 79.
160 Lukes 2006: 24.

who linked individualism to negative ideas: 'everyone for himself, and [...] all for riches, nothing for the poor', said Pierre Leroux (1797–1871); 'the remedy lies in association precisely because the abuse springs from individualism', vociferated Constantin Pecquer (1801–87); 'Communism is the protector of the individual, individualism his extermination', suggested Auguste Blanqui (1805–81). And Etienne Cabet (1788–1856) put it in absolute, dichotomist terms: 'Two great systems have divided and polarized Humanity ever since the beginning of the world: that of Individualism (or egoism, or personal interest), and that of Communism (or association, or the general interest, or the public interest).'[161] In broad terms, these negative views of individualism express the opposite idea of 'American individualism'. In French eyes, individualism destroys, rather than strengthens, society.

True, all these quotes are from nineteenth-century authors, and Lukes points out, too, that later socialists have used the term individualism in more complex ways, not always giving it a negative meaning. That was the case for Louis Blanc (1811–82), Charles Fourier (1772–1837) and Émile Durkheim (1858–1917), to whom 'individualism signified autonomy, freedom, and sacredness of the individual values which had hitherto taken a negative, oppressive, and anarchic form but could be henceforth only be preserved within a cooperative and rationally-organized social order'.[162] However, one can easily see that, according to Durkheim, the shift from a 'negative' to a 'positive' idea of individualism could *only* work if one considers individualism *as the source of a cooperative social order*. Swart explains that what socialists deplored was not the French Revolution per se (as the Reactionaries did), but 'the ruthless exploitation of man by man in the modern industry' and the 'economic doctrine of laissez faire'.[163] To them, it was not in France but England that the spirit of 'unfettered individualism' found its fullest expression.[164]

Lukes' historical study then presents the French liberal view of individualism, represented by Benjamin Constant (1767–1830), 'the most eloquent exponent of classical liberalism', and, of course, Tocqueville, 'who developed its most distinctive and influential liberal meaning in France'.[165] Embedded in the French ethos, Tocqueville's liberal mind deployed individualism with caution by severing the present (America) and the past (France), but not

---

[161] Quoted by Lukes 2006: 24.

[162] Lukes 2006: 25.

[163] Swart 1962: 81.

[164] See ibid: 82.

[165] Lukes 2006: 25–6. Constant's ideas, alongside those of Auguste Comte (1789–1857), the chief sociological positivist, were very influential in Brazil. See Carvalho 2005. And no wonder Constant favours the unity of jurisdiction in France. See Chavallier 1970: 96.

without remarking that individualism had 'corrosive effects' that could be 'counteracted by political participation at the local level'.[166] Tocqueville knew well enough that without counterbalances of collectivist ideas, individualism would lead to egoism.

By exploiting what he called a 'defensive' character of 'Frenchmen' individualism, Daniel Lerner has shown that the French seem to be more introspective about their individuality.[167] Unlike Americans, whose individualism would lead to a more communitarian life, French individualism would reveal itself in immobility (*l'immobilisme*) and in 'refus[al] of committing oneself to do something' (*refus de s'engager*).[168] What flows from this sort of passive behaviour is another aspect of the same negative sense of individualism, more introspective and, if one wishes, more egoistic.

French thought has generally expressed individualism by utilizing Durkheim's twin concepts of anomie and egoism, which represent 'the social, moral, and political isolation of individuals, their dissociation from social purposes and social regulation, the breakdown of social solidarity'.[169] This is not to say that Americans are selfish, egoistical individuals and have no sense of community, or that the French (or Brazilians) are altruistic people (a careful sociological survey may well prove otherwise). My only point is that individualism's positive and negative features are assumptions that shape legal systems and, consequently, public contract law.

In the US, a positive ethos of individualism has acted as a critical factor for theorists to dismiss any theory that threatens the reign of the self. If any specific theory conveys a minimal flavour of 'collectivism', 'state' or, even worse, 'socialism', the tendency is that it will not take hold in America.[170] Moreover, individualism serves as a barrier to any attempt to introduce a principle such as 'supremacy of the public interest', which, as I explained, has governed *le droit public* for a couple of decades in France, as well as in Brazil. The idea of the public sphere (the State) overcoming the individual, its private sphere, generally sounds in the US as aggression to the American self. On the contrary, in France individualism implies a negative viewpoint; it is like a sin.

In summary, the force of statelessness and the positive individualism in America operate together as a magnet, to repeat the metaphor I used before. American individualism rejects collective ideas and attracts individualistic theories. To Americans, whatever exalts their self-reliant individualism and

---

[166]   Joshua Mitchell 1995: 6.

[167]   See Lerner 1956.

[168]   See ibid: 189–90. See also Brault 1962 (agreeing with Lerner and depicting the notion of defensive French individualism).

[169]   Lukes 2006: 27. See also Swart 1962: 84.

[170]   See generally Hartz 1991 [1955]: chapters 8–9.

has an anti-state flavour will sound appealing and seductive. American culture favours the individual *over* the community and the state, and it is the strength of the former that is thought of as a way to keep the cohesion of the latter, not the contrary. Coke, Dicey and Pound have incarnated this spirit. Since the law must be equally applied, no prerogatives for the king or the state should be admitted. No public–private distinction is to be upheld. The individual, not the state, must be the protagonist of the economy and social life. The state has mainly negative rather than positive obligations; it must *not* invade the private sphere. Therefore, individual *liberal* rights – that is, *negative* rights, those that require mainly state *inaction* rather than state action – deserve high consideration. In contrast, *social* rights – that is, *positive* rights, those that mainly demand state *action* rather than inaction, such as housing, health care, education – seem to be foreign to American legal parlance.[171] The French and Brazilian general legal picture presents the opposite characteristics.

3.   COMBINING THE TWO FACTORS: BRIEF EXAMPLES

Louis Hartz (1919–86) said crudely that American liberal language 'does not *understand* the meaning of sovereign power'.[172] If 'sovereign state' is a tautological notion, as Loughlin put it,[173] then Americans do not understand the idea of state either. Notions like sovereignty and state run against the 'irrational Lockianism' or, more suggestively, against 'Americanism',[174] to borrow Hartz's words again.[175]

The word 'understand' carries heavy weight. It implies two things. First, understand means that the idea of 'sovereign power' (or state) is not part of the American liberal *mentalité*.[176] Second, it suggests that Americanism doesn't

---

[171] 'Social rights' is an important topic of public law in continental law today, and any citation of references would be incomplete. In this paragraph, I have only sketched a very complicated subject. And the common opposition between 'positive' and 'negative' rights is flawed. See Holmes & Sunstein 1999. The debate is besides my point. My only intention is to remark that in the US the *main idea* about the state is that it has *not to interfere* with private rights.

[172] Hartz 1991 [1955]: 7 (emphasis added).

[173] See Loughlin 2010: 184.

[174] Ibid: 11.

[175] Hartz (1991 [1955]: 9) identified the phenomenon of 'natural liberalism' as 'a remarkable force', or as 'the secret root from which have sprung many of the most puzzling of American cultural phenomena'.

[176] Unsurprisingly, all the above quotations are taken from the part of Hartz's classic book in which he expounds upon the American 'frame of mind'. See Hartz 1991 [1955]: 5–14. The section is called 'Natural Liberalism: The Frame of Mind'.

accept sovereignty (or state); in public contract law terms, Americanism doesn't accept sovereign immunity.

The American elevation of the value of an individualistic property, perhaps even above the whole society, is Lockean in origin. 'The great and *chief end*, therefore', wrote Locke in *The Second Treatise of Government* (1690), 'of men's uniting into commonwealths, and putting themselves under government, *is the preservation of their property*'.[177] Thus, one can see reflections of American individualism in children's inheritance rights, pre-contractual liability, criminal responsibility, just to name a few law fields.

In comparing civil and common law children's inheritance rights, Barbara Hauser noted that civilians' laws 'give automatic inheritance rights to children (equally)'. 'In the United States', she wrote, '*individualism is emphasized* and one has complete freedom to disinherit one's children (with limited exceptions in Louisiana, which followed French law when it was settled)'. Furthermore, the contrast is, again, with France: 'Parents in the United States thus also have the freedom to treat their children unequally. In the United States, we refer to the French system as a "forced heirship".'[178]

Unlike most European laws, American law is much more reluctant to impose pre-contractual liabilities, despite both having embraced the doctrine of estoppel. According to Allan Farnsworth, American Courts 'have declined to find a general obligation that would preclude a party from breaking off negotiations, even when success was in prospect'. While both the Uniform Commercial Code and the Restatement (Second) of Contracts supported a formulation of a general duty of good faith and fair dealing, at least by negative implication, the American courts do not extend the duty to negotiations.[179] In Europe, the doctrines of good-faith reliance and *venire contra factum proprium* (to act contrary to one's past behaviour), coupled with the German concept of *culpa in contrahendo* (fault in contracting, a doctrine created by Rudolph von Jhering as early as 1861), are usually accepted. In 'sources language', in the US, formal sources of law, being undefined on the matter, would allow an interpretation of the norm to include the duty of good faith to negotiations; material sources, however, silently guided the law to exclude the duty.

Moreover, it is hardly a coincidence that American criminal law is the only democracy that has upheld and still upholds capital sentences, the most retributive and individualistic form of punishment in modern Western his-

---

[177] Locke 1980 [1690]: § 124. Writing about the American 'natural liberalism', Hartz (1991 [1955]: 6) stated that 'a society which begins with Locke, and thus transforms him, stays with him, by virtue of an absolute and irrational attachment it develops for him'.

[178] Hauser 2003: 22.

[179] See Farnsworth 1987: 239; Lake 1994: 178.

tory.[180] No one ignores that modern criminal law was created and developed due to the barbarous, inhuman punishments perpetrated in ancient times and the Middle Ages, coupled with the even more barbaric cruelty of criminal procedural practices. This form of punishment is found today, in Western legal systems, only in the US criminal law. No responsibility for an individual act is attributed to the whole community. The philosophy, roughly stated, holds that the person must bear full responsibility for his or her actions. If the state must not interfere in individuals' lives, it cannot be blamed for individual mistakes. Collective responsibility runs against American individualistic philosophy. The guilty individual, not the social group or the state, must shoulder the burden for the individual's wrongdoing. Nevertheless, in constitutional law, the hallmark of the American culture, one sees the stain of individualism more clearly.

It is common sense that the individualistic philosophy, as a product of the Enlightenment, has played an essential role in shaping the US Constitution and American constitutional law, which has always emphasized and enforced the negative rather than the positive state duties and obligations; the state must *not interfere* with individual liberties. Unlike many European and South American Constitutions that embrace social rights,[181] the US Constitution is silent about the state's positive obligations, leaving this issue to the political arena. The state exists not to promote social rights but to permit individuals to develop their full capacities. The *autonomous* individual has the right not to be disturbed by the state and to develop his personhood freely. In short, the American Constitution 'incorporates a theory of personhood that is individualistic and self-regarding', which 'extols the ethic of individualism and, at the same time, exhibits a profound distrust of government power'.[182]

In *Deshaney v Winnebago County* (1989),[183] the Supreme Court supported this idea rather dramatically.[184] The issue was whether the state failed to rescue a toddler from his father when the county social service agency received several complaints, putting the state officials on notice that the child was in danger. The father's merciless beatings over two years caused the young boy to become comatose and severely mentally disabled. Chief Justice Rehnquist, speaking for the majority, said crudely, addressing the issue of protection

---

[180] For a brilliant study comparing criminal punishment in America and Europe, see Whitman 2003a.

[181] CFB/1988, Article 6: 'Education, health, work, habitation, leisure, security, social security, protection of motherhood and childhood, and assistance to the destitute, are social rights, as set forth by this Constitution.'

[182] Kommers 1991: 866–7.

[183] 489 US 189 (1989).

[184] See Kommers 1991: 867–8.

of liberty raised by the plaintiff (the child's mother) under the fourteenth amendment:

> [There's] noting in the language of the Due Process Clause [that] requires the State to protect the life, liberty, and property of its citizens against invasion by private actors. The Clause is phrased as a limitation of the State's power to act, not as a guarantee of [a] certain minimal level of safety and security [...] [Its] language *cannot fairly be extended to impose an affirmative obligation to the State* to ensure that those interests do not come to harm through other means.[185]

Had America embraced different conceptions of *individualism* and *state*, a different outcome could, I believe, have been reached in *Deshaney*. American law would then have been driven in an opposing direction, neither better nor worse per se, but remarkably different. Continental law jurists, primarily French and Brazilian, call it a 'more social', less individualistic direction. However, again, material sources were at work in *Dashaney*, informing the content of the dogmatic sources of law (in this case, the vague Due Process Clause of the US Constitution).

With this background in mind, it would be strange if American public contract law uncontroversially accepted the doctrine of sovereign acts. For the American legal community, SAD and the Unmistakability Doctrine are more willing to be viewed negatively than positively. Like government itself or sovereign immunity, SAD and the Unmistakability Doctrine are seen as a 'necessary evil', to borrow Gary Wills' suggestive expression.[186] These doctrines thus run against, I insist, the ever-present roots of Americanism.

In France, although an individualistic philosophy also fuelled the Napoleonic Code, a document also inspired by the Enlightenment and viewed as the actual 'constitution' of the French people,[187] a more collectivist idea of law holds from the Third Republic onwards. As Léon Duguit showed in 1912,[188] the individualism of the Napoleon Code has never been free from attack.[189] The

---

[185]   Ibid: 868 (footnote omitted) (emphasis added).

[186]   See Wills 2002.

[187]   There was, of course, more than one 'Enlightenment', as scholars have long noted (see eg also Dawson 1954).

[188]   See generally Duguit 1999 [1920]. I cite here the second edition of the book. The first edition was published in 1912, about which Duguit (1917: 21) wrote: 'I've tried to show elsewhere [referring to the 1st edition] how this purely individualistic and wholly metaphysical conception of the Code Napoléon disappeared progressively and how our civil law evolved toward a realistic and *social system*' (emphasis added).

[189]   About French individualism and the law, see Waline 1949. In a comparative historical and philosophical perspective, Dawson (1954: 276) compared the French and English bourgeoisie of the Enlightenment and correctly wrote that 'the French bourgeoisie looked to the state rather than to private enterprise for employment and social

entire legal system in France is fuelled by a more 'social' and 'collective' philosophy, which has had a deep impact on the law of *contrat administratif*.

This framework is crucial to my argument, for it structures all that follows. Again, stateless, individualistic societies like the American one tend not to welcome 'collectivist' or 'social' ideas. On the contrary, French philosophy favours the 'collective' or 'social' at the expense of individuals and their 'rights'. American liberal society does not favour the rhetoric of a strong state. American liberal language 'does not understand the meaning of sovereign power', remembering Louis Hartz's words in 1955. The 'intense', 'extreme', 'obstinate', individualism of American law,[190] which Pound described as the *Spirit of the Common Law* in 1932, results from a philosophy that has always been suspicious of state power and notions like 'sovereignty'. Quite the opposite has occurred in France and, to a lesser extent, in Brazil.

The first crucial difference is in both structure and methodology between French and American government contract law. American law has both poorly systematized the domain of public liability and remained both philosophically and methodologically attached to principles of private law. In contrast, French law has detached itself from private law and attempted to systematize the subject of state liability. As I will show, this role of systematization was in France undertaken by the doctrine, which has also played a crucial role in a broader intellectual movement that encompassed political theory, including the very concept of State. In the US, SAD and the Unmistakability Doctrine are *not* understood as part of a broader concept of state or governed by no-fault public liability or any other particular principle. The American law *mentalité* does not operate in terms of public–private law or fault-without-fault State liability or, as in France, of *égalité devant les charges publiques*, as we will shortly see. All these notions have a collectivist ethos. A stateless culture wouldn't construct – as a collective effort –an exorbitant doctrine of public responsibility. That runs against individualism. Worse, in Dicey's words, this would mean to accept the 'authoritarian' principles of *droit administratif*, which are foreign to the common law Liberal credo.

In jurisprudential terms, public law carries a sense of 'law of subordination',[191] to remember Radbruch's formula, which repulses the common law's spirit, to borrow Pound's famous title once again. For the Liberal view of the public–private dichotomy, there must be a 'penetration of the coördinative [*sic*] ideas of private law into public law, which is the essence of a government

---

advancement'. This idea both illustrates and helps to understand why the State has had such a powerful role in France.

[190]   The labels are all derived from Pound 1999 [1921]: 13–15.
[191]   See Radbruch 1950 [1932]: 153.

of laws'.[192] As Pound stated: '[c]onsociation, not subordination', is the hallmark of the common law; 'we are with one another, not over one another'.[193] Hence, any system of public responsibility is against the common law idea of liability. For common law lawyers' Liberal view, '[t]he state', said Radbruch accurately, 'in its business relationships [*Fiscus*] is subjected to private law. It assumes the same position as the individual by becoming a party in criminal and administrative procedure.' He then adds, touching the heart of our topic: 'That controversial legal conception, the "*public law contract*", would involve the state *placing itself on the same level as the individual*.'[194]

Notwithstanding these observations, to say that French law has constructed a different system of public liability or developed principles of *responsabilité sans faute* and opposed these features to the American concept of private law liability is only a descriptive assertion. It is necessary to know why France constructed its system, under what assumptions and principles.

The problem of state liability for sovereign acts must be understood within this context. Nevertheless, what strikes the comparatist is the following paradox. The basic principle of state liability in the US runs seemingly against the idea of protecting individuals' property, for American law still maintains sovereign immunity as a fundamental idea of its system of government liability. On the contrary, France and Brazil adopt, remarkably enough, the opposite philosophy.

---

[192] Ibid.
[193] Pound 1939: 475.
[194] Radbruch 1950 [1932]: 153 (emphasis added).

6. State responsibility in American public contract law

I have thus far stated that in the American *mentalité*, the individual is 'strong' while the state is 'weak'; that Americans favour the former at the expense of the latter; that in the Anglo-American world, the state is not to be responsible for individuals' fate, nor is it the protagonist in the public scene. Therefore, if the individual himself controls his destiny; if the state must be *laissez-faire*; if the individual is to be the master of his own life; then the individual alone must hold responsibility for his acts. And remember my point, which now has become, I hope, easier to be defended: the American philosophy of state irresponsibility results from this individualistic, stateless society.

In France, I have suggested, the opposite holds. The State is at the epicentre of social phenomena, being *the* protagonist of society; it plans the economy (*économie dirigée*), which is among its moral duties;[1] it amalgamates individuals. Therefore, if the State coordinates people's life; if it has a moral function to manage the economy; if it incites and guides people in the name of and towards *l'intérêt général*; if it is considered *responsible* for people's lives; and if it must provide for *services publiques* (more on this shortly); then the State must also be accountable for all its actions, including its wrongdoings and its legal actions. Brazil has primarily followed the French model.

SAD, the Unmistakability Doctrine, *fait du Prince* and *imprévision* are theories that ultimately deal with lawful activities of the state,[2] not with state wrongdoings. The state *can* and sometimes *must* act in a way that indirectly impairs its contracts. Public administration is continuous, not static, and public needs or even political interests don't wait for the right time to show up. What if the state does not act, say, to control the economy and fails to regulate interest rates during a period of high inflation caused by a world crisis? What if the state does not act to avoid the spread of a pandemic like SARS-CoV-2? Consider my hypothetical examples in Chapter 2. If the state fails to act in those situations, we will not hesitate to blame it.

Over the past two centuries, France has developed a system of public liability that differs from private responsibility (adopted in the common law world).

---

[1] See Dyson 1980: 97. See also Cohen-Tanugi 1985: 114–15.
[2] About the licit character of *fait du Prince*, see *Traité 2*: § 1295.

French law has set an *objective* and *public* system of State liability based on the liaison between the State activity and the particular. Brazil is only one among the many countries that have followed the French model. As will be demonstrated, French law was very early on launched to the vanguard of state liability, much because of its leading role in constructing theories that *favour* the responsibility of the State, thus providing for recoverability of eventual damages caused by State activity. This philosophy is only the backlash to the French Stateness and collective idea of society, and central to it is the highly ideological and political concept of *service public*, as we will see.

That is, of course, a crude simplification of a complex issue. It is, however, enough to serve as a starting point for my thesis, which is again dialectical: the backlash of American individualism and statelessness appears in the fact that American law keeps alive the spirit of the sovereign immunity doctrine – the state utilizes sovereign immunity as a mechanism to impose its force upon an ultra-individualistic legal culture that never accepted any sort of 'supremacy of the public', be that of kings, state or 'public law'. Anglo-American law, reluctant as it has been to accept the methodological, highly ideological, historically situated public–private law dichotomy, 'needs' the spirit of sovereign immunity and its related ideas such as SAD and the Unmistakability Doctrine. It is no wonder that recent academic work has invoked 'democracy' to fuel sovereign immunity: Americans need to protect the public interest with the catchwords they have built their Nation with.

The French collectivist 'State society' should also have forms to 'compensate' its Statenessness. In France more than anywhere else, the public–private law dichotomy has helped to shape the State's structure and facilitated the idea of a *droit exorbitante*, the *droit administratif*, of which the *contrat administratif* is a vital part. Having built a whole society on a strong concept of State, France has constructed a legal system that protects the individual (allegedly, more fully than Anglo-American nations). The uniquely French *Conseil d'État*, Napoleonic and totalitarian in its inception and designed to maintain the State's power,[3] has developed, alongside the systematic work of influent *publicistes*, a relatively coherent theory of public law that gained global attention. The basic assumption behind the State Council's philosophy has been to balance the *confessed and accepted existing historical* supremacy of the public interest, represented by the State, and the individual's rights, embedded in a collective ethos fuelled by the *public* notions of *service public* and *puissance public*. The theories of *fait du Prince* and *imprévision* must be understood within this scenario.

---

[3]   See generally, Burdeau 1995: 29–88.

True, as mentioned in the Introduction to this book, the neoliberal wave that has overtaken many Western legal systems in the past four decades did not spare France. It has, of course, changed *le droit public* and *les contrats administratifs*. But was it a tsunami – which requires changes in the tectonic plates?

Roughly stated, Brazil has followed the French model. The doctrine and courts have simply mimicked French ideas concerning the issues of state responsibility for sovereign acts. Brazilian theories of *fato do Príncipe* and *imprevisão* are gross copies of French homonymous doctrines. However, as we will see, Brazil was more generous than France in protecting contractors, having confusingly transformed the French model. Moreover, Brazil's continuous pendular movement from one leading model to another, again as mentioned in the Introduction, has recently pushed towards a more Liberal philosophy of State (in the Anglo-American sense of Liberalism), and the comparatist can perceive this move both in statutory language and in courts' decisions about public contracts. These subjects will be analysed later, however. I will now contrast the ideas of sovereign immunity and *responsabilité sans faute*, which are at the core of state responsibility for sovereign acts in the US, France and Brazil.

1. THE US AND THE SPIRIT OF SOVEREIGN IMMUNITY

'The starting point in Anglo-American jurisdictions', Hadfield stated referring to breach of government contracts, 'is the concept of sovereign immunity'.[4] Under the sovereign immunity doctrine, the government cannot be sued without its permission; that is, the government can be sued only if Congress has waived the government's immunity.[5]

The simplicity of this sentence encapsulates a power that is difficult to overestimate.[6] The first necessary observation is that sovereign immunity is not a mere procedural shield for the government, as its standard definition seems to imply. Instead, sovereign immunity's content is rather substantive. Although Congress has waived immunity from suit, the spirit of immunity,

---

[4]   Hadfield 1999: 471.

[5]   See eg Sisk 2016: 69; Randall 2002: 8.

[6]   The literature on either the origin or the actual meaning of sovereign immunity is abundant. It is impossible to cover all articles about the issue. Some remarkable studies must nevertheless be mentioned. For the origins of the doctrine in the common law world, see Borchard 1924; Pugh 1953. For the historical, political and philosophical foundations of the doctrine in comparative perspective, see Borchard 1926; 1927a; 1927b; 1928a. For a more recent approach to the doctrine, see Randall 2002; Jackson 2003; Sisk 2010; 2014; 2016.

as I've suggested repeatedly, remains alive and finds ways to re-emerge as the situation requires. From a comparative law perspective and concerning government procurement law, the function of avoiding or limiting government responsibility re-emerges through the SAD and the Unmistakability Doctrine, which are, in fact, sovereign immunity's corollaries.

Formal sources confirm that. The best example comes from the rationale of the petition of Winstar Corporation in *US v Winstar Corp.* (1996) (to be more fully explored later), the most critical and most recent case decided by the Supreme Court about the issue. The petition has linked, correctly, the Unmistakability Doctrine to sovereign immunity.

In truth, the government's notion of contract unmistakability misappropriates the nomenclature of a venerable and sensible rule of construction – that contract rights against the government cannot be implied or presumed, but must be 'expressed in terms too plain to be mistaken', as in *Jefferson Branch Bank v Skelly*, 66 US (1 Black) 436, 446 (1862) – and attaches it to an extraordinary claim of *governmental immunity* from liability for any contract breach occasioned by an act of Congress.[7]

My point is that doctrines and theories have heuristic functions and political aims; they are not constructed only to organize juridical materials. Alongside 'classification', which is crucial to *any* legal analysis,[8] doctrines and legal theories also have a productive, *normative* role; being part of a broader theory can be relevant, sometimes determinant, to interpret a legal doctrine and solve practical problems.[9] And remember, the consequence of the SAD and the Unmistakability Doctrine is the same as sovereign immunity: to avoid states' responsibility to pay damages.[10]

Here emerges a crucial and already mentioned difference between the theories of SAD or the Unmistakability Doctrine and the French (or Brazilian) *fait du Prince* or *imprévision*. In the US, SAD and the Unmistakability Doctrine are *defences* used *by the government* to avoid liability in contracts.[11] In France (and Brazil), on the contrary, the theories of *fait du Prince* and *imprévision* are constructions of the *Conseil d'État* (consecrated and adapted in Brazilian

---

[7]   1995 WL 17013389 Brief of Winstar Corporation and the Statesman Group, Inc., et al, in Opposition to Petition for Writ of Certiorari, at 16 (emphasis added).

[8]   See the impressive work by Vautrot-Schwarz 2009.

[9]   See Canaris 1995: 30–4.

[10]   See Sisk 2016: 327–31 (treating the 'sovereign act doctrine or defense' within the scope of sovereign immunity); Speidel 1963: 537 (correctly stating that the sovereign acts theory 'most clearly reflects the inherent conflict between public and private interests in government contracts' and demonstrating concern with the possible 'absolute immunity from suit for damages resulting from these protected [sovereign] acts'); Stack 1955 (treating *Horowitz v US* as '*Horowitz* rule of sovereign immunity').

[11]   See eg Morgan 1992; 226–32.

law) directed to *protect the contractor* and to allow compensation for losses in the case of the so-called administrative *alea* (*aléa administratif*, literally, 'administrative game of chance').[12]

These differences are anchored in the structures of the legal systems, being part of all legal actors' *mentalités*. For the comparatist interested in how material sources of law have influenced formal sources, mainly legal decisions, what is essential is to understand the reasons behind the differences, however similar the results in practical cases may be. I must therefore explore the origins and the meaning of sovereign immunity compared to the contrasting philosophy of *responsabilité sans faute*.

Yet let me invoke history to highlight the heuristic, normative function of a politically engaged reading of sovereign immunity.

The reaching of the English maxim 'the king can do no wrong' is disputed.[13] What seems indisputable after Janelle Greenberg's brilliant historical study is that the adage served different *ideological* and *political* ends in the past.[14]

The meaning of the maxim has varied along with history according to the needs of the lawyers who advocated for the various governments' particular, often conflicting concerns. For example, Tudor and early Stuart lawyers used the maxim to guarantee royal immunity and permit subjects to act against royal officials. However, by the end of the Civil War (1642–51), parliamentarians had combined the maxim with the 'king's two bodies' doctrine and transformed it into a very different instrument. The maxim should then 'protect only a lawful ruler, leaving a tyrant subject to ordinary process, including capital punishment'; it would be necessary in the Glorious Revolution (1688–9) as well, and early signs of the maxim's utility also appeared 'in sanctioning rebellion, deposition and transference of allegiance from James II to William and Mary'.[15]

It is, therefore, a historical mistake to base sovereign immunity on a single idea, that of avoiding the king's responsibility. Instead, as with many concepts and conceptions (public–private dichotomy is a paradigmatic example), the English maxim was used by lawyers according to their *political preferences*.

Similar upheavals seem to have permeated American law,[16] which is deemed to have misread English sovereign immunity in many aspects.[17] The application of the doctrine by American courts has been flawed since the

---

[12]   See Gaudemet 2020: 32.
[13]   See eg Fairgrieve 2003: 8.
[14]   See Greenberg 1991. The next paragraph derives freely from Greenberg.
[15]   See ibid: 216–28.
[16]   See Davis 1970: 395; Jackson 2003: 522; Pierce Jr 2002: 1.378.
[17]   See Jackson 2003: 531–2, 542–3; Pfander 1997: 914; Randall 2002: 26–30.

1820s. *Cohens v State of Virginia*,[18] decided in 1821, is considered the first case in which the Supreme Court touched, and denied, sovereign immunity doctrine,[19] although the Court used fickle language and regarded it only as state and not federal immunity.[20] In 1857, when the Supreme Court decided *Beers v Arkansas*, Chief Justice Taney announced that sovereign immunity was 'an established principle of jurisprudence in all civilised nations'.[21] But in 1879, speaking for a unanimous Court, Justice Miller said in *Langford v US*, a takings case, that '[w]e don't understand that either in reference to the government of the US, or of the several States, or of any of their officers, the English maxim has an existence in this country'.[22] Three years later, in *US v Lee* (1882), the Court flung open a paradox by granting that sovereign immunity had 'always been treated as an established doctrine', although acknowledging that there were 'abundant decisions' limiting sovereign immunity.[23]

These inconsistencies in the doctrine of sovereign immunity have remained throughout the twentieth century. Richard Pierce Jr's analysis of the Supreme Court cases in his *Treatise* is revealing:

> Over the last two centuries [...] the scope of potential governmental liability is dependent to some extent on the attitudes of judges and justices toward the doctrine of sovereign immunity. A Justice who believes that sovereign immunity is a good idea, either generally or in a particular context, is likely to adopt a narrow interpretation of a statutory provision that waives sovereign immunity. A Justice with the opposite view is likely to adopt an expansive interpretation of such a waiver.[24]

In a book-length article of 2002, Susan Randall blamed courts, scholars and legislation for what she called to be a history of historical and non-historical mistakes; she studied the *Federalist Papers*, the various documents of the framers, and the early, pre-1820s decisions of the Court and concluded that sovereign immunity was not the framers' intent. According to Randall, Article III of the Constitution itself, in its very first judicial interpretations, constituted

---

[18]   19 US 264 (1821).
[19]   See Jackson 2003: 523, footnote 5; Randall 2002: 31.
[20]   For a historical analysis of *Cohens*, see Randall 2002: 90–1.
[21]   *Beers v Arkansas*, 61 US 527, 529 (1857).
[22]   101 US 341 (1879), at 343.
[23]   106 US 196 (1882), at 250 (citing *US v Clarke*, 33 US 436 (1834); *US v McLemore*, 45 US 286 (1846); *Hill v US*, 50 US 386 (1850); *Nations v Johnson*, 65 US 195 (1960); *The Siren*, 74 US 152 (1868); *The Davis*, 77 US 15 (1869)). Davis (1970: 385) remarked that in *Lee* the Court professed the doctrine 'without judicial discussion of pros and cons'. About *Lee* and for a lengthy analysis of the nineteenth-century cases, see also Jackson 2003: 523–52. See also Randall 2002: 30–61, 85–98.
[24]   Pierce Jr 2002: 1.377. This is an old observation among scholars (see eg Pugh 1953: 477).

the sovereign's consent, both for the individual states and the US, to suit.[25] And '[e]ven cases well into the twentieth century found that Article III in itself constituted a waiver of sovereign immunity'.[26] After scrutinizing the Supreme Court's decisions, Randall also concluded that neither the frequently invoked 'efficiency of the government' nor the 'protection of the treasury' are reasons strong enough to support sovereign immunity.[27]

Others, however, disagree and invoke Alexander Hamilton's *The Federalist* n. 81,[28] as we will see shortly when dealing with the Unmistakability Doctrine. Some advocate that sovereign immunity is acceptable and normatively justifiable only if understood entangled with democracy, thus rejecting an all-or-nothing view of sovereign immunity and arguing, in a confessedly Dworkinian 'constructive' fashion, that the state must enjoy *some* immunity from suit.[29]

We do not need to solve the puzzle. Whatever the content of the sovereign immunity during the past two centuries in US law, the sole fact that scholars have been discussing it and, more importantly, that courts have been applying it (albeit inconsistently) clearly indicates that sovereign immunity's spirit is still in force. In seminal government contracts cases, the tension between 'congruence' and 'exceptionalism' is, in fact, a dispute between state responsibility and sovereign immunity. The stress is evident in *Lynch*, a case mentioned above and to be commented on shortly.

My claim, again, is that the American legal system has taken advantage of the sovereign immunity's tradition and rhetoric to compensate for the compelling pro-individualistic philosophy that reigns in the US. As for government procurement law, the SAD and the Unmistakability Doctrine, I insist, are vehicles used by the government and the courts to infuse a sense of 'public interest' into the public law scenario; functionally, they play the same role of sovereign immunity. Thus, American (government procurement) law needs doctrines like the SAD and the Unmistakability Doctrine to allow sovereign power to act in the name of the general welfare.

Nothing similar happens in France or Brazil, State cultures in which the supremacy of the public interest dominates. On the contrary, in these continental countries, the law needs vehicles that may counterbalance the State power. *Fait du Prince* and *imprévision* are the vehicles to protect contractors. In the

---

25 Randall 2002: 85–92. See also Seife 1996: 989–1032.
26 Ibid.: 92. Randall then exemplifies by citing and commenting upon *Monaco v Mississipi*, 292 US 313 (1934), and *Pennsylvania v Union Gas*, 491 US 1 (1989).
27 See ibid: 96–101.
28 See eg Sisk 2016: 73; Lash 2009: 1601–2. But see Schraub 2017: 6–7 (doubting that Hamilton had a clear definition on sovereign immunity).
29 See Brettschneider & McNamee 2015.

Liberal American legal system, SAD and the Unmistakability Doctrine have –
surreptitiously, if one wishes – the same function that the unwritten principle
of supremacy of the public interest has in the State-driven French and Brazilian
legal systems. I turn now to clarifying this dialectic.

1.1   The Sovereign Acts Doctrine (SAD)

As I stated earlier, SAD 'holds that the Government may not be held contractually liable for acts performed by it in its sovereign capacity'.[30] SAD's practical
importance is evident. Since its first appearance in two nineteenth-century
cases (commented on below), SAD has been, as far as government contract
cases are concerned, the defence most frequently invoked by the government
in courts.[31]

The Court of Claims first proclaimed the doctrine in 1865 in *Deming v US*
and *Jones v US*.[32] In *Deming*, the contractor had entered into two contracts
with the US to furnish daily rations for the Marine Corps throughout the period
1861–82. However, during the performance of the contracts, Congress enacted
two statutes imposing additional duties on some items to be supplied, thus
increasing the costs of the objects the contractor was to provide. Having fully
complied with the contract, the contractor sought money damages alleging that
the new conditions imposed by the US had changed the performance of the
contract. The Court's short rationale deserves full quotation:

> And herein is its fallacy: that it supposes general enactments of Congress are to be
> construed as evasions of his particular contract. This is a grave error. A contract
> between the government and a private party can't be *specially* affected by the enact-
> ment of a *general* law. The statute bears upon it as it bears upon all similar contracts
> between citizens, and affects it in no other way. In form, the claimant brings this
> action against the US for imposing new conditions upon his contract; in fact he
> brings it for exercising their sovereign right of enacting laws. But the government
> entering into a contract, stands not in the attitude of the government exercising its
> sovereign power of providing laws for the welfare of the State. *The US as a contrac-
> tor are not responsible for the US as a lawgiver.* Were this action brought against
> a private citizen, against a body corporate, against a foreign government, it couldn't
> possibly be sustained. In this Court the US can be held to no greater liability than
> other contractor in other Court.[33]

---

[30]   Latham 1975: 30.
[31]   See ibid.
[32]   Respectively, 1 Ct. Cl. 190 (1865) and 1 Ct. Cl. 383 (1865). For a scrutiny of
Deming and *Jones* and their implication for 'exceptionalism' in American government
contracts, see Schwartz 1996: 651–71. See also Morgan 1992: 224.
[33]   1 Ct. Cl. at 190 (emphasis added, except in the cases of *specially* and *general*,
which are in original).

Jones dealt with a similar problem. Two civil engineers contracted with the Commissioner of Indian Affairs to survey some districts described in the treaties between the US and certain Indian tribes. The contractors performed the terms of the contract, and the price was paid in full. However, the contractors alleged that, during the performance, certain 'obstructions and hindrances on the part of the US' rendered their survey more expensive, therefore allowing them to seek money damages. At stake was an executive rather than a legislative act. The Court's rationale in *Jones* was more generous than it had been in *Deming*. I quote the most relevant parts:

> The *two characters which the government possesses as a contractor and as a sovereign* can't be thus fused; *nor can the US while sued in the one character be made liable in damages for their acts done in the other.* Whatever acts the government may do, *be they legislative or executive,* so long as they be *public and general,* can't be deemed specially to alter, modify, obstruct or violate the particular contracts into which it enters with private persons [...] If the enactment of a law imposing duties will enable the claimant to increase the stipulated price of the goods he has sold to a citizen, then it will when the US are defendants, but not otherwise. If the removal of troops from a district liable to invasion will give the claimant damages for unforeseen expenses, when the other party is a corporate body, then it will when the US form the other party, but not otherwise. *This distinction between the public acts and private contracts of the government* – not always strictly insisted on in the earlier days of this Court – frequently misapprehended in public bodies, and constantly lost sight of by suitors who come before us, we now desire to make so broad and distinct that hereafter the two can't be confounded; *and we repeat, as a principle applicable to all cases, that the US as a contractor can't be held liable directly or indirectly for the public acts of the US as a sovereign.*[34]

The Supreme Court gave its imprimatur to SAD in *Horowitz v US* (1925),[35] the first case in which the Court expressly dealt with the subject. In *Horowitz*, the government had contracted to sell silk and ship it within a day or two, but it did not clearly comply with its promise because of an embargo on silk shipments by the US Railroad Administration. The claimant then sought damages for the loss suffered because of the delay. The Supreme Court cited *Deming* and *Jones* but added nothing to them.[36] Since then, SAD has experienced little change in

---

[34]　1 Ct. Cl. at 384–5 (emphasis added). As one can see from the excerpts quoted, in *Deming* the protection covered only executive action; but in *Jones* the Court extended the immunity to the executive acts as well. See Morgan 1992: 233; Schwartz 1996: 665.

[35]　267 US 458 (1925). For the importance of *Horowitz* in American 'exceptionalism', see Schwartz 1996: 671–4; Stack 1955.

[36]　See Schwartz 1996: 671. The Court limited its ruling to the lengthy quotation from *Jones* quoted in the text *supra*, plus the following part of the *Jones'* decision: 'In this court the US appear simply as contractors; and they are to be held liable only within the same limits that any other defendant would be in any other court. Though their sov-

American courts.[37] In short, it is from the language quoted above by the Court of Claims that SAD has evolved.

Scholars have tried to offer more precise guides for interpreting SAD since the second half of the past century. The studies of Daniel Stack, Peter Latham, Richard Speidel, Ronald Morgan, Joshua Schwartz, Michael Graf and Gillian Hadfield are some of the best examples of this effort.[38] As far as both coherence and essential guidelines for future decisions are concerned, Stark's and Latham's articles present a more optimistic view about the boards and courts' rulings,[39] while Morgan's, Schwartz's and Graf's works offer a less keen understanding about the state of the law.[40] But, as I will demonstrate shortly, if one takes as an example the most recent Supreme Court decision in the field, *US v Winstar Corp.* (1996),[41] the latter group's position seems more plausible.

Whatever side one takes, SAD is, as proved by the quotations above, a doctrine phrased in very open-ended words by the Supreme Court, which has not yet provided any clear guidance for the matter. In brief, SAD holds that the government is immune from liability so long as the external act impairing the contract is 'public and general'. It is easy to predict that such a broad standard can accommodate any *political choice*, precisely as sovereign immunity has done. Speaking in the sources' language, the absence of clarity in the formal sources invites material sources to sneak in.

My goal, again, is not to offer a contribution to fill the gap. Instead, I will pay closer attention to the theory of 'government's dual capacity', derived from *Deming*'s and *Jones*'s language quoted above, which holds, briefly, that the government can act as a contractor (government-as-contractor) and as sovereign (government-as-sovereign). If analysed, comparatively, from a continental viewpoint, the theory of dual capacity plays a role functionally

---

ereign acts performed for the general good may work injury to some private contractors, such parties gain nothing by having the US as their defendants.' *Horowitz*, 267 US at 461.

[37]   See Latham 1975: 32; Morgan 1992: 224.

[38]   See Stack 1955; Speidel 1963; Latham 1975; Morgan 1992; Schwartz 1996; Graf 1998. See also Nash & Cibinic 1991; Roe 1997; Madden & Gold 2000. None of this work stopped Hadfield (1999: 468) stating that 'government's liability for breach of contract is a topic that has received surprisingly little attention in the legal literature'.

[39]   See Stack 1955 (venturing to indicate, from the analysis of the thirty-year case law after *Horowitz*, a direction in which the doctrine should develop); Latham (1975: 34) ('The courts and Boards of Contract Appeals have developed the sovereign act doctrine to the point where it's now possible with substantial certainty to identify those acts which are sovereign in nature and to distinguish them from those which are not').

[40]   Morgan (1992: 273) undertook research on boards' and courts' decisions and found a great deal of inconsistency, insinuating that 'apparent chaos' has reigned in the field. I treat Schwartz's ideas later in the text.

[41]   518 US 839 (1996).

equivalent to the role played by the public–private law dichotomy for civilians, or, more specifically, by the old and dead dichotomy *actes d'autorité* et *actes de gestion* in the nineteenth-century French administrative law as a criterium for determining which jurisdiction should take the case, hence being crucial to establishing the applicable legal regime. The theory of dual capacity will also help me to illustrate the claim I made in Chapter 3 about the less systematic, more reactive, empirical character of US law. Remember that my focus was on the purposes a legal system wants to achieve and the consequence of less systematic thought in the American 'circumstantial exceptionalism'. Let me explain.

As we have seen, French and Brazilian public contract laws are structured on the public–private law dichotomy, which permits classifying contracts formed by the State in '*contrats administratifs*' (governed by public norms) and '*contrats privés de l'Administration*' (governed by private norms), and a set of principles derived from that division. American law of government procurement is not structured in this way. The 'theory' of dual capacity, however, compensates, in a less systematic, reactive mode, for the absence of the civilian structural dichotomy: as a contractor, the government is as responsible for breach as any other private party is; as a sovereign, however, the government is not responsible for the breach.

This Janus-faced figure of state has strong rhetorical force. On the one hand, it permits the Liberal credo to go free from criticism, since it bluntly affirms that government-as-contractor is equivalent to a private party; the state is thus not held 'superior' (in the 'continental' sense), but is *equal* to a private party and has no privileges. But on the other hand, the theory also permits the government to fulfil its public functions free from liability since it can act like a sovereign. This mechanism is very telling from a comparative law viewpoint. The clear scope of the theory of dual capacity is to free the government from liability for breach in cases where public welfare requires a government action (a sovereign act) in the name of the public interest. For example, in some situations during government contracts' performance, the government must act in the name of general purposes. The theory of dual capacity allows this action.[42] And it does so within a system that has never held a public–private law dichotomy, nor constructed a structural theory of *contrats administratif* versus *contrat privé de l'Administration*, as the French *publicistes* did, followed by Brazilian law.

---

[42] See Schwartz 1997: 558.

The dual capacity theory would be dismissible if the public–private law dichotomy were accepted in the US.[43] However, the *summa divisio* is perceived by the American *mentalité* as too continental, too French, too absolutist. It thus became necessary to create other mechanisms to serve as vehicles for sovereign (or public) purposes in the US. The ingenious notion of 'dual capacity' performs this function as an essential part of the SAD.

Again, theories in law are never value-free; they have purposes and, I repeat, perform normative functions. Moreover, the existence of a theory can be and frequently is determined by a practical necessity created by a lack of mechanisms to cope with a specific problem. In a comparative law light, what decided the creation of the SAD and its dual-capacity component was the statelessness of American society, its mistrust in governmental power, its strong individualism, and, mainly, the absence of a principle such as the supremacy of the public interest, which, in France and Brazil, was the result of the public–private law dichotomy.

In summary, in France and Brazil, as already suggested, the tension between government-as-contractor and government-as-sovereign is not solved by the theory of 'dual capacity', but in terms of the public–private law dichotomy: the *contrats administratifs*, governed by public law norms, would be equivalent to government-as-sovereign, while the *contrats privés de l'Administration*, governed by private law norms, would be equivalent to government-as-contractor. The structure is the following: in the *contrats administratifs*, the basic idea is that the sovereign, that is, the State (*l'Administration*), acts to protect and enhance the public interest, and there is a presumption that this interest is superior to individual interests. The Stateness of the culture is patent. Because American culture upholds the opposing philosophy, it was necessary to create 'dual capacity' to convey 'sovereign', public ideas and to free government from liability. The second, essential step was to say that whenever the government act is 'public and general', it can be considered a 'sovereign act', and therefore 'immune' from responsibility.

1.2   The Unmistakability Doctrine

The other doctrine that encompasses sovereign immunity's spirit and counterbalances 'Americanism' is the Unmistakability Doctrine, which some see as

---

[43]   Hadfield (1999: 470) apparently reaches the same conclusion: 'Recognizing that the law of government contract is and should be distinct form the private law of contract – indeed, that it's an instance of public, not private, law – resolves the apparent conflict between government-as-contractor and government-as-sovereign.'

a variation of SAD.[44] Like SAD, the origin of the Unmistakability Doctrine can be found, according to Graf, in the nineteenth-century federal cases 'in which courts grappled with the state's authority to abrogate existing contractual obligations entered into by previous state legislatures'.[45]

Vested rights issues then appeared. Briefly, the history of protecting vested rights in public contract cases begins in *Fletcher v Peck* (1810). The Contract Clause of the US Constitution,[46] originally drafted to protect private contracts, was extended to prohibit states from eliminating vested rights arising out of public contracts.[47] However, courts frequently refrained from taking this Liberal position in many subsequent decisions, despite Justice Marshall's dissenting opinions in *New Jersey v Wilson* (1812),[48] *Sturges v Crowninshield* (1919),[49] *Trustees of Dartmouth College v Woodward* (1819)[50] and *Ogden v Saunders* (1827).[51] In all these cases, had the Supreme Court adopted Justice Marshall's literal and Liberal interpretation of the contract clause, the states' ability to pass any legislation affecting economic interests eventually embodied in contracts would have been fettered.[52]

All these cases, however, referred to state-member rather than federal contracts. The first seeds of the Unmistakability Doctrine in federal public contracts were planted, according to Graf,[53] in *Union Pacific Rail Road Co. v US* (1878).[54] The issue was whether a statute which amended some terms of federal subsidy bonds and required that a private railroad corporation (created for public purposes and whose property was devoted mainly to public uses) set aside a portion of its income as a sinking fund to meet mortgage debts when they matured would be depriving the company of its property without due process of law, or if it would be improperly interfering with the company's vested rights. Despite having stated that '[t]he US are as much bound by their

---

[44]   See Schwartz 1996: 683–97. But see Graf 1998 (considering the SAD and the Unmistakability Doctrine as theories different in scope and purpose, to be applied in different situations: the SAD would be applicable to the market participant model of contract, while the Unmistakability Doctrine would be applicable to the quasi-regulatory model).

[45]   Graf 1998: 207.

[46]   US Constitution, art. I, § 10, cl 1 ('No State shall [...] pass any [...] Law impairing the Obligation of Contracts').

[47]   See Zigler 1984: 1449–51; Graf 1998: 207.

[48]   11 US (7 Cranch) 164 (1812).

[49]   17 US (4 Wheat) 122 (1819).

[50]   17 US (4 Wheat) 518 (1819).

[51]   25 US (12 Wheat) 213 (1927). I borrowed all examples from Zigler 1984: 1451.

[52]   See Zigler ibid.

[53]   See Graf 1998: 208.

[54]   *Union Pacific Rail Road Co. v US*, 99 US 700 (1878).

contracts as are individuals', the Supreme Court decided that Congress had reserved its power to amend the charter. The Court continued:

> If they repudiate their obligations, it's as much repudiation, with all the wrong and reproach that term implies, as it would be if the repudiator had been a State or a municipality or a citizen. No change can be made in the title created by the grant of the lands, or in the contract for the subsidy bonds, without the consent of the corporation. All this is indisputable.

However, this tribute to 'congruence' didn't impede the Court from reaching an 'exceptionalist' outcome. The Court held that contract clauses did not apply to the federal government and that it was 'unnecessary to decide what power Congress would have had over the charter if the right of amendment had not been reserved; for, as we think, that reservation has been made'.[55] *Union Pacific*, however, dealt with the Unmistakability Doctrine only indirectly, for the Court didn't expressly enunciate the government's immunity.

The official birth of the Unmistakability Doctrine dates back to 1982, when the Supreme Court decided the already mentioned *Merrion v Jicarilla Apache Tribe*.[56] In *Merrion*, the petitioners were 21 non-Indian lessees who, under leases granted them under the auspices of the Secretary of the Interior, produced oil and gas from within Jicarilla Apache's reservation. The lessees brought two suits, consolidated for trial, against the Jicarilla Apache Tribe, challenging the authority of the tribe to impose a severance tax on 'any oil and natural gas severed, saved and removed from Tribal lands'.[57] The Court upheld the authority of the tribe by reasoning that the tribe's sovereignty could be equated to the sovereignty of a city, state or federal sphere, in which an analogous situation would not cause them to lose their sovereign tax power merely because they supposedly failed to reserve this power expressly in a commercial agreement.[58] The Court then explicitly proclaimed the Unmistakability Doctrine: '[w]ithout regard to its source', the Court stated, 'sovereign power, even when unexercised, is an enduring presence that governs all contracts subject to the sovereign's jurisdiction and will remain intact unless surrendered in unmistakable terms'.[59]

However, as a 'doctrine', Unmistakability was more fully articulated in *POSSE*, unanimously decided by the Supreme Court in 1986.[60] In *POSSE*, the Court held that Congressional amendments to the Social Security Act

---

[55] All case quotations are from *Union Pacific* 99 US at 719–20.
[56] 455 US 130 (1982). See also Graf 1998: 209.
[57] *Merrion*, 455 US at 133.
[58] See ibid: 148. See also Graf 1998: 209; Schwartz 1996: 687.
[59] *Merrion*, 455 US at 148.
[60] 477 US 41 (1986).

prohibiting states' withdrawal of state and local government employees from participation in the system were legal, even though Congress had previously permitted the very withdrawal with two years' notice. Under the previous rule, states were afforded an option, which was to be exercised via an agreement between federal and state government, to enrol their employees in the system, withdrawal being permitted with previous notice. However, in prohibiting withdrawal, Congress's new statute specified that the rule would apply retroactively. The Court's complete statement is as follows:

> While the Federal Government, as sovereign, has the power to enter contracts that confer vested rights, and the concomitant duty to honor those rights, see *Perry v. US*, 294 U.S. 330, 350-354 (1935); *Lynch v. US*, 292 U.S. 571 (1934), we have declined in the context of commercial contracts to find that a 'sovereign forever waives the right to exercise one of its sovereign powers *unless it expressly reserves the right to exercise that power* in' the contract. *Merrion Jicarilla Apache Tribe*, 455 U.S. 130, 148 (1982). Rather, we have emphasised that '[w]ithout regard to its source, *sovereign power, even when unexercised, is an enduring presence that governs all contracts subject to the sovereign's jurisdiction, and will remain intact unless surrendered in unmistakable terms*'. *Ibid.* Therefore, contractual arrangements, including those to which a sovereign itself is party, 'remain subject to subsequent legislation' by the sovereign. *Id.* at 147.[61]

The same tension between private rights and sovereign state power remains. Despite having reached an 'exceptionalist' outcome, the Court has also expressly registered the congruence philosophy of honouring 'vested rights'. But no clear guidance is provided to say what 'capacity' (if sovereign or proprietary) should prevail, or what pole of the spectrum should be emphasized, and how it should so be. This *lack of guidance* is ultimately the hallmark of sovereign acts defences in American law.

The Court in *POSSE* invoked two cases that deserve mentioning: *Lynch v US*[62] and *Perry v US*.[63] *Lynch* and *Perry* are essential for my comparative analysis for several reasons. First, they expressly give voice to the idea of Unmistakability (hence in contrast with the 'congruence' philosophy) and use a sweeping pro-government language that fuels the rhetoric of 'exceptionalism', which causes a fundamental paradox. But *Lynch* and *Perry* help set the spectrum within which American law deals with the central problem of government contracts, although the cases offer, again and remarkably, no parameters whatsoever to establish what pole should prevail: the Court's rhetoric is broad enough to accommodate congruence *and* exceptionalism.

---

[61] 477 US at 52 (emphasis added).
[62] 292 US 571 (1934).
[63] 294 US 330 (1935).

Nevertheless, by posing the questions that the Court should answer, *Lynch* and *Perry* suggested, first, some limits for government immunity defences, and second, that some degree of leeway for sovereign acts is desirable.

As I will show later, *Lynch* and *Perry* were the leading cases that supported the plaintiffs' claims in *Winstar*,[64] when the Court rejected the government's theses based on SAD and the Unmistakability Doctrine, the two variations of sovereign immunity. In this sense, *Lynch* and *Perry* are fine examples of what I have been suggesting to be the American Liberal philosophy; in this sense, they are more 'naturally' American than are, for instance, *Jones*, *Deming* and *Horowitz*. Hence, from a comparative law perspective, *Lynch* and *Perry*, alongside *Winstar*, are the best available formal sources of the American Liberal *mentalité*. My point is that, in the absence of clearer guidance by the Court about the philosophy that should prevail, *Lynch* and *Perry*, together with *Winstar*, are consequences of 'Americanism'. To speak the language of the sources proposed in this book, material sources of Americanism infuse the content of formal, dogmatic sources – Court decisions, in this case.

Briefly, in *Lynch,* the plaintiffs asked for payment of insurance policies issued during the First World War under the War Risk Insurance Act of 1917.[65] However, in 1933 Congress enacted the Economy Act, which expressly repealed all laws granting or pertaining to yearly renewable term insurance. As presented by the Court, the issue was whether War Risk policies were 'gratuities', which could then 'be redistributed or withdrawn at any time in the discretion of Congress', or 'property', therefore able to 'create vested rights'.[66] The Court unanimously held that War Risk policies, 'being contracts', were property. The Court added: '*Valid contracts are property, whether the obligor be a private individual, a municipality, a state, or the US*. Rights against the US arising out of a contract with it are protected by the Fifth Amendment.' Then the Court phrased the congruence philosophy: 'When the US enters into contract relations, *its rights and duties therein are governed generally by the law applicable to contracts between private individuals*.'[67] And the Court emphasized soon after:

> To abrogate contracts, in the attempt to lessen government expenditure, would be not the practice of economy, but an act of repudiation. 'The US are as much bound by their contracts as are individuals. If they repudiate their obligations, it's as much

---

[64]   See Schwartz 1996: 637, 674. In *Winstar,* the most important defence presented by the government was the Unmistakability Doctrine, and not SAD. See Schwartz 1997: 487.

[65]   See *Lynch*, 292 US at 572.

[66]   See *Lynch*, 292 US at 576–7.

[67]   *Lynch*, 292 US at 579 (citations omitted) (emphasis added).

repudiation, with all the wrong and reproach that term implies, as it would be if the repudiator had been a State or a municipality or a citizen'.[68]

Classification comes in here, and *Lynch* is a revealing example of its importance and its epistemological function, coupled with the productive function of legal theories.

Interestingly, this 'strong version of congruence'[69] in *Lynch* was nevertheless infused with impressive 'exceptionalist' verbiage. First, the Court stated that '[c]ontracts between individuals or corporations are impaired within the meaning of the Constitution (art. 1, sec. 10, cl. 1) whenever the right to enforce them by legal process is taken away or materially lessened. A different rule prevails in respect to contracts of sovereigns'.[70] Then the Court invoked, remarkably, Alexander Hamilton in *The Federalist* 81: 'The contracts between a Nation and an individual are only binding on the conscience of the sovereign and have no pretensions to compulsive force. They confer no right of action independent of the sovereign will.'[71]

It is noteworthy that Hamilton's words in *The Federalist* 81 are found in the paragraph that begins by invoking sovereign immunity, which reads: 'It's inherent in the nature of sovereignty, not to be amenable to the suit of an individual *without its consent*.'[72] Together with James Madison's comments in the Virginia ratification debates and John Marshall's statements in those debates, these words have been *the* most crucial source invoked by the Supreme Court to uphold sovereign immunity since the 1820s. No wonder that scholars who are against sovereign immunity have not found any support for the doctrine they criticize in the Federalist Papers.[73] But all the same, the Court in *Lynch* decided the case in favour of congruence philosophy, while *in dicta* the Court paid tribute to the rhetoric of sovereign immunity.

Justice Brandeis's verbiage in *Lynch*, speaking for a unanimous Court, is the clearest example of the exceptionalist philosophy: 'The rule that the US may not be sued without its consent is all-embracing.' Finally, the Court completed its peroration:

> Although consent to sue was thus given when the policy issued, *Congress retained power to withdraw the consent at any time.* For consent to sue the US is a *privilege*

---

[68]   292 US at 580 (citation omitted).
[69]   Schwartz 1996: 677.
[70]   *Lynch*, 292 US at 580.
[71]   *Lynch*, 292 US at 580. See *The Federalist* n. 81 (2008 [1787–8]: 399).
[72]   *The Federalist* ibid.
[73]   See Randall 2002: 10–13, 71. Randall criticizes the Court's assessment of the founding generation's intent (at 14–26, 30–61, 70–85). For a recent criticism of sovereign immunity based on *The Federalist* n. 81, see Schraub 2017: 6–7.

accorded, not the grant of a property right protected by the Fifth Amendment. *The consent may be withdrawn*, although given after much deliberation and for a pecuniary consideration. *The sovereign's immunity from suit exists whatever the character of the proceeding or the source of the right sought to be enforced.* It applies alike to causes of action arising under acts of Congress, and to those arising from some violation of rights conferred upon the citizen by the Constitution [...] *For immunity from suit's an attribute of sovereignty which may not be bartered away.*[74]

Perry is a knotty case, about which 'most lawyers know nothing' – a case comparable to *Marbury v Madison* for New Deal historians, for it 'headed off a showdown with the Executive Branch by ruling that the bondholders were not entitled to damages even though their rights were violated'.[75] So, the opinion's dicta is important to us because the ruling left plaintiffs uncompensated, in a clear demonstration of the Court's pragmatism.

In *Perry*, the issue was whether Congress could abrogate norms that established the so-called gold clauses,[76] which existed in previous government obligations providing that the bonds acquired by the plaintiffs would be in the future paid 'in US gold coin of the present standard of value'.[77] However, a subsequent Congressional Joint Resolution provided that the 'gold clauses' were 'against public policy', the payment instead being made in 'coin or currency which at the time of payment is legal tender'.

The Court, which had earlier upheld Congress' power to abolish the gold clauses in *Norman v Baltimore & Ohio R.R.*, established an additional limit in *Perry* to the government's authority to impair its contracts and spread out its congruence view once again:

> There's a clear distinction between the power of the Congress to control or interdict the contracts of private parties when they interfere with the exercise of its constitutional authority and the power of the Congress to alter or repudiate the substance of its own engagements when it has borrowed money under the authority which the Constitution confers [...] To say that the Congress may withdraw or ignore that pledge is to assume that the Constitution contemplates a vain promise; a pledge having no other sanction than the pleasure and convenience of the pledgor. This Court has given no sanction to such a conception of the obligations of our government.

---

[74] *Lynch*, 292 U.S. at 580, 582 (citations omitted).
[75] Magliocca 2012: 1246. In short, *Perry*'s opinion affirmed the plaintiffs' right to recovery, but 'when opinion turned to damages, though, *Perry* did an about-face and held that the bondholders were entitled to nothing' (ibid: 1270).
[76] For two thoughtful analyses of *Perry* and the gold clauses cases, see Dawson 1935 (I thank Lima Lopes for this source); Hart Jr 1935.
[77] All quotations of *Perry* are to be found *in Perry*, 294 US at 347–53 (citations omitted).

The Court continued in its congruence philosophy: 'When the US, with con-stitutional authority, makes contracts, *it has rights and incurs responsibilities similar to those of individuals who are parties to such instruments*'. However, the Court also alluded to sovereign immunity by adding that '[t]here is no difference […] *except that the US can't be sued without its consent*'. Finally, facing the (exceptionalist) argument that the government could not, by con-tract, restrict its sovereign power, the Court stated that 'the right to make binding obligations is a competence attaching to sovereignty'.

That was all that the Court said about SAD and the Unmistakability Doctrine until 1996.

Merrion, POSSE, Lynch and *Perry* illustrate a battle between public law and private law values that revealed the traditions of congruence and exceptionalism. There is consensus among scholars that neither SAD nor the Unmistakability Doctrine are well-conceived and explained. In his seminal 1996 article *Liability for Sovereign Acts*, Joshua Schwartz labelled SAD a 'poorly delineated' doctrine, thus formulating the congruence–exceptionalism spectrum and proposing a set of standards to help the interpreter to solve the problem.[78] However, in *Winstar*, the case in which the Supreme Court could have provided more explicit guidance, it failed to do so, and the situation remains unclear at best.

1.3　*US v Winstar Corp.* (1996) and its Importance for Comparative Law

US v Winstar Corp., a regulatory-contract case, was 'the leading modern case on the scope of the sovereign acts and unmistakability doctrines'.[79] It was only the second time that SAD had reached the Supreme Court,[80] and apparently the fourth time that the Court expressly referred to the Unmistakability Doctrine.[81]

In *Winstar*, briefly, financial institutions sued the US, asserting breach of contract and constitutional claims arising from Congress's enactment of the Financial Institutions Reform, Recovery, and Enforcement Act of 1989 (FIRREA). FIRREA was designed to overcome a thrift crisis that began in the late 1970s. By imposing stricter capital requirements on thrifts, FIRREA

---

[78]　See Schwartz 1996: 691–702. In the post-*Winstar* era, Graf (1998: 255–76) pro-posed a different set of principles to tackle the issue. Schwartz criticized *Winstar* in 1997 and later commented on its ambiguous points (2000).

[79]　Schwartz 2022: 175.

[80]　See Nash & Cibinic 1996.

[81]　Besides *Merrion* and *POSSE*, the Court expressly addressed the Unmistakability Doctrine in *US v Cherokee Nation of Oklahoma*, 480 US 700 (1987). See Graf 1998: 211–12.

encouraged healthy financial institutions to take over failing thrifts. However, in an earlier response to a savings and loans crisis, where there were previous agreements between the Federal Home Loan Bank Board and the Federal Savings and Loan Insurance Corporations, some thrift institutions, such as Winstar Corp, had permitted these institutions to make use of more favourable accounting techniques to rescue failing thrifts. FIRREA considerably limited the use of these advantageous accounting mechanisms upon which the viability of the previous takeover transaction depended, thus impairing the thrift institutions. Plaintiffs then claimed that the application of the new requirements of FIRREA constituted a breach of the agreements they had entered into with the federal regulators.[82]

As David Toscano observed, 'the conflict between legislative prerogative and individual rights is not unique to the situation in which the rights infringed upon by legislation arise from government contracts: all legislation potentially generates tension between the command of the majority and the rights of individuals'.[83] That was the case in *Winstar*, which represented, 'in terms of the fundamental enforceability of government contract commitments [...] clearly the most important decision since the 1930s decisions'.[84]

On the eve of the Supreme Court's decision in *Winstar*, Schwartz wrote that the Court would have to 'apply and clarify a longstanding but poorly delineated principle known as the sovereign acts doctrine'.[85] The warning was based on the decisions taken in the previously cited cases (mainly *Jones*, *Deming*, *Horowitz*, *Lynch*, *Perry*, *Merrion* and *POSSE*), which offered, as demonstrated, only losing and conflicting jargon about state liability for sovereign acts. However, commentators said that the Supreme Court provided no clear guidance in *Winstar after the case was decided*.[86] Instead, the Court rejected both the SAD and the Unmistakability Doctrine as defenses, and it did so in a highly divided, somewhat confusing decision, having presented flawed arguments.

There are many thoughtful analyses and criticisms of *Winstar* by American scholars, which cannot all be delineated here.[87] However, for the comparatist,

---

[82]   For a resume of the facts in *Winstar*, see Schwartz 1997: 484–5; Graf 1998: 198–200; Wimberly & Amerling 1996: 127. For a detailed analysis of the purposes of government's policy toward the thrift industry in the 1980s, see Toscano 1992: 427–47.

[83]   Toscano 1992: 450.

[84]   Stouck & Lipson 1996: 315.

[85]   Schwartz 1996: 634; also at 637–8, 650–1, 697–702; Schwartz 2004: 2.

[86]   See eg Graf 1998; Schwartz 1997; 2000; 2021; Wimberly & Amerling 1996: 128; Sisk 2016: 327–31.

[87]   For a careful analysis of the Justices' opinions in *Winstar*, see Schwartz 1997; Graf 1998: 200–6. For a thoughtful criticism about the private law philosophy adopted in the case as far as the damages granted are concerned, see Hadfield 1999. For a criti-

Winstar is very telling for several reasons. First, *Winstar* mentions virtually all the important cases decided theretofore by courts about the government defences in state liability cases, thus offering a good sample of the histories of both SAD and the Unmistakability Doctrine. In this aspect, *Winstar* reflects the more 'reactive' feature of the common law reasoning. Second, most opinions in *Winstar*, mainly the plurality opinion, although somehow incoherent, indicate that private law values are predominant in American society and public contract law philosophy. Material sources are, again, governing the meaning of formal sources. Third, the arguments deployed by various Justices demonstrate both how pragmatic and how anti-theoretical American government contract law is. Fourth, the decision illustrates how little impact a view favouring the 'supremacy of the public interest' would have in court. Finally, and overall, the case offers a paradigmatic reference for a comparative law perspective, as far as the epistemological roots of exceptionalism are concerned.[88]

I will tackle these points interchangeably and exaggerate the importance of some passages of the decision and their implications to emphasize this comparative perspective. My intention, I repeat, is not to suggest any new formula to solve the problem of state liability in public contracts cases of any jurisdiction. The basic idea behind the following analysis is twofold: first, I wish to highlight the hidden reasons why the Court made the statements it did, to be highlighted shortly; second, I intend to discover the questions in response to which the statements were made. 'One of the more fertile insights of modern hermeneutics', wrote Gadamer, 'is that every statement has to be seen as a response to a question and that the only way to understand a statement is to get hold of the question to which the statement is an answer'.[89]

The first remark goes to the core of American exceptionalism. Facing a hallmark opportunity to say which 'philosophy' government contract law should *mainly* follow, the plurality opinion in *Winstar* seems to have indicated

---

cism of the potential problems created by the Court concerning future decisions on the liquidation of damages, to be solved by the lower courts, see Citron 2002. For a criticism of the confusion made by Justices in *Winstar* as far as the relationship between the SAD and the Unmistakability Doctrine are concerned, see Graf 1998: 206–38.

[88]   Justice Souter's plurality opinion commenced by clearly indicating that the Court was aware of the broader, important issue it would be dealing with: 'We took this case', he wrote, 'to consider the extent to which special rules, not generally applicable to private contracts, govern enforcement of the governmental contracts at issue'. *Winstar*, 518 US at 860 (Opinion of Souter J). Justice Souter then continues to say that the Court would address four defences presented by the government, among them the unmistakability doctrine of *POSSE* and the SAD of *Horowitz*.

[89]   Gadamer 2001b: 106.

that congruence, not exceptionalism, is the master.[90] Thus, according to the Supreme Court, private law philosophy must prevail *even in public contracts*: 'An even more serious objection', wrote Justice Souter, invoking the authority of *Lynch*,

> is that allowing the Government to avoid contractual liability *merely* by passing any 'regulatory statute' would flout the *general principle* that, '[w]hen the US enters into contract relations, its rights and duties therein are governed generally by the law applicable to contracts between private individuals'.[91]

And after that, remarkably enough, even though the Court has also recognized that government contracts are somehow unique, the plurality opinion emphasized the already examined congruence rhetoric offered by *Lynch* and *Perry*, while the Court could have used the same Janus-faced character of *Lynch* and *Perry* (letting aside *Horowitz*, an 'exceptionalist' case *par excellence*) to emphasize the opposite 'tradition' of exceptionalism.

This 'congruence paradigm'[92] reveals epistemological assumptions that unmask the material sources of law, the historical American Liberal option for private law values. *Winstar* confirms the vision deployed by Coke, Dicey, Pound – the most genuine examples of the Anglo-American anti-collectivist philosophy – an idea that was adopted by Shealey and Donnelly, who dealt with government contracts in the US in the 1910s–1930s (mentioned in Chapter 4), and is retained by most American scholars nowadays. Two lawyers resumed the ethos by writing that *Winstar* 'ultimately stands as a powerful reaffirmation of the *sanctity* of federal contract commitments and of the fundamental principle that *private contract law rules apply to public contracts as well*, even where the public contracts involve regulatory matters'.[93] In this vein, *Winstar* genuinely represents the spirit of the common law.

Alongside *Lynch* and *Perry*, Justice Breyer's concurring opinion quoted two nineteenth-century cases that deployed the same congruence rhetoric. '*The US*

---

[90]   I wrote 'seems to' in the wake of Schwartz 1997: 491 ('caution is warranted before concluding that *Winstar* indeed represents the triumph of the congruence ideal in government contracts'). See also Schwartz 2004: 2, footnote 3. The dissenting opinion clearly stated that the principal opinion 'drastically reduces the scope of the unmistakability doctrine, shrouding the residue with clouds of uncertainty, and it limits the sovereign acts doctrine so that it will have virtually no future application'. *Winstar*, 518 US at 924 (Rehnquist CJ dissenting).

[91]   *Winstar*, 518 US at 895 (quoting *Lynch v US*, 292 US at 579) (Opinion of Souter J) (emphasis added). Schwartz 1997: 491 (the plurality opinion 'was dominated in most respects by the congruence ideal').

[92]   Schwartz 1997: 493.

[93]   Stouck & Lipson 1996: 316 (emphasis added).

are as much bound by their contracts as are individuals. If they repudiate their obligations, it's as much repudiation, with all the wrong and reproach that term implies, as it would be if the repudiator had been a State or a municipality or a citizen',[94] the Court had said in the 1870s. In this sense, *Winstar* is only the revival of the same ideal. One of the 1870s cases quoted by Justice Breyer was the *Sinking Fund Cases* mentioned previously. As the plurality opinion could have done when it preferred the 'congruence' ideal of *Lynch* and *Perry* to the 'exceptionalist' ideal, and since the law was unclear at that point, Justice Souter could well have *chosen* – I take it as a positivist – the 'exceptionalist' rhetoric from the *Sinking Fund Cases*, in which the Unmistakability Doctrine and not the sweeping congruence language was consecrated.

Moreover, in a comparative law light, *Winstar* also implicitly reveals there is no room for speaking of or using any language similar to 'supremacy of the public interest' in the American mind. This principle – which came about, as I have shown, in the wake of the public–private law dichotomy and State societies – was permanently repealed by the common law jurisprudence. The philosophy of a transcendent, Rousseauian public interest would be invoked in the French or Brazilian systems, as has long been the case, to support the government's position. However, in the US this rhetoric simply does not fly, not only for the reasons already presented but also because a different conception of public interest dominates.

If words are slogans, the slogan of a superior public interest does not fit in the US. Recall Professor Schwartz's reaction to my provocative words mentioned at the beginning of this book (Schwartz himself is not an enthusiast of a sweeping congruence philosophy). A stateless society like the American one would not argue in favour of the government's immunity to liability by deploying an argument voiced in a language that runs against the society's Liberal nature, the American anti-abstract frame of mind, its more concrete way of thinking. Put differently, Americanism doesn't understand an argument based on the metaphysical, Rousseauian supremacy of the public principle.

Hence, the argument used by the government in *Winstar* should be, as it was, attached to another common law *tradition*, that of sovereign immunity – or of its functional equivalents, like the SAD and the Unmistakability Doctrine – which, although highly criticized and frequently misunderstood, has had some force in American courts. In other words, the only *tool* at the government's hand in *Winstar* was the citation of cases that invoked, directly or not,

---

[94] *Winstar*, 518 US at 912 (Breyer J concurring) (quoting *Sinking Fund Cases*, 99 US 700, 719, 25 L.Ed. 496 (1879); and *US v Klein*, 13 Wall. 128, 144, 20 L.Ed. 519 (1872)).

the still alive doctrine of sovereign immunity.[95] Speaking in comparative law terms, the government in *Winstar* had to circumvent the (very French) rhetoric of supremacy of the public interest, which triggers a general, collectivist, stateness ideal, to defend (the French would easily say), ironically, the very public interest, but differently (and, for Americans, correctly) understood.

By contrast, in France and Brazil the public interest argument has been unabashedly used by State, courts and jurists to allow State action that would otherwise be deemed as infringing individual rights. Societies that have historically accepted the State as *the* entity that should conduct the collectivity to the public good are much more willing to argue that the State acts 'naturally' for the sake of the superior public interest.

It is not that the government did not invoke the alleged 'public purpose' of FIRREA to escape from liability in *Winstar*. It surely did. One can read the language of public interest in the government's brief:

> Contracts entered into by government regulators with private parties promising specific regulatory treatment in the future may harmfully limit the ability of government to act to serve the *public interest*. The unmistakability doctrine protects against that danger [...] The unmistakability doctrine serves important public purposes. Contracts in which the government promises not to exercise its future regulatory authority in certain ways constitute a direct impairment of the government's ability to serve the *public interest*, should regulation of the sort prohibited by the contract become necessary or advisable at a later time.[96]

But the language employed in defence of the public interest is rather coy and sceptical. It may reflect a consciousness of the improbable success that this rhetoric would have in Court. 'Such scepticism is not surprising', wrote Schwartz before *Winstar* was decided, 'for a public interest criterion is subject to strong objections based both on political theory and on assessment of the institutional capabilities of courts'.[97]

A pause is again in order here. Schwartz's reasoning reveals the author's common law *mentalité*. In support of his position regarding the 'public interest criterion', the author cites in a footnote various works that advocate for a much more *pragmatic* view of the 'public interest', related either to interest groups' positions or (usually utilitarian) economic theories. This viewpoint about the public interest is what I believe to be at the deepest level of a comparative law analysis of public contracts (and many other public law subjects). As we will

---

[95]   For the arguments of the government in *Winstar*, see Brief of Petitioners, *US v Winstar Corp.*, 518 U.S. 839 (1996), 1996 WL 99716 **16–46 (1 March 1996).

[96]   See Brief of Petitioners, *US v Winstar Corp.*, 518 US 839 (1996), 1996 WL 99716 **11, 18 (1 March 1996) (emphasis added).

[97]   Schwartz 1996: 668.

see shortly, America's conception of public interest differs from the French idea of *intérêt général*, which founds the idea of *le droit public*. Despite Schwartz's more collective view of public contracts, he cannot escape from his common law frame of mind; he doesn't operate with the French conception of the *intérêt général*. The problem always lies in the assumptions.

We find ourselves – *voilà* – at the tectonic-plate zone of this comparative research, well below the surface: in *Winstar* the government's counsellors operated, perhaps unconsciously, with a *utilitarian conception* of the public interest, the 'only' conception understandable by American courts, the 'default' conception at judges' disposal. This conception favours competition and the free market, not a voluntarist, transcendental, Rousseauian interest of the State. Thus, Americans speak to the spirits of David Hume, Adam Smith and Jeremy Bentham, not to Jean-Jacques Rousseau.[98] I will return shortly to this central point.

For now, it must be remembered that the American reluctance to use public interest language to justify government actions only means that this specific language is strange to the American *mentalité*. It has never impeded the government from using other lines of thought to free itself from paying damages when allegedly acting 'in the public interest'. What the government has done in these, frequent, situations is to invoke theories, such as the SAD and the Unmistakability Doctrine, that *play the same role* played by the French and Brazilian voluntarist, transcendent public interest. In *Winstar*, these theories were unsuccessful. Yet, their *function* was ultimately the same.

In terms of the epistemology of public liability, one of the significant differences between a stateless culture and a State culture is this: while the latter departs from the assumption that the public interest is palpable and presumably legitimate and superior *because* the action emanates from the State, the former departs from the belief that the state is as responsible as a private party in breaking contract rules unless a specific rule or principle establishes otherwise.

The second comparative law remark highlights the importance of how the plurality opinion framed the problem of the liability for sovereign acts. The language used by the Court embodied a set of common law individualistic principles that would necessarily lead to a 'congruence' outcome. In the wake of the option favouring a private law philosophy and imbibed with the individualist ethos, the plurality emphasized the *promissory character* of the previous agreements between the financial institutions and the federal agencies.[99] The line of thought became theretofore syllogistic, and the importance of classification re-emerged.

---

[98] See Rangeon 1986: 200–7.
[99] See *Winstar*, 518 US at 868–9 (Opinion of Souter J).

The syllogism applied in *Winstar* was apparent. If, according to the spirit of the common law, the state is to be submitted to the same rules that guide private individuals, then a state promise is equivalent to a private promise. 'We read this [government's] promise', wrote J. Souter, 'as the law of contracts has always treated promises to provide something beyond the promisor's absolute control, that is, as a promise to ensure the promisee against loss arising from the promised condition's nonoccurrence'.[100] A revealing quotation from Holmes comes into plurality's opinion: 'Holmes's example is famous: "[i]n the case of a binding promise that it shall rain tomorrow, the immediate legal effect of what the promisor does is, that he takes the risk of the event, within certain defined limits, as between himself and the promise".'[101]

The congruence-rhetorical apparatus used by the Supreme Court should not be surprising. It is nevertheless remarkable that the 'Holmesian' congruence justification doesn't directly tackle the critical issue of whether special reasons exist for treating a government's promise differently from a private promise. Schwartz noted that the invocation of Holmes's analysis 'ultimately *circumvents* the operation of most of the Government's exceptionalist defenses'; when the Court *opted* for the congruence premise (something like 'public contracts equal private contracts; thus public promises shall be treated like private promises'), the Court quickly sidestepped the ultimate, most crucial question: wouldn't there be a justifiable reason, based on the 'public interest', or on 'sovereign reasons', to treat public promises differently from private promises?[102] The difficulty with all (legal) syllogisms is to reach a consensus on the premises. In this case, the entire problem is accepting the premise that

---

[100] *Winstar*, 518 US at 868–9 (Opinion of Souter J).

[101] *Winstar*, 518 US at 868–9 (Opinion of Souter J) (quoting Holmes, *The Common Law* (1881)) (footnote omitted). However, it's noteworthy that the dissenting opinion also quoted another Holmesian famous aphorism: 'But 75 years ago Justice Holmes [...] said that "[m]en must turn square corners when they deal with the Government".' Ibid: 937 (Rehnquist CJ dissenting) (internal citations omitted). 'The wisdom of this principle arises', Rehnquist continued, 'not from any ancient privileges of the sovereign, but from the necessity of protecting the federal fisc – and the taxpayers who foot the bills – from possible improvidence on the part of the countless Government officials who must be authorized to enter into contracts for the Government'. Holmes provided munition for both sides. Moreover, Holmes himself was deemed to be 'the most vigorous defender of the sanctity of the doctrine of State immunity'. Borchard 1924: 23–4. See also Alschuler 2000: 54 (citing Holmes's rhetoric in *Heard v Sturgis* (1888) ('there's no such thing as a right created by law, as against the sovereign who makes the law by which the right is to be created'), and in *The Western Maid* (1922) ('[T]he authority that makes law itself is superior to it [...] Sovereignty is a question of power'). For a criticism of Holmes's position in favour of sovereign immunity, see Borchard 1927b. The question, paraphrasing Laski, is to know whence the munition derives.

[102] Schwartz 1997: 495.

government is to be treated as a private party and that no difference exists between public and private contracts (or between public and private law).

The third aspect of *Winstar* that must be highlighted is the vested rights language the plurality adopted in part of its confusing reasoning. I do not have space to treat the multifaceted topic of 'rights' with care. Still, it must be emphasized (and further explored) that America's rights philosophy has been compelling. The same is not the case in France. Brazil is in a middle ground but now lies much closer to the American system. Based on individualistic, rights-based reasoning, the argument presented by the Court is, in its structure, Liberal[103] – Lockean, if one wishes.[104] A close reading of the plurality's opinion shows that the rights-based reasoning surprisingly *derived* vested rights *from* sovereignty, a strange (but revealingly American) move that somehow lacks the strength of sovereignty.

In *Winstar*, the plurality opinion, *aiming, consciously or not, at limiting the sovereign immunity,* referred to the capacity of the government to *bind itself* through the previous contract, which would restrict future Congresses and *create vested rights*.[105] Suggestively, the plurality linked the very notion of sovereignty to the government's capacity to contract – contracting would be 'of the essence of sovereignty' itself'.[106] This rhetoric is very telling, for it transforms the notion of sovereignty by putting it to the service of the rights talk. In a footnote, the Court makes a surreptitious leap of logic, quoting *Perry*: '[T]he right to make binding obligations is a competence attaching to sovereignty.'[107] Suppose one pushes the Court's argument to the extreme. In that case, she is compelled to infer that sovereignty, instead of immunizing the government, rather *requires* public contract performance (or, if that is impossible, full compensation). In short, the Court adopted the view that vested rights are not antagonistic to sovereignty; they are instead a by-product of a sovereign's expression.[108]

---

[103] See Raz 1986: 198–203.

[104] Rommen 1998 [1936]: 79 ('Locke's philosophy of law doesn't view the law as an objective order of norms out of which individual rights flow by intrinsic necessity; the rights of the individual are prior, and in them originates whatever order exists').

[105] '[I]t is clear that the National Government has some capacity to make agreements binding future Congresses by creating vested rights.' *Winstar*, 518 US at 876 (Opinion of Souter J) (citing *Perry* and *Lynch*).

[106] *Winstar*, 518 US at 884 (Opinion of Souter J) (quotation omitted, footnote citing *POSSE* and *Perry*).

[107] *Winstar*, 518 US at 885 (Opinion of Souter J) (quoting *Perry v US*, 294 US 330, 353 (1935)).

[108] This sort of compromise between rights and sovereignty is presented even by those who, like Loughlin, favour an autonomous idea of public law and think that sovereignty is a 'foundational concept' of public law. See Loughlin 2003: 86–7.

Many scholars have criticized *Winstar*. Michael Graf and Joshua Schwartz advocate a sort of 'proprietary-sovereign' approach to solving the intricate problem of government liability for sovereign acts.[109] Hadfield's words are telling: 'Recognising that the law of government contract is and should be distinct from the private law of contract – indeed, that it's an instance of public, not private, law – resolves the apparent conflict between government-as-contractor and government-as-sovereign.'[110] Hadfield's vocabulary is as French as it gets.

A French (or Brazilian) jurist would first classify the contract entered into by the State: were it a *contrat administratif,* then there would never be any doubt that the State would permanently conserve its power to change laws, even if this power is not 'reserved' in 'unmistakable' terms. Whether the private individual is to be compensated by the state action would be the next question. For a civilian mind, classification comes first; consequences follow from that.

As Samuel stated, '[c]lassification in law is not confined only to dividing up and categorising the areas of law itself. It's a much subtler process that reaches the heart of each subject.'[111] As far as government contract law is concerned, this statement is particularly true in relation to classifying a contract as 'public' or 'private'. Remember the dichotomies explored in Chapter 3. *Winstar* reflects them all.

2. ANOTHER PERSONAL STORY

I began this book with two personal stories and added another in Chapter 3. I will test the reader's patience by finishing this chapter with a final such story, and hope it can do justice to the general idea I have been trying to convey.[112]

It was spring of 2004, during my LLM at GW Law, just a month before the first meeting mentioned in the Introduction to this book. It was the last day of a seminary course on *Litigation with the Federal Government,* conducted by a public attorney, Jeffrey Axelrad, who had served as director of the US Department of Justice's Torts Branch from 1977 to 2003. The seminary, as we can imagine, evolved around the doctrine of sovereign immunity. In the first class, Axelrad gave us a brief theoretical idea about the subject. The rest of

---

[109] See Graf 1998; Schwartz 1997.

[110] Hadfield 1999: 470.

[111] Samuel 2003: 263, also 220–33. Classification, systematization and conceptualization are crucial to continental law, whose history is, as Samuel says, a history of *scientia iuris*. However, classification is traditionally not a topic that has attracted common lawyers' attention. See Samuel 1997: 448. On the importance of legal classification and qualification, see, in France, Bergel 2018: 105–42; Vautrot-Schwarz 2009.

[112] I've told it already, but in Portuguese, in Giacomuzzi 2011: 369–70.

the semester went by, with study of the many waivers of sovereign immunity consecrated in the American law and the probabilities of claimants' success in suing the government. Finally, in the last class, all students were asked to predict briefly whether sovereign immunity was to go or stay in US law.

There were no more than 10 or 12 of us, and I was the only foreign student. All my classmates were unanimous: sovereign immunity could not go, must not go. Instead, it was necessary to protect democracy, they timidly but clearly suggested. I was the only dissenter. A few years later, when I finished my doctoral degree, I understood my colleagues' answers. I cannot be positive, but I suspect they had in mind the protection of a public interest akin to that which I ventured to mention to my advisor a month later.

Would we be similar in our differences?

7. France and *la responsabilité sans faute*

'Without the State's intervention, an economic development strong enough is not possible in France. We do not have in our country a true class of business-men', said former French Prime Minister Lionel Jospin (1937–) on 24 October 1984.[1]

To better understand the functions of *fait du Prince* and *imprévision* in French law, the safest path is to approach State liability in French law more broadly.

As is tirelessly recalled in this book, *fait du Prince* and *imprévision* are, I repeat in soliloquy, subject to public law principles, that is, principles that differ from private law liability. While the common law world has never abandoned – as I have shown – the principles of private law liability, France has built an entire system of public liability completely severed from private law. This is common sense in terms of formal sources, but it is also only the tip of the iceberg.

We know that public–private liability in France goes back at least to *Blanco*, decided on 8 February 1873 and mentioned in Chapters 1 and 5 of this book. The *Tribunal des Conflits* held that the rules governing State liability should differ from the rules governing the *droit civil*. That leading case has been com-monly considered by *la doctrine* as being as crucial to *le droit administratif* as 1789 was to democracy.[2]

Decided in the wake of two previous decisions, *Rotchild* (1955) and *Dekeister* (1861), *Blanco* was not – as is also well known – really original; what remains unexamined, as the legal historian Grégoire Bigot recently demonstrated, is its political character.

At the beginning of the 1870s France was in political turmoil, with the End of the Second Empire (1852–70). The administrative jurisdiction was in great danger, and the battle over jurisdictional power hit its paroxysmal moment. The law of 24 May 1872 both reformulated *le Conseil d'État* (to detach it from the imperial regime) and reset *le Tribunal des Conflits* (which consists of

---

[1]   Apud Cohen-Tanugi 1985: 203.
[2]   See Bigot 2019: 40. What follows in the next four paragraphs is freely derived from the historical works of Chevallier 1970: 91–120, 197–217; and Bigot 2019: 58–9.

eight judges drawn equally from the State Council and the Court of Cassation), created by the 1848 Constitution to remedy the conflicts of jurisdiction between ordinary and administrative courts but shut down in the period of the Second Empire.

In the wake of this institutional reform, in a tort case decision rendered on 15 June 1972, just a few months before *Blanco* was ruled on, the *Court de cassation* (the highest Court of the ordinary jurisdiction) decided that, in the absence of an express, formal derogatory text (which didn't exist), the Civil Code and its general principles applied to the Administration. More crucially, *le Tribunal de conflit*, in a case named *Planque et Papelard v L'État* (1873), stated clearly, through the voice of the *commissaire du gouvernement* Perret, that there existed an 'absolute theory', encounterable in 'almost all decisions from the Lyon Court' and confirmed, Perret said, by the *Tribunal des Conflit*, that only the judiciary authority had jurisdiction over *all* questions on property issues, on contracts and quasi-contracts, torts and quasi-torts, without any distinction between those cases in which *l'État* would have acted as *puissance public* and those in which *l'État* would have acted as a private person. 'It's impossible', concluded the *Tribunal*, 'to more completely deny the existence of the administrative jurisdiction'.

Only 14 days later, *Blanco* was decided by the same *Tribunal* in the opposite direction. The words below were set out in the conclusions of *le commissaire du gouvernement* Edmond David, a *Conseiller d'État* in the *Tribunal*. I will quote the pertinent part and italicize the contrast:

> Considering that the liability that may fall upon the state for loss damage caused to individuals *by the acts of persons whom it employs in the public service cannot be governed by the principles laid down in the Civil Code to regulate the legal relationships between private individuals*; that this liability is *neither general nor absolute*; that it has its own unique rules that vary according to needs of the service and the *necessity to reconcile the rights of the state with private rights.*

What was behind this changing position? What material sources have operated underground?

Behind *Blanco*'s formal façade – as happens in many administrative law *arrêts*[3] – lurked not only political aspects; *Blanco* also opened a lens on the intrinsically *ideological* character of *le droit administratif.*[4] 'Ideology is insep-

---

[3]   See Fairgrieve 2021: 821.
[4]   This character has been tirelessly demonstrated by Chevallier 1979 and Plessix 2003a.

arably linked to law, to administrative law, to private law', wrote Plessix.[5] But, of course, ideology pervades *le droit des contrats administratifs*, too.

Briefly, *l'État Administratif* was, at the time of *Blanco*'s turmoil, eager to come to a decision that could pave the way to the consolidation of a new discipline,[6] *le droit administratif*, which would be based on *different principles* from those regulating private law – a discipline that would eventually influence many civilian legal systems in Europe and South American, Brazil among them. *Blanco*'s words, short and sharp as they were, served as an official impulse to develop different principles in essential areas of public law, such as state liability either in torts or contracts.

But no idea of State was offered in *Blanco*, and French law had no clear idea of State. France needed a new theory of the state to be able to build its uniqueness.

1.   *RESPONSABILITÉ SANS FAUTE* AND THE FRENCH CONCEPTION OF STATE

The period around the end of the nineteenth and the beginning of the twentieth century was a hectic one in the Western world. Industrial development and the concentration of the modes of production, social riots, political unrest and pressure, rapid economic growth and all sorts of social problems demanded social justice.[7] A new theory of State was necessary, and the publicists, with Léon Duguit at the forefront, offered it.[8] The State should be *engagé*.

This was the time of the French Third Republic (1870–1940). This period, known in France as *l'Âge d'Or*, was the apogee for French public law and the time at which the foundations of the classic *droit administratif* were constructed. The whole structure of the French State was remodelled. Consequently, the ideas about *droit administratif, contrat administratif* and State liability were remodelled, too. In short, *individualistic liberal ideas of the nineteenth century gave way to a more collectivist, social view of the law.*[9] America did not make this move, which was crucial to developing no-fault liability principles, in which *fait du Prince* and *imprévision* took place.

Not that the Third Republic was socialist. The contrary is true. It came alongside the then reigning Liberalism, which years before, in the 1820s, had been responsible for the very foundation of the course of *droit administratif.*[10]

---

5   Plessix 2003a: 488.
6   See Plessix 2020: 711–33.
7   See eg Belleau 1997: 381; Chevallier 1997: 9.
8   See generally eg Allison 1996: 59–66.
9   See Bigot 2002: 232.
10   See Burdeau 1995: 107.

'The Third Republic', said Richard Bellamy, 'marked the belated triumph of bourgeois liberal values'.[11] The development of the *droit administratif* is, in broad terms, heartily liberal.[12]

But 'Liberalism' in France has *never* had equal force to that which it has in America, or even the same meaning. French Liberalism was ever pregnant with *social* values,[13] thus distinguishing itself from the Anglo-American Liberal tradition.[14] As James Kloppenberg described, '[w]hereas Anglo-American liberalism seemed to culminate naturally in laissez-faire, in the French republican tradition, negative government, individualism, and the subordination of social and political questions to economics represented only a temporary aberration'.[15] Let me contextualize the socio-political liberal atmosphere from which the idea of *responsabilité sans faute* emerged.

Two interrelated dogmas dominated nineteenth-century public law: the power of the sovereign state and state irresponsibility, which was the rule even in France until the mid-nineteenth century.[16]

Sovereignty was a subject passionately debated at the beginning of the Third Republic.[17] The publicists led the debate to the following point: who was the sovereign? The Third Republic claimed to be the natural heir of the French Revolution. However, although the revolutionaries did not delineate any difference between popular sovereignty and national sovereignty,[18] the publicists of the Third Republic attempted to oppose the two notions. *La Nation française,*

---

[11]   Bellamy 1992: 60.

[12]   See generally Burdeau 1995: 106–8, 121–2.

[13]   See Bellamy 1992: 58–104; Coq 2015 166–8; Cohen–Tanugi 1985: 11.

[14]   See Kloppenberg 1986: 174–7. For a historical approach to Liberalism, examining the differences between French and Anglo-American notions of it, see Dawson 1954. For the many views of Liberalism, see Rosemblatt 2018.

[15]   Kloppenberg 1986: 175. Tocqueville is a good example of the social character of French Liberalism. Politically, he was undoubtedly a Liberal. Yet economically, his Liberalism was *sui generis*. Tocqueville advocated that State intervention was necessary in various fields, such as to diminish poverty, to construct railroads, to direct the economy, to avoid the dangers of absolute capitalism. About the (rather neglected) economic thought of Tocqueville, see the critical anthology organized by Benoît & Keslassy 2005.

[16]   About State irresponsibility in nineteenth-century France, see eg Burdeau 1995: 294; Dufau 2000: 220–3.

[17]   See Bigot 2002: 229. In addition to the other indicated sources, I derive what follows in the next two paragraphs freely from Bigot (at 229–37).

[18]   François Furet (1996: 77) quotes in length the words of the Pastor Rabaut Saint-Etienne, the Third Estate deputy from Nîmes, speaking 'on behalf of all' on 4 September 1789: 'The sovereign is a single and simple entity, since it's all men collectively, without any exception: therefore legislative power is one single and simple entity: and if the sovereign can't be divided, neither can legislative power.'

the sovereign, was *not*, so the publicists' argument advanced, the few who voted and lived in a specific time, that is, the electoral body. *La Nation* should be an abstract entity, detached from the contingent population. Thus, *la souveraineté* should be *nationale* and not *populaire*.[19] The former would represent the equilibrium to establish a representative regime, while the latter would imply conventional despotism. 'General will', so the argument goes, could not be confounded with 'legislative will'. The next step became easy to take with that grounding: *la souveraineté nationale* was amalgamated with the State. In short, *la Nation* and *l'État*, *l'État souverain*, the Sovereign State, formed the same thing.[20] Rousseau would have disagreed with that move, but I think only partially; his conception of *l'intérêt général* did not fade away.

The step of linking Nation and State allowed three essential consequences and a last crucial move. First, the State was able to play down the role of the Parliament and the citizens. Second, having incarnated *la Nation* and its needs, the State was legitimized to organize, protect and manage the abstract public interest, a move that helped to diminish the strength of the nineteenth-century individualist credo and favoured a collective, socialized view of the law. Last, the public power (*la puissance publique*) that characterized State activities throughout the nineteenth century became justified: the legitimate sovereignty of State represented a Nation that was diluted in *la puissance publique*. Hauriou's words are revealing: '*L'État* says: I'm a living personality, I'm the life of the nation, the general interest is incarnated in myself, and all its power whatever origin it may have, shall be exercised in my name, that is, in the name of the general interest.'[21]

The next crucial move was to pass from *l'État souverain* to *l'État de Droit*, that is, from the Sovereign State to the Rule of Law.[22] This move was pivotal, and I cannot set out the history at length here. However, I must remark that the French law is unique in submitting the State to the Law. In broad terms, the State could maintain its prestige while protecting individual rights. Let us return to the subject of State liability at the beginning of the twentieth century.

By then, remember, all civilized nations had debated the problem of State liability,[23] and the default rule was that the State was not responsible

---

[19]   Hauriou resumed this vision by saying in 1912 that 'the electoral body was not sovereign because it's not the nation'. In Bigot 2002: 230.

[20]   See Redor 1992: 93 (highlighting the doctrines of Carré de Malberg and Michoud and examining their importance for the construction of the identification of the nation with the State).

[21]   In Jones 1993: 203.

[22]   The translation from '*État de Droit*' into 'Rule of Law' is misleading. There's no equivalence in meaning between both concepts. See Heuschling 2002; Troper 1992.

[23]   See Pinto Correia 1998: 56.

for tort actions; the maxim '*le Roi ne peut mal faire*', the French version of the Anglo-Saxon 'the king can do no wrong', was in force in France, too.[24] Dominant in private law was the Aquilian *culpa*, whose subjective ethos was catapulted by the Napoleon Code to the general theory of delictual or even contractual liability;[25] remember the case *Planque et Papelard v L'État*, ruled on 14 days before Blanco.

Here emerges the political and legal importance of *Blanco*. Although we cannot find any guidance about what principles govern public law in *Blanco*'s language, we clearly know that they should not be 'laid down in the Civil Code'. If the subjective fault, that is, the private law *culpa,* could not guide state liability, then different public law principles should be developed. Moreover, *Blanco* also clearly said that private rights should be protected or 'reconciled' with the 'rights of the State'. In summary, to protect individuals' rights against the State's sovereign Power it was necessary to forge a theory of the State's objective responsibility, that is, liability without fault.

From here on, the history is well known: the *Conseil d'État* developed a set of principles through the twentieth century, with the invaluable guidance and systematization of the doctrine.[26] I will remark only on the main features of some theories that arose at the time. No equivalent idea was developed in the US,[27] in which, reflecting the common law tradition, 'there has historically been a marked reluctance to allow liability based upon risk or liability for lawful administrative acts',[28] as Duncan Fairgrieve wrote in 2021.

One aspect of the contrasting legal cultures must be emphasized: in British or American political thought, jurists have ever played a minute role, while in France the opposite holds, particularly concerning the theory of State.[29]

This was not accidental. Instead, 'it was inseparable from [French jurists'] identity as jurists'.[30] Among the French publicists of *l'Âge d'Or*, the two leaders were Maurice Hauriou (1856–1929), professor at Toulouse from 1882 to 1929, and Léon Duguit, professor at Bordeaux from 1986 to 1928.[31] In

---

[24]   See Allison 1996: 171; Borchard 1928a: 598.
[25]   See generally Pound 1953: 80–1; Samuel 2003: 264–5.
[26]   About the role of *la doctrine* in the development of *droit administratif,* see eg Burdeau 1995: 329–58; Pinto Correia 1988: 69–74.
[27]   About the development of a different set of principles of public responsibility in French law, see generally Plessix 2003a: 744–50.
[28]   Fairgrieve 2021: 818.
[29]   See Jones 1993: 149; Allison 1996: 74; Caillosse 1996: 958.
[30]   Jones 1993: 149.
[31]   Unsurprisingly, there are very few works of Maurice Hauriou available in English. See Hauriou 1918; 1970; 1983. For a fair idea of Hauriou's legal theory, see Gray 1983; 2010. For a historical study on both authors and their influence in the formation of *L'État,* see Blanquet & Milet 2015.

a way, they followed in the footsteps of Edouard Laferrière (1841–1901).[32] It is hardly an exaggeration to say that together they constructed the foundations of the most famous and widely imitated public law system in the Western world. The work of Duguit will interest us more deeply, for two linked reasons: first, because Duguit, based on Durkheim's ideas, founded his legal theory and philosophy upon the notion of 'social solidarity' (*solidarité sociale*), which became a leading force in French society; second, because Duguit launched and developed the idea of *service public*, a concept which became crucial to the French theory of State and served as one of the most potent catchwords in France.[33]

More importantly, the classic theory of *contrats administratifs* was built mainly based on cases that dealt with *services publics*. These ideas strongly contributed to developing the foundations of *responsabilité sans faute*, which is ultimately a collectivist, social idea of State liability.[34] The theories of *fait du Prince* and *imprévision* must be understood within this broader scenario.

2. LÉON DUGUIT AND THE IDEAS OF *SOLIDARITÉ SOCIAL* AND *SERVICE PUBLIC*; FRENCH SOCIAL VERSUS AMERICAN INDIVIDUALIST ETHOS

I stated that *le droit administratif* was constructed not only in courts but also by the work of some publicists (*la doctrine*). I also noted that, in the Golden Age, the French public law needed a theoretical basis other than the private Aquilian *culpa* to found a system of public liability. Duguit offered it.[35]

I will emphasize only the main steps taken to construct an objective concept of State no-fault liability, highlighting that none of Duguit's ideas were applied in the US,[36] a country in which the individualistic philosophy does not take

---

[32] Laferrière himself was not a professor, but an eminent member of the *Conseil d'État*. His *Traité de la jurisdiction administrative et des recours contentieux*, a two-volume work published in 1887–8, became a 'bible' for the members of the *Conseil*. See Burdeau 1995: 330. About the importance of Laferrière to the emancipation of public responsibility from private law parameters, see Plessix 2003a: 745; Jestaz & Jamin 2004: 113–14.

[33] See Chevallier 1997: 10–11; Foulquier 2011: 51.

[34] See François Burdeau 1995: 320–1.

[35] Bigot 1985: 226–48. See also Pinto Correia 1998: 74–5.

[36] For an overview of Duguit's influence on *droit administratif*, see Jèze 1932. Common law scholars have paid attention to Duguit's work at the beginning of the twentieth century. *L'État, le droit objectif et la loi positive* (1901) was translated into English in 1916 together with works of other French legal philosophers, namely Alfred Fouillée, Joseph Charmont and René Demogue. See Wigmore et al eds 1921: 237–344.

a sympathetic view of notions such as *social solidarity* and does not even work with the concept of *service public*.[37] More importantly, I'll stress the *political and ideological character* of *le service public*, which is, in its origin and fundamentally, a typically French institution constructed to justify *l'État*, and consequently the French *étatisme*. Thus, *le service public* and *l'État* can be viewed as co-dependent institutions.[38]

Duguit was a sociological positivist. Émile Durkheim (1858–1917), the great French sociologist, was Duguit's colleague at Bordeaux from 1901 to 1914 and significantly influenced Duguit.[39] One of Durkheim's fundamental ideas, *la solidarité sociale*, exposed in his seminal 1893 book *De la division du travail social*, inspired the first chapter of *L'État, le droit objectif et la loi positive*, Duguit's first great book about the State, published in 1901.[40] In this work Duguit introduced into law his (or Durkheim's) notion of 'social solidarity', which he never abandoned and upon which he founded his entire legal theory.[41] The role of the State was to promote *la solidarité sociale*, which was above the State.[42] It is a means–end relation.[43] For Duguit, social solidarity was a *fact*, not a moral rule, a Christian duty of charity or a republican slogan;

In 1916, Brown published an accurate essay on Duguit's jurisprudence. In 1918, the editors of the *Illinois Law Review* wrote a short inventory of Duguit's works in a foot-note opening his article entitled *Compensation for Losses of War*, mentioning works of Duguit translated into English thus far. One of them, *The Law and the State*, is a lengthy 185-page study published in vol 31 of the *Harvard Law Review* (1917), containing a good deal of Duguit's jurisprudence and political theory. *Columbia Law Review* pub-lished other four articles, called *Objective Law*, in a row in 1920–1. In 1922 Elliott wrote *The Metaphysics of Duguit's Pragmatic Conception of Law*. Roger Bonnard (1878–1944), one of Duguit's most eminent disciples and a professor at Bordeaux, had his article on Duguit's theory translated into English in 1930, two years after Duguit's death.

[37] Of course, there are public services in the US. What I'm claiming is that the French conception of *service public* is foreign to American Liberalism. My point, again, is that the idea of *service public* served as the foundation of French public law. See generally Chevallier 1997: 9–10.

[38] I derive what follows massively from Foulquier 2011; Chevallier 2018; Esplugas–Labatut 2018.

[39] See Bigot 2002: 228; Allison 1996: 61; Jones 1993: chapter 6; Loughlin 1992: 110.

[40] See Duguit 2003 [1901]: 23–79. Duguit opens the chapter footnoting that he was 'largely inspired, in this chapter, by the excellent book of M. Durkheim, *De la division du travail social*, 1893, although we brush aside many ideas there exposed' (at 23). For a study on Durkheim's idea of 'law as an index of social solidarity', see Lukes & Scull 1984: 33–8.

[41] See eg Le Fur 1932: 175; Loughlin 1992: 110–11; Pinto Correia 1988: 76–7.

[42] See Laski 1932: 122–3.

[43] See ibid: 124.

it could very well indirectly found a norm, but it was not primarily a norm.[44]
Based on Durkheim, Duguit saw in the *solidarité sociale* an objective motto
that could replace the subjective, chimerical, improvable, metaphysical notions
of 'sovereignty', 'general will' or 'individual rights', which founded most of
modern democratic republics (America among them). Duguit emphasized, in
short, the social character of law, opposing it to its individualistic roots.[45]

In his famous *Les Transformations du Droit Public*, of 1913, he posed a normative claim about the transformation of public and private law: 'they are the
result of similar causes and can be summarized by the same formula: a juridical system of a realist, socialist order replaces the previous juridical system of
a metaphysical, individualist order.' In the book's conclusion, Duguit deemed
to have proved his claim: 'Thus, as in private law, the modern public law rests
entirely on a realist, socialist conception [of legal system].'[46] A few years
later, in a series of lectures at Columbia University from December 1920 and
February 1921, Duguit bluntly stated – in the Tenth Lecture, *La conception
solidariste de la liberté* – that this conception could be resumed in the following words: 'liberty is no longer a right, it's a duty.'[47]

The first remark to be made is comparative. Duguit's (and Durkheim's)
sociological positivism is based on a collectivist ideology rather than the individualistic ideology that founded American Liberalism.[48] Remember that the
Third Republic, the period in which the classic theory of *contrat administratif*
was ultimately constructed (and the theories of *fait du Prince* and *imprévision*
were launched),[49] was dominated by liberal values. Still, French Liberalism,
unlike the American type, elevated *solidarity* to a moral phenomenon,[50] putting
it at the epicentre of a theory that wished to avoid egoism (or individualism in
its negative form) and promote communitarian values. The contrasting opinions of Durkheim and Herbert Spencer (1820–1903) – both leading positivists
– are revealing: for the Frenchman, the social should supplant the individual,
and social change was inherently led by an 'organic solidarity' and not, as the
English liberals proclaimed, by moral forces. Durkheim felt Spencer erred in
saying that the individual came prior to society; for Durkheim, the contrary
was true.[51]

---

44 See Duguit 2003 [1901]: 23–4; Laski 1932: 122.
45 See Laski 1932: 126.
46 Duguit 1913: XI, 280.
47 Duguit 1921: 141.
48 See Loughlin 1992: 112–13; Laski 1932: 126.
49 See Drago 1979: 152.
50 See Durkheim 1999 [1893]: 21.
51 See Bellamy 1992: 94–6.

In defence of these social values, Duguit aimed to dethrone 'sovereignty' and put in its place, at the summit of the legal system, the concept of *service public*, which is full of ideology. Within this collectivist atmosphere, one can better understand the second significant move in the Third Republic: constructing a new theory of State based on the idea of *service public*.[52]

As Jacques Chevallier explained, *le service public* in France is a myth.[53] The myth is so potent and uniquely French that it became a model of society. Behind the words is an entire conception of State that would render any comparison misleading. It is well known that '[o]ne would seek in vain, in American law', wrote Lucien Rapp, 'for the notion of public service. Soon one finds in American law the notion of universal service. However, one knows that the notion of *service public* in the sense of French case law is not equivalent to the notion of universal service.'[54]

Le service public is, again, a highly ideological concept, being intimately tied to the conception of *l'intérêt général* and *solidarité sociale*.[55] As Michel Guénaire summarized, the French call *service public à la française* the outcome of a conjugation of political, economic and juridical realities.[56] In addition, the notion was first constructed in the juridical camp. Politically, the notion was linked to the place that the State occupied in the Nation's development.[57] Economically, the *service public* has designed a combination of interventions by the State, counties (*collectivités locales*) and public enterprises, which has had a significant impact on the national economy.[58] Legally, the *service public* was, as mentioned, the basis of a new notion of State.

---

[52]   See generally Guénaire 2005 (even identifying service public and *solidarité collective* at 55). Touzeil-Divina 2019: 160–1.

[53]   See Chevallier 1997: 8. In what follows in the next two paragraphs, I derive freely from Chevallier's work. See also Rangeon 1986: 23; Foulquier 2011: 45; Touzeil-Divina 2019: chapter 4.

[54]   Rapp 1997: 159. For the British experience with the idea of *service public*, see Bell 1997.

[55]   See Rangeon: 24–5.

[56]   See Guénaire 2005: 52–3.

[57]   Guénaire (2005: 52) correctly remarks that 'the difficulty that our European partners have had to understand our conception of *service public* goes back undoubtedly to this original link between State and *service public*. The State has harbored a voluntarist conception of national solidarity with the *service public*.' In fact, this miscomprehension of the *service public à la française* by the foreign peoples is caused by weak historical knowledge about French law. French civilization has since the Middle Ages been vested with 'the insertion of the public life in the scope of law', a fundamental element nicely captured by Mestre (1985: 19) in his historical study.

[58]   See Guénaire 2005: 52–3. Durkheim has recognized a positive duty of the State, which had the moral and economic role. See Allison 1996: 60.

Moreover, the idea of *service public* allowed French law to detach the public from private liability.[59] The argument was thus constructed: since the State is based on social solidarity and has to provide public services for the people, there must be a sort of 'social insurance' to protect eventual losses that the individual could suffer when utilizing public services. Thus, the primary concern is *not* the supposedly existent individual 'right' to be compensated for a loss, but a State *duty* to provide not only for services but also for compensation when the services have poorly functioned.

At the basis of State liability without fault lies the fundamental principle of *égalité devant les charges publiques*.[60] This equality, extracted from Article 13 of the Declaration of the Rights of Man of 1789, became *the* basis of either fault or no-fault State liability.[61] Thus, if the Nation – or the State – was sovereign; if it was founded upon social solidarity; if it had to provide for *services*; and if all citizens should equally bear public burdens, then a single injured individual alone could not be responsible for the eventual damage caused by the whole collectivity, that is, by the State – or by the Nation.

In short, the French conception of no-fault liability is imbibed in a whole new theory of State, a State that should be *responsible* and *subject* to the law. The linked ideas of *solidarité* and *service public* formed this new structure and created a collectivist ethos which opposed Anglo-American Liberalism.[62] The theory of no-fault liability is part of this.

Bringing these ideas to the camp of *contrat administratif* and taking the Anglo-American individualism as a parameter, the comparatist faces two very different scenarios in the American and French legal systems. Briefly, in a 'State society' in which the State manages private lives and coordinates the economy (*économie dirigée*), individuals need protection when the omnipresent State, via external activities, impairs contractors' rights or expectations. The *Conseil d'État* has thus responded to these needs with the theories of *fait du Prince* and *imprévision*.

3.   *FAIT DU PRINCE* AND *IMPRÉVISION*

Let me start with some quick reminders.

I stated that *fait du Prince* and *imprévision* are, in contrast to SAD and the Unmistakability Doctrine, theories originally constructed by courts to protect

---

[59]   See Duguit 1927: 178–9. See also Duez & Debeyre 1952: 419.

[60]   See Gaudemet 2020: 196–7. In English, see Brown & Bell 1998: 194. In Portuguese, see Pinto Correia 1988: 80–3.

[61]   See Pinto Correia 1988: 83 (citing Laubadère, Vedel, Duez & Debeyre and Waline).

[62]   See Guénaire 2005: 61.

the contractor against the power of the State. The primary reason for that crucial difference was that French 'State society' needed theories to protect contractors from counterbalancing its collective ethos.

But there is also a 'publicist' reason for that protection: the continuity of the performance of *le service public*, which cannot be stopped. For example, suppose the State existed to render *services publics*. In that case, they cannot be controlled either by States' own activities, that would eventually affect public contract relations (*fait du Prince*), or by external events that would ultimately impair them (*imprévision*). So, fuelling the 'counterbalance' idea of protecting contractors' rights, there is a collective idea of the *continuité du le service public*.

Moreover, *fait du Prince* and *imprévision* fall within what French law calls *responsabilité sans faute*, that is, no-fault liability. This liability flourished in the twentieth century and represents an essential difference between French law and Anglo-American systems of public liability,[63] either contractual or delictual. It also marks a crucial difference within the French system between *droit administratif* and *droit civil*.[64] The coexistence of two responsibilities, namely *responsabilité pour faute* (fault liability) and *responsabilité sans faute* (no-fault liability), in contractual relations is 'the great originality of theory of contractual liability in *droit administratif*. It has no equivalent in private law.'[65]

In the wake of all the arguments presented so far, no-fault liability is presented as the backlash, in fact as 'the consequence, if not the counterpart, of the exorbitant powers inherent to the nature of the *puissance public* and to the [public] functions that [the public administration] carries out'.[66] *Fait du Prince* and *imprévision* are the express recognition of the exorbitant powers of the public Administration, which are 'inherent to the nature' of the State. This 'nature' requires different principles of liability. In brief, the appearance of an entirely different basis for State liability became possible in France *because* the French culture has accepted and incorporated the exceptional, sovereign character of the State.[67] *Fait du Prince* and *imprévision* are thus the *juridical means* to perform, and mainly maintain, the State's most important (for Duguit, its only) activity: *les services publics*.

---

[63] As for English law, see eg Fairgrieve 2003: 136–7 ('In contrast [to the French system], the English judiciary has – until recently – shown a marked reluctance to allow negligence liability of public authorities, let alone any extension into liability based on risk or liability for lawful administrative action').

[64] See Gaudemet 2020: 196–205.

[65] *Traité 1*: § 766; also § 757; Terneyre 1989: 141.

[66] Terneyre 1989: 141.

[67] See Beaud 2004: 46.

I will deal first with *fait du Prince,* although some observations are also applicable to *l'imprévision.* After all, both theories are part of a broader theory, *la théorie des sujétions imprévues.*[68]

3.1   *Fait du Prince*

In private law there is a theory of *fait du Prince,* too. But its meaning and scope are different.

In private law, *fait du Prince* is a variation of the theory of *force majeure* ('superior force'). However, both provide from the same 'legal category' (*catégorie juridique*), operating under the same conditions (there must be a total impossibility of performance derived from an unpredictable fact to avoid liability) and producing the same effects, namely, the termination of the contract freeing the debtor to pay breach damages.[69]

In *droit administratif,* the conditions and consequences are diverse from private law.[70] *Fait du Prince* needs an aggravation of the contractor's situation caused by a *regular* State activity and not the total impossibility of performance. As for the consequences, in some cases *fait du Prince* will oblige State to pay damages. The question is in what circumstances the public responsibility for damages arises, but the fundamental difference between public and private law liabilities is set from the outset.

In brief, *fait du Prince* is a theory that falls within a broader idea of State liability for legal activity, which was constructed, as I stated earlier, within a particular context and influenced by a positive idea of State. The philosophy behind the theory of *fait du Prince* is that the whole community shall bear the burden of the public service. Therefore, the State, that is, the entire Nation, shall support the contractor's losses when *un fait du Prince* occurs. If it does, the contractor is to be fully compensated (*indemnisation intégrale*).[71] For a comparative law perspective, however, it is essential to recognize the epistemological differences between *fait du Prince* and its 'functional equivalents' in order to understand what is at stake when a jurist or a lawyer deals with the problem of sovereign acts.

In contrast to SAD, *fait du Prince* requires from the interpreter an *active construction,* in the sense that the jurist departs from the idea that the State

---

[68]   See Brenet 2011: 251–5.
[69]   See Badaoui 1955: 1; Richer & Lichère 2019: 274; Hourson & Yolka 2020: 120.
[70]   On *fait du Prince,* the classic book is Badaoui 1955. See also Duez & Debeyre 1952: 570–2; Laubadère 1956a: 390–4; *Traité 2*: §§ 1290–1323; Richer & Lichère 2019: 274–8; Terneyre 1989: 150–66. In English, see Brown & Bell 1998: 207–8; Langrod 1955: 344; Mewett 1958: 232–3; JDB Mitchell 1954: 193–8.
[71]   See Gaudemet 2020: 428.

may, in the name of the general interest, interfere with contractors' status, *unless* some conditions – provided by the theory of *le fait du Prince* – are met. If these conditions apply, then the contractor is entitled to recover. In other words, the fundamental difference appears in the first assumption made by the interpreter. While the French jurist departs from the idea that in a *contrat administratif* the State – always acting in the name of the *intérêt général* – can indirectly modify contractors' situation in the name of the general interest *because* what is at stake is a *public law* relationship, the American lawyer departs from the assumption that the state shall be treated equally to the private party. Accordingly, the French had to construct a theory *to protect contractors* and compensate the *always incorporated prerogatives of the State*, based on the predominance of public law principles, a State that provides for *les services publics*; hence, French law invented the French law theory of *fait du Prince*. In contrast, American law had to construct a theory to *shield the government* from liability and compensate the widespread ultra-individualistic American ethos, based on the predominance of private law principles*;* hence, SAD emerged.

Like SAD, however, the theory of *fait du Prince* (sometimes also called *fait de l'Administration*) is deemed to be somehow confused. When it comes to the 'elements' of *fait du Prince*, the case law and the doctrine are flawed, although they are not as poor as SAD is. Scholars had tried to systematize this 'obscure problem' since the mid-twentieth century,[72] when André de Laubadère labelled *fait du Prince* as 'one of the most confusing' theories of *droit administratif.*[73] The confusion remains.[74]

One of the problems was already mentioned: often, *fait du Prince* is understood broadly enough to encompass the *pouvoir de modification unilatérale*, that is, the power of the unilateral change. In this case, *fait du Prince* is said to be understood *lato sensu*. All modifications in the contracts' performance, either internal or external, would be a manifestation of a 'Sovereign Act'.[75] This is, for instance, the position of Badaoui.[76]

Others adopt a stricter view of the theory, in which *fait du Prince* is said to be understood *stricto sensu*. This is, for example, the position of André de

---

[72]   Badaoui 1955: 199.
[73]   Laubadère 1956b: § 910.
[74]   See eg *Traité 2*: § 1291 ('the most confused theories of the *droit des contrats administratifs*'); Chapus 2001: § 1384 ('very uncertain' case law); Brenet 2011: 255 ('obscure theory'); Richer & Lichère 2019: 284–5) (examining the case law, and concluding that no 'total certitude' exists); Ubaud-Bergeron 2019: 330–1 (a theory that lacks uniformity in the scholarly analysis).
[75]   See the explanation of Terneyre 1989: 115, 150. See also Laubadère 1956b, § 910; *Traité 2*: § 1292; Brenet 2001; Richer & Lichère 2019: 275.
[76]   See Badaoui 1954: 395.

Laubadère, Franck Moderne, Georges Vedel and Pierre Delvolvé[77] and, more recently, Philippe Terneyre – the first author to systematize State contractual liability after Badaoui[78] – and Christophe Guettier.[79] For them, *fait du Prince* and *pouvoir de modification unilatérale* vary in kind, scope and consequences. The principal difference is that *fait du Prince* requires that the contractor suffers a 'special damage' to recover, while in the *pouvoir de modification unilatérale* the contractor must always be reimbursed.[80] Besides that, *fait du Prince*, as noted in Chapter 2, refers to an external alteration of the contract, while *pouvoir de modification unilatérale* is internal to the *contrat administratif* itself.

In systematizing law, *la doctrine* elaborated, from the courts' decisions and scholarly commentaries, some elements or conditions to applying the theory of *fait du Prince*,[81] however uncertain they may be.[82] First, the action that triggers compensation under *fait du Prince* must be imputable to the contracting Administration, not any other public authority. Second, the act must be unforeseeable at the time the *contrat* was signed. Finally, and more importantly, the 'nature' of the act itself, the very State intervention, is to be susceptible to trigger compensation under the theory of *fait du Prince*. I will briefly expose the two first conditions, and deal more closely with the last.

The first condition says that the *fait* must be imputable to the contracting State authority (*collectivité contractante*). If the *fait dommageable* (harmful act) does not emanate from the same contracting authority (for instance, *contrat* and *fait* originated from the Ministry of Agriculture and Food) but from another State authority (*contrat* firmed by any *établissement public*, but the *fait* emanated from the Ministry of Economy, Finance and Recovery), then the contractor cannot invoke the theory for compensation. However, it is still possible to recover under the theory of *imprévision*,[83] which sometimes overlaps with *fait du Prince* but differs in essential points. Nevertheless, courts did not always require this condition.

In *Tanti* (1924), following an earlier case, *Cie. Marseillaise de Navigation* (1904), the *Conseil d'État* ruled that compensation for damages were due under *fait du Prince* 'whatever the authority that has caused them'.[84] This

---

[77]   See Laubadère 1956a: § 911; *Traité 2*: § 1292. See also Richer & Lichère 2019: 275.
[78]   See Terneyre 1989: 150–1.
[79]   See Guetier 2008: 417–19.
[80]   See Terneyre 1989: 115.
[81]   See *Traité 2*: §§ 1296–1323; Terneyre 1989: 151–4.
[82]   See Brenet 2011: 255 ('it's impossible to determine the elements with certitude').
[83]   See *Traité 2*: § 1300.
[84]   Ibid. Terneyre (1989: 151) cites many other cases in the same direction.

ampler interpretation of the first condition favours the contractors. However, it has been restricted ever since. The crucial point is to know what 'contracting State authority' means, or 'who' the *autorité contractante* is.

Since the mid-twentieth century, this first condition seems to have been interpreted more strictly than was the case in *Tanti*. Laubadère said in his 1956 *Traité*,[85] updated in 1984 by Moderne and Devolvé,[86] that the question was straightforward – it was impossible to apply the *fait du Prince* when the *fait* is not provided by the contracting Administration (*administration contract-ante*) – supporting his vision with the case *Ville de Toulon*, decided in 1949 by the *Conseil d'État*. In *Ville de Toulon*, the *Societé du gaz et de l'électricité du Sud-Est* invoked the theory of *fait du Prince* in seeking compensation for losses caused by a State measure that ordered turning off lights during wartime hostilities. The Court negated the claim by saying that 'the reduction of income [was] uniquely due to exceptional circumstances, [which were] independent of the parties'.[87] Interestingly, no language exists in the Court's opinion invoking 'wartime circumstances' to avoid compensation (more on wartime circumstances below). Lurking behind the scene was the Statenessness of French law. However, the *Conseil d'État* alluded to the possibility of partial recovery through the doctrine of *imprévision*,[88] pushing the pendulum again to the congruence side and offering contractors a chance of some economic relief.

An analogous situation occurred in *Compagnie du chemin de fer de Bayonne à Biarritz* (1971).[89] In *Biarritz*, the *concessionnaire* claimed damages for being obliged to make gratuitous transportation during wartime. The *Conseil d'État* rejected the claim by saying that this obligation was independent of the author-ity that had made the *concession*.[90] Remarkably, the wartime circumstances, which could be invoked to avoid State liability if the case were before an American court, were not addressed. More recently, the *Conseil d'État* ren-dered a similar decision in *Soc. civ. des Néo-Polders* (1997).[91] In *Néo-Polders*, the plaintiff claimed damages based on harmful consequences caused by a town planning regulation. The Court denied by saying that the State was the author of the rule, not the contracting authority (probably the county).

---

[85] See Laubadére 1956b, § 918.
[86] See *Traité 2*: § 1300.
[87] Quoted by Laubadère 1956b: § 919; *Traité 2*: § 1300. See also Guettier 2008: 562.
[88] See Laubadère 1956b: § 919; *Traité 2*: § 1300.
[89] CE 20 Oct. 1971, Rec. 624, quoted by *Traité 2*: § 1300; and by Richer & Lichère 2019: 276.
[90] See *Traité 2*: § 1300; Richer & Lichère 2019: 276.
[91] CE 29 Dec. 1997, quoted by Richer & Lichère 2019: 276.

But what, in the end, is to be understood as '*autorité contractante*'? Laubadère, Moderne and Devolvé stated that this expression is to be understood in *sens large*; that is, to invoke *fait du Prince* it is enough that the sovereign act has emanated from a government office or agency (*organe*) of the 'public person' (*personne publique*) that entered into the contract.[92] That means that State authorities are 'strangers' (and therefore do not trigger *fait du Prince*) to the contracts entered into by *départements*, communes and *établissements publics*.[93] However, a contract signed by one secretary of State (*ministre*) is not strange to a sovereign act of another secretary.[94]

It is easy to see that this issue has to do with the structure of the State itself, and consequently with the relationship between federal and state power, the design of the government agencies and their independence vis-à-vis the federal or local government, and ultimately with the political problem of decentralization. The more decentralized the French State becomes, and the more independent the local power turns out to be, the more 'strange' the *personne public* will be vis-à-vis the other *personne public*, from which the eventual sovereign act would derive. Accordingly – and herein lies a paradox – the more centralized the French State becomes, the greater the possibility of applicability of *fait du Prince*, that is, the more protection contractors would have. This theoretical path can be seen as a result of the Stateness culture of French law. Thus, the robust and centralized State shall vigorously protect contractors, too.

Let me insert a comparative flavour here. In scholarly work on the Brazilian doctrine, the reader may bump into statements like this: 'In federal states, like ours, the *fato do príncipe* only takes form if the act or fact comes from the contracting Public Administration. If the act has another origin, the eventual inconveniences will be solved by the theory of *imprevisão*.'[95] We will see, however, that nothing in the written text of the LLCA/1993 (the only one applicable when the statement was uttered) authorizes that difference. Thus, the scholar only mimicked the French law in clear vassalage. Moreover, it is doubtful whether a country of continental dimension like Brazil should reasonably import *tout court* a doctrine from a unitary country like France.

Back to French law: the second condition is that the *fact* must be unforeseeable when signed. Laubadère expressed this requirement in 1956: 'If the intervenient act could have normally been foreseen when the contract was

---

[92]   *See Traité 2*: § 1301.

[93]   The first two (*départements* and *communes*) are tiers of local government. *Établissements publics* are also *personnes publics*, but are governed by a 'principle of specialty' (*principe de spécialité*), which limits their power and intervention to certain domains established by statutes. See Gaudemet 2001: § 86.

[94]   See Laubadère et al 1984; § 1301.

[95]   Gasparini 2009: 749–50.

signed, it's presumable that the contractor would have taken it into consideration, notably to establish the price.'[96]

The *leading case* is said to be *Pouillard* (1926), in which the *Conseil d'État*
put bluntly that 'in October of 1919, the plaintiff couldn't ignore the economic
conditions such as the rise of both the labour force's cost and the coal's cost,
which required the public power to authorise a new rising of the railroad
prices'.[97] Terneyre remarks that the application of this condition is sometimes
very harmful to contractors. For instance, the *Conseil d'État* decided that if an
additional clause is added to the contract after the *fait*, the contractor cannot
benefit from the theory of *fait du Prince*.[98] Even worse, no recovery is due even
when the contractor in good faith ignored the intervention of *fait du Prince*.[99]

But it is in the last condition that the main problem lies. For various reasons,
all contracting public authorities (*personnes publics*) face practical situations
in which they must act as *Prince*, in the name of the *intérêt général*. However,
in some cases the 'sovereign act' cannot be performed without just compensation; hence, *fait du Prince* applies. Since the types of State action that can give
rise to compensation under *fait du Prince* are many, it is convenient to divide
the possibilities into two broad categories: (1) the general measures (statutes,
réglements); and (2) particular measures (individual acts, material acts).[100]

Under the umbrella of general measures (*mesures générales*), we can classify the actions taken by the State itself and measures taken by all *collectivités
publiques*. The two common examples of general measures taken by the State
itself are legislative and administrative acts. On the other hand, the *collectivités publiques* regularly take general measures that ultimately impair *contrats
administratifs* indirectly, mainly through exercising the police power. As in the
US, these actions can be analysed under the umbrella of 'sovereign acts'. In
terms of case law, the American counterparts are *Deming* and *Jones*, examined
in Chapter 6.

---

[96]   Laubadère 1956b: § 916. See also Terneyre 1989: 153; *Traité 2*: § 1298.
[97]   CE 14 May 1926, *Pouillard*, quoted by Laubadère 1956b: § 916; Terneyre 1989:
153. However, here the doctrine splits over the certainty of this condition. Terneyre
(1989: 153) says that the case law is 'certain', citing four other cases decided by the
Conseil d'État.
[98]   CE 15 Dec 1922, *Ville de Rennes*; CE 13 Dec 1961, *Ministre des Travaux
Publics v Société Nacionale de Construction*, quoted by Terneyre 1989: 153.
[99]   See Terneyre 1989: 153.
[100]   I borrow the classification from Terneyre 1989: 154–63. In what follows I derive
freely from Terneyre's systematic work. Similar classification can be found in *Traité 2*:
§ 1303.

As for the legislative acts,[101] the general rule is that the contractor can always seek damages for legislative acts if the *contrat* itself contains such a provision; in contrast, if the *contrat* excludes the possibility for damage claims, *fait du Prince* can't be invoked.[102] The problem arises when the contract is silent. The first answers given to the question whether the State should be responsible for the public and general legislative act were negative: only particular actions could trigger *fait du Prince.* General measures established by statutes were considered a sovereign act (*acte de souveraineté*), and as such, the State was held not liable.[103]

Two cases illustrate this position. In 1908, in *Noiré et Beyssac*, the *Conseil d'État* held that, if the statute has a 'general character', no compensation is due by the State.[104] In 1928 the *Conseil* rendered another decision along these lines, *Compagnie des scieries africaines*, holding that only a specific *fait*, a particular measure, could give rise to compensation under *fait du Prince.*[105] In this sense, the *Conseil d'État* used rhetoric similar to that used by the American Court of Claims in *Jones.* Nevertheless, this position is no longer held by courts or by publicists.

In some cases, dealing with general measures established by statutes, *fait du Prince* was recognized, and (full) compensation was granted to contractors.[106] True, French courts haven't frequently applied *fait du Prince* for State legislative acts, and the elements of the theory remain, as I noted, unclear and hard to define. Still, since 1906 State liability has been held as at least possible,[107] and the doctrine, although acknowledging the 'large empiricism of the case law',[108] was able to set out some standards to address whether *fait du Prince* is applicable in the case of State contractual liability for legislative action. In my comparative perspective, it is important to emphasize that behind the idea of compensation, which is more favourable to contractors, is the principle of *égalité devant les charges publics*, based as it is – and here lies the paradox – in the French 'Stateness' philosophy.

---

[101] The statute itself can obviously establish compensation for contractors, which is not uncommon. See *Traité 2*: § 1305) (citing three cases).

[102] See Terneyre 1989: 155 (citing various cases in both ways); *Traité 2*: §§ 1308–10.

[103] See *Traité 2*: § 1307 (citing the classic works of Laferrière and Teissier).

[104] See ibid.

[105] CE 9 Mar. 1928, *Cie des scieries africaines*. See Laubadère 1956b: § 922; *Traité 2*: § 1304. General measures would fall within the domains of the theory of *imprévision*. See ibid.

[106] See *Traité 2*: § 1305.

[107] See Terneyre 1989: 155–6.

[108] Laubadère 1956b: § 932; *Traité 2*: § 1314.

Since the leading case *La Fleurette* (1938), the general rule is that extra-contractual State liability for legislative acts can be recognized provided, first, that the damage is both 'special' and of 'sufficient gravity', and second, that the statute has not excluded compensation expressly or implicitly.[109] In *La Fleurette*, a 1934 statute that aimed to protect milk industries prohibited the fabrication and commerce of all products that were not exclusively made of pure milk. La Fleurette, an enterprise that manufactured a product called 'Gradine', composed of milk, peanut oil and egg yolk, had to stop production because of the new statute. The *Conseil d'État* held that the charge to stop producing was created in the general interest and that the whole community, not *La Fleurette* alone, should support it.

Behind *La Fleurette* lurks the collective idea of *égalité devant les charges publiques*. The damage caused by the legislation was so essential and grave (*La Fleurette* had to stop production) and so particular (*La Fleurette* seems to have been *the only* firm touched by the article first of the statute) that the *Conseil d'État* decided that the *charge publique* should be supported by the public purse.

Along the same lines, in 1939 the *Conseil d'État* decided *Compagnie des Chemins de fer de l'Ouest*, a typical case of a general measure taken by a legislative act that impaired a *contrat administratif*. In 1935, a decree-law raised taxes at the rate of 10 per cent overall public charges (*dépenses publics*), and the application of this general measure to the *Compagnie des Chemins de fer de l'Ouest* caused a reduction of the annual payment due by the State to the *Compagnie*, payment that was established by a *contrat* between the parties in 1909. That was a typical case of *fait du Prince législatif*, a legislative sovereign act. What is remarkably interesting in this case is that the *commissaire du gouvernement*, Monsieur Josse, led the opinion of the *Conseil*. According to the *commissaire du gouvernement*, the mere fact that a contract between the parties doesn't impede the State from elevating the taxes via *décret*, but the contractor should have the right to recover. At stake was exactly, said Josse, the State legislative intervention in a *contrat administratif*. The indemnification was due by the State, said Josse, unless there was a legislative equivalent measure expressly excluding compensation.[110]

However, this is not to say that any public and general act, either legislative or executive, triggers full compensation in France. As Guettier nicely put it, it is necessary to see that *fait du Prince* 'was not instituted in the [contractors'] sole interest, but in the interest of the whole collectivity: it's by comparing the regime of *fait du Prince* in public law and in private law that one grasps all its

---

[109]   See Terneyre 1989: 154–5; GAJA/2021: 307–14 (for this and next paragraph).
[110]   See Laubadère 1956b: § 923; Traité 2: § 1305; Terneyre 1989: 156.

dimension'.[111] The *Conseil d'État* has frequently held that the theory of *fait du Prince* cannot apply to the domain of fiscal measures (*mesures fiscales*, such as an increase in general taxes), of social measures (*mesures sociales*, such as the enactment of statutes establishing employment-related accident compensation or maxim hours of working or minimum wage) or of monetary and economy-related measures (*mesures économiques ou monétaires*, such as export regulations).[112] Therefore, at least in this broad and superficial sense, it may very likely be that scrutiny of the case law would reveal that French and American legal systems reach similar outcomes concerning cases involving fiscal, social and economic measures. However, French law has presented many cases in which compensation to contractors was issued, as we will soon see.

French law has mitigated the State power to take general measures, either legislative or executive, through the theory of *fait du Prince*. Concerning legislative measures, French law has established other criteria for the application of *fait du Prince*. Compensation is due either when the statute 'affects an element that one can consider as essential, determinant in the conclusion of the *contrat*',[113] that is, an element without which the contractor wouldn't have accepted at the time the *contrat* was signed, or if the statute 'modifies an essential element of the *contrat*'.[114] In addition, another element is necessary: the loss suffered by the contractor must be *unique*.[115] As one can see, these words are general and offer unclear guidance to the interpreter.

In searching for similarities between French and American systems, one can compare this requirement with the American standards of SAD. In stateless America, SAD is applicable (and the government is held irresponsible) if and only if the statute is 'public and general'. In France, *fait du Prince* is applicable (and therefore the State is held responsible) if and only if the damage is 'special' and presents 'sufficient gravity'. Thus, one could say that the French words are as broad and open-ended as the American 'public and general' criterion. However, what must be noted is that the *purpose* of the doctrine and courts in systematizing the field is led by a necessity to *protect the contractor*, not to shield the State from liability.

Similar standards can be applied if a general government act (*acte de gouvernement*), like an international convention and not legislation, is in play. The landmark case apropos the State liability for government 'international' act is *Compagnie Générale d'Énergie Radio-Eléctrique*, decided by the *Conseil*

---

[111] Guettier 2008: 419.
[112] See *Traité 2*: § 1307 (citing many cases).
[113] Laubadère 1956b: § 929; *Traité 2*: § 1311; Terneyre 1989: 156.
[114] See Terneyre 1989: 156.
[115] Ibid: 156.

d'État in 1966,[116] in which the Court equalized, as far as the legal effects are concerned, international conventions (provided they are lawfully and regularly incorporated in the system) and domestic statutes. Put differently, international conventions can also trigger *fait du Prince* and give full compensation if the damage is unique and presents sufficient gravity.

In *Radio-Eléctrique*, the plaintiff owned the broadcasting fittings of *Post Parisien*, which were used by the Germans during the occupation of Paris during the Second World War. After the war, *Radio-Eléctrique* asked the French State for damages, alleging that the Hague Convention of 1907, which was regularly incorporated in the French legal system, allowed indemnity. The Court agreed with the argument that an international convention lawfully incorporated in the system could prompt State liability but negated the claim under the argument that the plaintiff had not proven particular prejudice or a sufficient degree of damage. As for contractual liability for 'international' government acts, in the sense they could trigger *fait du Prince*, it seems reasonable to say that State liability is possible, despite the strict requirements imposed by the case law.[117]

There are also general measures that other *collectivités publiques* can take. Terneyre didactically classifies them as two, both being expressions of the State police power: measures dealing with *police administrative* and measures dealing with *police économique*.[118] Regarding the *police administrative*, it is inevitable that, in terms of extra-contractual (tort) liability, French law affirms the possibility of State liability either in cases in which *l'Administration* acts with a gross fault (*faute lourde*) or in cases in which the principle of *égalité devant les charges publiques* is violated.[119] Regarding contractual liability, the case law is very scarce, but it's possible to find examples affirming State liability.

In *Société du Parking de la Place de la Concorde* (1982), the following facts were considered by the *Conseil d'État*. Paris had given a *concession de stationnement* to a private enterprise that should manage the parking space near the *Place de la Concorde* in Paris. However, Paris took no measures (*measure de police*) to prevent irregular parking around the concession area, thus modifying an 'essential element' of the *contrat administratif*. What mattered for the application of the theory of *fait du Prince*, therefore, was that the *mesure de police administrative* had, positively or negatively, 'modified an essential element of the *contrat*', and had not been merely 'incidental' to the

---

[116] See GAJA/2021: 534–41.
[117] See Terneyre 1989: 158–9.
[118] See Terneyre 1989: 159–62.
[119] See Terneyre 1989: 159 (citing CE 7 Dec. 1979, *Société Les Fils Henri Ramel*).

conditions of the performance of the *contrat*. In short, the *fait du Prince* 'must have modified the state of affairs (*l'état des choses*) according to which the *contrat* was signed'.[120]

The greatest support for the theory of *fait du Prince* nevertheless comes from the day-to-day activity of *police économique*. In a 'State society', in which the economy is planned (*dirigé*), the probability that a *contrat administratif* will be impaired by a State action is high. Consequently, there can be two types of general measure under the umbrella of *police économique*: fiscal measures (*mesures fiscales*) and 'planned economy' measures (*mesures d'économie dirigée*).

At the beginning of the twentieth century, the *Conseil d'État* had various opportunities to rule that specific special fiscal measures, having changed the general economy of the *contrat*, gave rise to State responsibility.[121] The conditions to apply the theory of *fait du Prince* in these cases were twofold: first, a significant change in the *contrat* (*bouleversement du contrat*); second, special damage (*spécialité*).[122] Today, most contracts have clauses dealing with the subject, but nothing impedes courts from using the same rationale to establish State responsibility.

The support *par excellence* for the theory of *fait du Prince* is the area of *économie dirigée* (planned economy), notably so-called price freezing (*blocage de prix*).[123] Terneyre states that, however strict the conditions to impose compensation, the *Conseil d'État* held that *fait du Prince* should apply, for instance, in a case in which the State has cut fiscal benefits for export goods, considering that these benefits were an essential condition of the *contrat*, a condition without which the contractor would not have accepted the work.[124] The same was true in a case in which the State had frozen toll prices, thus causing losses to the *concessionaire d'autoroutes* to which the *contrat* had consented in not imposing any price control.[125] In these cases, what mattered was that an essential condition of the *contrat* was modified; *but for* this condition, the contractor would not have engaged in the performance.

What is ultimately at the basis of the theory of *fait du Prince*? If the State is *sovereign* and the action is lawful, what is the source of this State obligation to pay damages? French doctrine has been struggling with this subject, and two

---

[120] Terneyre 1989: 160.
[121] See Terneyre 1989: 161 (citing many cases decided by the *Conseil d'État* at the beginning of the twentieth century).
[122] Terneyre 1989: 161.
[123] See ibid.
[124] See Terneyre 1989: 162 (citing CE 7 Oct. 1970, *Lavigne*).
[125] See Terneyre 1989: 162 (citing CE 13 May 1977, *Compagnie Financière et Industrialle des Autoroutes*; CE 9 Feb 1979, *Société des Autoroutes Rhône – Alpes*).

explanations have been presented.[126] The first, defended, among others,[127] by Gaston Jèze[128] and Georges Péquignot,[129] is that at the basis of any contractual relation there is an *équilibre financier du contrat*, that is, a financial balance of the contract.[130] In broad terms this principle, also called 'financial equation' (*équation financière*), is deemed to exist either explicitly or implicitly in all *contrats administratifs*. It establishes that, whenever the initial balance of the contract is broken, the contractor has the right to full pecuniary compensation, provided that certain conditions are met.[131] That is the most common foundational explanation for *fait du Prince*, which is considered the typical figure of *équilibre financier*.[132]

This principle was set up in the conclusions of the *commissaire du government* Léon Blum (1872–1950) adopted by the *Conseil d'État* in *Compagnie générale française des tramways* (1910), mentioned in Chapter 3 as a politically important case. In *Tramways*, there was a *contrat de concession de service public* between a government department and a tramway company. The local prefect of *Bouches-du-Rhône*, whose power to regulate the trains' timetable was indisputable, augmented the number of trains that should operate in response to increasing demand for the public service of transportation. A few years before, the *Conseil d'État* had rendered two decisions in analogous cases. In *Compagnie des Chemins de Fer Écon. du Nord* (1903), and in *Compagnie des tramways de Paris* (1905), the Council had decided that *l'autorité administrative* could not impose on the *concessionnaire* any duty that exceeds contractual obligations: if the contract of *concession* had stipulated that the contractor (*le concessionnaire*) would put into service a certain number of trains, the prefect could not unilaterally increase this number.[133]

---

[126] See Laubadère 1956b: § 943; Terneyre 1989: 163.
[127] See Terneyre 1989: 163.
[128] See Jèze 1927: 230.
[129] See Péquignot 2020 [1945]: 408–56.
[130] See Vidal 2005.
[131] For a general view, see eg Gaudemet 2001: § 1473. In English, see Brown & Bell 1998: 206–7.
[132] See Laubadère 1956b: § 943; Laubadère 1956a: 391. According to some, one way to explain the theory of *équilibre financier* is this: there would be in all *contrats* a tacit clause expressing a *presumed intention* of the parties in the sense that the financial contractual *equilibrium* could never be broken. It's not difficult to note that the 'presumed intention' is still a reminiscence of the will theory in contract law. This idea gives to the *équilibre financier* a taste of private, subjective relationship, thus pushing the theory to the private law side. Laubadère will say that this linkage is 'gratuitous' and that such an explanation is an 'easy type'. See Laubadère (1956a: 392).
[133] See Burdeau 1995: 282.

Léon Blum's conclusion in *Tramways* changed this view and caused a revolution in the idea of *concession de service public*.[134] Based on the idea of *service public* – here lies the importance of the notion – Blum expounded that the prefect had the power to alter the contract according to the public interest; but in reverse – and here is the backlash – the State should compensate the contractor.

According to Blum, if the *économie finacière* of *le contrat de concession* is menaced or destroyed because of the inherent powers held by the State, the contractor has a right to compensation. The *contrat administratif de concession*, the argument goes, is not a private contract; it has its peculiarities, and they are always concerned with the public interest; it's the idea of *service public* that governs all changes, either internal or external to the *contrat* itself; however, the contractor has always the right to be fully compensated.[135] The language used in the case by Blum affirmed the existence in the *contrat administratif* of an 'honest equivalence' (*équivalence honnête*), which was 'of the contracts' essence' and should be maintained.[136] Blum's words are worth quoting in full:

> It's of the essence of every *contrat de concession* to seek and carry out, as fair as possible, equality between the advantages that are granted to the *concessionaire* and the responsibilities that are imposed on him [...] The advantages and the responsibilities must be balanced to form the counterpart of the probable benefits and foreseen losses. Thus, in every *contrat de concession* is implicated, like a calculation, the honest equivalence between what is granted to the *concessionaire* and what is demanded from him [...] This is what we call the commercial and financial equivalence (*l'équivalence financière et commerciale*), the financial equation (*l'équation financière*) of the *contrat de concession*.

Although related in *Tramways* to a contract of *concession de service public*, this principle soon after spread to all *contrats administratifs*.[137]

The second explanation simply sees *fait du Prince* as a consequence of the *responsabilité contractuelle de l'Administration*. The State is responsible because it entered into a contract and caused damages to the contractor. The *commissaire du government* Romieu presented this simple position in *Bardy* (1905), as did Achille Mestre (1874–1960) in a doctrinal piece.[138]

---

[134]   See ibid: 283.

[135]   See GAJA/2021: 133.

[136]   See *Traité 1*: § 718 (also for the quotation below). This idea is as well known and foundational to the French system as it is criticized. Vidal (2005: 6–11) points out the criticisms at the beginning of his study.

[137]   See *Traité 1*: § 717.

[138]   See Laubadère 1956b: § 943; Terneyre 1989: 164.

The most commonly held theoretical position, developed by André de Laubadère, combines the two ideas.[139] *Fait du Prince* is to be classified as an example of State contractual liability without fault. For one part, the 'contractual' aspect appears when we remember the previously explained requirement that *fait du Prince* can be triggered only if the so-called *fait dommageable* (harmful act) provides by the contracting State authority. The no-fault part is explained by a functional analogy between the notions of *équilibre financier* and *égalité devant les charges publiques*. As Laubadère explained, in State contractual liability the notion of *équilibre financier* plays a similar function to that of *égalité devant les charges publiques* in State extra-contractual liability. As Terneyre summarized, the idea of *égalité devant les charges publiques* received, in the contractual domain, the name of *fait du Prince*.[140] It functions as an objective criterion that requires no subjective scrutiny of *culpa* to trigger State liability and gives a collective aspect to the subject. For comparative purposes, I will return to the problem of *l'équilibre financier* shortly.

The political aspect of *Tramways*, however, remained relatively unexplored until recently. In his article in the GAPJA mentioned in Chapter 3, Jean-Arnaud Mazères shed light on what I have been calling material sources of law in *Tramways*.[141]

By using, revealingly, Michael Foucault's notion of *gouvernmentalité*, Mazères calls our attention to some new interconnected social realities that have formed the idea of the nascent Welfare State, to which *le service public* was a crucial part. First, it was necessary to distinguish *l'État souverain* from *l'État gouvernante*. This move was essential: it permitted severing the monolithic, abstract, sovereign function of *reigning* from the function of *governing*, that is, of serving (hence *service public*) concrete individuals, however universal services are, not only in public transportation, as in *Tramways*, but also in education, health, security, communication and so on. Therefore, the notion of *gouvernmentalité* paves the way for understanding the political dimension of the 'public' not as an abstract notion but as a concrete, alive (*vivant*) reality that demands attention.

Second, from the notion of *gouvernmentalité*, and following the previous idea of concrete reality, a new dichotomy of *peuple* and *population* would spring, usually melded into one. The 'people', sometimes conflated with the Nation, alludes to the idea of an undifferentiated sum, an abstraction that usually refers to the logic of power in constitutional law. The idea of *population*, according to Mazères (always following Foucault), evokes the notion of

---

[139] See Laubadère 1956b: § 943.
[140] See Laubadère 1956b: § 848; Terneyre 1989: 165–6.
[141] See Mazères 2019, from whom I derive freely in the next two paragraphs.

human beings '*vivants et agissants*'; that is, the population is not a given, fixed entity, but a reality dependent on a series of variables such as nature, social and economic character, and legal, political and ideological aspects. This is precisely the idea conveyed, says Mazères, in the conclusions of *Tramways* when Léon Blum educes the particularity of a '*mode de gestion d'un service public à besoins variables*'; the necessities of the population vary, which requires new management of public service. *Gouvernmentalité*, in Foucault's sense, is not a question of 'reigning over a people' (*reigner sur un peuple*) but of 'acting in favour of a population' (*agir pour une population*). In this perspective, *le service public*, Mazères concludes, 'is not only a new sphere of State's action, it's a new form of State's being; as an expression of *gouvernmentalité*, it's a new form of State'.[142] This is a profound move, for it accommodates, theoretically, the concrete necessities of a population to the transcendental idea of *l'intérêt général*.

Tramways, as a formal source of law, is well known as the leading case in which the *Conseil* has inaugurated a new era in the history of *le droit des contrats administratifs*, planting the seeds of *le principe de mutabilité du contrat administratif*, that is, the contract's mutability principle. In addition, however, the untold political foundations of the case reveal a uniquely French conception of State, whose theoretical structure is entirely foreign to American *mentalités*. And last but not least, *Tramways* was not a wartime case at all.

The other leading theory to protect contractors is *la théorie de l'imprévision*, to which we now turn.

3.2   *L'imprévision*

Although some authors have identified the origins of *imprévision* in the nineteenth century,[143] the leading case in French administrative law on *l'imprévision* was *Compagnie générale d'éclairage de Bordeaux*, decided by *le Conseil d'État* in 1916.[144] As we will see later, the theory is now consecrated in Articles L. 6, 3°, R. 3135-5 of the CCP/2018.[145]

---

[142]   Mazères 2019: 86–7.
[143]   See Vidal 2005: 119–26.
[144]   See GAJA/2021: 184–92; *Traité 2*: §§ 1332–1402; Chapus 2001: §§1385–9; Y Gaudemet 2001: §§ 1488–93; Guettier 2008: 422–37; Richer & Lichère 2019: 266–70. In English, see eg JDB Mitchell 1950: 197–8; Langrod 1955: 344; Mewett 1958: 230–2; Brown & Bell 1998: 208–9. In Portuguese, see eg Meirelles 2010: 320–2; Giacomuzzi 2011: 280–90; Loureiro 2020: 206–2016. For a comparison between France and Brazil, see Barbosa 2019.
[145]   See CCPComm/2021: 70–1, 1474–7.

In *Gaz de Bordeaux* there was a *contrat de concession* between a gas company and the city of Bordeaux, in which the company should supply gas for the lighting of the streets of Bordeaux. However, because of the striking rise in the prices of coal caused by the First World War (the cost of a ton of coal increased from 35 francs in January 1915 to 117 francs in March 1916), the company asked for compensation. The *Conseil d'État*, after having established the necessary conditions of the *contrat de concession*, stated that *la puissance public, le concédant* (that is, the city of Bordeaux) should protect the public interest, and the only way to do that was to compensate the contractor for the losses imposed by the abrupt change in circumstances. Moreover, it would not be reasonable to foresee such a change in prices when the *contrat de concession* was formed.

Briefly, *l'imprévision* holds that, if supervening abnormal and unforeseen circumstances arise after the formation of the *contrat*, rendering the performance increasingly more costly, the contractor cannot rescind the *contrat* but is entitled to an indemnity (called *indemnité d'imprévision*) from the State, which has to 'divide the loss' with the contractor. The unforeseen circumstances must be *external* to the parties of the *contrat* and cannot be of such a strength that the performance of the *contrat* would be rendered impossible. If the alteration makes the performance of the *contrat* impossible, then the theory applicable is *force majeure*, which exempts both parties from obligations. Moreover, *l'état d'imprévision* (the 'state of unforeseeability') is always provisory and can't last indefinitely. Moreover, the unforeseeable changes apt to trigger compensation under *imprévision* can be triggered by general and specific measures, either legislative or executive.[146] Although the theory of *imprévision* originated in a case that dealt with a *contrat de concession*, it has been applied to all *contrats administratifs* for decades.[147]

Less simple than *fait du Prince*,[148] *l'imprévision* is a vast topic, which can be analysed from different angles and perspectives. It could, for instance, be viewed, together with *fait du Prince* and *force majeure*, as a conclusion of an evolutionary process, a sort of modern version of the Roman *rebus sic stantibus* clause, in contrast to *pacta sunt servanda*.[149] But would that equivalence be historically reliable and theoretically helpful?

---

[146] About the application of *imprévision* caused by increase in price or salaries or by general measures, either legislative or executive, see *Traité 2*: § 1348 (citing many cases).

[147] See *Traité 2*: §§ 1338–9; GAJA/2021: 184–92 (citing many cases).

[148] See *Traité 2*: § 1332.

[149] See Cunha 1995: 37; Barbosa 2019: 9–17.

One could also study *l'imprévision* from the internal comparative perspective of public and private contracts,[150] in which case it would be noted that, unlike *fait du Prince*, *l'imprévision* was a theory with no equivalent in *droit privé* until very recently, applying only to *droit administratif.* This situation, however, changed in 2016, with the new Article 1.195 of the *Code Civil*, which now expressly consecrates *l'imprévision* (the Brazilian Civil Code of 2002 consecrates *rebus sic stanbitus* in Article 317, but it is debatable whether it blesses *imprevisão*).[151] From this perspective, an exciting question springs: would *l'imprévision* be founded on the same principles in both public and private law? Classic commentators answered in the negative: in *droit privé*, *l'imprévision* would be applied upon equity, good faith, reasonable interpretation of the parties' will or other private law concepts.[152] They are certainly not foreign to *droit administratif* but were not the public law primary concern, at least in the theory's inception in *Gaz de Bordeaux*.

Does that difference persist nowadays? Wouldn't *l'imprévision* be an excellent example of the unity of contracts? After all, aren't public and private contracts subject to the same economic incertitudes? Don't we live in a Liberal culture that moderates the public–private dichotomy?[153] From this perspective, many further points arise: How does *l'imprévision* fit in the theory of *aléas* in *droit administratif*?[154] If economic efficiency is the new *Deus ex machina* of the Western world, the new standard of public law (the Brazilian Constitution has expressly consecrated 'efficiency' as a legal principle in Article 37), what is the role of *l'imprévision* in this scenario?

I do not think we need to solve all these questions (or others derived from them). But we will necessarily bump into some of these problems below, for they touch the foundations of public contracts and unveil interesting comparative law points. But let me first present the main features of the classic view of *imprévision*. I will then make further observations about the comparative perspective and *l'équilibre financier.*

The main reason why *imprévision* exists in *droit administratif* is to preserve *les besoins du service public*, that is, the needs of the public service. Put simply: it is for the sake of the continuity of the *service public* that the State has to compensate the contractor for losses suffered when an abrupt and

---

[150] As in Labrot 2016.
[151] I follow Ferreira da Silva 2007: 179.
[152] See *Traité 2*: § 1333.
[153] See Labrot 2016: 615–22.
[154] For a comparative study on *l'aléa* in French and English public contracts, see Gabayet 2015.

unforeseeable change in circumstances occurs.[155] The spirit amalgamates State and contractor, so the classic view holds, in *collaboration* towards a common good, and the idea of *service public* encompasses this spirit.[156] Behind this idea is Durkheim's and Duguit's genuine philosophy of *solidarité sociale*, harboured by Léon Blum and known as 'a form of official philosophy' of the Third Republic.[157] In sum, *l'intérêt général* requires the continuity of the public service, and this public law idea, absent from private law – remember the heuristic functions of the dichotomy – is what *primarily* drives State liability to compensate contractors' losses; it follows that the contractor, which has the 'right' to compensation when *imprévision* occurs, *cannot stop* providing for the public services.[158] If the contractor, while facing an *aléa* that would supposedly trigger *imprévision*, does not provide services, the contractor is in breach and is no longer entitled to compensation.[159] The *contrat administratif* is not terminated if *imprévision* applies, as public services cannot cease. Therefore, it is easy to see that *imprévision* applies *mainly* to a particular type of *contrat administratif*, namely, the *concession de service public*. However, it can be invoked in other sorts of *contrats*, too.

Some comparative observations fit here. The most obvious is related to the wartime circumstances, which could lead the comparatist to find a resemblance between American and French origins of exceptionalism. But this link is to be taken with a grain of salt for at least three reasons. First, in France, this circumstance is used in favour of the contractor. Second, for the French, legal reasoning is moved by the *duty of the State* to provide for services which would otherwise be suspended if the contract were rescinded. Third, and subtler, unlike in American law, *le droit administratif* at the time had already begun to forge a theoretical structure of public contracts, in which wartime circumstances were indeed taken into consideration, but merely as another circumstance – important, undoubtedly – that has perhaps, accelerated the growth of a nascent systematic theory, not as *the* main circumstance.

I am by no means saying that wartime circumstances had no impact on the decisions of the *Conseil d'État*. On the contrary, as François Burdeau says, '[i]t is a clear idea in the Western tradition that there's a law (*un droit*) adapted to

---

[155] See *Traité 2*: §§ 1333, 1376; Chapus 2001: § 1385; Gaudemet 2001: § 1489; Guettier 2008: 427. But see Vidal 2005: 826.

[156] See *Traité 2*: § 1373; Gaudemet 2001: § 1489; Langrod 1955: 341–2.

[157] See Grand 2008: 489.

[158] See *Traité 2*: §§ 1333, § 1371; Gaudemet 2001; §§ 1489, 1492; Guettier 2008: 427.

[159] CE 5 Nov 1982, *Société Propetrol*, in GAJA/2021: 189.

peacetime and another for the times of necessity and peril'.[160] What I'm saying is that *imprévision* was not an ad hoc theory caused *only by* wartime circumstances; it was a critical gear in the more fantastic enterprise of constructing a new State.

Administrative courts, however, rarely apply *l'imprévision*, as meeting its requirements has been a challenge.[161] First, the upsetting (*bouleversement*) of the *contrat* must have been caused by an *aléa économique* (literally, 'economic game of chance'), that is, the change in circumstances that trigger *imprévision* must be economic in origin. Second, the *aléa* is to be 'unforeseeable' (*imprévisible*) at the moment of contract formation (which, of course, varies depending on the type of the contract). Third, an element is related to the *déficit d'exploitation*: the contractor's loss must exceed a 'price limit' (*dépassement du prix-limite*), which is, in brief, the margin of a reasonably foreseeable rise in the price of the *contrat*. Fourth, there must be an 'upsetting of the contract's economy' (*bouleversement de l'économie du contrat*), which must not be a simple loss or an *aléa ordinaire*, but rather *extraordinaire*. Like the 'price limit' element, the *bouleversement* can't be defined a priori and conceptualized in abstract terms.[162] I will briefly comment on some features to shed comparative law light on the subject.

The economic *aléa* can be caused by an increase in prices or salaries (the most common factors of *imprévision*), by a drop in revenue, and so forth. These changes can be originated by strictly economic causes (such as a rise in prices due to scarcity of a product, offering-and-demand rule or a monetary depreciation) or by natural causes (cataclysms, cyclones).[163] The critical question one may pose is this: if the contractor's theory of *imprévision* can be invoked due to an economic *aléa*, what is the difference between *imprévision* and *fait du Prince*? What is the relation between the two theories?

The theories sometimes overlap (such as in cases of a rise in prices).[164] However, a general rule is that *fait du Prince* is applicable when the sovereign act emanates from the contracting authority, while *imprévision* is applicable when the act stems from another public authority or a cause external to the

---

[160] Burdeau 1995: 304 (Burdeau then analyses *la jurisprudence* of the wartime and its influence at 313–15). The most complete study of wartime cases is Vidal 2005: 169–274.

[161] See Labrot 2016: 613–15.

[162] I borrowed the requirements from *Traité 2*: §§ 1345, 1350–1, 1360–1 (citing many cases).

[163] See *Traité 2*: §§ 1345–6. The *Conseil d'État* has recognized *imprévision* for natural cataclysm in *Compagnie française des câbles télégraphiques*, decided on 21 April 1944. See also Guettier 2008: 424.

[164] See *Traité 2*: § 1347; Guettier 2008: 427–9.

contractual parties. Moreover, *fait du Prince* is certainly more interesting for the contractor because it provides full compensation, while *imprévision* does not. Hence, *imprévision* is subsidiary to *fait du Prince*; if the latter does not apply, the former can still be invoked.[165]

It's interesting to consider that the *Conseil d'État* deemed *imprévision* (and *fait du Prince*) to be a theory 'of public order' (*d'ordre public*); it could not be bargained out, that is, parties could not make adjustments such that the theory would not apply.[166] In the same vein, the *Conseil d'État* decided that, even though standard clauses of readjusting prices and tariffs commonly exist in the *contrats* nowadays (which would make *imprévision* an obsolete theory), it is still possible to apply the theory of *imprévision* in favour of the contractor.[167] This position of the *Conseil* was, theoretically, favourable to contractors.

Notwithstanding, caution is in order here. The 'Statenessness' of the French culture is always present, and it has been easy for courts to limit compensation under *imprévision*. If judges read each element of the theory strictly, compensation will not be provided. For instance, if the Court is willing to emphasize the public character of the *concession de service public* and understands, say, that the loss suffered by the contractor was not unforeseeable at the time of the *contrat*'s formation,[168] or that it didn't cause a *bouleversement de l'économie du contract*, the contractor can ultimately be left without compensation.

It has been stated that the *bouleversement* plays a 'selective draconian role' in limiting compensation under *imprévision*.[169] Again, my point is not to advocate for or against one system (French) over the other (American). I do not believe that the comparatist can abstractly state, from case law only, that one system provides for stronger protection to contractors than the other. My point is that the collective ethos of French public law is the counterforce of *imprévision*, which is, for its part, the way the French legal system was found to compensate its 'publicness'. Behind all elements of *imprévision* (or of *fait du Prince*) may lie, in every single case, reasons that are hidden from the justification offered by courts and the doctrine.

---

[165] See *Traité 2*: §§ 1353–4; Guettier 2008: 424–5.

[166] See *Traité 1*: § 1364. See also Gaudemet 2001: § 1490 (citing CE 10 March 1948, *Hospice de Vienne*). In English, see Langrod 1955: 344.

[167] See *Traité 2*: § 1365; Chapus 2001: § 1389 (citing CE 19 Feb 1992, *SA Dragages et Travaux Publics*).

[168] For actual examples, see GAJA/2021: 184–92.

[169] See Guettier 2008: 426, 428. Nevertheless, as a 'rare application' of the theory, the author cites *Commune de Staffelfelden*, decided by the CE on 14 June 2000, in which the *commune* was ordered to pay 850,000 francs to *la société Sogest* after it was verified that the *déficit d'exploitation* suffered by the contractor, which provided water to the community, was related to accidental pollution that imposed on the contractor a production cost that exceeded the price the consumers were charged.

As time passed, *contrats* began to include clauses providing for readjustments of prices and tariffs. This phenomenon, a sort of 'incorporation' of the theory into the *contrat* itself, has undoubtedly led to diminished application of *imprévision* in courts,[170] so much so that Guettier recently stated, before the promulgation of the CPP of 2018, that *imprévision* was likely 'to be put in the museum of courts' inventions'.[171]

In a way, however, the most crucial formal source of law, *la Loi*, has proved him wrong: the CCP of 2018 expressly consecrates the theory, reuniting all the conditions in the broad language of Articles L. 6, 3° (as a general norm), R. 3135-5 (specifically for *concessions*), thus confirming the everlastingness of *l'imprévision*.

It has been said that the CCP has followed the European Union Directive 2014/24/UE, Articles 72, 1, (c) and 109,[172] which put into words all the essential elements of *imprévision* exposed thus far. Yet is this not simply a consequence of the unification of law not only in private contracts but also in public procurements? Is it not a mere example of a movement towards *un droit Européen des contrats publics*?[173] How much weight the EU liberal ethos has had in the positivation of *imprévision*, or the whole French conception of *service public*, in the CCP is debatable.

Although many scholars have been advocating the death of *le service public à la française*, there is reasonable room to maintain that the EU Services of General Interest, in its initial consumer spirit, were elevated to the idea of universality, which is, in the end, nothing more than the French ideas of *égalité* and *continuité*.[174] No wonder that this political and philosophical conception flourished and was nurtured in the country that first developed a collective idea of State, the land of Delamare, Domat, Gérando, Lafferière, Hauriou, Duguit, Jèze, Laubadère. And isn't it that collective ethos that some English socialists, such as Laski, admired?

It has been understood for more than a century that *l'imprévision* is a necessary mechanism not only to maintain the contract's financial equilibrium but also, and mainly, to retain a particular idea of the State, a State that provides for services and that cannot leave its collaborators without help whenever it is necessary to keep public services going. Emphasis was traditionally put on the continuity of the *service public*, which was very early, unsurprisingly, consecrated by the *Conseil d'État* as a *principe fondamental* in *Synd. Nat. des*

---

[170] See Chapus 2001: § 1388.
[171] Guettier 2008: 428. But see Chapus ibid; GAJA/2021: 191 (stating that 'the principles posed by the case *Gaz de Bordeaux* maintain all their impact and value').
[172] See CCPCom/2021: 70–1, 1474–7.
[173] See Amilhat 2014: 333–454.
[174] See Plessix 2020: 631.

chemins de fer de da France et des Colonies (1913), and later by the *Conseil constitucionnel* as a constitutional principle (25 July 1979, apropos of the *continuité du service public de la radiotétévision*).[175]

On the other hand, the continuity can be viewed as only a particular expression of *l'intérêt général*.[176] A liberal critic may, however, contend that if we put aside the ideological factor, the whole theory of *imprévision* is based on fragile premises. For example, what to say about the contracts that are not tied to public services? In these cases, the compensation cannot be based on the continuity of the service, unless we venture to say that all public contracts are at least *indirectly* tied to a *service public*, when the actual, direct basis for compensating contractors would be the financial equilibrium per se, a factor connected to the internal economy of the contract and principles such as good-faith reliance, derived primarily from private law.

So, the liberal critic would say that continuity of public service as foundational of *imprévision* may be reasonably contested even in the concessions. It is a fact that the classic *doctrine* identifies the public interest with the 'cause and goal' (*cause* and *but*) of all administrative contracts and that continuity is the result of that idea. Yet why would that be so? From the necessity of continuing service does not follow tout court an obligation of compensation by the State unless we insert the idea of financial equilibrium into the equation. Put differently, the State does not need to compensate *because* of the continuity, Liberals would say, but because it has to maintain the financial equilibrium of the contract to keep the service operating in the name of the public interest. Liberals could even invoke Blum's language in *Tramways*, the 'honest equivalence', which caused a revolution in public contract law theory and was one of the 'most original' causes of contractors' compensation.[177]

This readjustment in reasoning, subtle and profound, pushes the pendulum to the congruence side and helps to put the parties on an equal footing: the very idea of the State's superiority is called into doubt.[178] Thus, the continuity principle, originated in public law as a unique instrument of a new theory of State, becomes less relevant.

This doctrinal move twists the foundations of the subject and operates at the level of material sources, having profound consequences, especially when we face the critical contemporary problem of *risk*. Who would bear the risks of a public contract, especially a long-term contract such as *le concession*?

---

[175] See CCPCom/2021: 69.
[176] See Vidal 2005: 831. In this and the next paragraph, I derive freely from ibid at 778–846.
[177] See Gaudemet 2001: § 1471.
[178] This is Vidal's conclusion 2005: 771.

We know that the expression 'honest equivalence' of the contract reflects a general principle and an essentially static vision of the equilibrium.[179] True, 'honest equivalence' was deemed to take the form not of a mathematical equation but of 'equity', a calculation subject to a 'reasonable interpretation' of the *contrat*,[180] in an effort not to equate it to 'profit' or 'economic equality' of parties, being always indispensable to scrutinize contractual allocation of risks.[181]

But suppose that the contract does not precisely allocate the risks (or does so in an unclear fashion). In that case, all judges will have are 'principles', 'standards' or any other normative tool. In the end, they will either consciously use doctrinal theories, themselves fuelled by material sources, or unconsciously follow material sources tout court to provide substance to the law. In these (mostly hard) cases, emphasizing the ethos of solidarity pushes the pendulum to the exorbitance side, or towards distributive instead of commutative justice, to use philosophical jargon.

Put differently, for a French jurist, the State has always been *engagé*, and the financial equilibrium can be viewed, to the limit, as an instance of State Power. Thus, adapting Bertrand de Jouvenel's formula mentioned in Chapter 2, French law places Power over rights. Comparatively, an American lawyer, devoid of a collective *mentalité* and embedded in the most pro-Market Western society, as put in Chapter 2, has no difficulty emphasizing rights over Power and seeing financial equilibrium as a source of contractors' rights.

That is why Steven Schooner, a leading American government procurement law scholar, can state that, in the US, '[w]e promote *competition* because we believe in the power of the market place'; and, in a footnote, to complete: 'We believe that the marketplace thrives because of *human self-interest*, which proves far more effective than legislated or regulated mandates or policies.'[182] No wonder that, while Schooner quotes Adam Smith's *Wealth of Nations* in the same footnote, Plessix, in analysing the importance of *l'intérêt générale* in French law, has voiced: 'Nobody ignores the influence in the French thought: Jean-Jacques Rousseau.'[183] All this plays a role when formal sources are unclear in answering a specific case.

Brazilian law is an excellent example of a pendular system in the area, as we will see in Chapter 8.

---

179   See Vidal 2005: 7.
180   See *Traité 1*: § 717 (citing CE 10 Apr. 1935, *Ville de Toulon*).
181   See Guettier 2008: 262–7.
182   Schooner 2002: 104 (emphasis in original), footnote 4 (emphasis added).
183   Plessix 2020: 617.

8. Brazil: *fato do Príncipe* and *teoria da Imprevisão*

'The celebration of the centennial of the Brazilian Republic (1889–1989) was marked by a few events of academic or civic nature and no enthusiasm whatsoever. It has been observed that the bicentennial of the French Revolution aroused more interest in the people of Brazil', wrote the Brazilian historian José Murilo de Carvalho (1939–) in 1991.[1]

Brazil has never had an original conception of the state. On the contrary, even before the Empire (1882–89), in colonial times (1500–1882), Brazil looked for models overseas.[2] The eagerness to reproduce on Brazilian soil what happened in foreign countries was not a phenomenon restricted to the conception of state; it began with the importation of philosophies. That should not surprise us, especially in colonies and developing countries. History is not a succession of independent events, and cultural heritage has always broken geographic boundaries. Nor is it surprising that its colonizers' ideas have influenced a colonial country such as Brazil; its enthusiasm to reproduce other cultures in its territory is, therefore, far from unique.

As stated in the Introduction to this book, the two cultural models Brazil has followed most closely since – and even before – its independence from Portugal in 1822 were the Anglo-American and the French.[3] The Brazilian elite has ever since been influenced by the cultural worlds of England (and later the US) and France, be it in politics, economics, morals or laws. All these influences left profound marks in Brazilian law.

The most influential model of State and law for the formation of independent Brazil was the French, running from the founding of the Empire, highly centralized as it was,[4] to the Republic (1889 – on). Nevertheless, Brazilian Eclecticism has always left some room for Anglo-American 'statelessness'. From the 1990s onwards, however, Anglo-American Liberalism has been finding its way through Brazilian law; nowadays it is stronger than ever before, including in public contract law.

---

[1] Carvalho 1991: 139.
[2] See Carvalho 2006: 381; Weffort 2006: 135–6.
[3] See Costa 1956: 49–75; Carvalho 2006: 382.
[4] See Souza 1960 [1962]: 429; Carvalho 2005.

1.   BRAZILIAN 'STATENESSNESS' AND ITS RELEVANCE TO GOVERNMENT CONTRACT LAW

In Brazilian colonial times Portugal was a small country to which the bourgeois revolution had come late, and whose government was based on a centralized bureaucracy. While English and American elites were formed of individuals who worked in the private sector, the Portuguese elite was formed of nobles and aristocrats, and depended materially on the State structure. Public jobs were often the only source of income for many people.[5]

In 1808, Portugal's royal family – escaping from Napoleon's invasion of Portugal – sought refuge in Brazil, which hosted its colonizer and inherited part of its State apparatus for a period of 14 years. Historical reasons eventually 'forced' the Portuguese Prince Pedro, the oldest child of the King of Portugal, to proclaim the colony's independence; the Prince became Dom Pedro I, the first emperor of Brazil. With this unusual independence, declared as it was by the son of its original master, Brazil inherited 'royal blood', and all that comes with it. At that time, not even *le droit administratif* was formed as a discipline in France, let alone the concept of *service public*.

An absolutist conception of the State was among Portugal's legacies. At the inception of Brazilian independence, the State's role became central to the country's development; the elite was formed by the State, worked for the State, lived through the State. In short, the formation of Brazilian life *depended entirely on* the State. Accordingly, the primary purpose of the foundation of the first law schools in the 1820s was to forge the correct maintenance of the State structure, not to mobilize civil society.[6] As a result, the birth certificate of Brazilian law schools comes with the stamp of the State, not that of civil society or individual rights.

In this vein, the French model of the State became very useful: the basis of the Brazilian State, the formation of its political philosophy, and, as a result, the development of Brazilian administrative (contracts) law should be (and remain) *mainly* French.[7]

---

[5]   See Carvalho 2006: 25–47 (most arguments are available in English in Carvalho 1972); 1991 (on the Brazilian elite).

[6]   See Mota 2006: 135.

[7]   About the cultural influence France has had over Brazil, see Costa 1956: 56–8, 74–5, 80. England has had a crucial role in Brazilian intellectual history, too. Free trade with American independent countries was very economically important for England, and this interest led England's effort in freeing European colonies, Brazil among them. Free trade has had not only economic but also cultural consequences: for a long period, Brazil has imported ideas and doctrines from England. See ibid: 60.

At the beginning of the nineteenth century, France exported its culture to Europe and the Western world. As Roger Picard (1884–1950) wrote in *Le Romantisme Social* (1944), France's mission was to 'awaken, instruct, and guide other nations'.[8] Once awakened in 1822, Brazil accepted instruction and guidance. This influence lasted for more than a century. At the end of the nineteenth century, a cultivated Brazilian citizen aimed to be a European, preferably a Frenchman.[9]

It is a fact that, from the nineteenth century onwards, Brazil has imported many foreign ideas from abroad, having been influenced by a myriad of contradictory philosophies. Yet, the principal doctrines have come from Paris.[10] Brazilian philosophical curiosity, says Paulo Arantes in a book called *An Overseas French Department*, has always been 'at the mercy of ideological tides of the metropolis [France]'.[11]

The statement, however, doesn't mean that Brazil has had a coherent or linear philosophy throughout its history. The contrary is true.[12] 'One can't speak of Brazilian philosophy or Brazilian Philosophers as distinguished from thinkers. We have neither. We've not even a philosophical mind',[13] wrote Coutinho in the 1940s. He wished to free Brazilian philosophy from its 'colonial complex' and build 'cultural autonomy'. In 1973, Vita echoed this statement by saying that Brazilian historiography was 'predominantly destitute of theories'. In 1994, Arantes added that in Brazil philosophy has had 'a subaltern place in the evolution of the whole national culture'.[14]

But the alternative to the French model has always been the Anglo-American one and its opposing visions of State and individual. As Mota observed, in the first half of the nineteenth century Brazil was, in fact, 'an informal part of British Empire'.[15] Since then, the battle between French Statenessness *versus* Anglo-American Statelessness has been continuously present in Brazilian life. This posture would later be labelled Eclecticism.

---

[8]   Quoted by ibid: 80.
[9]   See Rolland 2004: 237, 239.
[10]   See Costa 1956: 81; Vita 1973: 538.
[11]   Arantes 1994: 61.
[12]   Brazil has had no genuine philosophy; even today it does not have a strong philosophical tradition. As a colony, it would be surprising if Brazil has had an independent philosophy. It's astonishing that a sort of 'colonial mentality' remains inculcated in Brazilian philosophy, which since colonial times has been willing to import – often uncritically – foreign movements. See Coutinho 1943: 187.
[13]   Coutinho 1943: 192.
[14]   Vita 1973: 542; Arantes 1994: 21.
[15]   Mota 2006: 100.

In nineteenth-century Brazil, *l'Éclectisme* was the most influential philosophy imported from France.[16] Vita's assertion set the tone: 'Eclecticism was the only attempt at a philosophical hegemony in all of the history of ideas of the country, and it was practically "officialised" in Imperial Brazil.'[17] Thus, Eclecticism is either a method or a school: as a method, it can be seen either as a reunion of compatible parts of different philosophical systems by mere juxtaposition of the same systems, neglecting their non-compatible parties, or as a conciliation of seemingly opposing philosophical thesis by discovering a superior viewpoint; as a school, it was once linked to the school of Alexandria (*l'École d'Alexandrie*), later becoming synonymous with the school of Victor Cousin (1792–1867), also called Spiritualistic Eclecticism, which became part of the history of ideas in nineteenth-century France.[18]

Cousin was a prominent figure, 'the founder and the director of the dominant school of French Philosophy'.[19] As the French Minister of Public Education after 1840 and being a lecturer at the Sorbonne, his book *Du vrai, du beau et du bien* (1853) was at the centre of French thought; Cousin's ideas, however, seem to have been more a matter of rhetoric and eloquence than anything else,[20] and his doctrine, 'if doctrine one can call this *fusion without method and without critic*',[21] faded away after his death.[22] What matters is not the accuracy of Cousin's philosophy but its influence in Brazil, where *Ecletismo* has always found a way to *accommodate* seemingly opposing philosophical theses *without method and without criticism*. The explanation for having tried to conciliate two opposing political philosophies like the French and Anglo-American is therefore historical. But, yet again, the most decisive influence was the French.

Mirroring French State and Law, Brazil created in its monarchical period a State Council, which was abolished together with the proclamation of the Republic in 1889.[23] Although the *Conselho de Estado* was coloured with Brazilian peculiarities (even before its independence in 1822 Brazil had had a State Council, which had nevertheless been seldom put to work), it was

---

[16] See generally Costa 1956: 89–111.
[17] Vita 1973: 539.
[18] See Lalande 2002 [1921]: 258–60.
[19] Simon 1965: 46.
[20] See Kloppenberg 1986: 17.
[21] Cruz Costa 1956: 94.
[22] See Kloppenberg 1986: 17. Vita (1973: 538) associates Eclecticism with 'vacuous verbalism, elegiacal lyricism and the rhetorical superficiality'.
[23] Brazilian monarchy had three State Councils. The first, called the 'Council of Procurators', was created by Dom Pedro I in 1822 and was dissolved in 1823; the second lasted from 1823 to 1834; the third and final one lasted from 1942 to 1889. From 1834 to 1841 there was no State Council. In 1910, 1920 and 1933 there were unavailing attempts to recreate it. See Rodrigues 1978; Carvalho 2006: 357–90.

influenced by the French *Conseil d'État* and the French conception of State. Remarkably, the same debates that occurred in France about the legitimacy of the *Conseil d'État* were seen in Brazil, particularly charges as to the alleged usurpation of the judiciary functions by the *Conseil.*[24]

Like in France, and unlike in the US,[25] the Brazilian Empire nurtured the idea that a group of strong civil servants would be apt to run the State and administer the *res publica*.[26] Brazil took its first public servants from Coimbra, Portugal's most famous university, which was since the fourteenth century influenced by the French ethos and, of course, based its teaching on Roman law; as in France, jurists in the Brazilian Empire became, more than any other professional category, the most influential class in the formation of the country.[27] Machado de Assis (1839–1908), the greatest Brazilian novelist, wrote in *Brás Cubas* (1881): 'This time', the father said to the son, 'you're going to Europe. You're going to study at a university, probably Coimbra. I want you to be a serious man, not a loafer and a thief.'

All these factors would be expected to a strong influence on Brazilian law and, particularly, public law.

With this structure imported from France, the Brazilian administrative law would resemble *le droit administratif.* I have already commented on French law's influence on Brazilian administrative law scholars during the Brazilian Empire, mainly Pimenta Bueno and Paulinho de Souza. This influence has lasted ever since. As in France, Brazilian *contrato administrativo* is part of *direito administrativo*, which is itself part of *direito público.* It follows that all consequences deriving from this dichotomy were (and still are) present in Brazilian law, too.

The syllogistic method was applied in Brazilian law in the nineteenth century. Antônio Joaquim Ribas (1818–90), one of the administrative law pioneers during the Empire,[28] wrote in 1866 that the science of *direito administrativo* should be explained through the 'synthetic method', which proceeds 'from the more general to the less general synthesis'; this was so because of the 'incontestable superiority of the synthetic method'.[29] A set of definitions of concepts given by French (Gérando and Laferrière) and Brazilian jurists

---

[24]   See Rodrigues 1978: 231–3.
[25]   See Rangeon 1986: 202.
[26]   See Costa 1956: 79.
[27]   See Carvalho 2006: 61–117; Caccia et al 2006: 240–50, 301–2; Lopes 2014: 157.
[28]   For a historical appreciation of Ribas' work, see Guandalini Jr 2016: 192–202.
For an analysis of administrative law during the Empire, see Almeida 2015: 197–225.
[29]   Ribas 1866: 12. About the deductive method in Brazilian legal culture in the nineteenth century, see Lopes 2002: 338.

follows.[30] In remarkable contrast to the Anglo-American philosophy of state, Ribas, writing about the nature of the political Power, stated:

> Power is *not*, therefore, a necessary evil [...] [or] an implacable enemy [...] against which society must constantly be warned and on the watch for; Power is an institution indissolubly linked to the substance of society and *indispensable* for its existence; it's a protecting principle of all licit interests; [it is an] *auxiliary* of human activity; [...] [It's] the *tutor* of physical or moral individualities, which *don't have* the intelligence, the will, or the necessary strength to watch over themselves.[31]

For Ribas, the State Power must *watch over individuals* because they have neither intelligence nor strength nor will to do so. Later on, Ribas, mourning the same principles that Souza had advocated, stated: 'The governmental centralisation can't be seriously objected; it's [a] condition of the life, strength, and national glory'.[32] Viveiros de Castro (1867–1927), the first great administrative law scholar of the Brazilian Republic and STF Associate Justice (1915–27), thought of the State 'not as a necessary evil, a strawman, but as a powerful actor of social well-being'.[33]

These are all French ideas, and Brazilian liberals of yesterday and neoliberals of today don't like them. We can't forget, however, that our State – frequently despotic, almost always unjust and inefficient – has often acted as *the* inducer of new values that in the long run would change society for the better.[34]

Back to history: the books of Pimenta Bueno, Souza, Ribas and Castro said nothing about public contract law. That is understandable. In France, no theory of public procurement had yet been developed. Plessix explains that the theory of public contracts has not merely imitated the theory of private contracts. Historically, from the end of the eighteenth century to the beginning of the twentieth, no effort was made by publicists to conceptualize the *contrats administratifs*. There was no theory of *contrats administratifs* because there was no theory of *droit administratif*, even though there was a theory of *contrats privés*. The roots of *contrats administratifs* are, therefore, *not* the roots of *contrats privés*.[35]

If France were still building its premises, Brazil would not take the lead. Remember that Jèze had written a *Théorie Générale des contrats de l'administration* and not a General Theory *du contrat administratif* – this appeared only

---

[30]   See Ribas 1866: 12–17.
[31]   Ibid: 47–48 (emphasis added).
[32]   Ibid: 85.
[33]   Viveiros de Castro 1914: 27.
[34]   See Weffort 2006: 334.
[35]   Plessix 2003a: 723–44.

in 1945 with the remarkable work of Péquignot, who 'planted the tree'.[36] It is remarkable, however, that Brazilian public contract law consecrated without objection the principles of 'superiority of the public interest' and 'inequality of the parties' very early. These maxims became axioms for an almost unanimous doctrine and for courts, which pronounced them clearly throughout the twentieth century.

Unsurprisingly, the idea of *service public* is strong in the Brazilian conception of State and law. As in France, the Brazilian theory of *serviço público* had a grip in the first half of the twentieth century. In 1938, Themístocles Brandão Cavalcanti (1899–1980), perhaps the most influential scholar of his generation and later STF Associate Justice (1967–9), defined *direito administrativo* as a 'set of juridical principles and norms that govern the organisation and functioning of public services'.[37] Again as in France, public service theory facilitated acceptance of the no-fault liability principles in Brazilian public law. As for the government contract law itself, Cavalcanti followed the same line and said that what distinguishes public from private contracts was that the administration used the former to perform public services. 'To conclude, therefore, we can say that the concept of a government contract is intimately linked to the concept of public service.'[38]

Cavalcanti's work had an essential mark on Brazilian's government contract law. At the time (the 1930s), and as it was the case in France, Brazilian doctrine about government procurement law was at its inception. In France, only Duguit's, Hauriou's and, more systematically, Gaston Jèze's ideas had been presented; Cavalcanti briefly commented on all of them and concluded that government procurement law deserved more attention, lamenting the lack of more significant elements to form a more consistent doctrine.[39]

While Cavalcanti did not construct a Brazilian theory of government contracts (his book was about administrative law as a whole, not about government contracts specifically), he nevertheless confirmed the basis upon which Brazilian government contract law would later last: talking about the public–private dichotomy – upon which the whole edifice of *direito administrativo* was erected – Cavalcanti said that it should be the focus of serious criticism. He nevertheless did not want to exalt the private sphere (as American Liberalism would do), nor did he wish to suppress the dichotomy (as American 'Realists' would advocate for); he instead wanted to elevate the public Power – the separation of the two branches of law was difficult, because 'the pre-

---

[36] See Richer in the Introduction to Péquignot 2000: 5, 17.
[37] Cavalcanti 1938: v. 2, 3.
[38] Ibid: 100–01.
[39] See ibid: 92–5, 100.

dominance of the public interest [was] so vast', that, theoretically, private law could only be delimited by exclusion.[40] Cavalcanti was only giving voice to Francis Bacon's formula, quoted, unsurprisingly, by Radbruch: *Jus privatum sub tutela juris publici latet* (private law latently rests under the tutelage of public law).[41]

Ever since, either in generic works about *direito administrativo* or in specific books and articles about government procurement, the French basis of *droit administratif*, with all its axioms and corollaries, has pervaded Brazilian formal sources of law, either at the academic level or in courts' decision or statutes. 'In Brazilian law', maintains Celso Bandeira de Mello, 'scholars based their works on French authors. But, as the French professors of administrative law do little more – most of them and since a long-time – than to systematise their case law, Brazilian professors, through indirect roots, theorise about the French case law'.[42]

My point cannot be more straightforward. Following the French lead, Brazil incorporated a set of ideas, values and principles that aimed at forming a coherent system; the public–private dichotomy became inherent to Brazilian legal epistemology; public law deals with a Rousseauian public interest, which *morally and legally* is superior to the private interest; different principles should guide public law and private law; public contract law, being part of *direito administrativo* – hence of public, not private law – follows public law principles as well. As a result, Brazilian legal epistemology has historically been as French as it could be. Of course, it is impossible to highlight all scholarly works and court decisions,[43] but I will mention a few influential authors.

In 1941, Franco Sobrinho (1916–2002) stated bluntly that the parties are not at the same level in a public contract. 'The Public Administration is in all privileged',[44] he wrote, drawing ideas from the then French coryphaeus in the field, Gaston Jèze, 'the most realist of the French scholars'. And the author added: the 'tendency of the modern juridical [meaning the civil law world] thought is to accept that the public law contract is unequal and different from

---

[40]   See ibid: 12. In 1941, in the first Brazilian book specifically on *contratos administrativos*, Lyra Filho (1941: 37–57) conducted an inventory of the works before 1940, enumerating the Brazilian law schools in which the subject of *contratos administrativos* was covered: Out of 15 law schools, 11 offered at least one topic about the subject. Lyra Filho then analysed the works of all Brazilian professors who dealt with the subject of *contratos administrativos*: all did little more than copy foreign doctrines.

[41]   Radbruch 1950 [1932]: 152.

[42]   Mello 2021: 574.

[43]   A good example is the STF decision on a concession case in RMS 1.138, ruling on 24 May 1950, in which the court based its ruling on Cavalcanti and many French (among other Brazilian and foreign) authors.

[44]   See Sobrinho 1941: 423.

the civil or commercial contract, ie, the private law contract.' The public contract, so the rationale goes, is dominated by the goal, the driving idea of the public service. Moreover, private law would then be publicized or, better, *socialized.* Thus, Sobrinho concluded: 'Whatever socialising emerging theory brings in its program of action the conversion of Private Law into Public Law.' But there is more.

Invoking Radbruch, Sobrinho reminds us that individuals exist for the whole, not the contrary. Crowning his French peroration, Sobrinho said that what was certain was that the French school juridical affection lived in the 'laudable attempt to 'de-individualise' Private Law', meaning that individualistic feature of private law was to be combated. 'The private sense is not interesting to the State', he asserted later. In addition, after having glanced over the Italian, German and French systems (glorifying the latter), Sobrinho supportively quoted a French author, Bernatzik: 'Rigorously speaking, *the individual has no rights against society.*' Therefore, all 'administrative acts' should be studied not through private law lenses but to capture the 'higher interest', as if the act were 'an authoritarian intervention of the State in the private sphere'.[45]

Another excellent example of Brazilian vassalage is the first article to address *fato do Príncipe*, written in 1964 by Cretella Júnior. Remarkably, no Brazilian case or scholar was mentioned; Cretella derived *everything* from French doctrine, citing only one French case; he simply informed Brazilians what *fait du Prince* was to the French by describing the theory and its complexities, questions, origin, phases, and effects.

Cretella's rhetoric sharply contrasted with American ideas of government procurement. Cretella frankly stated, first, that in government contracts, the liberty of the contracting parties, that is the freedom of contract, 'doesn't exist'. Second, he said that the inequality of the parties is 'evident'. Third, because public administration has to 'tutor the public interest', it must put itself 'in a superior plan to, if needed, act unilaterally and use its *imperium* to modify, compulsively enforce, and even rescind the contract, whenever the high interests of society are at risk'.[46]

In 1968, Cretella was also a pioneer in writing an article on administrative law principles. He attempted to systematize the principles and canons that should guide Brazilian administrative law. Exposing the Cartesian, deductive mind of continental jurists, Cretella wrote that an effort should be made to construct an 'articulated pyramid' of principles, at whose summit would rest 'the supreme guiding maxim' of administrative law, 'the *predominance of the public interest* over the private interest, accompanied by the *principle*

---

[45]   Ibid: 426–35 (emphasis added).
[46]   Cretella Júnior 1964: 23–4.

of legality'. According to Cretella, the principle of supremacy of the public interest was not restricted to administrative law but was rather 'common to all public law, in its different instances'. The hierarchy should begin with these axioms and then descend to 'smaller and secondary principles'; this effort was a preliminary, necessary step to be taken 'in a given moment of the scientific enterprise, [a moment] in which a discipline overcomes the empirical phase, structuring itself in a more rigorous plan'.[47] This effort in shaping a hierarchy of principles able to found the 'distinctive discipline' of *direito administrativo* was necessary, Cretella concluded, to distinguish some public law institutes from their private law counterparts, thus separating the two camps.[48]

With the exception of one Italian author mentioned in a footnote (Ranelletti), the arguments deployed in Cretella's article rest on Brazilian and French authors, thus following a legal ideology a century old, representing a line of thought that lasted for decades in public contracts,[49] still vivid and dominant in courts. Also, the article, following a tradition of the same length, doesn't mention Brazilian courts' decisions but instead comments on French leading cases and doctrines. The Anglo-American case method had not influenced Brazilian scholars at this time.

The first serious attempt to organize government procurement law in Brazil was set out in a book written by Hely Lopes Meirelles (1897–1990), one of the most influential authors of Brazilian administrative law in the last quarter of the twentieth century. His classic book on government procurement, *Licitação e Contrato Administrativo* ('Public Bidding and Government Contract'), appeared in 1973, and the last edition (the 14th) was published in 2006. The book is still of some influence in courts – including the STF – which in Brazil, contrary to the US and France, abundantly quote and cite scholarly works, as if they were mandatory sources of law. Meirelles was the most significant intellectual influence on many statutes and by-laws promulgated in the 1970s

---

[47]   Cretella Júnior 1968: 2, 4 (emphasis in original).

[48]   See ibid: 10.

[49]   In the 1970s, see eg Meirelles 1973: 181–93 (explaining that a public contract is characterized by the 'supremacy of power' of the public administration, which acts in the name of the public interest and therefore is subject to public, not private, law principles). In the 1980s, see eg Barros Júnior 1986: 9–23 (analysing the doctrines of Jèze and Laubadère and justifying the existence of public law contracts based on the supremacy of the public interest). In the 1990s, see eg Mello 1991: 205–13 (referring to the Brazilian vassalage to French doctrine and attesting the inequality of the parties and the supremacy of the public interest); Pellegrino 1990: 179–80 (attesting the French influence on Brazilian administrative law and government contract law, confirming the supremacy of the public interest and advocating the supremacy of power); Tácito 1997: 617–19 (affirming the supremacy of the public interest and the parties' inequality, citing the most significant French doctrine).

and 1980s which (despite Meirelles' death in 1990) served as the theoretical basis for subsequent federal Statutes, including LLCA/1993 and LLCA/2021. All these critical legal norms have Meirelles' impression on them.

Highly influenced by the French doctrine, Meirelles always recognized the supremacy of the Administration's Power and its privileges in public contracts, marked by its 'exorbitant clauses' and its public character.[50] Jèze, Laubadère and Bonnard are Meirelles's main sources. Moreover, Meirelles never abandoned his basic principles,[51] which are still followed by the STF.

In 1981, Franco Sobrinho began his book on public contracts by saying that difficulties in the theory (and practice) of government contracts no longer existed; for him, it was plain that different principles should guide public and private contracts. Public contract law, he maintained, was driven by the *ratio publicae utilitas*; public interest should therefore dominate juridical relations. Public procurement, Sobrinho repeatedly reminded readers, is about two fundamental notions: public interest as the motive and public service as the goal.[52]

Unsurprisingly, the most important formal legal source in Brazil has reflected the public–private dichotomy and its corollaries. Article 54 of LLCA/1993 reads: 'The administrative contracts treated hereby are regulated by the clauses and precepts of public law; the principles of the general theory of contracts and the private law dispositions are supplementary.' The same norm is present in Articles 89 of LLCA/2021, the most recent Brazilian statute at the time of writing.

However, as we will see in the next section, liberal waves were always present in Brazilian public law. The scenario of French predominance so far illustrated has been changing since the last decade of the twentieth century: as always, when material sources change, the whole structure of law changes too.

2. THE LIBERAL ANTIDOTE FOR BRAZILIAN STATENESSNESS

Anglo-American law has also been pervasive throughout Brazilian history, alongside the dominant French influence in Brazilian administrative law.

If Brazil was, as mentioned, 'an informal part of British Empire' in the first half of the nineteenth century, the Brazilian Republic was born in 1889 under the name 'United States of Brazil'; in 1891, the STF (Brazilian Supreme Court) was created, not by chance mimicking the American model, while the State Council was suppressed. In the Old Republic (1889–1930), the US law's

---

50   See Meirelles 1973: 182–93.
51   See Meirelles 2006: 193–206.
52   Sobrinho 1981: 3–4, 56–8, 67–8, 153, 275.

constitutional liberalism echoed in Brazil: the pendulum had shifted to the American side.[53]

In fact, while it was only in its youth,[54] US administrative law also influenced Brazilian law at the time: even though US government procurement law could not have had a grip in Brazil (we have seen that it was born in the 1910s–20s, at least as a scholarly effort), it is remarkable that the American public utilities regulatory system has had sway in Brazil.[55]

It has repeatedly been said that America doesn't 'understand' the idea of state. A book popular in the US captured this contrast nicely: 'The idea of *l'état*, the state, and its representatives, the *hauts fonctionnaires*, has a significance in France that is incomprehensible to Americans, for whom it means, at best, the post office.'[56] As a consequence, US law doesn't work with the idea of *service public*.

The closest functional equivalent for *service public* is the notion of *public utility*, which is the American mechanism for providing for goods and services that aren't commonly provided for the private sector in most modern economies but are more 'public' in character: electric lighting and power, gas, all sorts of communication, public transportation, water supplies, and so on. But public utilities and *service public/serviço público* are by no means identical concepts, and the official translation of the Brazilian Constitution by the Federal Senate converting *serviço público* into *public utility services* and not *public service* (see the next paragraph) is a gross mistake. In comparative law, translation matters.

Following the French model, in Brazil the State provides public services. But, and this is crucially important, Brazil has elevated the public–private dichotomy to constitutional status: while Article 173 excludes the State from the direct exploitation of economic activities except for the 'cases set forth by the Constitution' or 'whenever needed to the imperative necessities of the national security or a relevant collective interest, as defined by law', Article 175 establishes that it 'is incumbent upon the Government, as set forth by law, to provide public utility services [*serviços públicos*], either directly or by concession or permission, which will always be through public bidding'.[57] Thus, apropos the public service, the State is the master. Comparatively,

---

[53]   See Giacomuzzi 2017a: 239–45. I derive freely from this study, which is full of Brazilian sources. See also Almeida 2015: 44–50 (referring to the Liberalism/Statism dichotomy in the formation of Brazilian administrative law). For a comparison between American and Brazilian federal judiciary system, see Lopes 2006: 188–98.

[54]   See Dickinson 1927.

[55]   See Loureiro 2007: 11–165; Giacomuzzi 2017a: 230–7.

[56]   Gopnik 2000: 113–14.

[57]   See the official translation at www2.senado.leg.br/bdsf/handle/id/243334.

the American public utilities regulatory system, in short, departs from the opposing starting point: public utilities are services and goods not provided by the state but more or less regulated by public authorities.[58] The master is the private sector.

In the 1930s, Brazilian law was at a crossroads. For critical public services such as electricity, telephone and water power, it was necessary, for strategic purposes, to choose between the two models at stake: American or French. Brazil opted for the latter. Odilon Braga (1894–1958), Minister of Agriculture (1934–37) in Getúlio Vargas' administration (1930–45), presided over a Commission to draft a Bill to redesign the system of public service, as determined by the Constitution of 1937, Article 147. In a lengthy (99 pages) study, Braga detailed the hybrid historical influence of both US and French systems of public utilities and *service public* in Brazilian law and referred to the 'infiltration of the American law' in the contractual system; for him, Brazil could not follow the American model at the risk of 'retroceding to the liberalism before 1848'. The French model should be adopted, for this was 'the notion that emerges from the traditional realities of our administrative law'. The pendulum shifted again to the French side.[59] But it would move once again some half a century later.

As we have seen, from the 1990s onwards, following the Liberal wave and in the wake of the shaken structure of the State, Brazilian jurisprudence and public law have been increasingly more interested in American law literature. As a result, Pragmatism, Realism and Utilitarianism now pervade Brazilian scholarly studies as never before, mainly in administrative law doctrinal work. There have even been efforts to remake Brazilian administrative law with new foundations.[60]

The next section demonstrates how the liberal spirit has sneaked into Brazilian public contract law and helped to redesign the French theories of *fait du Prince* and *imprévision* in its own confusing way.

3. *FATO DO PRÍNCIPE, TEORIA DA IMPREVISÃO* AND 'FINANCIAL EQUILIBRIUM OF THE CONTRACT' IN BRAZILIAN LAW: THE TIP OF AN INCONSISTENT LEGAL SYSTEM?

We have seen that, like the French, the Brazilian legal system has ever recognized antidotes for exceptionalism. In fact, all the efforts made by the French

---

[58] For an early study, see Bradford 1924: 10.
[59] See Giacomuzzi 2017b: 240–1.
[60] See Binembojm 2006.

doctrine to compensate the vast Power granted to the State (that is, all no-fault liability principles and ideas that came along with the theory of public service) were broadly and naturally accepted in Brazilian law, which has imported principles such as the *égalité devant les charges publiques*, the 'equality of all citizens in bearing public burdens', or risk responsibility, and so forth. The consequence of the transplant of French principles was the acceptance of French ideas such as *l'équilibre financier du contrat* (in Portuguese, *equilíbrio financeiro do contrato*), which includes, of course, the adoption of theories like *fait du Prince* and *imprévision (fato do Príncipe* and *imprevisão)*.

But Brazilian law has evolved in such a way that it has turned out to be fertile terrain for comparatists, reflecting the difficulties of legal transplants and revealing the importance of material sources for legal methodology and epistemology.

Let me start by quoting the formal sources, highest norm first.

Article 37, clause XXI, of the CFB/88 expressly states that the 'effective conditions of the bid' shall remain unaltered. The text reads:

> Except for the cases specified in law, public works, services, purchases and disposals shall be contracted by public bidding proceedings that ensure equal conditions to all bidders, with clauses that establish payment obligations, *maintaining the effective conditions of the bid*, as the law provides, which shall only allow the requirements of technical and economic qualifications indispensable to guarantee the fulfilling of the obligations. [emphasis added]

The vast majority of scholars, with the imprimatur of the STF, defend the idea that the words 'maintaining the effective conditions of the bid' amount to the 'financial equilibrium' (*equilíbrio econômico-financeiro*), that is, that the French *l'équilibre financier du contrat* has been inserted in the text of the Constitution to protect contractors in *all* public contracts.[61]

Brazilian ordinary laws of collaboration contracts and concessions do consecrate the financial equilibrium by using express words *equilíbrio econômico-financeiro*: LLCA/1993 (Articles 57, §1°; 65, II, 'd' and §6°); LLCA/2021 (many times, but mainly Articles §§4° e 5°; 104, §2°; 124, I, 'd'); LGC (Articles 9°, §§ 2°, 4°; 10; 11, sole paragraph).[62]

---

[61] See eg Meirelles 2010: 266; Meirelles et al 2020: 209; Binenbojm 2019: 161.

[62] As Bockmann Moreira claimed (2019), the logic of financial equilibrium should operate differently in contracts of collaboration (LLCA/2021; LLCA/1993) and contracts of long duration such as concessions (LGC/1995) and PPP/2004. But that isn't, unfortunately, the dominant interpretation among scholars yet. The subject is besides my point in this book. Financial equilibrium of public contracts is a vast, nuanced topic. However, it has got Brazilian legal scholars' attention only recently, much due to the

In addition, *fato do Príncipe* and *imprevisão* are consecrated in ordinary laws, either explicitly mentioning the very expression or using indirect language. *Fato do Príncipe* is mentioned expressly in LLCA/2021 (Article 124, I, d); LLCA/1993 (Article 65, I, d); PPP/2004 (Article 5º, III). *Imprevisão* is mentioned as 'supervening unforeseeable facts' in LLCA/2021 (Article 124, I, d) and LLCA/1993 (Article 65, I, d), or as 'extraordinary economic alea' in the Law of PPP/2004 (Article 5º, III).

At the outset, let me remark on an innovation. The LLCA/2021, Article 124, II, 'd', while consecrating *imprevisão* and *fato do Príncipe*, also states that 'respected, in any case, [shall be] the objective risk allocation established in the contract'. This idea follows a new pattern of the LLCA/2021, which mentions a matrix of risks (Articles 6º, XXVII) as a 'necessary clause' (Article 92, IX) to government procurements. This norm, absent in the LLCA/1993, reflects a more horizontal, equal-footing view of public contracts.

Apart from that, Brazilian law gives its imprimatur to French doctrines. But Brazilian formal sources are, I repeat, very confusing, and the antidote to Statenessness turns out to be stronger here than in the French case.

A Brazilian Supreme Court case, *Brazil v VARIG*, decided in 2014,[63] is perhaps the best example of confusion. The decision contains many important rulings, one unanimous, most not.

In the unanimous part, STF ratified a decades-old interpretation that financial equilibrium as a constitutional norm came out of the text of Article 37, XXI, of the CFB/88, quoted above, following an almost unanimous doctrine, as mentioned.

Nothing in the plain text of CFB/1988, however, authorizes this reading.[64] The contrary holds. The express words of Article 37, XXI ('maintaining the effective conditions of the bid'), historically contrasted with the words of the anterior Constitution (of 1967), which did contain an express clause establishing that the rates of public service should 'assure the financial equilibrium of the contract' (Article 160, II), consecrate only *pacta sunt servanda* and suggest that CFB/1988 leaves the subject to the ordinary law (which indeed contains express protection, as we have seen). How can we explain that, in a country that has followed French statenessness, the STF and most scholars have elevated, through interpretation, a right to compensate contractors to the constitutional level?

---

influence of congruence philosophy. See articles in Bockmann Moreira (ed) 2019; Alencar 2019; Loureiro 2020.
[63]   STF, RE 571.969, 12 March 2012.
[64]   See Alencar 2019; Loureiro 2020: chapter 2.

Throughout its history, the Brazilian government has unfortunately been strongly unjust concerning its broad duties related to fundamental rights of its people and with respect to abuses of Power, contractual included. It's fair to suppose that the Stateness rhetoric has contributed to a 'State's despotism'. An excellent way to balance excessive Power and individual rights is to elevate the latter to the highest legal status. It was, therefore, easy to formally solve the problem by reading in the Constitutional text what is not expressly there, namely, the idea of financial equilibrium of the contracts, however vague this formula may be. It is better to have a right in the Constitution than in ordinary law, especially in a Constitution that consecrates, as the Brazilian one does, a so-called eternity clause in Article 60, § 4°, IV, providing that 'No proposal of amendment shall be considered which is aimed at abolishing individual rights and guarantees'. STF, in short, chose to make contractual rights eternal to compensate for Statenessness.

But *VARIG*, a near billion-dollar case, contains non-unanimous parts too, which are the most interesting. Remember that VARIG, *Viação Aérea Rio-Grandense*, founded in 1927, was the first, most famous Brazilian air transport company; it stopped operating in 2006.[65]

Briefly: in *VARIG*, the company sued the federal government in 1993 for losses allegedly caused by a government economic plan called *Cruzado*, implemented by the Brazilian federal government in 1986, which froze the prices of airline tickets sold in Brazil but not the rising operational costs. Under Brazilian law, VARIG operated a concession of air transportation and sought damages under the financial equilibrium theory. The majority of the Court, led by Justice Cármen Lúcia, a former administrative law scholar, agreed.

Justice Lúcia's short opinion begins by classifying *VARIG* as a State responsibility for a lawful action case, which was, she added, 'by no means a novelty'. According to her, if a lawful State action, although general, has caused a loss to a specific contractor for exceptional circumstances (VARIG could've raised prices but for the general economic plan), the State should pay damages in the name of the contract's financial equilibrium. According to the majority, the theory of *imprevisão* should apply to compensate the contractor.

The minority disagreed, employing, in my opinion, more plausible arguments. First, there was a causal divergence. VARIG's collapse, wrote the first dissenter, Justice Joaquim Barbosa (who holds a PhD in public law from the University of Panthéon-Assas), was caused mainly by the company's internal disarrangements, not by the State freezing tariffs. Financial equilibrium, said Barbosa (who agreed that it was a constitutional norm), did not amount to a static equation based on the tariffs at the beginning of the contract, and the

---

[65]   On Varig's history, see Moreira & Ferrer 2012.

State couldn't be responsible for the success of any private company; the rest of society couldn't be charged for VARIG's incompetence in conducting its business. General legislative measures, Barbosa wrote, could not generate compensation, as STF itself had decided earlier; the economic plan, which had been put in place to address a high annual inflation rate (229.9 per cent in March 1984), was implemented to the benefit of all society and, more importantly, did not impair VARIG specifically.

Justice Barbosa's reasoning was as French as it could be – even the French quotations in Barbosa's opinion were not translated into Portuguese![66] However, what is comparatively remarkable is that Barbosa cites various French authors mentioned throughout this book (Jèze, Hauriou, Chapus, Guettier, Richer) and French cases, such as *La Fleurette* and *Gaz de Bordeaux*. *L'imprévision* couldn't be applied, concluded Barbosa, because some of its requirements, like the *bouleversement* (upsetting) of the economic substance of the contract and the circumstances' unforeseeability (*imprévisibilité*) at the moment of contract formation, weren't met.

In short, the linear, simplistic arguments of the majority won the day in court, having deployed a French idea, *l'équation financière*, to help the congruent philosophy prevail. The more articulate, detailed application of a centenarian French public law theory deployed by dissenters wasn't enough for the government to protect the public interest, as Justice Barbosa vented. As a result, *VARIG* succeeded in a near billion-dollar case, which ended up benefiting VARIG's former employees to the detriment of the exchequer, backed by everybody's purse. I doubt that the French Council would have rendered this decision.[67]

Justice Barbosa, however, called attention to another peculiarity of *imprevisão*, already mentioned: it couldn't trigger full compensation to contractors; only *fait du Prince* could. *VARIG* ignored this doctrinal difference, and the majority didn't say a word about the subject. Curiously enough, Brazilian statutory law, despite having imported French doctrines, treats the compensation in both *fato do Príncipe* and *imprevisão* in the same article of collaboration contract laws, LLCA/2021 (Article 124, I, d), and LLCA/1993 (Article 65, I, d), thus suggesting the same legal consequence for both.[68] To make things even

---

[66] It is noteworthy that CFB/1988 states in Art. 13: 'Portuguese is the official language of the Federative Republic of Brazil.'

[67] Lima Lopes warned me that *VARIG* could have been framed as a money and finance law, instead of a public contract law case, and the result could then have been rendered differently, perhaps in the same direction of the Gold Clause cases in the US. Remember that *Perry* (commented on in Chapter 6) was a Gold Clause case.

[68] For a recent study demonstrating that the Brazilian *imprevisão* is more willing to compensate contractors than the French *imprévision*, see Barbosa 2019.

more confusing, no word about *fato do Príncipe* and *imprevisão* appears in the Law of Concessions, LGC/1995.

Put differently, whereas statutory law in Brazil suggests that *fato do Príncipe* and *imprevisão* cause the same effect in the collaboration contracts, both theories providing full compensation to contractors, in France a distinction operates, either for *marchés* or *concessions*: *fait du Prince* triggers full compensation, while *imprévision* triggers only partial compensation. Brazilian doctrine, however, based on the French distinction, has explained the differences between *fato do Príncipe* and *imprevisão* since the seminal article by Caio Tácito (1917–2005) in 1960 entitled 'The financial equilibrium in the concession (*concessão*) of public service'.[69]

I believe that the 'imperfect transplant' from the French matrix to Brazil can be explained in terms of the hierarchy of norms: since the CFB/1988 is the 'highest norm', and once the STF reads it as containing the norm of financial equilibrium, *this* shall be the principle whence *fato do Príncipe* and *imprevisão* derives, considering that these latter principles are established in a statute, an inferior norm. Moreover, the statutory language, treating, as we have seen, *fato do Príncipe* and *imprevisão* interchangeably, contributed to a later reluctance, or rather a confusion of the doctrine and of courts, in clearly defining and distinguishing the two theories.

Recent decisions of the Brazilian Superior Court of Justice (*Superior Tribunal de Justiça* – STJ) confirm the vision that the financial equilibrium is a pillar of public procurement law.[70] For example, in *Moura Informática Ltda.* (2002),[71] the Court stated that 'the novel culture about the *contrato administrativo* encompasses, as nuclear to the legal regime, the protection of the financial-economical equilibrium of the public law contract, which is inferred from the specific statutes'. Thus, *Moura* was not only a typical case of application of *imprevisão* but also a fine example of how Brazilian law deals with the subject of contractual equilibrium, *fato do Príncipe* and *imprevisão*.

Moura Informática, a computer firm contractor, had won a public bid (*licitação*) to provide and instal software products in computers of the Fifth Federal Regional Court (*Tribunal Regional Federal da 5ª Região* – TRF5) in 1998. In the period between the award and the beginning of the contract's performance, a new governmental economic policy, handed down at the beginning of 1999, supervened and abruptly devaluated the *Real* (Brazilian

---

[69]   See Tácito 1997 [1960].

[70]   STJ has the power and the duty to unify and harmonize the interpretations of all federal and state courts' decisions with respect to federal law, having the final say on federal statutory law. STF is competent to judge constitutional cases.

[71]   STJ, 19 Nov 2002, ROMS 15.154 – PE, *Moura Informática Ltda. v Juiz Presidente do TRF 5a Região*.

currency), which caused a sharp increase in software prices (all were imported from the US). Although recognizing that the new State monetary policy had injured the contractor, the TRF/5 had negated Moura's claim to readjust the contract under the argument that the monetary depreciation was considered part of the risk of the contractor's activity.

The STJ granted the contractor's claim by applying the theory of *imprevisão*. The Court used (in a bamboozling fashion, however) all rhetorical weapons at hand, cited doctrinal works about the *rebus sic stantibus* clause and claimed that the abrupt change of the currency's value 'irrefutably character-ized' the so-called administrative *aléa*, thus triggering the theory *imprevisão*, which imposes on the State the duty to compensate contractors' losses fully. *Moura's* rationale presents two curious factors. The Court mentioned the difference between *fato do Príncipe* and *imprevisão*, supporting its arguments via doctrinal works suggesting that they would cause different practical results. Surprisingly, the Court alluded to financial equilibrium as a 'novel culture' of Brazilian government procurement, forgetting that financial equilibrium was expressly established as early as 1967 on constitutional grounds, even disregarding many inferior court decisions and doctrinal works. The STJ also remarked on the *exceptional character* and the 'unforeseeableness' of the supervening change in economic policy as an indispensable element of *imprevisão*, and implicitly alleged the *bouleversement* (upsetting) of the eco-nomic substance of the contract, thus indicating that, as far as the elements of the *imprevisão* are concerned, Brazilian law has faithfully copied the French matrix. It's interesting to note that although the general character of the State action was manifest (a change in monetary policy affects all indistinctly), the State was held liable for the special damages caused to the contractor under the theory of *imprevisão*.

From a dialectic, comparative perspective, it's also interesting to analyse a recent decision of the same Court handed down in 2005, *Moinhos de Trigo Indígena S/A v União and BACEN.*[72] In *Moinhos de Trigo*, no government contract existed. However, the State's objective liability was at stake, and the doctrine of *fato do Príncipe* was invoked in dicta to deny contractors claims for damages. As in *Moura*, in *Moinhos de Trigo* the contractor suffered from an abrupt change in the government's monetary policy, which devalued the currency at the beginning of 1999. The contractor (Moinhos de Trigo), an importer of goods, sought damages from the federal government and the Central Bank (BACEN), alleging it had suffered a significant decrease in profits because of the real's abrupt devaluation. The Court, in contrast to its

---

[72] STJ, 15 Mar 2005, RE 614.048 – RS, *Moinhos de Trigo Indígena S/A v União and BACEN.*

decision in *Moura* (a case in which a government contract was involved), held that the State could not be liable for having undertaken a general monetary policy that aimed to benefit the entire population and to save the country from economic crisis. In dicta, the STJ ambiguously said that 'the *fato do Príncipe* is arguable internally between particulars and externally by the State, provided that the alleged unforeseeable and damaging fact was dependent, in substance, on international, unforeseeable conjectures'. It is hard to determine the meaning of this excerpt. From the context, one can infer that it aimed to support the rationale, which overall rejected the damage claim. A concurring opinion, however, seems to clarify the Court's holding, which maintained that 'the losses suffered by enterprises due to variations of currency's rate are risks inherent to the activities they undertake', and that 'in [the Brazilian] economic system there's no legal possibility to, because of variations of currency's rate, hold the State liable as if it were a form of socialisation of losses and privatisation of profits'.

In both cases, the State's act could be considered as 'public and general'. The State was challenged on the same grounds, and the same issue was at stake. The same Court reached, however, opposing results. In *Moura*, a case in which the government was contractually involved, the contractor received compensation under the theory of *imprevisão*. In contrast, in *Moinhos de Trigo*, a case in which no contractual relationship existed between the State and the private party, the claimant remained uncompensated. Thus, from the perspective of these two very recent cases, government contractors in Brazil, unlike in the US,[73] benefit more than private contractors when the State passes a statute or takes other action affecting the public.

Five months before *Moura* was ruled on, the STJ decided *Palheta Refeições Coletivas Ltda. v Petrobrás.*[74] *Palheta* is a strong case to show how grey the areas of the doctrines of *imprevisão* and *fato do Príncipe* are and how vital the force of supremacy of the public interest rhetoric can still be in Brazil. At stake in *Palheta* was the same principle of financial equilibrium of the contract. Palheta Refeições, the contractor, provided food services for Petrobrás, the largest Brazilian government enterprise. To address inflationary problems, in 1994 Congress passed a Federal law instituting a new 'inflation index' (*indexador*), called URV. Among other monetary *general* measures, the law sus-

---

[73] In the US, Cibinic et al (2016, ch 3, VI) state that sovereign acts doctrine is based 'on this theory that Government contractors shouldn't benefit more than private contractors when the Government passes a statute or takes other action affecting the public'. In France, it's plain that *contrats administratifs* offer, in some cases, more protection to contractors than the *contrats de droit privé* would do.

[74] STJ, 11 Jun 2002, RE 169.274 – SP, *Palheta Refeições Coletivas Ltda. v Petrobrás.*

pended specific contractual clauses of price adjustment for one year. Palheta sought a price adjustment following the contract's specific clause, alleging that the theories of *fato do Príncipe* and *imprevisão* should govern the case. After citing Cretella's definition of government procurement and Maria Sylvia Di Pietro's 'exorbitant clause' doctrine,[75] the Court denied the contractor's motion using exceptionalist rhetoric. The Court, in its reasoning, first recalled that in government procurements, the controlling principle is the supremacy of the public interest over the private interest. Next, the Court recognized that the contractual equilibrium as an 'immutable' principle of government procurement, and that this principle was based 'on the same idea of equity that founds the theory of State no-fault liability or, still, on the same idea that justifies the indemnity for takings'.[76] However, said the Court in a somewhat confusing way, citing Meirelles' work, neither *fato do Príncipe* nor *imprevisão* were characterized, because the element of *bouleversement*, the upsetting of the economic substance of the contract, was not perfected and neither was the unforeseeability requirement. In dicta the Court, revealing its exceptionalist bias, said that the contractor had a vested right to the contractual equilibrium but had no right to apply any specific index to readjust the contract's prices. This index, said the Court, 'was fixed by the sovereign government as an act of *imperium*'. In *Palheta*, the Court opted for exceptionalism over congruence, having applied purely French rhetoric to emphasize the *imperium* of public interest despite paying tribute to the strength of financial equilibrium. One could say that *Palheta* is as ambiguous as *Lynch* and *Perry* are. However, in the outcome, Brazil has opted for exceptionalism in *Palheta*, while America has opted for congruence in *Lynch* and *Perry*.

Another decision illustrating Brazilian cultural vassalage is *Estado do Paraná v Rodovia das Cataratas S/A*, decided by the Fourth Federal Regional Court (*Tribunal Regional Federal da 4ª Região* – TRF4) in 2005.[77] *Cataratas* also reveals much of what I have explained about the differences in *mentalité* between American lawyers and civil law jurists regarding neglecting or adoring facts and favouring or deploring general ideas.

Apparently (the facts are all but clear), a concessionaire ('Rodovia das Cataratas S/A') of a public service consisting in building and managing a highway in the state of Paraná asked for an adjustment to the toll price, since the concessionaire had constructed the road in a wider dimension than the original contract would have established. This fact (of doing more than the

---

[75] Di Pietro was professor of *direito administrativo* at USP (University of São Paulo state) and a prominent pupil of Cretella.

[76] In this part, the court cites Hely Meirelles' work on government contracts.

[77] TRF4, 30 June 2005, AR no AI 2004.04.017706-6/PR, *Estado do Paraná v Rodovia das Cataratas S/A.*

contract required), remarkably enough, received little attention by the Court. Instead, the Court (besides neglecting the facts) quoted, and commented on uncritically, a good deal of the French doctrine, from Laubadère, Moderne and Devolvé's *Traité* to Jean de Soto, Marcel Waline, Jean Rivero and many other French authors' work on the importance, in the concession, of the principle of the contract's financial equivalence. Unfortunately, like the STF in *VARIG*, the Court did not translate the French works quoted. The outcome favoured the contractor, but more important is to call attention to the Court's confusing rhetoric in deploying classic French doctrine to justify applying a (supposedly existent) Brazilian constitutional principle.

In *Democracy in America*, Tocqueville wrote about the French aptitude and taste for general ideas, which 'has become a passion so unrestrained that it must be satisfied in the slightest thing. I learn each morning upon waking that a certain general and eternal law has just been discovered that I had never heard of until then'.[78] It was 1840. A few years later, in 1854, Charles Dickens (1812–79), the most popular English novelist at the time, wrote the introductory paragraph in *Hard Times*: 'Now, what I want is, Facts. Teach these boys and girls nothing but Facts. Facts alone are wanted in life. Plant nothing else, and root out everything else. You can only form the minds of reasoning animals upon Facts: nothing else will ever be of any service to them.'[79]

In *Cataratas*, the TRF4's reasoning gave voice to the French aristocrat and neglected the English genius.

---

[78] Tocqueville 2010 [1840]: 730.
[79] Dickens 2004 [1854]: 9.

9. Termination for convenience of the government

In Chapter 2, I mentioned 'internal exceptionalism' and its most relevant example, termination for convenience. That is the topic of this chapter.

As noted, all three legal systems currently allow, with minor differences in language, the government to terminate contracts for its convenience – for reasons of 'the government's interest' (US) or '*intérêt général*' (France) or '*interesse público*' (Brazil). Thus, on the surface, the three legal systems look similar. However, we are seeing only the tip of the iceberg. This final chapter shows that termination for the government's convenience in the three legal systems is based on different assumptions and follows different paths.

In American law, termination for convenience runs against the individualist private law *mentalité*, which favours market and companies rather than the state; having no legal norm similar to the 'supremacy of the public interest' like in Brazil and France, convenience termination is viewed as an 'arbitrary', unwelcome governmental power, to which most scholars oppose. A significant part of the debate in courts and in scholarly work restricts the discussion as to whether convenience termination should be confined to wartime circumstances. The argument is straightforward: since this power has appeared in wartime contracts, it should be limited to war circumstances; *but for* the war, so the argument goes, termination for convenience should not have existed; the exceptional element alone cannot mean that exceptionalism must triumph in all government procurement law; in short, exceptionalism can't be extended to peacetime procurement.

Moreover, 'the government's interest', even if understood as meaning the 'public interest',[1] is viewed as a sweeping concept that ends up granting government undesirable discretionary power; it holds no positive meaning and incarnates no leading force. It may well be widely used by contracting officers to perform public functions, but public interest rhetoric has never served to run the nation. On the contrary, it has served purposes that run against the

---

[1]   The *Reference Book* 2021, entry 'Public Interest', reads: 'In the interest of the United States. This term is frequently used when broad authority is granted to an officer of the government.'

American individualistic credo. Remember: the American conception of general interest is utilitarian, not Rousseauian.

In France, *le pouvoir de résiliation* is inserted in a legal system that departs from the opposing conceptions of State and general interest of its American functional equivalent. No wonder, therefore, that this power has been widely accepted, even when it was not expressly consecrated in the CCP/2018. The debates over the *pouvoir de résiliation unilatérale* have moved around the limits of the power to terminate a *contrat administratif*. Still, no one dares to confine it to wartime circumstances. The idea of the State as a provider of *service public* facilitates welcoming convenience termination, which is viewed as *necessary*, not arbitrary.

Brazil is somehow in between the two poles, presenting a third, hybrid vision of the subject. We have seen that the Brazilian idea of State and public law was originally French. In the past three decades or so, as mentioned in the Introduction to this book, the Liberal ideology has been pushing Brazilian's pendulum to the US side: ideas about the State, the foundations of administrative law, government contracts and, consequently, convenience termination have been liberalized. I intend to demonstrate that Brazilian law's choices concerning convenience termination are but the consequence of a move in ideological assumptions.

Termination for convenience is a multifaceted topic in all three countries, and I won't comment on the various technicalities and procedures that governments must follow to terminate contracts. Much can be said about how, when, if and what steps are to be taken by each country's government to give or receive the termination notice, about the initial conference that shall be conducted between the parties or about the inventory and the settlement proposal. I concede that a careful study of these topics or a detailed study on what legal problems and legal rights and duties can emerge from them could reveal a tendency towards either congruence or exceptionalism in each legal system. Procedural issues do impact substantive matters, and a simple difference in, say, which party should support the burden of proof about the damages can indeed determine the outcome. However, an analysis of all the technicalities and procedures governments would not be pertinent to this study, for reasons already emphasized.

Instead, I will make brief comments on the leading cases to extract from them the underlying philosophy governing the government's convenience termination, taking advantage of the already studied epistemology. I will start with the US and demonstrate that termination for convenience is dominated by the following obsessions: first, how to limit the government's power (or right) to terminate a contract; second, what to do to allow a full possible recovery of damages to the private contractors when termination for convenience takes place. Congruence philosophy acts both as a magnet and as a starting point.

1.   TERMINATION FOR CONVENIENCE IN THE US

As mentioned in Chapter 2, the standard US Termination for Convenience Clause is asserted by FAR 52.249-1 through 52.249-5. The sweeping clause grants the government the right to terminate the contract 'in the government's interest'. There are no other criteria, either in statutes or regulations, to guide contracting officers in deciding whether and when to terminate a contract.

The language of the FAR is revealing. There is no mention of an abstract 'public interest', but rather a more concrete 'government interest'. Government and its interests change in the real world, and so does the public interest. These changes may dictate termination for convenience. At the limit, the FAR's language reveals that American pragmatic thinking is preferable if compared to a Platonic/Rousseauian ideal of general interest. But let me spare the language-worldview vocabulary and get into more actual comparative observations.

In practice, the greatest impact for the contractor, where the 'exceptionalism' ultimately lies, is that 'in general anticipatory profits are not recoverable when a termination for convenience of the Government is invoked. Therefore, the recovery of anticipated profit is precluded. Thus, this mandatory provision confers a major contract right on the government with no commensurate advantage to the contractor.'[2]

While in ordinary common law contracts the entire profit that would be earned had the contract been fully completed is due to the 'innocent' party,[3] in government procurement the contractor's recovery is based on incurred costs plus some reasonable amount of profit on those incurred costs.[4] In other words, the contractor's recovery is limited to the contract price for completed services, the costs incurred on work already performed, the profits earned on work already performed and the costs of termination.

In the respective entry of the leading reference book in the field, we read: 'This long-standing right allows the government to withdraw from a contract without having to pay the contractor the profit and fixed overhead it would have earned had the contract gone to completion.'[5] And the opening sentence of an influential handbook is revealing: 'The Termination for Convenience Clause is one of the most unique provisions contained in government con-

---

[2]   Cibinic et al 2016: chapter 11.
[3]   See Andrews & Peacock 1979: 282 (citing many cases); Perlman & Goodrich 1978: 4 (citing scholarly work).
[4]   See Cibinic et al 2016: chapter 11, VI.
[5]   Nash et al 2021: entry *Termination for Convenience*.

tracts. *In no other area of contract law* has one party been given such complete authority *to escape from contractual obligations*.'[6]

Let me exaggerate the importance of the italicized words. They subtly reveal that 'contract law' forms a *unity*. It is the same unity, you remember from the Introduction, that Benoît Plessix referred to as being a 'fashion' and against which the *Conseil d'État* would be 'the best rampart'. For the American mainstream, contract law is an 'area' into which government contracts should fit; but 'most unique[ly]', Termination for Convenience 'escape[s] from contractual obligations', that is, escapes from the congruence philosophy that dominates contract law, to use Schwartz's suggestive spectrum. Just below the surface of the handbook's opening sentence are, I think, assumptions shared by *all* lawyers and scholars, even those who more willingly accept exceptionalist philosophy. The assumptions were unfolded already, but I would like to stress that scholarly work has, historically, *ever*, unsurprisingly and revealingly, attacked Termination for Convenience.

Recall James Donnelly's premise in the 1920s: 'Governments are bound to observe the same rule of conduct in their contractual relations with their citizens as they require citizens to observe with each other. Accordingly, they become bound by their contracts the same as individuals.'[7] On Termination for Convenience, he pointedly wrote:

> Public bodies have no sovereign right to rescind agreements at their mere pleasure. Such contracts can only be rescinded under the same conditions and subject to the same liability as natural persons. There's not one law for the sovereign and another for the subject. When the sovereign engages in business and the conduct of business enterprise and contracts with individuals, when such contracts come before the court for construction, the rights and obligations of the parties must be adjusted upon the same principles as if both contracting parties were private persons. Both stand upon equality before the law and the sovereign is merged in the dealer, contractor and suitor. After a contract has been lawfully entered into, it can't be annulled by a public body by reconsidering its approval. A contract creates fixed and perfect legal obligations, wholly detached from a *locus pœnitenciœ* and not subject to reconsideration. It's a contradiction in terms to speak of a contract revocable at will of a contracting party.[8]

Soon after in his Treatise, there is a one-paragraph section about the 'Reserved Right to Terminate',[9] in which Donnelly added a pejorative 'arbitrary' to the word 'termination': 'Where the public body reserves the right to terminate the

---

6   Cibinic et al 2016: Chapter 11 (emphasis added).
7   Donnelly 1922: § 82 (internal quotations omitted).
8   Donnelly 1922: 353 (citing *People v Stephens* and *People ex. rel. Graves v Sohmer*).
9   Ibid: 354–5.

contract, the exercise of the option pursuant to such provision will be strictly construed. It may reserve the *arbitrary right* of termination or the right to annul for failure to properly perform the work.'[10]

This credo reflected some court decisions thus far taken in American history. Yet Donnelly not only stated his opposition to the State's allegedly arbitrary right to terminate a contract, but also remained silent about *US v Corliss Steam Engine Company*,[11] decided by the Supreme Court in 1875, in which the Court affirmed, apparently for the first time in the US history, the government's right to terminate a contract for its convenience.

Whether this omission was deliberate, I cannot tell. What I can tell is that Donnelly's *mentalité* in the 1920s has somehow lasted to this day. It reveals America's willingness to support congruence instead of exceptionalism, even though subsequent cases and regulations have expressly granted to the government the power to terminate contracts for its convenience. From a comparative law perspective, what matters is that congruence philosophy still lurks behind the scene of the most scholarly work, even though nowadays termination for convenience is fully consecrated in the FAR.

The invention of the word 'exceptionalism' by Joshua Schwartz, who is ideologically more sympathetic to the state or public values than most scholars in the field, reveals this. In contrast, those who favour the private sector (most scholars) seem to merely *tolerate* termination for convenience (like SAD and the Unmistakability Doctrine). That is why scholars have been denouncing the government's right to terminate the contract as 'almost unrestricted'[12] or 'virtually unlimited';[13] it is said that, in theory, 'the contractor is put in the same position he would have been in had he not received the contract at all'.[14] One commentator wrote that the clauses grant government an 'almost uncontrolled discretion'.[15] The language reveals Americanism.

The story of termination for convenience and its philosophy can be briefly told. The irrelevance of the public–private dichotomy for the theory of government contracts has already been mentioned, and the combined historical and ideological factors were used to tentatively explain why termination for convenience in the US has remained an issue restricted to military procurement for a century. Now I will explore the subject more fully.

---

[10]   Ibid: 354 (emphasis added) (internal quotations omitted).
[11]   91 US 321 (1875).
[12]   Andrews & Peacock 1979: 274.
[13]   Petrillo & Conner 1997: 338.
[14]   Perlman & Goodrich 1978: 4.
[15]   Lerner 1980: 711.

Although the precise origin of termination for convenience is obscure,[16] the doctrine mentions that the first appearance of the institute in American law was the already quoted *US v Corliss Steam Engine Company* (1875).[17] *Corliss* was a Civil War (1861–5) case. Justice Stephen Field (1816–89), speaking for a unanimous court, held that the Secretary of the Navy, having the duty 'to enter into numerous contracts for the public service', also had the power to require the termination of the contract 'when from any cause the *public interest* require[d] such suspension'. Thus, the inherent sovereign authority of the state was invoked.[18] However, as Schwartz remarked, the Court's emphatic language made 'clear the importance of the military context to the result reached'. The case 'thus testifies powerfully to the particularized impact of the military context of procurement on the development of exceptionalist doctrine'.[19]

Nevertheless, as stated in Chapter 4, termination for convenience was not extended to civilian contracts for almost a century after *Corliss*. Instead, between 1875 and the Second World War, statutes and regulations were enacted, most of them in response to or originated from wartime necessities, granting the government the power to terminate or modify military contracts. That was the case of the Urgent Deficiency Appropriation Act (1917), the Dent Act (1919), the Contract Settlement Act (1944) and the Armed Services Procurement Act (1947).[20] A possible explanation that a comparativist can offer to understand this congruential scenario is based on the reigning private law philosophy that has governed the American legal system, so well represented by Donnelly's blunt phrase in 1922: 'Our concept of government is founded on the principle of *individualism*.'[21]

After the Second World War, however, termination for convenience gradually spread through regulations into peacetime contracts and civilian contracts, and such clauses are now mandatory in most federal contracts.[22] Investigating the reasons for this expansion is a work far beyond my capacity. Yet, it would not be far from the truth to intimate that, aside from pragmatic reasons, the idea

---

[16]　See Petrillo & Conner 1997: 338.

[17]　91 US 321 (1875). Most scholars cite *Corliss* as the first case dealing with termination for convenience. See Cibinic et al 2016: chapter 11, I; Lerner 1980: 712; Petrillo & Conner ibid; Schwartz 2004: 56. It is nevertheless noteworthy that in *US v Speed*, 75 U.S. 77 (1868), a case that also arose out of a Civil War contract, the Supreme Court had already dealt with termination for the Government's convenience. See LaBrum 1943: 7.

[18]　See L Lerner 1980: 714.

[19]　Schwartz 2004: 59, 63.

[20]　I borrow the sequence of Acts from Petrillo & Conner 1997: 339. See also Young 1984: 894–6.

[21]　Donnelly 1922: 50.

[22]　See Petrillo & Conner 1997: 339–40.

of a more active state may have played a role in the expansion of termination for convenience for civilian procurements.[23] In any event, what seems to be clear for a comparatist is that, even if 'exceptionalist' rules granting express power to the government to terminate contracts for its convenience were enacted, the reaction of the courts and the doctrine still favours congruential philosophy.

Two cases deserve mentioning, both decided by the former Court of Claims: *Colonial Metals Co. v US* (1974)[24] and *Torncello v US* (1982).[25] In these cases, the Court fought over the limits of the right to terminate the contract. In short, the main issue was whether the use of the clause should be confined to cases in which a change in circumstances (as happens during wartime) has occurred. *Colonial Metals* found this condition unnecessary, thus pushing the pendulum towards 'exceptionalism', but it was in this respect expressly overruled by an ambiguous *en banc* Court in *Torncello*, which forced the pendulum towards 'congruence' again.

In *Colonial Metals*, the Court stated that the language of regulations had granted a pure discretion to the Contracting Officer to terminate contracts: 'The language of the clause gives the contracting officer the "fullest of discretion to end the work" in the interest of the Government.' Briefly, the Navy contracted for a supply of copper ingot from a contractor, but soon after this the government terminated the contract to get a better price from another source.[26] The Court decided that if the government had found a better price or a more advantageous contract elsewhere, no matter if the Navy 'knew or ought to have known that a better price was available before the contract was signed', the Contracting Officer could have terminated the contract in the government's 'best interest'. 'Termination to buy elsewhere at a cheaper price', the Court said, 'is essentially such a termination as has repeatedly been approved'. Thus, 'the Government alone', the Court stated bluntly (in a language that sounded very French), 'is the judge of its best interest in termination [of] a contract for convenience, pursuant to the discretionary power reserved by the clause to the Government's contracting officer'.

---

[23]　President Franklin Roosevelt tried in 1944 to introduce a 'Second Bill of Rights' in the US, granting a set of economic and social rights (food, clothing, recreation, decent home, medical care, good education and others) to individuals. Moreover, it was not by chance that, during the New Deal, the idea that government bureaucrats would be able to determine the public interest was held up by some supporters of the public administration. See Cohen-Tanugi 1985: 114–15. France has never abandoned this idea.

[24]　204 Ct. Cl. 320, 494 F.2d 1355 (1974).

[25]　231 Ct. Cl. 20, 681 F.2d 756 (1982).

[26]　I just paraphrase the resume by Claybrook Jr 1997: 564.

Colonial Metals is crucial because, in a sense, as commentators stated clearly, it 'grants Government a unilateral right to repudiate contracts – even retrospectively – at any time, for any reason, and without paying damages'.[27] A common law criticism based on *equality* is easy to make: contractors cannot terminate contracts when prices rise.[28] However, the same court posed limits to a convenience termination. Aside from the government's 'bad faith', which may well be 'virtually impossible' to prove,[29] or 'some other wrong to the plaintiff or illegal conduct',[30] the most common limit has come wrapped in a historical argument. *Torncello* offered it.

The *Torncello* Court cited on eight occasions the work of Cibinic and Nash, two outstanding authors who have severely criticized the unlimited use (or abuse) of the government's power to terminate the contract and who are more identified with the private sector than with the public authority.[31] However, *Torncello* was an *en banc* decision. A plurality of three judges formed the majority, and three other sitting judges concurred in the result, each having written a separate opinion. As in *Winstar*, the Court did not offer a clear guide for the matter. The judges' reasoning revealed a lack of consistency in the convenience termination theory and permitted further confusing and contradictory decisions.[32]

In any event, the plurality in *Torncello* pushed the pendulum back to the congruence side, revealing a robust common law approach and offering critics of termination for convenience a good argument. The Court emphasized the historical circumstances in which termination for convenience of the government arose, stressing the Civil War origin of the restriction to military procurement. After having perused the most significant range of decisions about the subject, the *Torncello* Court affirmed that *Colonial Metals* 'appear[ed] to be an aberration in the precedents of the courts' and 'marked a dramatic departure from the development of convenience termination as a method of risk allocation'. Briefly, the court's reasoning suggested that, during wartime, circumstances frequently change dramatically, and that it in this case it would be 'clearly [...] against the public interest' to continue a contract.[33] Thus, by linking wartime and changing circumstances, congruence philosophy supported some form of the 'changed circumstances' test.[34] Those who criticize 'exceptionalism' insist

---

27 Petrillo & Conner 1997: 343–4.
28 See Perlman & Goodrich 1978: 6.
29 Cibinic et al 2016: Chapter 11, II (citing courts' and boards' cases).
30 *Colonial Metals*, 494 F.2d at 1361.
31 As is known, American courts are unwilling to cite scholarly works.
32 See Petrillo & Conner 1997: 346.
33 *Torncello*, 681 F.2d at 768.
34 See Petrillo & Conner 1997: 347.

on the wartime argument and urge that peacetime government contracts should 'mimic commercial practice', limiting convenience termination 'to contracts for weapons systems, wartime requirements, or other uniquely governmental needs'.[35] Wartime circumstances could not have spoken louder. Language unveils ideology.

But the rationale, theoretically, doesn't help much. The question about the parameters to measure the changed circumstances criteria remains, as well as the inquiry about the necessary liaison between war and changing circumstances, to name just two evident problems. The standard of pricing is the most obvious example. How much 'changing' legitimizes termination for convenience? Would a cap in the percentage of the total cost be a fair criterion? Should the cap be the same for all contracts? As for the liaison between war and changed circumstances, would it not be fair to think that, say, an economic depression can devastate a nation's wealth at least as much as a war can? Or a pandemic such as Covid-19? If so, wouldn't it be reasonable to permit termination for reasons other than war-based ones? The doctrine, reflecting the decisions of the courts and boards, suggests that *Torncello*'s teaching is ambiguous,[36] with later decisions narrowing its reach.[37]

French criticism of the previously mentioned American syllogism would nevertheless be addressed not to the minor premise, but the major one: a *contrat administratif* is not a private contract. Thus, the application of the same rules and principles doesn't follow. The government can permanently terminate a contract for its convenience, whether the conditions have changed because of external or internal circumstances or whether the government's policy has changed. In the background of the French reasoning lies not an *individualistic* idea of government but a collectivist one.

The last case to be mentioned here is *Krygoski Construction Co. v United States*,[38] decided by the United States Court of Appeals for the Federal Circuit in 1996. *Krygoski* narrowed the reaching of *Torncello* and suggested that the government may terminate contracts for its convenience without having to justify its action by reference to a change in circumstances, thus apparently again pushing the pendulum away (perhaps not so strongly, though) from the congruence side.[39]

---

[35]   Ibid: 371–2.

[36]   See ibid: 348.

[37]   See eg Cibinic et al 2016: 1064–7 (citing many boards' and courts' decisions limiting the scope of *Torncello*).

[38]   94 F.3d 1537 (Fed. Cir. 1996), *cert. denied*, 117 S. Ct. 1691 (1997).

[39]   As Schwartz noted, '*Krygorski* independently underscores the key role played by military procurement in the development of the termination for convenience doctrine' (2004: 65).

After *Krygoski*, however, the scenario became perhaps even fuzzier than it was with *Torncello*.[40] The 'changed circumstances' test apparently suggested by the plurality in *Torncello* was repudiated. Supporters of congruence have stated that '*Krygoski* doesn't delineate meaningful limits on the government's right to terminate for convenience' and urged for a 'simpl[e] return to *Torncello*'s "changed circumstances" test',[41] while defenders of exceptionalism have insinuated that the exceptionalist approach retained its force.[42]

No matter which side one takes, it is fair to say that termination for convenience runs counter to American Liberalism. In a recent article, Bruce Page Jr attacks convenience termination on many grounds, claiming that the better policy to adopt should include expectation damages in the composition of the just compensation in convenience termination cases.[43] No wonder that Page's arguments, backed by American case law history, run from utilitarian morals to economic analysis. The article's argument can be encapsulated in the following passage: 'My [...] question [...] is whether the law of government contracts generally, and each government contract in particular, improve, even if only marginally, the well being of Americans.'[44]

Adam Smith sings backstage.

2.   FRANCE: *POUVOIR DE RÉSILIATION UNILATÉRALE SANS FAUTE*

As previously stated in Chapter 2, *le pouvoir de résiliation unilatérale sans faute* ('the power to unilaterally rescind the contract without [contractor's] fault'), consistently recognized by French law since the mid-nineteenth century at least, is nowadays found in the CCP/2018, Articles L. 6, 5°, L. 2195-3.

The statutory language used to justify *le pouvoir de résiliation* is the Rousseauian *intérêt général*. The rationale is straightforward: a *contrat administratif*, as performed in the name of *l'intérêt général*, can also be terminated in its very name.[45] 'Like the power to make changes (*modification unilatérale*), the power to terminate the contract finds both its source and limits in the general interest.'[46] The lingo is quintessentially French: *l'intérêt général* is the telos and the limit of the State action.

---

[40]   See Petrillo & Conner 1997: 360.
[41]   Ibid: 369–70.
[42]   See Schwartz 2004: 66–7.
[43]   See Page 2008.
[44]   Ibid: 4.
[45]   See Richer 2002: 22.
[46]   GAJA/2021: 131. See also Richer ibid: 29.

In 1958, the *pouvoir de résiliation unilateral sans faute* was solemnly recognized by the *Conseil d'État* in *Distillerie de Magnac-Laval*, the 'best illustration' of the State prerogative.[47] In commenting on this leading post-Second World War case, I will call attention to how the divergent comparative foundations we have already discussed in this book contribute to shifting the focus of the legal reasoning from the wartime circumstantial character of the case to the structural, systematic exceptionalism that governs French law. Put differently, the ongoing discussion held in the US about the liaison between wartime (or military) contracts and exceptionalism is foreign to French *mentalités*. The ferment of termination for convenience in *contrats administratifs* is not the wartime circumstances, but the idea of *service public*.

In 1944, soon after the liberation of Paris from Nazi Germany, the State established legal norms aiming at both developing the production of industrial alcohol and permitting the State to buy part of the production at a specific price; that is, the production and sale of alcohol was at the time under State regulation (*production planifiée*). The advantageous conditions of production led numerous agricultural producers to buy a large quantity of beet cultivated soil. Still, soon after, the State found it could no longer keep on buying the production without burdening the public treasury. Consequently, following a Law of 11 July 1953, which granted the State specific power, a decree (*décret*) was issued on 9 August 1953 either lowering or suppressing the amount of alcohol already purchased, thus harming contractors. The Distillerie de Magnac-Laval sued the State, arguing that the Decree was illegal for terminating contracts, thus infringing contractors' rights.[48]

The *commissaire du government* Kahn, whose conclusions were only partially followed by the *Conseil*, maintained that laws and decrees had given the government the power to reduce alcohol production. Therefore, the emphasis should be on regulating and planning the economy rather than on the eventually existent contract right. 'The production of alcohol is a regulated production (*production planifiée*)', said Kahn; under this perspective, 'the contract occupies necessarily, compared to the regulation, a secondary place'.[49] Kahn went further, stating that even if the circumstances weren't the ones at stake, the *nature juridique* of the *contrats administratifs* would not be affected; *l'Administration* could have terminated the contract anyway. The *résiliation* is thus a 'normal prerogative' of *l'Administration*, and the French doctrine, unlike in

---

[47]   See Terneyre 1989: 147; Brenet 2011: 249; CCPcom 2021: 73.

[48]   For the facts and ruling, see Lachaume et al 2020: 582–92, from which I derive also the following paragraph.

[49]   Quotations from the conclusion of the *commissaire* Kahn, in vol 1958 *Actualité Juridique – Droit Administratif*: 285–6.

the US, finds no difficulty in labelling this power as 'discretionary',[50] 'quasi immune'.[51] Yet Kahn suggested that only the legislator could *generally* terminate contracts in the name of the general interest, while the Administration could do it only individually. While accepting most of Kahn's rationale, the *Conseil* didn't follow, in this last part, Kahn's conclusions, and decided that government could generally and unilaterally terminate contracts.

The structure of the legal reasoning in *Magnac-Laval* is as French as it could be, beginning with the controlling catchwords used: 'State power', 'special character of the public law', 'intrinsic inequality of the parties'. The rhetoric has only confirmed the French preconceived jurisprudence regarding the State's *inherent* power to terminate the contract (*mettre fin au contrat*) whenever it wishes during the contractual relation (*en tout état de cause*), as public law rules are applicable (*en vertu des règles applicables*) to the *contrats administratifs*.[52] 'We can't forget', wrote a group of scholars commenting on *Magnac-Laval* in 2020, 'that [*le pouvoir de résiliation*] bases itself on the supremacy of the general interest over the private and individual interests'.[53]

This idea is as anti-American as it could be. The premise of the French legal reasoning holds the opposite ideology to that prevalent in the US. The State can, in principle, terminate any *contrat administratif*. Exceptionalism, not congruence, is the governing ideology. Unlike in the US, it is not a problem for the French to accept government's power to modify or terminate contracts. Wartime is a minor circumstance that triggers State policy and influences economic planning. It is not the main reason for the exceptional rule. In French law, it is unnecessary to invoke the war to accept *exorbitance*.

The Rousseauian conception of *intérêt général* fuels French law and makes 'natural' the acceptance of convenience termination. That is why *la jurisprudence* has not confined the power to terminate the *contrat* to the 'good functioning of the public service'. *L'intérêt général* can be invoked to terminate contracts when *l'Administration* abandons a previous project, or when there is a change in regulation that must be followed, or for budgetary purposes, or if there is a necessity to reorganize, or even suppress, the functioning of public service.[54]

---

[50]   See Gaudemet 2001: § 1468.
[51]   Richer 2002: 28.
[52]   The French words italicized in the text are used by the *Conseil d'État* and are those most commonly quoted by the French doctrine to explain the institute of termination for convenience in France.
[53]   Lachaume et al 2020: 589.
[54]   See Richer & Lichère 2019: 241–2 (citing appropriate cases).

Yet *l'intérêt général* and *intérêt du service* are usually equated,[55] and *l'équilibre financier* is not the only principle founding full recoverability. The State shall compensate the contractor also 'on the very interest of the public service itself of whom the contractor is definitely the collaborator'.[56] Lurking behind this idea are Durkheim's and Duguit's philosophies. It is not the 'right' of the contractor that is taken as the foundation of the *équilibre financier*, but the *interest of the public service itself*. The contractor is a *collaborator* and not a *right holder* against the State.

The *collaboration* versus *right* contrast is not casual. Duguit himself negated the idea of 'right' and criticized the individualistic doctrine, which he attributed to Locke.[57] Duguit dismissed the individualistic philosophy of 'rights' as 'theoretically inadmissible' and a 'purely metaphysical proposition', which could not 'be supported by any direct proof'. Man 'can't live alone, has never lived alone, can live only in society, and has never lived except in society', Duguit wrote. 'Therefore the idea of the social man is the only possible starting point of juridical doctrine.' For Duguit, the individualistic doctrine of rights, which holds that men are born with rights that they can assert *against* society and the state, is contradictory because no man can have rights *before* entering the society; if men have rights, it is *because* they live in a community. Thus, Duguit affirms, the individualistic doctrine 'supposes and opposes two contradictions, the sovereignty of the State and the autonomy of the individual'. This contradiction is the reason why countries such as France and Germany have made the 'prodigious effort [...] to maintain intact the sovereign of the State and at the same time to protect the autonomy of the individual'.

Whatever one may think of Duguit's philosophy, what matters is to note that his ideas *against* the 'metaphysical', individualist doctrine of 'rights' facilitated the French notion of State power, and therefore made more complex the acceptance of the very philosophy of 'rights' in French public law, hence in France *droit administratif*.[58] Not that Duguit supported the concepts of sovereignty and State. The contrary is true:[59] he was a critic of both concepts and even of the concept of *imperium*.[60] In that respect, his ideas were not adopted. Yet, the State must be limited, and Duguit has based the limits on the concept

---

[55]   See Chapus 2001: § 1377; Cohen-Tanugi 1985: 110–11.

[56]   *Traité 2*: § 720.

[57]   See Duguit 1917: 10–26, 103–18, also for quotations in this paragraph.

[58]   For a brilliant study about the rights of the 'administered' (*administrés*), see Foulquier 2003 (analysing the contribution of Duguit at 58–62, 146–51, 181–5, 470–2).

[59]   See Duguit 2003 [1901]: 227–318.

[60]   See Duguit 1999 [1913]. At this point, his ideas did not succeed. The French idea of State remains strong today. Nevertheless, what matters here is Duguit's rejection of the individualistic conception of rights.

of *service public*, not on rights. He wrote that the transformation of public law was to be made by substituting the anterior metaphysical and individualistic order for a *realist and socialist juridical system*.[61] The ends pursued by Duguit and the (American) Liberals, namely limiting state power, were the same; yet the means and the philosophy used were entirely different.

One last comparative remark. As I wrote in Chapter 3, French law seems to have guaranteed to the contractor, since – I repeat – at least the nineteenth century, broader compensation for damages than American law does. Courts, supported by the doctrine, have established that the contractor can fully recover its damages when termination takes place. This is the principle of 'full compensation' (*réparation* or *compensation intégrale*),[62] established in *Tramways* as early as 1910, according to which the contractor has the right to be compensated not only for the work performed but also for anticipatory profits, that is, not only for *damnum emergens*, but also for *lucrum cessans*.[63]

This broader recoverability in France can be attributed, though not exclusively, to the principle established very early in the *droit administratif* – that is, the principle of *l'équilibre financier du contract* – already studied, which is, in a sense, the flip side of a whole conception of *exorbitance* represented by the very idea of *contrat administratif* and its corollaries, such as the power to change or terminate a contract.[64]

3.   BRAZIL: *RESCISÃO UNILATERAL DO CONTRATO* (UNILATERAL RESCISSION OF THE CONTRACT) IN THE PUBLIC INTEREST

Until the past decade, there were no significant theoretical and historical studies about public contracts in Brazilian law,[65] let alone any on termination for convenience. Instead, as noted throughout this book, most studies used to copy and paste existing French studies.

---

[61]   See ibid: XI, 281.

[62]   See Chapus 2001: § 1382.

[63]   See GAJA/2021: 133; Gaudemet 2001: § 1468 (citing CE 10 Nov 1927, *Guinard*); Guettier 2008: 395 (citing CE 23 May 1962, *Ministres des Finances des Affaires Économiques c/ Société Financière d'exploitation industrielles*); Richer 2002, at 232 (citing CE 24 Jan 1975, *Clerc-Renaud*); Terneyre 1989: 301; Symchowics 2002: 32 (citing CE 7 Aug 1874, *Hotchkiss et Koolidge*, and mentioning that uncertain and indirect damages are nevertheless excluded).

[64]   See *Traité 2*: § 720.

[65]   The first studies are Giacomuzzi 2011; Almeida 2012; Rosilho 2013; Moura 2014.

I will not seek to fill the gap. However, I will call attention to the pendular movement between the exceptionalist and congruential poles of the spectrum, since termination for convenience is a good example.

As in the US and France, nineteenth-century Brazilian legal sources, either primary or secondary, were scarce. As stated in Chapter 8, during the period of Empire no scholar treated the subject of government procurement.[66] Brazil had to wait for its intellectual matrix. Before the second half of the past century Brazil had started to deal with government procurement more systematically. This was in the period when the French ideology dominated.

However, at the beginning of the twentieth century, Ruy Barbosa (1849–1923), 'the most legitimate of Brazilian liberals, truly prodigious jurisconsult',[67] would advocate his 'faith' in private contracts invoking French *and* American secondary sources. In two lawyering opinions published in the 1910s about State liability for breaching contracts, Barbosa, the mind behind the first Brazilian Republican Constitution in 1891, equated public with private contracts. This idea has echoed in some court decisions. In the first opinion in 1911, what was at stake was a termination of a construction procurement (*empreitada*), and Barbosa emphasized that only by mutual agreement could the contract court be rescinded.[68] And he was emphatic in 1918, in an opinion about State liability in a government procurement case: 'When entering into a contract, the State is subject to the civil law norms, if no special laws exist.'[69] In the same vein, emeritus jurisconsult and commercialist lawyer Carvalho de Mendonça (1861–1930), in a lawyer's opinion from 1916, wrote, based on the STF decisions rendered in 1898, 1902 and 1904, that the State did not have the 'unconstitutional, exorbitant, odious power [… to] arbitrarily terminate [a concession contract]'.[70] Remember that the Old Republic coincided with Brazil's first shift in its conception of State to the American side, as we saw in Chapter 8.

As Ruy Cirne Lima (1908–84), an administrative law scholar and one of the great Brazilian jurists, stated, this was a time in which there reigned 'exotism, more political than legal' in Brazilian administrative law; a time in which Decree 848 of 11 October 1890, oddly enough, determined that the principles of the *common law* should govern the then incipient regime; the result would

---

[66] See Sobrinho 1981: 125.

[67] Lynch 2014: 16.

[68] See Barbosa 1912. See decisions in the Law Report *Revista dos Tribunais* vol 33, at 3–17, n 176.

[69] Barbosa 1918. It is remarkable that Barbosa dated the opinion in American style, putting the month before the day ('Agosto 29, 911'), and not the usual continental style (29 de Agosto de 1911).

[70] Mendonça 1920: 75.

have been that 'the incertitude of this contradiction is the incertitude of legal categories of our administrative law'; the Old Republic, Cirne Lima explained, 'didn't contribute much for the advance of the science of administrative law'.[71]

Moreover, the Brazilian liberalism of the Old Republic, as Raymundo Faoro (1925–2003) wrote, '*deserved to be put in quotes, for being peculiar*'; it was, since its origin, 'officially directed from above, as an appendix of the State'. A Liberalism of façade, I add. 'In Brazilian practice, the liberal, besides the distortion caused by the State character, would go astray in masks of many types and colours.'[72]

The first norm dealing with public contracts was the Federal Code of Public Accountability, Decree 4.536 of 1 January 1922, which said very little about public contracts.[73] However, this Decree was soon regulated by Federal Decree 15.783 of 8 November 1922, in which one can read in Article 766 the following words: 'The administrative contracts are regulated by the same general principles of private contracts concerning to parties' will of agreement and object, being obeyed, however, the norms prescribed in this Chapter as to the formation, approval, and performance.' And Article 788 reads: 'For the grave motive of public interest and interest of the State, the Minister can refrain from performing any contract, however lawful it may be.' In short, and to use the sources' language, positive Brazilian norms early revealed the ambiguity of the legal system's philosophy.

True, this ambiguity only reflects the inherent complexity of the subject. However, it is fair to say that the French philosophy of State, which had inspired Brazil since its infancy, was always present. 'The State', said Brazilian Supreme Court in 1908, 'although entering into a contractual relationship with a private person, is not divested of its rights and capacities that constitute its very quality of power',[74] thus opposing the opinions of both jurisconsults mentioned above.

From the 1930s on, the same idea was advocated by Cavalcanti in 1936, who maintained that 'this doctrine is universally accepted'. Two years later, the Court of Appeals of the State of Goiás bluntly consecrated the French legal ethos in saying that 'due to the world transformations and new forms of political framing, in which [the] social interest is everywhere preponderant, the anachronic theory that considers concessions as private contracts is to be

---

[71]   Cirne Lima 2007: 64, 96.
[72]   Faoro 2007: 102, 74, 158.
[73]   Four articles of the Code (arts 54–57) were dedicated to it. For a brief inventory of the sparse, unsystematic Brazilian legislative treatment to the subject before 1922, see Tácito 1997: 744. For the history of Brazilian public contract laws from the Decree 4.536/1922 to the LLCA/1993, see Rosilho 2013.
[74]   Quoted in Cavalcanti 1936: 183 and Sobrinho 1981: 437.

disregarded'. Concessions, the court said, 'should be considered as public contracts', in which 'preponderates the general interest, represented by the public service, [which] can't be surpassed by the particular interest of the concessionaire'.[75]

The Federal Code of Public Accountability was followed by the Decree-law 200 of 25 May 1967, which contains some rules about public procurement, but none about termination. Finally, the first norm to deal with public contracts more systematically was the Decree-law 2.300/1986, which established specific rules about termination (and changes), 'thus validating what was only a doctrinal recommendation', as Meirelles wrote.[76]

The Decree-law 2,300/1986 crudely exposed the Frenchness of Brazilian law, then still dominant. In the Chapter on contracts, Article 44 separated public from private contracts; this would later be repeated in Article 54 of LLCA/1993 and 89 of LLCA/2021, quoted in the previous chapter. In Articles 68, XIII and 69, I of the Decree-law 2,300/1986, termination was expressly consecrated 'for reasons in the interest of public service', the contractor being considered 'a real collaborator of the public service'.[77] The Decree's 'motivation' (an official declaration about the motives for enacting the norm) mentioned a leading French work on *droit administratif*, André de Laubadère's *Traité du Droit Administratif* of 1973, and stated that the termination in the name of public interest is founded on the 'interest of the public service' and that the contractor is a 'collaborator'. Meirelles, the mind behind the Decree-law, wrote that the State power to alter or terminate contracts was inherent to its authority and could be exercised even if the contract was silent, thus echoing French law. Unsurprisingly, Meirelles expressly advocated the superiority of the public interest throughout his life.[78]

Meanwhile, Brazilian doctrine did little more than add glosses to French doctrine. In 1987, one year after Decree 2,300 was enacted, a commentator wrote that a horizontal relation characterized private contracts while public contracts were governed by a *vertical* relation, meaning that inequality of the parties was the hallmark of the latter. Thus, while no party could terminate a private contract, the government could permanently terminate *contratos administrativos* in the name of the public interest. What founds this prerogative, said the author, was 'the central precept of the whole structure of administrative law (*direito administrativo*), which is the prevalence of the *public interest* over the *private interest*'. Remarkably enough, the author then

---

[75] In *Revista Forense* 36/321.
[76] Meirelles 1987: 158.
[77] Ibid: 301.
[78] See See Meirelles 1990: 325, 156–8, 301.

invoked the 'authority' of a Roman maxim: *salus populi suprema lex est* ('let the safety of the people be the supreme law').[79]

This ethos was overwhelmingly dominant in Brazilian law from the end of the Old Republic to the last decade of the twentieth century, at the level of both formal and material sources. Consequently, termination for convenience in Brazilian government procurement law has revealed remarkably strong exceptionalism, mimicking the French philosophy of State.

The LLCA/1993, in force until 4 April 2023, was promulgated in a transitional time. In the 1990s, the Liberal wave mentioned throughout this book invaded Brazilian public law, and public contracts were not spared. True, Law 8,666 keeps exceptional norms in force. It establishes all the prerogatives mentioned in Chapter 2 and the government's specific power of 'unilateral rescission' (Article 58, II, 78, XII), this being the functional equivalent of the American termination for convenience. The legal text permits termination for 'reasons of high relevancy, well known public interest, [provided that these reasons are both] justified and determined by the agency's head to which the contractor is subordinated and taken in the respective administrative proceeding'.

While LLCA/1993 said nothing else about the proceeding requirements, and despite the 'administrative proceeding' regulated very late in Brazilian history by Law 9,784/1999, courts have invoked the constitutional text to protect contractors in termination cases. Thus, in *Sérgio L M Ferreira v the State of Rio Grande do Sul*, decided by the Court of Appeals of Rio Grande do Sul on 31 March 1999,[80] the government terminated a contract for its convenience. Still, no procedure was followed or notice given or hearing conducted. Yet the Court decided that, although the statutory language of LLCA/1993 was silent about the right to be heard, CFB/88 provided in Article 5°, LV[81] that a defendant has the right of full defense even in administrative proceedings, which means '[a] right to at least be heard', in the court's words.

Besides the procedural protections, the transcendental, open-ended 'public interest' clause was qualified by the expressions 'high relevancy' and 'well known'. These are not empty words. The statutory language suggests that the mere reference to the public interest was insufficient to terminate a contract for the government's convenience.

It would be too naïve to think that, in a very ideological field, the addition of two new adjective locutions ('high relevancy' and 'well known') could shift

---

[79]   See Araújo 1987: 135, 139 (emphasis in original), 140.

[80]   AC 597.232.651/TJRS.

[81]   The clause reads: 'Litigants, in judicial or administrative processes, as well as defendants in general, are ensured of the adversary system and of full defense, with the means and resources inherent to it.'

a century of Statenessness. But it was a grain of congruence in an exceptionalist soil. Subtleties in formal sources may be viewed as reflections of changes in material sources of law. There was already in course, slowly but steadily, a subtle shaking in material sources of law, as suggested in the Introduction; the liberal wave was pushing the pendulum to the congruence side.

The germ of congruence has blossomed. As suggested in the Introduction, from the early 1990s on, Brazilian law experienced a nascent movement towards Liberal values that shook the Brazilian political and legal structure. It was not by chance that scholarly criticism of the century-old principle of 'supremacy of the public interest' began in 1998; neither was it a coincidence that one of the leading scholars in the field, Marçal Justen Filho, dethroned the supremacy principle and put in its place, as foundations of administrative law, 'the protection of fundamental rights and the human dignity'. Marçal's radical move took place between 2004 and 2008,[82] and has been influential on a large part of the scholarly work.

Yet the most crucial blow suffered by the abstract principles, mostly the supremacy of the public interest, was Law 13,665/2018, which added many articles to the Decree-law 4,657/1942, known as the 'Introductory Law to the Brazilian Normative System' (*Lei de Introdução às Normas do Direito Brasileiro* – LINDB). Law 13,655/2018 is, potentially, a revolution in the Brazilian legal order, for it attempts to bring – as never before in Brazilian history – a sense of pragmatism and consequentialism into law. In a way, the spirit of the New LINDB is encapsulated in the famous aphorism of Holmes in his dissenting opinion in *Lochner v New York* (1905): 'General principles do not decide concrete cases.'[83] This idea permeates Brazilian public law nowadays as a legal standard expressly written in the New LINDB. I will make only two remarks.

First, Article 20 reads: 'In administrative, controlling, and judicial spheres, it shall be no decision based on abstract legal values without considering the practical consequences of the decision.' Thus, what seems evident to American sensibilities was deemed necessary to be expressly written in a statutory text in Brazil.

Second, in Articles 21, sole paragraph, 23, and 26, §1, I, the Law subtly suggests a shift in the conception of public interest, from the Rousseauian to the utilitarian, in expressly using the plural '*interesses gerais*', general interests. In this book's language, the New LINDB is the best example of formal sources reflecting a move in the tectonic plates of material sources of law.

---

[82] See Marçal 2004; 2005; 2008.
[83] See Sundfeld & Giacomuzzi 2018.

Moreover, the actual LLCA/2021, Article 137, expressly states that any contract extinction must be preceded by a formal decision in a due process, and Clause VIII maintains the termination power for 'reasons of public interest, justified by the head of the agency in the respective administrative proceeding', thus suppressing the qualifiers 'high relevancy' and 'well known'. This suppression, however, may be deceiving if isolated from the new standards established in the New LINDB. From the dogmatic legal viewpoint, at least, it is no longer necessary to qualify the 'public interest' as of 'high relevancy' or 'well known'. As an abstract value, the public interest must be confronted with the concrete life.

The subtleties of the move towards congruence could also be noted in the LGC/1995, which regulates the Concessions. Articles 35, II, and 37 establish that the granting authority can retake the service from the concessionaire 'for reasons of public interest, through specific authorizing law and after previous compensation'. The legislative intention is clear: besides the previous compensation, there must be legislative interference through specific legislation to terminate the concession. In concessions, it is not the sole Power of the Administration that counts.

Let me try a few words about compensation.

Its extension is expressly regulated by Laws 8,666/1993, Article 79, § 2 and LLCA/2021, Article 138, §2°, using similar language. In case of unilateral rescission for the sake of public interest, the Laws state that the contractor has the right to recover for the 'damages regularly proved' plus the warranty given, the costs incurred and payments due for work already performed, and the expenses of termination.[84] Nothing in the law says expressly that the anticipated profits are recoverable. It is a question of legal interpretation whether the expression 'damages regularly proved' includes *lucrum cessans*, that is, the loss of anticipated profit, or only *damnum emergens*, that is, the actual realized loss. Revealingly, most scholarly works and courts decisions have been taking the statutory language in its broader sense, thus allowing anticipatory profits to be recoverable,[85] advancing congruence philosophy.

To sum up, although still using exceptionalist language, not abandoning any State prerogatives and maintaining the language of 'public interest', the Brazilian legal procurement system has slowly and steadily pushed towards congruence philosophy, either by enacting laws that establish new standards of public law interpretation that deflate a Rousseauian understanding of public interest and recommend a consequentialist reading of laws or by inserting in

---

[84]   I have paraphrased clauses I, II and III of art 79, § 2, LLCA/1993, and clauses I, II and III of art 138, § 2, LLCA/2021.

[85]   See Justen Filho 2021: 1500 (citing cases from STJ).

legal texts many horizontal norms that encourage equality between State and contractors, leaving the solution of contractual problems to the parties. No wonder that a recent scholarly article, echoing the Liberal ethos, has questioned the exceptional character of the exorbitant clauses, that is, the core of public contract law.[86]

However, Brazilian legal history shows that the pendulum's recent swing to the congruence side may not be its last. The strong Statenessness of Brazil is always lurking behind the scenes.

---

[86] See Câmara & Souza 2020.

Conclusion to *Foundations of Public Contracts*

At the end of the Introduction to this book, I mentioned Benoît Plessix's idea about contract law being the common concept archetype for a currently fashionable attitude towards the unity of law, unity meaning the mastering of liberal, private law parameters, following the predominant ideological force in the Western world from the 1980s onwards. If the contract is an archetypical concept in law, it would be surprising if public contract theory had not been affected by the same intellectual mood. But, I asked, would the liberal wave be strong enough to alter the French and Brazilian conception of administrative contracts?

Revolutions in law are rare, at least in peaceful times. Since the law is a conceptual discipline, revolutions are better made through concepts: new meanings are attributed to old ones; original concepts are constructed, others are attacked. Moreover, when revolutions happen, they don't start at the surface of the formal sources; they operate at the foundational level, in material sources of law. The more adamantine a concept is in a legal system, the more complex it is to remove or alter it. It follows that the stability of law, one of its most important goals, depends on the firmness of its foundations – and that is why, paraphrasing Laski's advice to Holmes set out in the Introduction, we need to know the material sources whence law derives. In this book, I've tried to delve into these sources to discover what they were or are and how firm they remain.

From that perspective, the Brazilian legal system is more willing to change its conception of public contracts and accept liberal values than is the French system. As the history has shown, Brazilian law has, in a pendular move, been shifting its model of State between French Statenessness and American statelessness, finding itself today in a liminal moment: it is by no means a coincidence that formal sources, from recently enacted laws to scholarly work and legal decisions, have unbosomed the American neoliberal ethos that lies at the foundations of the move.

Nevertheless, from a comparative law viewpoint, that hesitation is less shocking than an eventual transformation of the concept of *le contrat administratif*, vitally entrenched in the French legal system as such. As we have seen, in France, unlike in the US, an entire legal structure, different from the common law, was constructed to accommodate *le droit politique, le droit administratif* and, consequently, *les décisions unilatérales de l'Administration* and *les contrats administratifs*.[1] It is not easy to sap all that structure, constructed as it was to support a kvelled system of administrative justice, which, unsurprisingly, Tocqueville opposed, as an institution of the Old Regime.[2]

Nowadays, the common criticism in France, which has spread to Brazil, is well known: that entire structure, departing from the public–private law dichotomy, is a byproduct of an authoritarian State that, so critics claim, doesn't respect individual rights and democracy. It is not an accident that, as shown by Norbert Foulquier, French *droit administratif*, cradled by ideology, avoided referring to 'rights of the administered' (*les droit publics subjectifs*) until the last strong liberal wave in the 1990s.[3] Of course, *le droit administratif* did protect contractors' rights, and perhaps better than the US law did; but the liberal, individualistic rhetoric of rights was avoided in France.

My impression is that, of all these criticisms, the most fundamental is directed to what I called in Chapter 3 'the deepest stage of public contract law foundations': the conception of the general interest. There is a '[clash] between two legal cultures', as advanced by the *Rapport Public du Conseil d'État* in 1999. This clash operates at the level of *mentalités*, thus at the level of the *longue durée*. Accordingly, they are anchored deeply in legal minds.

The dispute over the conception of public interest has reached Rousseau's soil, stirring up French legal scholarship to such a degree that some have proposed that the public interest should be *rejected* as the criterion of *contrats administratifs*.[4] Others, however, advanced a subtler move. In 2006, in a prize-winning *thèse de doctorat* more than 1000 pages in length, Guylant Clamour, framing the subject by detailing the concepts of *intérêt général* and *concurrence*, solved the battle by melding the latter into the former. Private interests and the marketplace are not in a priori opposition to the general interest. This move came through in the form of a new concept, with a new name: *intérêt général néo-moderne*. It is a revolution through the concepts mentioned above. The French hubris at whose core is a transcendent conception of *l'intérêt général* is therefore called into question. According to the neo-modern general interest, *l'intérêt général*, for centuries adamantine to *le droit administratif*, is no longer monolithic but fragmented into a plurality of public interests, responding to a political philosophy deeply embedded with liberal, pluralist values.[5]

---

[1] See generally Plessix 2003a: 715–21. For a recent study on the power of Administration's unilateral decision and democracy, see Testard 2018.
[2] See Tocqueville 1998 [1856]: 132–5. See also Jaume 2005: 32–8.
[3] Foulquier 2003: 694, 1164.
[4] See Gartner 2006.
[5] See Clamour 2006: passin, mainly §§ 297–437, 1373–81.

That idea conveys a strong utilitarianism, as we can easily sense. As a conceptual invention, although still in its inception, it has a normative, heuristic function with potentially enormous consequences. If incorporated by French law, particularly *le Conseil d'État*, it will shift the tectonic plates of one the most influential legal systems in the continental world. In Brazilian law this general idea has already germinated – as we saw in Chapter 9 – even in public contracts specifically,[6] with the suggestion that private law principles and values should dominate and the principle of public interest supremacy should be rethought. We have reached the most foundational level of a legal system.

Yet that is not a novelty either. In a historical preface to Tome 26 of the *Archives de Philosophie de Droit*, published in 1981 (suggestive title: *L'utile et le juste*), the French legal philosopher Michel Villey (1914–88) remembered a frequently neglected truism: the principal source of public law is a byproduct of a philosophy 'from which the legal professors have received the [philosophical] systems'.[7] Villey's main target was French professors of public law, *les publicistes*. For Villey, there would be a 'publicists' Calvary' consistent in a gap, a very uncomfortable contradiction between the experience of the publicists and the legal philosophy which they nevertheless followed and taught, and largely refused to call into question.

By examining the three legal systems' administrative and public contract law literature, what is perhaps new is the idea that French publicists may have nowadays surmounted that Golgotha. I am sure, however, that most Brazilian publicists, unfortunately, still neglect Villey's warnings. And I sense that this debate does not often appear in American legal academia, at least not among public contracts scholars. That happens, I venture to suggest, not only because government contract law is 'somewhat mundane', as William Rehnquist said, but also because the reigning liberalism has not yet been seriously threatened as the prevailing ideology.

As mentioned in Chapter 1, I am not suggesting that law cedes its authority to moral or political theories of a particular philosophy and therefore incorporates its teachings, thus solving the problem. Again, adapting Weber's methodological teaching, law's *preliminary analysis* shares common concepts with the other disciplines, but it later adapts them to legal institutional necessities of the law itself. According to Guy Oakes, for Weber sociocultural disciplines, including law, are 'an arena in which a struggle over methods, basic concepts and presuppositions is waged', resulting in a 'perpetual flux of problematics

---

[6]   See eg Ferraz 2017.
[7]   Villey 1981: 2.

and a constant redefinition of concepts'.[8] Yet to redefine crucial concepts like public contracts, we need to understand the 'specific problematic', which 'constitutes an unquestioned, although not unquestionable set of assumptions'.[9] The more fundamental assumptions of public contracts, and the presuppositions of and conditions for their maintenance or change, were the object of this study.

In his concluding remarks about the relationship between *l'intérêt général* or public and *les intérêts particuliers* in the colloquium on *l'intérêt général dans les pays de common law et de droit écrit* mentioned in Chapter 3, Didier Truchet stated: 'Much more than a juridical problem, it is a political problem, in the noblest sense of the term, or, as we say nowadays, a problem of values. That confers it fundamental social consequences and makes it so difficult to solve.'

I couldn't agree more. The problem's solution, whatever it is, can only be grasped if we understand the foundations of public contract law. Before being legal, the foundations are social, historical, philosophical. In short, they are Political, in the broadest sense of the term.

The irony of all theorizing, Oakeshott once observed, lies in 'its propensity to generate, not an understanding, but a not-yet-understood'.[10] I don't pretend to have offered an understanding about the foundations of public contracts, but I hope I have improved our endless not-yet-understood.

---

[8]   Oakes 1977: 13 (the quotations marks for Weber's words in *Gesammelte Aufsätze zur Wissenschaftslehre,* 3rd ed, 1968, are omitted).
[9]   Ibid.
[10]   In Loughlin 2003: vii.

References

Alencar, Letícia (2019), *Equilíbrio na Concessão* (Forum).

Alexander, Larry (1993), The Public/Private Distinction and Constitutional Limits on Private Power, 10 *Constitutional Commentary* 361.

Allison, John (1996), *A Continental Distinction in the Common Law. A Historical and Comparative Perspective on English Public Law* (Oxford).

Almeida, Fernando Dias (2012), *Contrato administrativo* (Quartier Latin).

Almeida, Fernando Dias (2015), *Formação da Teoria do Direito Administrativo no Brasil* (Quartier Latin).

Alschuler, Albert (2000), *Law Without Values. The Life, Work, and Legacy of Justice Holmes* (Chicago).

Amhlaigh, Cormac Mac (2015), Defending the Domain of Public Law, in CM Amhlaigh, C Michelon and N Walker (eds), *After Public Law* (Oxford) 103.

Amilhat, Mathias (2014), *La notion de contrat administratif. L'influence du droit de l'Union européene* (Bruylant).

Amselek, Paul (1982), Brèves réflexions sur la notion de 'sources du droit', 27 *Archives de Philosophie du Droit ('Sources' du droit)* 251.

Andrews Jr, Harris and Peacock, Robert (1979), Terminations: An Outline of the Parties Rights and Remedies, 11 *Public Contracts Law Journal* 269.

Arantes, Paulo Eduardo (1994), *Um Departamento Francês de Ultramar. Estudos sobre a formação da cultura filosófica uspiana (Uma experiência dos anos 60)* (Paz e Terra).

Araújo, Edmir (1987), *Contrato Administrativo* (Revista dos Tribunais).

Arieli, Yehoshua (1964), *Individualism and Nationalism in American Ideology* (Harvard).

Aristotle (2004), *The Nicomachean Ethics* (Penguin Classics, trans JAK Thompson).

Auby, Jean-Bernard and Mark Freedland (eds) (2004), *La Distinction du Droit Public et du Droit Privé: Regards Français et Britanniques – The Public Law/Private Law Divide: Une Entente Assez cordiale?* (LGDJ).

Auby, Jean-Bernard (2004), Le Rôle de la Distinction du Droit Public et du Droit Privé dans le Droit Français, in J-B Auby and M Freedland (eds), *La Distinction du Droit Public et du Droit Privé: Regards Français et Britanniques – The Public Law/ Private Law Divide: Une Entente Assez cordiale?* (LGDJ) 19.

Auby, Jean-Bernard (2006), Les Problèmes Posés par le Développement du Contrat en Droit Administratif Comparé, in Guylain Clamour and Marion Ubaud-Bergeron (eds), *Contrats Publics – Mélanges en l'honneurs de Professeur Michel Guibal* vol I (Faculté de Droit de Montpellier) 411.

Auby, Jean-Bernard (2021), Public/Private, in P Cane et al (eds), *The Oxford Handbook of Comparative Administrative Law* (Oxford) 467.

Ávila, Humberto (1998), Repensando o princípio da supremacia do interesse público sobre o particular, 24 *Revista Trimestral de Direito Público* 159.

Badaoui, Saroit (1955), *Le Fait du Prince dans les Contrats Administratifs en Droit Français et en Droit Égyptien* (LGDJ).

Barbosa, Letícia (2019), *La Théorie de l'Imprévision dans les Contrats de Concession de Service Public* (Université Paris II).

Barbosa, Rui (1912), Parecer, 1 *Revista dos Tribunais* 39.

Barbosa, Rui (1918), Contrato de Empreitada – Responsabilidade Civil do Estado, 29 *Revista Forense* 74.

Barnes, Javier (2019), The Evolution of the Public/Private Divide, in J-B Auby (dir) *Le futur du droit administratif – The future of administrative law* (LexisNexis) 81.

Barros Júnior, Carlos (1986), *Contratos Administrativos* (Saraiva).

Batiffol, Henri (1979), *Problèmes de Base de Philosophie du Droit* (LGDJ).

Beaud, Olivier (1990), La notion d'État, 35 *Archives de Philosophie du Droit* 119.

Beaud, Olivier (1994), *La Puissance de L'État* (PUF) .

Beaud, Olivier (2004), La Distinction entre Droit Public et Droit Privé: Un Dualisme qui Résiste aux Critiques, in J-B Auby and M Freedland (eds), *La Distinction du Droit Public et du Droit Privé: Regards Français et Britanniques – The Public Law/ Private Law Divide: Une Entente Assez cordiale?* (LGDJ) 29.

Beauregard, Henry (1965), Termination for Convenience as Breach of a Government Contract, 7 *Boston College Industrial and Commercial Law Review* 259.

Beauté, Jean (1992), La Théorie Anglaise de la Couronne, 15 *Droits* 113.

Beauthier, Régine and De Broux, Pierre-Olivier (2012), Un regard historien: sources du droit, sources du pouvoir?, in I Hachez et al (dirs), *Les sources du droit revisités*, vol 4 (Théories des sources du droit) 715.

Beiser, Frederick (2002), *German Idealism. The Struggle Against Subjectivism, 1781–1801* (Harvard).

Bell, John (1997), L'expérience britannique, 1997 *L'actualité Juridique – Droit Administratif* 130.

Bell, John (2002), Comparing Public Law, in A Harding and E Örücü (eds), *Comparative Law in the 21st Century* (Kluwer Academic Publishers) 235.

Bell, John (2011), Legal Research and the Distinctiveness of Comparative Law, in MV Hoecke (ed), *Methodologies of Legal Research. Which Kind of Method for What Kind of Discipline?* 155.

Bellamy, Richard (1992), *Liberalism and Modern Society: A Historical Argument* (Pennsylvania).

Belleau, Marie-Claire (1997), The 'Juristes Inquiets': Legal Classicism and Criticism in Early Twentieth-Century France, 1997 *Utah Law Review* 379 .

Benoît, Jean-Louis and Keslassy, Éric (2005), *Alexis de Tocqueville. Textes économiques* (Pocket).

Bergel, Jean-Louis (2018), *Métholodogie Juridique* (PUF, 3rd ed).

Bezançon, Xavier (2001), *Essai Sur Les Contrats de Travaux et de Services Public* (LGDJ).

Bienvenu, Jean-Jacques (1985), Tendances de la doctrine contemporaine en droit administratif, 1 *Droit* 153.

Bigot, Grégoire (2000), Les mythes fondateurs du droit administratif, 16 *Revue Française de Droit Administratif* 527.

Bigot, Grégoire (2002), *Introduction historique au droit administratif depuis 1789* (PUF).

Bigot, Grégoire (2019), Tribunal des conflits, 8 février 1873, Blanco, in T Perroud et al (eds) *Les grands arrêts politiques de la jurisprudence administrative* (LGDJ) 40.

Binenbojm, Gustavo (2006), *Uma Teoria do Direito Administrativo. Direitos Fundamentais, Democracia e Constitutionalização* (Renovar).

Binenbojm, Gustavo (2019), Isenções e Descontos Tarifários de Caráter Essencial em Serviços Públicos Concedidos: Requisitos de Validade e Eficácia, in EB Moreira (ed), *Tratado Do Equilíbrio Econômico-Financeiro* (Fórum, 2nd ed) 159.

Bird, Colin (1999), *The Myth of Liberal Individualism* (Cambridge).

Bix, Brian (1999), H.L.A. Hart and the Hermeneutic Turn, 52 *Southern Methodist University Law Review* 167.

Birocchi, Italo (1996), La distinzione 'ius publicum/ius privatum' nella dottrina della scuola culta (François Connan, Hugues Doneau, Louis Charondas Le Caron), 23 *Ius Commune* 139.

Blanquet, Jean-Michel and Milet, Marc (2015), *L'invention de l'État. Léon Duguit, Maurice Hauriou et la naissance du droit public moderne* (Odile Jacob).

Bluntschli, Johann (1885), *The Theory of the State* (Oxford).

Bobbio, Norberto (1982), Kelsen e les sources du droit, 27 *Archives de Philosophie du Droit ('Sources' du droit)* 135.

Bobbio, Norberto (1985), *Stato, governo, società. Per una teoria generale della politica* (Einaudi).

Bobbio, Norberto (1995) [1979], *O Positivismo Jurídico. Lições de Filosofia do Direito*, Nello Morra (ed) (Ícone, M Publiesi et al trans).

Bockmann Moreira, Egon (2019), Contratos Administrativos de Longo Prazo: A Lógica de Seu Equilíbrio Econômico-Financeiro, in EB Moreira (ed), *Tratado Do EquilíbrioEconômico-Financeiro* (Fórum, 2nd ed) 89.

Bodin, Jean (1945 [1566]), *Method for the Easy Comprehension of History* (WW Norton, B Reynolds trans).

Bonnard, Roger (1930), The Doctrine of Duguit on Law and the State, 4 *China Law Review* 193.

Borchard, Edwin (1924), Government Responsibility in Tort, 34 *Yale Law Journal* 1.

Borchard, Edwin (1926), Government Responsibility in Tort, IV, 36 *Yale Law Journal* 1.

Borchard, Edwin (1927a), Government Responsibility in Tort, V, 36 *Yale Law Journal* 757.

Borchard, Edwin (1927b), Government Responsibility in Tort, VI, 36 *Yale Law Journal* 1039.

Borchard, Edwin (1928a), Governmental Responsibility in Tort: VII, 28 *Columbia Law Review* 577.

Borchard, Edwin (1928b), Theories of Governmental Responsibility in Tort, 28 *Columbia Law Review* 734.

Bourdieu, Pierre (1991), The Peculiar History of Scientific Reason, 6 *Sociological Forum* 3.

Bradford, Ernst (1924), The Field of Regulation, in M Cooke (ed), *Public Utility Regulation* (Ronald) 9.

Brault, Gerald (1962), French Culture: Some Recent Anthropological and Sociological Findings, 36 *The French Review* 44.

Brenet, François (2011), Les contrats administratifs, in P Gonod, F Melleray and P Yolka (eds), *Traité de droit administratif* Tome 2 (Dalloz), 217.

Brettschneider, Corey & McNamee, David (2015), Sovereign and State: A Democratic Theory of Sovereign Immunity, 93 *Texas Law Review* 1229.

Brown, Jethro (1916), The Jurisprudence of M. Duguit, 32 *Law Quarterly Review* 170.

Brown, Neville and Bell, John (1988), *French Administrative Law* (Oxford, 5th ed).

Burdeau, François (1989), *Histoire de l'administration française. Du 18e au 20e siècle* (Montchrestien).

Burdeau, François (1980), *Traité de sciences politiques*, Tome I (LGDJ, 3rd ed).

Burdeau, François (1995), *Histoire du droit administratif* (Presses Universitaire de France).

Caccia, Natasha et al (2006), Os Juristas e a Construção do Estado Liberal, in CG Mota (ed), *Os Juristas na Formação do Estado-Nação Brasileiro* (Quartier Latin) 147.

Caillosse, Jacques (1996), Droit public–privé: sens et portée d'un partage académique, *Actualité Juridique – Droit Administratif* 955.

Caillosse, Jacques (2017), *L'État du droit administratif* (LGDJ, 2nd ed).

Caillosse, Jacques (2019), Le traitement doctrinal de la jurisprudence administrative: l'euphémisation du politique in T Perroud et al (eds) *Les grands arrêts politiques de la jurisprudence administrative* (LGDJ) 19.

Câmara, Jacintho (2019), Contratos Administrativos, in MSZ Di Pietro (ed), *Tratado de Direito Administrativo* (Revista dos Tribunais, 2nd ed) 319.

Câmara, Jacintho and Souza, Ana Paula (2020), Existem cláusulas exorbitantes nos contratos administrativos?, 279 *Revista de Direito Administrativo* 185.

Canaris, Claus-Wilhelm (1995), *Función, estructura y falsación de las teorías jurídicas* (Civitas, D Brückner and JL de Castro trans).

Canaris, Claus-Wilhelm (2002 [1983]), *Pensamento Sistemático e Conceito de Sistema na Ciência do Direito* (Calouste Gulbenkian and AM Cordeiro trans, 3rd ed) (Portuguese translation of the 2nd German ed *Systemdenken und Systembegriff in der Jurisprudenz*).

Cane, Peter (1987), Public Law and Private Law: A Study of the Analysis and Use of a Legal Concept, in J Eekelaar and J Bell (eds), *Oxford Essays in Jurisprudence. Third Series* (Oxford) 57.

Canedo, Marguerite (2004), L'exorbitance du droit des contrats administratifs, in F Melleray (ed), *L'exorbitance du droit administratif en question* (Faculté de droit et des sciences sociales de Poitiers) 125.

Carvalho, José Murilo de (1972), Political Elites and State Building: The Case of Nineteenth-Century Brazil, 24 *Comparative Studies in Society and History* 378.

Carvalho, José Murilo de (1991), The Unfinished Republic, 48 *The Americas* 139.

Carvalho, José Murilo de (2005), *Pontos e Bordados: Escritos de história e política* (UFMG).

Carvalho, José Murilo de (2006), *A Construção da Ordem – Teatro de Sombras* (Civilização Brasileira, 4th ed).

Cassese, Sabino (2000), *La construction du droit administratif – France et Royaume-Uni* (Montchrestien, J Morvillez-Maigret trans).

Cavalcanti, Themístocles Brandão (1938), *Instituições de Direito Administrativo Brasileiro* Vol 2 (Freitas Bastos).

Chapus, René (1999), Signification de l'arrêt Blanco, in *L'administration et son juge* (PUF) 29.

Chapus, René (2001), *Droit Administratif Général* vol 1 (Montchrestien, 15th ed).

Chevallier, Jacques (1970), *L'Élaboration historique du principe de séparation de la juridiction administrative et de l'administration active* (LGDJ).

Chevallier, Jacques (1979), Les Fondements Idéologiques du Droit Administratif Français, in J Chevallier (ed), *Variations Autour de l'Idéologie de l'Intérêt Général* vol. 2 (PUF) 3.

Chevallier, Jacques (1988), Le droit administratif, droit de privilege? 46 *Pouvoirs* 57.

Chevallier, Jacques (1995), Presentation, in *Public/Privé* (PUF) 5.

Chevallier, Jacques (1997), Regards sur une évolution, *L'Actualité Juridique – Droit Administratif* 8.

Chevallier, Jacques (2001), Doctrine ou science?, *Actualité Juridique – Droit Administratif* 603.

Chevallier, Jacques (2015), Déclin ou Permanence du Mythe de L'Intérêt Général?, in *L'Intérêt Général: Mélanges en L'Honneur de Didier Truchet* (Dalloz) 83.

Chevallier, Jacques (2018), *Le droit administratif* (PUF, 11th ed).

Chevallier, Jacques (2019), *Science administrative* (PUF, 6th ed).

Chevrier, Georges (1952), Remarques sur l'introduction et les vicissitudes de la distinction du 'jus privatum' et du 'jus publicum' dans les œvres des anciens jurists français, *Archives de Philosophie du Droit – Nouvelle Série* 5.

Chiassoni, Pierluigi (2016), *El discreto placer del positivismo jurídico* (Universidad Externado de Colombia).

Chiassoni, Pierluigi (2021), From Savigny to Linguistic Analysis: Legal Positivism through Bobbio's Eyes, in T Spaak and T Mindus (eds), *The Cambridge Companion to Legal Positivism* (Cambridge) 325.

Church, William (1967), The Decline of the French Jurists as Political Theorists, 1660–1789, 5 *French Historical Studies* 1.

Cirne Lima, Ruy (2007), *Princípios de Direito Administrativo* (Malheiros, 7th ed rev by Paulo Pasqualini).

Citron, Roger (2002), Lessons from the Damages Decisions Following *United States v. Winstar Corp.*, 32 *Public Contracts Law Journal* 1.

Cibinic Jr et al (2011), *Formation of Government Contracts* (Cheetah, 4th ed).

Cibinic Jr et al (2016), *Administration of Government Contracts* (Cheetah, 5th ed).

Clamour, Guylain (2006), *Intérêt général et concurrence. Essay sur la pérennité du droit public en économie de marhé* (Dalloz).

Clark, David (1999), The Use of Comparative Law by American Courts, in Ulrich Drobnig and Sjef van Erp (eds), *The Use of Comparative Law by Courts – XIVth International Congress of Comparative Law* (Kluwer Law International) 297.

Clark, David (2012), History of Comparative Law and Society, in DS Clark (ed) *Comparative Law and Society* (Edward Elgar Publishing) 1.

Claybrook, Jr, Frederick (1997), Good Faith in the Termination and Formation of Federal Contracts, 56 *Maryland Law Review* 555.

Clemmy, Friedrich (2016), *Histoire doctrinale d'une mise en discours: des contrats de l'administration au contrat administratif (1800–1960)* (University of Toulouse).

Cohen, Morris (1927), Property and Sovereignty, 13 *Cornell Law Quarterly* 8.

Cohen, Morris (1936), On Absolutism in Legal Thought, 84 *University of Pennsylvania Law Review* 681.

Cohen-Tanugi, Laurent (1985), *Le droit sans l'Etat. Sur la démocratie en France et en Amérique* (PUF, 3rd ed).

Coq, Véronique (2015), *Nouveles recherches sur les fonctions de l'intérêt général dans la jurisprudence administrative* (L'Harmattan).

Costa, João Cruz (1956), *Contribuição à História das Idéias no Brasil* (José Olympio).

Coutinho, Afrânio (1943), Some Considerations on the Problem of Philosophy in Brazil, 4 *Philosophy and Phenomenological Research* 186.

Cretella Júnior, José (1964), Teoria do 'Fato do Príncipe', 75 *Revista de Direito Administrativo* 23.

Cretella Júnior, José (1968), Princípios Informativos do Direito Administrativo, 93 *Revista de Direito Administrativo* 1.

Cretella Júnior, José (1990), *Direito Administrativo Comparado* (Forense, 3rd ed).

Cretella Júnior, José (2001), *Dos Contratos Administrativos* (Forense).

Cretella Júnior, José (2006), *Das Licitações Públicas* (Forense, 18th ed).

Creveld, Martin van (1999), *The Rise and Decline of the State* (Cambridge).

Cunha, Thadeu (1995), A teoria da imprevisão e os contratos administrativos, 201 *Revista de Direito Administrativo* 35.

Curran, Vivian Grosswald (1998a), Cultural Immersion, Difference and Categories in U.S. Comparative Law, 46 *American Journal of Comparative Law* 43.

Curran, Vivian Grosswald (1998b), Dealing in Difference: Comparative Law's Potential for Broadening Legal Perspective, 46 *American Journal of Comparative Law* 657.

Curran, Vivian Grosswald (2006), Comparative Law and Language, in M Reimann and R Zimmermann (eds), *The Oxford Handbook of Comparative Law* (Oxford University Press) 675.

Custos, Dominique (2017), La formulation de l'intérêt public en droit administratif Américain, in GJ Guglielmi (dir), *L'intérêt général dans les pays de* common law *et de droit écrit* (Panthéon-Assas) 67.

Dawson, John (1935), Gold Clause Decisions, 33 *Michigan Law Review* 647.

Dabin, Jean (1969), *Théorie Générale du Droit – Nouvelle Édition* (Dalloz).

Davis, Kenneth Culp (1970), Sovereign Immunity Must Go, 22 *Administrative Law Review* 383.

Dawson, Christopher (1954), The Historical Origins of Liberalism, 16 *Review of Politics* 267.

Delamare, Nicolas (1705), *Traité de la Police*, Tome Premier (Jean & Pier e Cot).

Diamant, Alfred (1951), The French Council of State: Comparative Observations on the Problem of Controlling the Bureaucracy of the Modern State, 13 *Journal of Politics* 562.

Dias, José de Aguiar (1995), *Da Responsabilidade Civil* vol 2 (Forense, 10th ed).

Dickens, Charles (2004 [1854]), *Hard Times* (Barnes & Noble).

Dickinson, John (1927), *Administrative Justice and the Supremacy of Law* (Harvard).

Dijon, Xavier (2012), Le regard jusnaturaliste: la nature humaine, source du droit, in I Hachez et al (Dirs), *Les sources du droit revisités*, vol 4 (Théories des sources du droit) 809.

Dimock, Marshall (1933), The Development of American Administrative Law, 15 *Journal of Comparative Legislation and International Law* 35.

Donnelly, James Francis (1922), *A Treatise on the Law of Public Contracts* (Little, Brown).

Drago, Roland (1979), Paradoxes sur les Contrats Administratifs, in Études offertes à Jacques Flour (Répertoire du Notariat Defrénois) 151.

Drago, Roland (1990), Le Contrat Administratif Aujourd'hui, 12 *Droits* 117.

Dubos, Olivier (2019), Le droit administratif contra la théorie de l'État, in J-B Auby (dir) *Le futur du droit administratif – The future of administrative law* (LexisNexis) 135.

Dubouis, Louis (1996), Le droit communautaire a-t-il un impact sur la definition du droit administratif?, *L'Actualité juridique – Droit Administratif* 102.

Duez, Paul and Debeyre, Guy (1952), *Traité de Droit Administratif* (Dalloz).

Dufau, Valérie (2000), *Les Sujétions Exorbitantes du Droit Commun en Droit Administratif. L'administration sous la contrainte* (L'Harmattan).

Duffy-Meunier, Aurélie (2017), La conception Britannique de l'intérêt général, in G Guglielmi (dir), *L'intérêt général dans les pays de* common law *et de droit écrit* (Panthéon-Assas) 47.

Dufour, Alfred (1982), La théorie des sources du Droit dans l'École du Droit historique, 27 *Archives de Philosophie du Droit ('Sources' du droit)* 85.

Dufour-Kowalska, Gabriel (1982), Philosophie du fondement et fondement du Droit, 27 *Archives de Philosophie du Droit ('Sources' du droit)* 191.

Duguit, Léon (1913), *Les Transformations du Droit Public* (Armand Colin).

Duguit, Léon (1917), The Law and the State, 31 *Harvard Law Review* 1.

Duguit, Léon (1927), *Traité de Droit Constitutionnel* vol 1 (E. de Boccard, 3rd ed).

Duguit, Léon (1999 [1913]), *Les Transformations Générales du Droit Privé depuis de Code Napoléon* (Mémoire du Droit, 2nd ed).

Duguit, Léon (2002 [1921]), *Souveraineté et Liberté* (Mémoire du Droit).

Duguit, Léon (2003 [1901]), *L'État, le droit objectif et la loi positive* (Dalloz).

Durkheim, Émile (1999 [1893]), *Da Divisão do Trabalho Social* (Martins Fontes, E Brandão trans).

Duxbury, Neil (2001), *Jurists and Judges. An Essay on Influence* (Hart).

Dworkin, Ronald (1986), *Law's Empire* (Harvard).

Dworkin, Ronald (1996), *Freedom's Law* (Harvard).

Dworkin, Ronald (2006), *Justice in Robes* (Harvard).

Dyson, Kenneth (1980), *The State Tradition in Western Europe. A Study of an Idea and Institution* (Martin Robertson).

Eckert, Gabriel (dir) (2021), *Code de la commande publique 2021 commenté* (LexisNexis 2nd ed).

Elias, Norbert (2000 [1939]), *The Civilizing Process. Sociogenetic and Psychogenetic Investigations*, E Dunning et al (eds) (Blackwell, Jephcott trans).

Elliott, William (1922), The Metaphysics of Duguit's Pragmatic Conception of Law, 37 *Political Science Quarterly* 639.

Esplugas-Labatut, Pierre (2018), *Le service public* (Dalloz, 4th ed).

Estorninho, Maria (1990), *Réquiem pelo Contrato Administrativo* (Almedina).

Estorninho, Maria (1999), *A Fuga para o Direito Privado* (Almedina).

Ewald, William (1994), The American Revolution and the Evolution of Law, 42 *The American Journal of Comparative Supplement* 1.

Ewald, William (1995), Comparative Jurisprudence (I): What Was It Like To Try a Rat? 143 *University of Pennsylvania Law Review* 1889.

Fairgrieve, Duncan (2003), *State Liability in Tort. A Comparative Law Study* (Oxford).

Fairgrieve, Duncan (2021), Criminal and Civil Liability, in P Cane et al (eds), *The Oxford Handbook of Comparative Administrative Law* (Oxford) 811.

Fairgrieve, Duncan et al (eds) (2002), *Tort Liability of Public Authorities in Comparative Perspective* (British Institute of International & Comparative Law).

Faoro, Raymundo (2007), Existe um pensamento político brasileiro?, in F Comparato (Org), *A República Inacabada* (Globo) 25.

Farnsworth, Allan (1987), Precontractual Liability and Preliminary Agreements: Fair Dealing and Failed Negotiations, 87 *Columbia Law Review* 217.

Fauvarque-Cosson, Bénédicte (2006), Comparative Law in France, in M Reimann and R Zimmermann (eds), *The Oxford Handbook of Comparative Law* (Oxford University Press) 35.

Ferraz, Sergio (2017), Por Uma Nova (e Diferente) Lei de Licitações, in A Wald et al (eds), *O Direito Administrativo na Atualidade* (Malheiros) 1105.

Ferreira da Silva, Jorge Cesa (2007), *Adimplemento e Extinção das Obrigações: Comentários aos Arts. 304 a 388 do Código Civil* (Revista dos Tribunais).

Fletcher, George (1997), What Law Is Like, 50 *Southern Methodist University Law Review* 1599.

Fortsakis, Théodore (1987), *Conceptualisme et Empirisme en Droit Administratif Français* (LGDJ).

Foulquier, Norbert (2011), Le Service Public, in P Gonod, F Melleray and P Yolka (eds), *Traité de droit administratif* Tome 2 (Dalloz) 46.

Foulquier, Norbert (2003), *Les droits publics subjectifs des administrés. Émergence d'un concept en droit administratif français du XIXe au XXe siècle* (Dalloz).

Franco Sobrinho, Manoel de Oliveira (1941), O contrato administrativo. Noção e Fundamentos, 83 *Revista dos Tribunais* 416.

Franco Sobrinho, Manoel de Oliveira (1981), *Contratos Administrativos* (Saraiva).

Frankenberg, Günter (1985), Critical Comparisons: Re-thinking Comparative Law, 26 *Harvard International Law Journal* 411.

Frankenberg, Günter (1998), Remarks on the Philosophy and Politics of Public Law, 18 *Legal Studies* 177.

Frankfurter, Felix (1938), Foreword, 47 *Yale Law Journal* 515.

Freedland, Mark (2004), The Evolving Approach to the Public/Private Distinction in English Law, in J-B Auby and M Freedland (eds), *La Distinction du Droit Public et du Droit Privé: Regards Français et Britanniques – The Public Law/Private Law Divide: Une Entente Assez cordiale?* (LGDJ) 101.

Friedrich, Carl (1939), The Deification of the State, 1 *Review of Politics* 18.

Fromont, Michel (2010), L'évolution du droit de contrat de l'Administration – Différences théoriques et convergences de fait, in R Noguellou (ed) *Droit comparé des contrats publics* (Bruylant) 263.

Frydman, Benoît (2011), *Les Sens des Lois. Histoir de l'interprétation et de la raison juridique* (Bruylant, 3rd ed).

Furet, François (1984), Introduction, in *In the Workshop of History* (Chicago, J Mandelbaum trans) 1.

Furet, François (1996), *The French Revolution, 1770–1814* (Blackwell, A Nevill trans).

Gabayet, Nicolas (2015), *L'aléa dans les contrats públics em droit anglais et droit français* (LGDJ).

Gadamer, Hans-Georg (2001a), *Gadamer in Conversation. Reflections and Commentary)* (Yale University Press, RE Palmer ed and trans).

Gadamer, Hans-Georg (2001b), Hermeneutics as Practical Philosophy, in *Reason in the Age of Science* (MIT Press, FG Lawrence trans) 88.

Gadamer, Hans-Georg (2004), *Truth and Method* (Continuum, J Weinsheimer and DG Marshall trans, 2nd ed).

Gadamer, Hans-Georg (2005), *La Dialéctica de Hegel* (Cátedra, M Garrido trans, 6th ed).

Gallie, Walter (1956), Essentially Contested Concepts, *Proceedings of the Aristotelian Society* 167.

García-Villegas, Mauricio (2006), Comparative Sociology of Law: Legal Fields, Legal Scholarships, and Social Sciences in Europe and the United States, 31 *Law & Society Inquiry* 343.

Garner, James (1919), Administrative Reform in France, 13 *American Political Science* 17.

Gartner, Fabrice (2006), Des rapports entre contrats administratifs et intérêt général, *Revue Française de Droit Administratif* 19.

Gaudemet, Jean (1995), *Dominium – Imperium*. Les Deux Pouvoirs dans la Rome Ancienne, 22 *Droits* 3.

Gaudemet, Yves (2001), *Traité de Droit Administratif* Tome 1 (LGDJ, 16th ed).

Gaudemet, Yves (2020), *Droit Administratif* (LGDJ, 23rd ed).

Gavison, Ruth (1992), Feminism and the Public/Private Distinction, 45 *Stanford Law Review* 1.

Gérando, Joseph-Marie (1829), *Institutes du Droit Administratif Français, ou Élémens du Code Administratif, Réunis et Mis en Ordre* vol 1 (Nève).

Gerber, David (1992), Idea-Systems in Law: Images of Nineteenth-Century Germany, 10 *Law & History Review* 153.

Giacomuzzi, José Guilherme (2011), *Estado e Contrato* (Malheiros).

Giacomuzzi, José Guilherme (2017a), O serviço de táxi é serviço público? Em torno de conceitos e da esquizofrenia no direito administrativo brasileiro, 68 *Revista de Direito Administrativo e Constitucional* 209.

Giacomuzzi, José Guilherme (2017b), Uma Breve Genealogia do Interesse Público, in A Wald et al (eds), *O Direito Administrativo na Atualidade* (Malheiros) 635.

Gierke, Otto von (1900 [1881]), *Political Theories of the Middle Age* (Cambridge, FW Maitland trans).

Glendon, Mary Ann et al (1994), *Comparative Legal Traditions. Texts, Materials and Cases* (West Group, 2nd ed).

Glenn, Patrick (2006), Aims of Comparative Law, in JM Smits (ed) *Elgar Encyclopedia of Comparative Law* 57 (Edward Elgar Publishing).

Goltzberg, Stefan (2018), *Les Sources du Droit* (PUF, 2nd ed).

Gopnik, A (2000), *Paris to the Moon* (Random House).

Gordley, James (1981), European Codes and American Restatements: Some Difficulties, 81 *Columbia Law Review* 140.

Gordley, James (1998), Codification and Legal Scholarship, 31 *University of California Davis Law Review* 735.

Gordley, James (2017), Comparison, Law, and Culture: A Response to Pierre Legrand, 65 *American Journal of Comparative Law* 133.

Gordon, Robert (1983), Legal Thought and Legal Practice in the Age of American Enterprise, 1870–1920, in *Professions and Professional Ideologies in America* 70 (NCU Press 1983).

Goyard-Fabre, Simone (1982), Les sources du droit et la 'révolution copernicienne': quelques réflexions sur Kant et Rousseau, 27 *Archives de Philosophie du Droit (sources du droit)* 67.

Goyard-Fabre, Simone (1989), *Jean Bodin et le Droit de La Republique* (PUF).

Goyard-Fabre, Simone (1997), *Les principes philosophiques du droit politique moderne* (PUF).

Graf, Michael (1998), The Determination of Property Rights in Public Contracts after *Winstar v. United States*: Where has the Supreme Court Left Us?, 38 *National Resources Journal* 197.

Grand, Vincent (2008), *Léon Blum (1872-1950): Gouverner la République* (LGDJ).

Gray, Christopher (1983), Critique of Legal Theory. From Rousseau to Kelsen: Maurice Hauriou on his Predecessors, 14 *Rechtstheorie* 401.

Gray, Christopher (2010), *The Methodology of Maurice Hauriou* (Rodopi).

Green, Leslie (2012), Introduction, in HLA Hart, *The Concept of Law* (Oxford, 3rd ed).

Green, Leslie (2021), Positivism, Realism, and Sources of Law, in T Spaak and T Mindus (eds), *The Cambridge Companion to Legal Positivism* (Cambridge) 39.

Greenberg, Janelle (1991), Our Grand Maxim of State, 'The King Can Do No Wrong', 12 *History of Political Thought* 209.

Greenberger, Gerald (1979), Lawyers Confront Centralized Government: Political Thought of Lawyers during the Reign of Louis XIV, 23 *American Journal of Legal History* 144.

Grossfeld, Bernhard (1990), *The Strength and Weakness of Comparative Law* (Oxford, T Weir trans).

Guandalini Jr., Walter (2016), *História do Direito Administrativo Brasileiro. Formação (1821-1895)* (Juruá).

Guénaire, Michel (2005), Le service public au cœur du modèle de développement français, 134 *Le Débat* 52.

Guettier, Christophe (2008), *Droit des contrats administratifs* (PUF, 2nd ed).

Guglielmi, Gilles (2017), Introduction: Les habits neufs de l'intérêt général, in G Guglielmi (dir), *L'intérêt général dans les pays de* common law *et de droit écrit* (Panthéon-Assas) 15.

Guglielmi, Gilles (1991), *La Notion d'Administration Publique dans la Théorie Juridique Française. De la Révolution à l'Arrêt Cadot (1789–1889)* (LGDJ).

Guldi, Jo and Armitage, David (2014), *The history manifesto* (Cambridge).

Guimarães, Fernando Vernalha (2003), *Alteração Unilaterial do Contrato Administrativo* (Malheiros).

Haarscher, Guy (1998), Autorité et Raison en Philosophie, in P Vassart et al (eds), *Arguments d'Autorité et Arguments de Raison en Droit* 249 (Nemesis).

Hacker, PMS (1977), Hart's Philosophy of Law, in PMS Hacker and J Raz (eds), *Law, Morality, and Society: Essays in Honour of H.L.A. Hart* (Clarendon) 1.

Hadfield, Gillian (1999), Of Sovereignty and Contract: Damages for Breach of Contract by Government, 8 *South California Interdisciplinary Law Journal* 467.

Harlow, Carol (1980), 'Public' and 'Private' Law: Definition Without Distinction, 43 *Modern Law Review* 241.

Hart, HLA (1983 [1954]), Definition and Theory in Jurisprudence, in *Essays in Jurisprudence and Philosophy* (Clarendon) 21.

Hart, HLA (1983), Introduction, in *Essays in Jurisprudence and Philosophy* (Clarendon) 1.

Hart, HLA (2012 [1961]), *The Concept of Law* (Clarendon, 3rd ed).

Hart Jr, Henry (1935), The Gold Clause in United States Bonds, 48 *Harvard Law Review* 1057.

Hartz, Louis (1991 [1955]), *The Liberal Tradition in America* (Harvest, 2nd ed).

Hauriou, Maurice (1918), Interpretation of the Principles of Public Law, 31 *Harvard Law Review* 813.

Hauriou, Maurice (1970), *The French Institutionalists: Maurice Hauriou, Georges Renard, Joseph T. Delos*, A Broderick (ed) (Harvard, M Welling trans).

Hauriou, Maurice (1983), *Tradition in Social Sciences* (Ann Arbor, CB Gray trans).

Hauser, Barbara (2003), Born a Eunuch? Harmful Inheritance Practices and Human Rights, 21 *Law & Inequality* 1.

Hegel, GWF (1991 [1821]). *Elements of the Philosophy of Right*, AW Wood (ed) (Cambridge, HB Nisbet trans).

Helmholz, Richard (1992), Use of Civil Law in Post-Revolutionary American Jurisprudence, 66 *Tulane Law Review* 1649.

Heuschling, Luc (2002), *État de droit – Rechtsstaat – Rule of Law* (Dalloz).

Hobbes, Thomas (1994 [1668]), *Leviathan* (E Curley ed, Hackett).

Hobbes, Thomas (2005 [1666]), *A Dialogue Between a Philosopher and a Student, of the Common Laws of England* (A Cromartie ed, Oxford).

Hoeflich, Michael (1997) *Roman & Civil Law and the Development of Anglo-American Jurisprudence In The Nineteenth Century* (Georgia).

Hoecke, Mark Van (2004), Deep Level of Comparative Law, in M Van Hoecke (ed), *Epistemology and Methodology of Comparative Law* (Hart) 165.

Hoecke, Mark Van (2011), Legal Doctrine: Which Method(s) for What Kind of Discipline?, in M Van Hoecke (ed), *Methodologies of Legal Research* (Hart) 1.

Hoecke, Mark Van (2015), Methodology of Comparative Legal Research, *LaM* DOI: 10.5553/REM/.000010.

Hoecke, Mark Van (2017), Is There Now Comparative Legal Scholarship?, 12 *Journal of Comparative Law* 271.

Hoecke, Mark Van and Warrington, Mark (1998), Legal Cultures, Legal Paradigms and Legal Doctrine: Towards a New Model for Comparative Law, 47 *International & Comparative Law Quarterly* 495.

Holdsworth, William (1983 [1925]), *Sources and Literature of English Law* (William Hein).

Holmes, Stephen and Sunstein, Cass (1999), *The Cost of Rights. Why Liberty Depends on Taxes* (WW Norton).

Horwitz, Morton (1992), *The Transformation of American Law, 1870–1960* (Oxford).

Hourson, Sébastien and Yolka, Philippe (2020), *Droit des Contrats Administratifs* (LGDJ, 2nd ed).

Howe, Mark DeWolfe (ed) (1953), *Holmes–Laski Letters – The Correspondence of Mr. Justice Holmes and Harold J. Laski 1916–1935*, vols 1–2 (Harvard).

Husa, Jaakko (2014), Research Designs of Comparative Law, in M Adams and D Heirbaut (eds), *The Method and Culture of Comparative Law. Essays in Honour of Mark Van Hoecke* 53.

Husa, Jaakko (2015), *A New Introduction to Comparative Law* (Bloomsbury).

Hutchinson, Allan and Monahan, Patrick (1987), Democracy and the Rule of Law, in AC Hutchinson and P Monahan (eds), *The Rule of Law, Ideal or Ideology* (Carswell) 97.

Hutton, Patrick (1981), The History of Mentalities: The New Map of Cultural History, 20 *History and Theory* 237.

Jackson, Vicky (2003), Suing the Federal Government: Sovereignty, Immunity, and Judicial Independence, 35 *George Washington International Law Review* 521.

Jacquemet-Gauché, Anne (2013), *La responsabilité de la puissance public em France et em Allemagne* (LGDJ).

James, Herman (1946), *The Protection of the Public Interests in Public Contracts* (Public Administration Service).

James, William (1975 [1907]), *Pragmatism and the Meaning of Truth* (Harvard).

Jaume, Lucien (2005), Tocqueville dans le Débat entre le Droit de l'État et le Droit de la Société, in M Carius et al (eds), *La pensée juridique d'Alexis de Tocqueville* 27 (Artois).

Jestaz, Philippe (1993), Source delicieuse … (Remarques en cascade sur les sources du droit), 92 *Revue Trimestrielle de Droit Civil* 73.

Jestaz, Philippe (2015), *Les sources du droit* (Dalloz, 2nd ed).

Jestaz, Philippe and Jamin, Christophe (2004), *La doctine* (Dalloz).

Jèze, Gaston (1932), L'Influence de Léon Duguit sur le Droit Administratif Français, 12 *Archives de Philosophie du droit et de Sociologie juridique* 135.

Jèze, Gaston (2004 [1930]), *Les principes généraux du droit administratif* Tome 2 (Dalloz, 3rd ed).

Jèze, Gaston (2005 [1925]), *Les principes généraux du droit administratif. La technique juridique du droit public français*. Tome 1 (Dalloz).

Jones, Stuart (1993), *The French State in Question. Public Law and Political Argument in the Third Republic* (Cambridge).

Jones, John (1970), *Historical Introduction to the Theory of Law* (Greenwood).

Jouvenel, Bertrand de (1993 [1945]), *On Power* (Liberty Fund, trans JF Huntington).

Justen Filho, Marçal (2019), *Comentários à Lei de Licitações e Contratos Administrativos* (Revista dos Tribunais, 18th ed).

Justen Filho, Marçal (2021), *Comentários à Lei de Licitações e Contratos Administrativos. Nova Lei 14.133/2021* (Revista dos Tribunais).

Kahn-Freund, Otto (1974), On Uses and Misuses of Comparative Law, 37 *Modern Law Review* 1.

Kantorowics, Hermann (1932), The Concept of the State, 35 *Economica* 1.

Kelley, Donald (1974), History, English Law and the Renaissance, 65 *Past and Present* 24.

Kelsen, Hans [2006] (1949), *General Theory of Law & State* (Transaction).

Kelsen, Hans [1960] (1967), *The Pure Theory of Law* (California, Max Knight trans).

Kennedy, Duncan (1997), *A Critique of Adjudication* (Harvard).

Kennedy, Duncan (1982), Stages of the Decline of the Public/Private Distinction, 130 *University of Pennsylvania Law Review* 1349.

Keohane, Nannerl (1980), *Philosophy and the State in France. The Renaissance to the Enlightenment* (Princeton).

Kischel, Uwe (2019), *Comparative Law* (Oxford, trans A Hammel).

Kloppenberg, James (1986), *Uncertain Victory. Social Democracy and Progressivism in European and American Thought, 1870–1920* (Oxford).

Kommers, Donald (1991), German Constitutionalism: A Prolegomenon, 40 *Emory Law Journal* 837.

Kramer, Matthew (1999), In Praise of the Critique of the Public/Private Distinction, in *In the Realm of Legal and Moral Philosophy. Critical Encounters* 112 (Macmillan).

Krent, Harold (1992), Reconceptualizing Sovereign Immunity, 45 *Vanderbilt Law Review* 1529.

Krygier, Martin (1986), Law as Tradition, 5 *Law and Philosophy* 237.

Labrot, Émilie (2016), *L'imprévision. Étude comparée droit public-droit privé des contrats* (L'Harmattan).

LaBrum, Harry (1943), Termination of the War Contracts for the Government's Convenience, 18 *Temple Law Quarterly* 1.

Lachaume, Jean-François et al (2020), *Droit administratif. Les grandes decisions de la jurisprudence* (PUF, 18th ed).

Lake, Ralph (1994), *Letters of Intent and Other Precontratual Documents: Comparative Analysis and Forms* (Butterworth, 2nd ed).

Lalande, André (2002 [1921]), *Vocabulaire technique et critique de la philosophie* (PUF).

Langrod, Georges (1955), Administrative Contracts: A Comparative Study, 4 *American Journal of Comparative Law* 325.

Larenz, Karl (1997 [1991]), *Metodologia da Ciência do Direito* (Calouste Gulbenkian, J Lamego trans, 6th ed).

Lash, Kurt (2009), Leaving the Chisholm Trail: The Eleventh Amendment and the Background Principle of Strict Construction, 50 *William and Mary Law Review* 1577.

Laski, Harold (1919), *Authority in the Modern State* (Yale).

Laski, Harold (1932), La Conception de L'État de Léon Duguit, 1–2 *Archives de Philosophie du droit et de Sociologie juridique* 121.

Latham, Peter (1975), The Sovereign Act Doctrine in the Law of Government Contracts: a Critique and Analysis, 7 *University of Tol. Law Review* 29.

Laubadère, André de (1956a), Les éléments d'originalité de la responsabilité contractuelle de l'administration, in *L'Évolution du Droit Public – Études Offertes à Achille Mestre* (Sirey) 383.

Laubadère, André de (1956b), *Traité Théorique et Pratique des Contrats Administratifs* (LGDJ).

Laubadère, André de et al (1983–4), *Traité des Contrats Administratrifs*, vols 1–2 (LGDJ, 2nd ed).

Le Fur, Louis (1932), Le Fondement du Droit dans la Doctrine de Léon Duguit, 1–2 *Archives de Philosophie du droit et de Sociologie juridique* 175.

Legendre, Pierre (1992), *Trésor Historique de L'État en France. L'Administration classique* (Fayard).

Legendre, Pierre (2005), *Le Désir Politique de Dieu* (Fayard).

Legohérel, Henri (1991), *Histoire du droit public français, des origines à 1789* (PUF, 2nd ed).

Legrand, Pierre (1995a), Antiqui Juris Civilis Fabulas, 45 *University of Toronto Law Journal* 311.

Legrand, Pierre (1995b), Comparative Legal Studies and Commitment to Theory, 58 *Modern Law Review* 262.

Legrand, Pierre (1996a), Comparer, 2 *Revue Internationale de Droit Comparé* 279.

Legrand, Pierre (1996b), European Legal Systems Are Not Converging, 45 *International & Comparative Law Quarterly* 52.

Legrand, Pierre (1996c), How to Compare Now, 16 *Legal Studies* 232

Legrand, Pierre (1997), The Impossibility of 'Legal Transplants', 4 *Maastricht Journal European & Comparative L*aw 111.

Legrand, Pierre (1999a), John Henry Merryman and Comparative Legal Studies: A Dialogue, 47 *American Journal of Comparative Law* 3.

Legrand, Pierre (1999b), *Le droit comparé* (PUF).

Legrand, Pierre (2002), Public Law, Europeanisation and Convergence: Can Comparatists Contribute?, in P Beaumont et al (eds)*, Convergence and Divergence in European Public Law* 225 (Hart).

Leiter, Brian (2012), In Praise of Realism (and Against "Nonsense" Jurisprudence), 100 *The Georgetown Law Journal*, 865.

Leiter, Brian (1997), Rethinking Legal Realism: Toward a Naturalized Jurisprudence, 76 *Texas Law Review* 268.

Lerner, Daniel (1956), Interviewing Frenchmen, 62 *American Journal of Sociology* 187.

Lerner, Lawrence (1980), Tying Together Termination for Convenience in Government Contracts, 7 *Pepperdine Law Review* 711.

Lichère, François (2020), *Droit des contrats publics* (Dalloz, 3rd ed).

Llewellyn, Karl (1989 [1933]), *The Case Law System in America*, P Gewirtz (ed) (Chicago, Michael Ansaldi trans).

Llorens, François (1984), Le pouvoir de modification unilatérale et le principe de l'équilibre financier dans les contrats administratifs (commentaire de l'arrêt du Conseil d'État du 2 février 1983, Union des transports publics régionaux et urbains*), Revue Française de Droit administrative* 45.

Lobban, Michael (2018), Legal Formalism, in MD Dubber and C Tomlins (eds) *The Oxford Handbook of Legal History* (Oxford) 419.

Lobingier, Charles (1942), Administrative Law and *Droit Administratif*. A Comparative Study with an Instructive Model, 91 *University of Pennsylvania Law Review & American Law Register* 36.

Locke, John (1980 [1690]), *The Second Treatise of Government*, CB Macpherson (ed) (Hackett).

Logoff, Martin (1997), A Comparison of Constitutionalism in France and the United States, 49 *Maine Law Review* 21.

Long et al (2021) *Les grands arrêts de la jurisprudence administrative* [GAJA] (Dalloz, 23rd ed).

Lopes, José Reinaldo de Lima (2002), *O Direito na História* (2nd rev ed, Max Limonad).

Lopes, José Reinaldo de Lima (2004), *As Palavras e a Lei* (FGV).

Lopes, José Reinaldo de Lima (2006), *Direitos Sociais* (Método).

Lopes, José Reinaldo de Lima (2014), *Naturalismo Jurídico no Pensamento Brasileiro* (Saraiva).

Loughlin, Martin (1992), *Public Law and Political Theory* (Oxford). Loughlin, Martin (2003), *The Idea of Public Law* (Oxford).

Loughlin, Martin (2000), *Sword & Scales. An Examination of the Relationship Between Law & Politics* (Hart).

Loughlin, Martin (2010), *Foundations of Public Law* (Oxford).

Loughlin, Martin (2013), The Nature of Public Law, in C M Amhlaigh, C Michelon, and N Walker (eds), *After Public Law* (Oxford) 11.

Loughlin, Martin (2017), *Political Jurisprudence* (Oxford).

Loughlin, Martin (2018), The Historical Method in Public Law, in MD Dubber and C Tomlins (eds) *The Oxford Handbook of Legal History* (Oxford) 984.

Loureiro, Gustavo (2020), *Estudos sobre o equilíbrio econômico-financeiro dos contratos de concessão* (Quartier Latin).

Loureiro Filho, Lair (2001), Evolução e Fundamentos da Responsabilidade Pública no Direito Brasileiro, 36 *Revista Trimestral de Direito Público* 203.

Lucy, William (1997), *The Common Law According to Hegel*, 17 *Oxford Journal of Legal Studies* 685.

Lukes, Steven (2006), *Individualism* (ECPR Press Classics, new introduction).

Lynch, Christian (2014), *Da monarquia à oligarquia* (Alameda).

Lyra Filho, Tavares (1941), *Contratos Administrativos* (Imprenta).

MacCormick, Neil (2008), *HLA Hart* (Stanford, 2nd ed).

Macmillan, Hugh (1937), Two Ways of Thinking, in *Law and Other Essays* (Cambridge) 76.

Madden, Thomas and Gold, Andrew (2000), Supreme Court Holds Government to Same Standard as Private Party in Breach Action: Future of 'Sovereign Acts' Doctrine in Doubt, 27 *Government Contractor* 277.

Mairal, Hector (2003), Government Contracts under Argentine Law: A Comparative Law Overview, 26 *Fordham International Law Journal* 1716.

Mannheim, Karl (1954), *Ideology and Utopia* (Routledge, L Wirth and E Shils trans).

Marmor, Andrei (2006), Legal Positivism: Still Descriptive and Morally Neutral, 26 *Oxford Journal of Legal Studies* 683.

Martinich, Aloysius (2005), *Hobbes* (Routledge).

Mattei, Ugo (1992), Common Law: *Il diritto anglo-americano* (UTET).

Máynez, Eduardo García (2000 [1940]), *Introducción al Estudio del Derecho* (Porrúa 2000, 5th ed).

Mazères, Jean-Arnaud (2019), Compagnie générale française des tramways, in T Perroud et al (eds) *Les grands arrêts politiques de la jurisprudence administrative* (LGDJ) 76.

Meirelles, Hely (1973), *Licitação e Contrato Administrativo* (Revista dos Tribunais).

Meirelles, Hely (1987), *Licitação e Contrato Administrativo* (Malheiros, 7th ed).

Meirelles, Hely (1990), *Licitação e Contrato Administrativo* (Malheiros, 9th ed).

Meirelles, Hely et al (2010), *Licitação e Contratos Administrativos* (Malheiros, 15th ed).

Meirelles, Hely et al (2020), *Direito Administrativo Brasileiro* (Malheiros, 44th ed).

Mello, Celso Antônio Bandeira de (1981), *Elementos de Direito Administrativo* (Revista dos Tribunais).

Mello, Celso Antônio Bandeira de (2021), *Curso de Direito Administrativo* (Malheiros, 35th ed).

Mendonça, Carvalho de (1920), A Cláusula Resolutiva Expressa nos Contratos, 33 *Revista Forense* 74.

Merryman, John (1968), The Public Law–Private Law Distinction in European and American Law, 17 *Journal of Public Law* 3.

Merryman, John and Pérez-Perdomo, Rogelio (2007), *The Civil Law Tradition: An Introduction to the Legal Systems of Europe and Latin America* (Stanford, 3rd ed).

Mestre, Jean-Louis (1985), *Introduction historique au droit administratif français* (PUF).

Mestre, Jean-Louis (2021), France: The Vicissitudes of a Tradition, in P Cane et al (eds), *The Oxford Handbook of Comparative Administrative Law* (Oxford) 23.

Mewett, Alan (1958), The Theory of Government Contracts, 5 *McGill Law Journal* 222.

Magliocca, Gerard (2012), The Gold Clause Cases and Constitutional Necessity, 64 *Florida Law Review* 1243.

Michaels, Ralf (2019), The Functional Method of Comparative Law, in M Reimann and R Zimmerman (eds), *Oxford Handbook of Comparative Law* (Oxford University Press, 2nd ed) 345.

Mineur, Didier (2010), *Carré de Malberg. Le positivisme impossible* (Michalon).

Mitchell, JDB (1950), Limitations on the Contractual Liability of Public Authorities, 13 *Modern Law Review* 318.

Mitchell, JDB (1965), The Causes and Effects of the Absences of a System of Public Law in the United Kingdom, 1965 *Public Law* 95.

Mitchell, JDB (1954), *The Contracts of Public Authorities. A Comparative Study* (London).

Mitchell, JDB (1951), The Treatment of Public Contracts in the United States, 9 *University of Toronto Law Journal* 194.

Mitchell, Joshua (1995), *The Fragility of Freedom. Tocqueville on Religion, Democracy, and the American Future* (Chicago).

Moreira, Maurício and Ferrer, Jr, Celso (2012), Varig Case: The Downfall of a Brazilian Icon, 2 *Journal of Airline and Airport Management* 51.

Moreira Neto, Diogo (2014), *Curso de Direito Administrativo* (Forense, 16th ed).

Morgan, Ronald (1992), Identifying Protected Government Acts under the Sovereign Acts Doctrine: A Question of Acts and Actors, 22 *Public Contracts Law Journal* 223.

Mota, Carlos Guilherme (2006), Do Império Luso Brasileiro ao Império Brasileiro, in *Os Juristas na Formação do Estado-Nação Brasileiro* (Quartier Latin) 21.

Moura, Mauro (2014), *A Autonomia Contratual da Administração Pública* (GZ).

Mousourakis, G (2019), *Comparative Law and Legal Traditions. Historical and Contemporary Perspectives* (Springer).

Nagle, James (1999), *A History of Government Contracting* (GWU, 2nd ed).

Noguellou, Rozen (2010), France, in R Naguellou (ed), *Droit comparé des contrats publics* (Bruylant) 675.

Nash, Ralph and Cibinic, John (1991), The Sovereign Acts Defense: Is It Being Fairly Applied?, 10 *Nash & Cibinic Repport* 55.

Nash, Ralph and Cibinic, John (1996), Supreme Court Decides Winstar: 'Unmistakability' Doctrine and 'Sovereign Acts' Defense Deliberated, 10 No. 8 *Nash & Cibinic Repport* 42.

Nash, Ralph et al (2021), *The Government Contracts Reference Book* (Cheetah, 5th ed).

Nehl, Hans (2006), Administrative Law, in JM Smits (ed) (2006) *Elgar Encyclopedia of Comparative Law* (Edward Elgar Publishing) 18.

Nettl, John (1968), The State as a Conceptual Variable, 20 *World Politics* 559.

Nietzsche, Friedrich (1998 [1888]), *The Twilight of the Idols* (Oxford, D Large trans).

Nohara, Patricia and Marrara, Thiago (2018), *Processo Administrativo. Lei 9.784 Comentada* (Revista dos Tribunais, 2nd ed).

Oakes, Guy (1977), Introductory Essay, in Weber, Max, *Critique of Stammler* (Free Press, G Oakes trans, 2nd ed) 1.

Örücü, Esin (1987), An Exercise on the Internal Logic of Legal Systems, 7 *Legal Studies* 310.

Örücü, Esin (2004), *The Enigma of Comparative Law: Variations on a Theme for the Twenty-first Century* (Springer).

Ost, François and Van De Kerchove, Michel (1994), *The Legal System Between Order and Disorder* (Oxford, Iain Stewart trans).

Page Jr, Bruce (2008), When Reliance Is Detrimental: Economic, Moral, and Policy Arguments for Expectation Damages in Contracts Terminated for the Convenience of the Government, 61 *Air Force Law Review* 1.

Papaux, Alain and Cerutti, Davide (2020), *Introduction au droit et à la culture juridique* (Schulthess).

Parker, David (1989), Sovereignty, Absolutism and the Function of the Law in Seventeenth-Century France, 122 *Past and Present* 36.

Pekelis, Alexander (1943), Legal Technique and Political Ideologies: A Comparative Study, 41 *Michigan Law Review* 665.

Pellegrino, Carlos (1990), Os Contratos da Administração Pública, 179–80 *Revista de Direito Administrativo* 68.

Péquignot, Georges (2020 [1945]), *Théorie Générale du Contrat Administratif* (Mémoire du droit).

Perlman, Matthew and Goodrich Jr, William (1978), Termination for Convenience Settlements – The Government's Limited Payment for Cancellation of Contracts, 10 *Public Contracts Law Journal* 1.

Perrin, Florence (2014), *L'intérêt général et liberalism politique* (Fondation Varenne).

Perriquet, Eugène (1884), *Les Contrats de L'État* (LGDJ).

Perrone-Moisés, Leyla (ed) (2004), *Do Positivismo À Desconstrução. Idéias Francesas na América* (Edusp).

Petit, Jacques and Frier, Pierre-Laurent (2020), *Droit Administratif* (LGDJ 14th ed).

Petrillo, Joseph and Conner, William (1997), From *Torncello* to *Krygoski*: 25 Years of the Government's Termination for Convenience Power, 7 *Federal Circuit Bar Journal* 337.

Pfander, James (2003), Government Accountability in Europe: A Comparative Assessment, 35 *George Washington International Law Review* 611.

Pfander, James (1997), Sovereign Immunity and the Right to Petition: Toward a First Amendment Right to Pursue Judicial Claims Against the Government, 91 *Northwestern University Law Review* 899.

Pfersmann, Otto (2001), Le Droit Comparé Comme Interprétation et Comme Théorie du Droit, 2 *Revue International de Droit Comparé* 275.

Picard, Étienne (1996), L'influence du droit communautaire sur la notion d'orde public, *L'Actualité juridique – Droit Administratif* 55.

Pierce Jr, Richard et al (1999), *Administrative Law and Process* (Foundation, 3rd ed).

Pierce Jr, Richard et al (2002), *Administrative Law Treatise* vol 3 (Aspen Law & Business, 4th ed).

Pimenta Bueno, José Antônio (1978 [1857]). *Direito Público Brasileiro e Análise da Constituição do Império* (Senado Federal).

Pinto Correia, Maria Lúcia (1998), *Responsabilidade do Estado e Dever de Indenizar do Legislador* (Coimbra).

Pires, Maria Coeli Simões (2005), *Direito Adquirido e Ordem Pública. Segurança Jurídica e Transformação Democrática* (Del Rey).

Plessix, Benoît (2003a), *L'utilisation du droit civil dans l'élaboration du droit administratif* (Panthéon-Assas).

Plessix, Benoît (2003b), Nicolas Delamare ou Les Fondations du Droit Administratif Français, 38 *Droits* 113.

Plessix, Benoît (2011), La part de la doctrine dans la création du droit des contrats administratifs, 2011 *Revue Droit Administraif* 46.

Plessix, Benoît (2020), *Droit administratif général* (LexisNexis 3rd ed).

Pollock, Frederick (1923), The Contact of Public and Private Law, 1 *Cambridge Law Journal* 255.

Ponthoreau, Marie-Claire (2005), Le Droit Comparé en Question(s) entre Pragmatisme et Outil Épistémologique, 1 *Revue International de Droit Comparé* 7.

Poscher, Ralf (1908), The Influence of French Law in America, 3 *Illinois Law Review* 354.

Poscher, Ralf (1930), The Revival of Comparative Law, 5 Tulane Law Review 1.

Poscher, Ralf (1931), The Ideal Element in American Judicial Decision, 45 *Harvard Law Review*, 136.

Poscher, Ralf (1933), Hierarchy Of Sources And Forms In Different Systems Of Law, 7 *Tulane Law Review*, 475.

Poscher, Ralf (1937), What is the Common Law? in *The Future of Common Law* (Harvard) 3.

Poscher, Ralf (1939), Public Law and Private Law, 24 *Cornell Law Quarterly* 469.

Poscher, Ralf (1944), Law and the State. Jurisprudence and Politics, 57 *Harvard Law Review* 1193.

Poscher, Ralf (1946), Sources and Forms of Law, 21 *Notre Dame Lawyer*, 247.

Pound, Roscoe (1953), *An Introduction to the Philosophy of Law* (Yale).

Poscher, Ralf (1955), Comparative Law in Space and Time, 4 *American Journal of Comparative Law* 70.

Poscher, Ralf (1956), Codification in Anglo-American Law, in B Schwartz (ed) *The Code Napoleon and the Common-Law World* (NYU) 267.

Poscher, Ralf (1999 [1932]), *The Spirit of the Common Law* (Transaction).

Poscher, Ralf (2009), The Hand of Midas: When Concepts Turn Legal, or Deflating the Hart–Dworkin Debate, in J Hage and D Pfordten (eds), *Concepts in Law* (Springer) 99.

Poscher, Ralf (2019), Hermeneutics and Law, in MN Forster and K Gjesdal (eds), *The Cambridge Companion to Hermeneutics* 326.

Priel, Dan (2020), Analytic Jurisprudence in Time. Philosophy of Law as an Integral Part of Philosophy: Essays on the Jurisprudence of Gerald J. Postema (Thomas Bustamante and Thiago Lopes Decat eds, 2020), Osgoode Legal Studies Research Paper, Available at SSRN: https://ssrn.com/abstract=3552355.

Pugh, George (1953), Historical Approach to the Doctrine of Sovereign Immunity, 13 *Louisiana Law Review* 476.

Radbruch, Gustav (1950 [1932]). Legal Philosophy, in *The Legal Philosophies of Lask, Radbruch, and Dabin* (Harvard, Kurt Wilk trans) 43.

Radbruch, Gustav (1962), *Lo Spirito del Diritto Inglese* (Giuffrè, A Baratta trans).

Raiser, Ludwig (1990), Il Futuro del Diritto Privato, in *Il Compito del Diritto Privato*, CM Mazzoni (ed), Giuffrè, M Graziadei trans).

Randall, Susan (2002), Sovereign Immunity and the Uses of History, 81 *Nebraska Law Review* 6.

Rangeon, François (1986), *L'idéologie de l'intérêt général* (Economica).

Rapp, Lucien (1997), L'expérience américaine, *L'actualité Juridique – Droit Administratif* 159.

Raz, Joseph (1986), *The Morality of Freedom* (Oxford).

Raz, Joseph (1992), The Relevance of Coherence, 72 *Boston University Law Review* 273.

Redor, Marie-Joëlle (1992), L'État dans la Doctrine Publiciste Française du Début du Siècle, 15 *Droits* 91.

Reimann, Mathias (1998), Stepping out of the European Shadow: Why Comparative Law in the United States Must Develop Its Own Agenda, 46 *American Journal of Comparative Law* 637.

Reimann, Mathias (1989), The Historical School Against Codification: Savigny, Carter, and the Defeat of the New York Civil Code, 37 *American Journal of Comparative Law* 95.

Reitz, John (2012), Comparative Law and Political Economy, in DS Clark (ed), *Comparative Law and Society* (Edward Elgar Publishing) 105.

Ribas, Antônio (1866), *Direito Administrativo Brasileiro* (FL Pinto & C).

Richardson, William (1882), History, Jurisdiction, and Practice of the Court of Claims of the United States, 7 *Southern Law Review New Series* 781.

Richer, Laurent and Lichère, François (2019), *Droit des Contrats Administratifs* (LGDJ 11th ed).

Richer, Laurent (2002), La résiliation unilatérale: motifs et procedures de rupture, 16 *L'Actualité de la Commande et des Contrats Publics* 22.

Rigaudière, Albert (1997), Pratique politique et droit public dans la France des XIV et XV siècles, 41 *Archives de Philosophie du Droit* 83.

Riley, Patrick (1986), *The General Will before Rousseau: The Transformation of the Divine into the Civic*. New Jersey (Princeton).

Riley, Patrick (2001), Rousseau's General Will, in P Riley (ed), *The Cambridge Companion to Rousseau* (Cambridge) 124.

Riley, Patrick (2015), The General Will before Rousseau: The Contributions of Arnauld, Pascal, Malebranche, Bayle, and Bossuet, in J Farr and David Williams (eds), *The General Will: The Evolution of a Concept* (Cambridge) 3.

Ripert, Georges (1955), *Les Forces Créatrices du Droit* (LGDJ).

Rodrigues, José Honório (1978), *Conselho de Estado. O Quinto Poder?* (Senado Federal).

Roe, Mary Katherine (1997), Conoco Inc. v. United States: A Narrowing of the Sovereign Acts Doctrine?, 3 *Ocean & Coastal Law Journal* 275.

Rohr, John (1995), *Founding Republics in France and America. A Study in Constitutional Governance* (Kansas).

Rolland, Denis (2004), A Crise de um Certo Universalismo: O Modelo Cultural e Político Francês no Século XX, in L Perrone-Moisés (ed), *Do Positivismo À Desconstrução. Idéias Francesas na América* (Edusp) 237.

Rommen, Heinrich (1998 [1936]), *The Natural Law. A Study in Legal and Social History and Philosophy* (Liberty Fund, Thomas R Hanley trans).

Rosemblatt, Helena (2018), *The Lost History of Liberalism* (Princeton).

Rosilho, André (2013), *Licitação no Brasil* (Malheiros).

Roubier, Paul (1951), *Théorie générale du droit. Histoire des doctrines juridiques et philosophie des valeurs sociales* (Sirey, 2nd ed).

Rousseau, Jean-Jacques (1979 [1762]), *Emile, or On Education* (Basic Books, A Bloom trans).

Rousseau, Jean-Jacques (1994 [1762]), *The Social Contract* (Oxford, C Betts trans).

Rowen, Herbert (1961), 'L'État c'est moi': Louis XIV and the State, 2 *French Historical Studies* 83.

Ryan, Magnus (2003), Freedom, Law, and the Medieval State, in Q Skinner and Bo Stråth (eds), *States & Citizens. History, Theory, Prospects* (Cambridge) 51.

Ruelle, Annette (2012), Le regard de la romaniste: La *forme* normative ou la guerre comme *raison* du droit, in I Hachez et al (dirs), *Les sources du droit revisités*, vol 4 (théories des sources du droit) 755.

Sacco, Rodolfo (1991a), *La Comparaison Juridique au Service de la Connaissance du Droit* (Economica).

Sacco, Rodolfo (1991b), Legal Formants: A Dynamic Approach to Comparative Law, 39 *American Journal of Comparative Law*, 1.

Sacco, Rodolfo (1991c), Legal Formants: A Dynamic Approach to Comparative Law (Installment II of II), 39 *American Journal of Comparative Law*, 343.

Samuel, Geoffrey (1983), Public and Private Law: A Private Lawyer's Response, 46 *Modern Law Review* 558.

Samuel, Geoffrey (1997), Classification of Obligations and the Impact of Constructivist Epistemologies, 17 *Legal Studies* 448.

Samuel, Geoffrey (1995), Ontology and Dimension in Legal Reasoning, in Zenon Bankowski et al (eds), *Informatics and the Foundations of Legal Reasoning* 205 (Kluwer Academic).

Samuel, Geoffrey (1998a), Comparative Law and Jurisprudence, 47 *International & Comparative Law Quarterly* 817.

Samuel, Geoffrey (1988b), Governmental Liability in Tort and the Public and Private Law Distinction, 8 *Legal Studies* 277.

Samuel, Geoffrey (2011), Does One Need an Understanding of Methodology in Law Before One Can Understand Methodology in Comparative Law? in MV Hoecke (ed), *Methodologies of Legal Research. Which Kind of Method for What Kind of Discipline?* 177.

Samuel, Geoffrey (2003), *Epistemology and Method in Law* (Ashgate).

Samuel, Geoffrey (2005), L'Esprit de Non-Codification: Le *Common Law* Face au Code Napoléon, 41 *Droits* 122.

Samuel, Geoffrey (2014a), *An Introduction to Comparative Law Theory and Method* (Hart).

Samuel, Geoffrey (2014b), What is Legal Epistemology? in M Adams and D Heirbaut (eds), *The Method and Culture of Comparative Law. Essays in Honour of Mark Van Hoecke* (Bloomsbury) 23.

Samuel, Geoffrey (2018a), *Rethinking Legal Reasoning* (Edward Elgar Publishing).

Samuel, Geoffrey (2018b), What Is (Or Perhaps Should Be) the Relationship between Legal History and Legal Theory? Review of: Law in Theory and History: New Essays on a Neglected Dialogue by Del Mar, Maksymilian and Lobban, Michael. Comparative Legal History. *Accessed online with permission* on August 18th 2020 at http://kar.kent.ac.uk/66144/.

Sanches, Ricardo and Angel, Daniel (2010), Brésil/Brazil, in R Noguellou (ed), *Droit comparé des contrats publics* (Bruylant) 431.

Sandevoir, Pièrre (1964), *Études sur le recours de pleine jurisdiction* (LGDJ).

Schiavone, Aldo (2017), *Ius. L'invenzione del Diritto in Occidente* (Einaudi).

Schmidt, Folke (1965), *The German Abstract Approach to Law. Comments on the System of the Bürgerliches Gesetzbuch* (Almqvist & Wiksell).

Schwartz, Bernard (1952), French and Anglo-American Conception of Administrative Law, 6 *Miami Law Quarterly* 433.

Schwartz, Bernard (1956), The Code and Public Law, in *The Code Napoleon and the Common-Law World* (NYU) 247.

Schwartz, Joshua Ira (1996), Liability for Sovereign Acts: Congruence and Exceptionalism in Government Contracts Law, 64 *George Washington Law Review* 633.

Schwartz, Joshua Ira (1997), Assembling Winstar: Triumph of the Ideal of Congruence in Government Contracts Law? 26 *Public Contracts Law Journal* 481.

Schwartz, Joshua Ira (2000), The Status of Sovereign Acts and Unmistakability Doctrines in the Wake of Winstar: An Interim Report, 51 *Alabama Law Review* 1177.

Schwartz, Joshua Ira (2002), Learning from the United States' Procurement Law Experience: On 'Law Transfer' and Its Limitations, 11 *Public Procurement Law Review* 115.

Schwartz, Joshua Ira (2003), Public Contracts Specialization as a Rationale for the Court of Federal Claims, 71 *George Washington Law Review* 863.

Schwartz, Joshua Ira (2004), The Centrality of Military Procurement: Explaining the Exceptionalist Character of United States Government Procurement Law (https://papers.ssrn.com/sol3/papers.cfm?abstract_id=607186).

Schwartz, Joshua Ira (2010), États Unis/United States, in R Noguellou (ed) *Droit comparé des contrats publics* (Bruylant) 613.

Schwartz, Joshua Ira (2022), *Cases and Materials for a Survey of Government Procurement Law*, forthcoming.

Sefton-Green, Ruth (2002). Compare and Contrast: Monstre a Deux Têtes, 1 *Revue International de Droit Comparé* 85

Seife, Rodolphe (1996), The King is Dead, Long Live the King! The Court-Created American Concept of Immunity: The Negation of Equality and Accountability under Law, 24 *Hofstra Law Review* 981.

Sérvulo Correia, José Manuel (1987), *Legalidade e Autonomia Contratual nos Contratos Administrativos* (Almedina).

Sève, René (1986), Système et Code, 31 *Archives de Philosophie du Droit* 77.

Shapiro, Martin (1972), From Public Law to Public Policy, or The 'Public' in 'Public Law', 5 *Political Science* 410.

Shapiro, Martin (1981), *Courts. A Comparative and Political Analysis* (University of Chicago).

Shealey, Robert Preston (1919), *The Law of Government Contracts* (Ronald Press).

Shealey, Robert Preston (1938), *The Law of Government Contracts* (Federal Publishing, 3rd ed).

Shimomura, Floyd (1985), The History of Claims Against the United States: The Evolution From a Legislative to a Judicial Model of Payment, 45 *Louisiana Law Review* 625.

Siems, Mathias (2018), *Comparative Law* (Cambridge, 2nd ed).

Schleifer, James (2010), Notes in E Nolla (ed) *Democracy in America/Historical-Critical Edition of* De la démocratie en Amérique (Liberty Fund, JT Schleifer trans).

Schooner, Steven (2001), Fear of Oversight: The Fundamental Failure of Businesslike Government, 50 *American University Law Review* 627.

Schooner, Steven (2002), Desiderata: Objectives for a System of Government Contract Law, 11 *Public Procurement Law Review* 103

Shklar, Judith (1987), Political Theory and The Rule of Law, in AC Hutchinson and P Monahan (eds) *The Rule of Law, Ideal or Ideology*, Carswell) 1.

Shklar, Judith (1969), *Men & Citizen: A Study of Rousseau's Social Theory* (Cambridge).

Schraub, David (2017), Finding the 'Sovereign' in 'Sovereign Immunity': Lessons from Bodin, Hobbes, and Rousseau, *Critical Review*, 1 DOI: 10.1080/08913811.2017.1403730.

Simmonds, Nigel (1984), *The Decline of Juridical Reason. Doctrine and Theory in the Legal Order* (Manchester).

Simon, Walter (1965), The 'Two Cultures' in Nineteenth-Century France: Victor Cousin and Auguste Comte, 26 *Journal of the History of Ideas* 45.

Sisk, Gregory (2003), The Tapestry Unravels: Statutory Waivers of Sovereign Immunity and Money Claims Against the United States, 35 *George Washington International Law Review* 602.

Sisk, Gregory (2010), The Inevitability of Federal Sovereign Immunity, 55 *Villanova Law Review* 899.

Sisk, Gregory (2014), Twilight for the Strict Construction of Waivers of Federal Sovereign Immunity, 92 *North Carolina Law Review* 1245.

Sisk, Gregory (2016), *Litigation with the Federal Government* (West Academy).

Slesser, Henry (1936), *The Law* (Longmans, Green & Co).

Smith, Loren (2003), Why a Court of Federal Claims?, 71 *George Washington Law Review* 773.

Smith, Adam (1976 [1776]), *An Inquiry into the Nature and Causes of the Wealth of Nations* (Oxford).

Sordi, Bernardo (2014), Sur La Valeur Normative De La Doctrine Juridique Dans Le Système Administratif, 60 *Droits* 169.

Sourzat, Lucie (2019), *Le Contrat Administratif Résilient* (LGDJ).

Souza, Paulino José Soares de (1960 [1862]), *Ensaio sobre o Direito Administrativo* (Rio de Janeiro).

Spaak, Torben and Mindus, Patricia (2021), Introduction, in T Spaak and T Mindus (eds), *The Cambridge Companion to Legal Positivism* (Cambridge) 1.

Speidel, Richard (1963), Implied Duties of Cooperation and the Defense of Sovereign Acts in Government Contracts, 51 *Georgetown Law Journal* 516.

Stack, Daniel (1955), The Liability of the United States for Breach of Contract, 44 *Georgetown Law Journal* 77

Stahl, Jacques-Henri (2017), De l'identification et des usages de l'intérêt général par le juge administratif, in G Guglielmi (ed), *L'intérêt général dans les pays de la common law et de droit écrit* 155.

Stouck, Jerry and Lipson, David (1996), *United States v. Winstar Corp*: Affirming the Application of Private Contract Law Principles to the Federal Government, 6 *Federal Circuit Bar Journal* 315.

Sundfeld, Carlos Ari (2014), *Direito Administrativo para Céticos* (Malheiros, 2nd ed).

Sundfeld, Carlos Ari and Giacomuzzi, José Guilherme (2018), O Espírito da Lei 13.655/2018: impulso realista para a segurança jurídica no Brasil, 62 *Revista de Direito Público da Economia* 39.

Swart, Koenraad W (1962), 'Individualism' in the Mid-Nineteenth Century, 23 *Journal of History of Ideas* 77.

Symchowics, Nil (2002), L'indemnité de résilition, 16 *L'Actualité de la Commande et des Contrats Publics* 31.

Tácito, Caio (1977), Presença Norte-Americana no Direito Administrativo Brazileiro, 129 *Revista de Direito Administrativo* 21.

Tácito, Caio (1997a), A Nova Lei das Licitações, in *Temas de Direito Público* vol 1 (Renovar) 741.

Tácito, Caio (1997b), Contrato Administrativo, in *Temas de Direito Público* vol 1 (Renovar) 617

Tácito, Caio (1997 [1960]), O equilíbrio financeiro na concessão de serviço público, in *Temas de Direito Público* vol 1 (Renovar) 199.

Tardieu, André (1927), *France and America. Some Experiences in Cooperation* (Riverside).

Terneyre, Philippe (1989), *La Responsabilité Contractuelle des Personnes Publiques en Droit Administratif* (Economica).

Terneyre, Philippe (1996), L'Influence du droit communautaire sur le droit des contrats administratifs, *L'Actualité juridique – Droit Administratif.*

Testard, Christophe (2018), *Pouvoir de decision unilatérale de l'Administration et démocratie administrative* (LGDJ).

Testu, François Xavier (1998), La distinction du droit public et du droit privé est-elle idéologique?, 1998 *Recueil Dalloz* 345.

Tocqueville, Alexis de (2010 [1935–40]), *Democracy in America/Historical-Critical Edition of* De la démocratie en Amérique Schleifer, E Nolla (ed) (Liberty Fund, JT Schleifer trans).

Tocqueville, Alexis de (1998 [1856]), *The Old Regime and the Revolution* vol 1 (Chicago, AS Kahan trans).

Touzeil-Divina, Mathieu (2019), *Dix mythes du droit public* (LGDJ).

Toscano, David (1992), Forbearance Agreements: Invalid Contracts for the Surrender of Sovereignty, 92 *Columbia Law Review* 426.

Triepel, Heinrich (1986 [1926]), *Derecho público y política* (Civitas, 2nd ed, JL Carro trans).

Troper, Michel (1992), Le Concept D'État de Droit, 15 *Droits* 51.

Troper, Michel (1994), Autorité et raison en droit public français, in *Pour Une Théorie Juridique de l'État* (PUF) 107.

Troper, Michel (2004), La Distinction public-privé et structure de l'ordre juridique, in J-B Auby and M Freedland (eds), *La Distinction du Droit Public et du Droit Privé: Regards français et Britanniques – The Public Law/Private Law Divide: Une Entente Assez Cordiale?* (LGDJ) 183.

Troper, Michel (2021), The French Tradition of Legal Positivism, in T Spaak and T Mindus (eds), *The Cambridge Companion to Legal Positivism* (Cambridge) 133.

Truchet, Didier (2017), L'intérêt général demeure-t-il une exception française?, in G Guglielmi (ed), *L'intérêt général dans les pays de la* common law *et de droit écrit* 211.

Tsuk Mitchell, Dalia (2007), *Architect of Justice: Felix S. Cohen and the Founding of American Legal Pluralism* (Cornell).

Turkel, Gerald (1988), The Public/Private Distinction: Approaches to the Critique of Legal Ideology, 22 *Law & Society Review* 801.

Turpin, Colin (1982), Public Contracts, in *International Encyclopedia of Comparative Law* vol 7 (Siebeck, Tübingen & Nijhoff).

Ubaud-Bergeron, Marion (2019), *Droit des contrats administratifs* (LexisNexis, 3rd ed).

Ullmann, Walter (1949), The Development of the Medieval Idea of Sovereignty (1949) 64 *English Historical Review* 1.

Ullmann, Walter (1975), *Medieval Political Thought* (Peregrin Books).

Uhlmann, Eric et al (2009), American Moral Exceptionalism, in J Jost, A Kay and H Thorisdottir (eds) *Social and Psychological Bases of Ideology and System Justification* (Oxford) 27.

Unger, Roberto Mangabeira (1983), The Critical Legal Studies Movement (1983) 96 *Harvard Law Review* 561.

Valcke, Catherine (2004), Comparative Law as Comparative Jurisprudence: The Compatibility of Legal Systems, 52 *American Journal of Comparative Law* 713.

Vautrot-Schwarz, Charles (2009), *La Qualification Juridique en Droit Administratif* (LGDJ).

Vidal, Laurent (2005), *L'Équilibre Financier du Contrat dans la Jurisprudence Administrative* (Bruylant).

Villain-Courrier, Anne-Élisabeth (2004) *Contribution générale à l'étude de l'éthique du service public en droit anglaise et français comparé* (Dalloz).

Villey, Michel (1957), Essor et décadence du volontarisme juridique, 1957 *Archives de Philosophie du Droit* 87.

Villey, Michel (1962), *Leçons d'Histoire de la Philosophie du Droit* (Dalloz).

Villey, Michel (1964), La genèse du droit subjectif chez Guillaume d'OCCAM, 9 *Archives de Philosophie du Droit* 97.

Villey, Michel (1981), Préface historique, 26 *Archives de Philosophie du Droit* 1.

Villey, Michel (2001), *Philosophie du droit: Définitions et fins du droit – Les moyens du droit* (Dalloz).

Viveiros de Castro (1914), *Tratado de Sciencia da Administração e Direito Administrativo* (Jacinto RS, 3rd ed).

Vita, Luís Washington (1973), The Meaning and Direction of Philosophical Thought in Brazil, 33 *Philosophy and Phenomenological Research* 531.

Voegelin, Eric (1989 [1936]), *The Collected Works of Eric Voegelin* vol 4: *The Authoritarian State. An Essay on the Problem of the Austrian State* (Missouri, R Hein trans).

Vogenauer, Stefan (2019), Sources of Law and Legal Method in Comparative Law, in M Reimann and R Zimmerman (eds), *Oxford Handbook of Comparative Law* (Oxford University Press, 2nd ed) 878.

Waline, Marcel (1949), *L'Individualisme et le Droit* (Domat Montchrestien, 2nd ed).

Watson, Alan (1983), Legal Change: Sources of Law and Legal Culture, 131 *University of Pennsylvania Law Review* 1121.

Watson, John (1892), The Critical Philosophy and Idealism, 1 *Philosophical Review* 9.

Webber, Max (1977), *Critique of Stammler* (Free Press, G Oakes trans, 2nd ed).

Weffort, Francisco (2006), *Formação do Pensamento Político Brasileiro* (Ática).

Weinrib, Ernest (1995), *The Idea of Private Law* (Harvard).

Whitfield, Stephen (1988), Characterizing America, 21 *The History Teacher* 479.

Whitman, James (1990), *The Legacy of Roman Law in the German Romantic Era. Historical Vision and Legal Change* (Princeton).

Whitman, James (2003a), *Harsh Justice. Criminal Punishment and the Widening Divide between America and Europe* (Oxford).

Whitman, James (2003b), The Neo-Romantic Turn, in P Legrand and R Munday (eds), *Comparative Legal Studies: Traditions and Transitions* (Cambridge) 312.

Whitman, James (2017), The Hunt for Truth in Comparative Law, 65 *American Journal of Comparative Law* 181.

Wigmore, John et al (eds) (1921), *Modern French Legal Philosophy, by A. Fouillée et al.* (Macmillan, FW Scott and JP Chamberlain trans) 237–344.

Williams, David (2007), *Rousseau's Platonic Enlightenment* (Pennsylvania State).

Williams, David (2014), *Rousseau's Social Contract: An Introduction* (Cambridge).

Williams, David (2015), The Substantive Elements of Rousseau's General Will, in J Farr and DL Williams (eds), *The General Will: The Evolution of a Concept* (Cambridge) 219.

Wimberly, Gerald and Amerling, Kristin (1996), The Sovereign Acts Doctrine after *Winstar*, 6 *Federal Circuit Bar Journal* 127.

Wolin, Sheldon (1989), *The Presence of the Past. Essays on the State and the Constitution* (Johns Hopkins).

Wolin, Sheldon (2001), *Tocqueville Between Two Worlds. The Making of a Political and Theoretical Life* (Princeton).

Young, Stephen (1984), Limiting the Government's Ability to Terminate for Its Convenience Following *Torncello*, 52 *George Washington Law Review* 892.

Zigler, Michael (1984), Takings Law and the Contract Clause: A Taking Law Approach to Legislative Modification of Public Contracts, 36 *Stanford Law Review* 1447.

Zoller, Élisabeth (2017), Avant-propos, in G Guglielmi (dir), *L'intérêt général dans les pays de* common law *et de droit écrit* (Panthéon-Assas) 9.

Zweigert, Konrad and Kötz, Hein (1998), *Introduction to Comparative Law* (Clarendon, T Weir trans, 3rd ed).

Index